What Were Your Parents Doing Back Then?

Youth and Drugs in a Southern California Beach Community From 1970 into the 21st Century

Jeremiah Lowney

University Press of America,® Inc.
Lanham · New York · Oxford

University Press of America,® Inc.
4720 Boston Way
Lanham, Maryland 20706
UPA Acquisitions Department (301) 459-3366

12 Hid's Copse Rd.
Cumnor Hill, Oxford OX2 9JJ

Printed in the United States of America
British Library Cataloging in Publication Information Available

Library of Congress Cataloging-in-Publication Data

Lowney, Jeremiah, 1939-
What were your parents doing back then? : youth and drugs in a Southern California beach community from 1970 into the 21st century / Jeremiah Lowney.
p. cm
Includes bibliographical references and index.
1. Youth—California—San Diego—Social conditions—Longitudinal studies. 2. Youth—Drug use—California—San Diego—Longitudinal studies. 3. Counterculture—California—San Diego. I. Title.

HQ796 .L69 2001 305.235'09794'985—dc21 2001053040 CIP

ISBN 0-7618-2123-6 (pbk. : alk. paper)

The paper used in this publication meets the minimum requirements of American National Standard for Information Sciences—Permanence of Paper for Printed Library Materials, ANSI Z39.48—1984

DEDICATION

This book is dedicated in memory of Jim Cameron, Mark Starvish, Jim Alquire and Rodney Batt as well as in honor of the many living participants who have shared their life stories and made this research possible.

CONTENTS

LIST OF TABLES

PREFACE

In writing this book, I have attempted to walk a fine line between making it interesting and appealing to students and the general public and sacrificing the scholarly basis of the research. It is my hope that professors, graduate students and other scholars will benefit from the research. Likewise, I have attempted to gain the attention of undergraduate students who may be inspired to seize their own opportunities to conduct sociological research for succeeding generations. The combination of qualitative and quantitative methods in a longitudinal study is, unfortunately, rather unique in most social scientific studies. I trust my work will fill a some small portion of this void. Moreover, parents and those who work with young people ought to find much in the book that will be useful for them. A great deal of what I have accomplished has been the result of unexpected opportunities and the encouragement of my own professors and colleagues.

In 1970, during the heyday of the youthful drug subculture, I became acquainted a group called the Wall Gang. I began to research the group in a community of San Diego that I refer to as Golden Beach. Under the guidance of Dr. Robert Winslow of San Diego State University, I employed a qualitative technique of sociological research, termed "nonparticipant observation." I continued my contacts with the Wall Gang during the time of my doctoral studies at the University of Kentucky.

In 1975, I returned to Golden Beach to begin a more systematic and in-depth 10-month period of research for my dissertation. Using a "snowball" technique, I used my contacts and rapport with members of the Wall Gang and others to introduce me to a younger cohort. The younger cohort, males between 14 and 21 years of age, either used drugs with varying degrees of frequency or were among the very few "non-users." During this phase of the research I combined quantitative, statistical analysis with a continuing qualitative method of nonparticipant observation. As in my succeeding visits in 1978 and 1981, I had a considerable amount of freedom to research alcohol and other drug use among young people because I had been given a "Grant of Confidentiality" by the United States Department of Justice. The results during this period set the stage for continuing research.

I returned to Golden Beach in 1978, not only to follow up on the previous subjects, but also to add an additional cohort of 20 females. The patterns among the females were not markedly different from those of the males.

During the "cocaine epidemic" and its aftermath in the 1980s, I returned to Golden Beach several times – most notably during the summer of 1981. By this time, the patterns of drug use and other behaviors, became increasingly consistent among those with varying degrees of involvement in the drug subculture.

In 1985, I entered the seminary at the Catholic University of America to begin studies for the Roman Catholic priesthood. I had some initial concerns that this decision and my subsequent ordination as a priest might evoke less openness from those in my research. The opposite proved true. The former members of the "Old Wall Gang" and others who knew me well were more open than ever and all but expected that I would become a priest.

During the 1990s, I returned frequently to the beach area. I was able to contact 80 percent of the original subjects, and interview several of their teenage sons and daughters.

Throughout the entire 31 years, the importance of family has stood paramount. The role of a father, or father figure, had the most direction effects, positive or negative, on young people's use of drugs and other behaviors. The father figures were not necessarily biological fathers. They included coaches, clergy, teachers, stepfathers and mothers. Most noteworthy was "Super-Mom," Mrs. Mary Gilroy. She fulfilled the roles of both a father and a mother in an exemplary fashion. Those sons and daughters who felt that they did not have an adequate father figure in their lives most often mentioned that they were deprived of "caring discipline."

The family influenced the young peoples lives in other, indirect, ways. Some parents encouraged their children to be active in church and school, including athletics and other extracurricular activities. These activities provided the young people opportunities to associate with others who were less likely to be heavily involved in drugs or other deviant behaviors.

What follows is their story, but it also has become my story. Because of my close association with them, they have touched my life and shaped my own journey. Many claim that I have done the same for them. In all, we have become, and remain, good friends. My journey with them has been emotional and rewarding. In the past several months, as I have reviewed and recalled many of our interactions, conversations and letters, I have found myself laughing, weeping, smiling or aching. I hope I am able to adequately portray to others the depth of their struggles, growth and overall goodness that I have come to understand.

ACKNOWLEDGMENTS

It is difficult to acknowledge all of those who have assisted me over the past 31 years and during the written compilation of my research.

I begin with those who encouraged my initial research. Dr. C. Dale Johnson of San Diego State University who told me in 1970 to "keep notes" on the Wall Gang because "you might want to do a Master's Thesis on them sometime." Dr. Johnson directed me to a Juvenile Delinquency course taught by Dr. Robert W. Winslow. Dr. Winslow directed me in an initial independent study. He became my mentor and encouraged my progress in this and related sociological research and studies.

Dr. Robert Straus of the University of Kentucky became my mentor during my doctoral years. Dr. Straus' background in alcoholism and use of case studies provided me with invaluable assistance. Dr. Thomas J. Garrity and Dr. John Haley assisted me in statistical and quantitative analysis, always keeping me "objective."

I have received financial support and leave time from various institutions including the University of Richmond, Spring Hill College and Carroll College. I especially wish to thank the Faculty Development Committee of Carroll College who provided me with what limited funds were available during the summers of 1996 through 1998. I also wish to thank the Rank and Tenure Committee of Carroll College for recommending my sabbatical leave to write this book. I thank Carroll's vice-president of academic affairs, Dr. Jim Trudnowski, and our interim president, Fr. Steve Rowan, who approved my sabbatical and provided me with additional encouragement.

Others have assisted in more informal, but, at times, even more important ways. Paul Dorrance, owner of Headmaster in Helena, Montana, was available to me, at any hour, to provide me with advice and help on computer matters. He donated countless hours to this effort. Pat Ryan, the copy editor at *The Montana Standard*, assisted in proofreading in spite of his very busy schedule and his own necessary time as a father. My former student, Jon Flynn, helped proofread Chapter 8. He provided valuable insights as to how to present some very technical data in order that it would be more comprehensible to undergraduate students. Many members of the Carroll College faculty have been very supportive. For several years, Dr. Ann Perkins, of the Psychology Department has urged me to write this book. Dr. Richard Lambert and Dr. Mark Smillie of the Philosophy

Department have both been personally supportive and willing to provide me with a ready piece of advice. Mrs. Marie Vanisko, my neighbor and a member of the Mathematics Department, has also been very supportive and helpful. I appreciate the support of my fellow priest-faculty, especially Fr. Joe Harrington, Professor Emeritus of Biology, and Fr. Dan Shea, Department of Language and Literature.

None of this could have been accomplished without the participation and support of the wonderful people in Golden Beach. Many were subjects of the research. Others have supported me throughout the years in many ways. In order to assure confidentiality, I thank them in the pseudonyms that I have utilized herein. I especially single out the Bayer family, my second family. In addition, others who are members of the "five families," Mrs. Mary Gilroy and her sons, the Dunn's, the Jones family and the Roe family. Pat and Luke have constantly been available to provide me with the latest information about the "Old Wall Gang," the wall crew and their current group, the "Golden Beach Seawall Social Club." All the members of that group have a special place in my heart. Finally, I wish to thank the fine staff and welcoming parishioners of St. Patrick's Church. Without their assistance, the last several years of research would have never been possible. I appreciate the advice and support of the "the Monsignor." I thank the pastor, Fr. Paul, who also provided me invaluable support. I encourage him and the parish to continue their wonderful ministry in Golden Beach, especially their good efforts among the young people.

PROLOGUE

It is July 7, 2000, I'm driving from the freeway to Golden Beach.[1] I view the traffic, the conservative tone of the community, the greatly increased wealth, and the conventional haircuts, dress, and general way of life. My mind drifted back to 1968.

I recall my first entrance into Golden Beach. I could distinguish the young from the older according to several criteria. Young males had hair below their ears or shoulder length. The exceptions were those in the military whose buzz cuts separated them from other youth.

The older generation condemned the “rock and roll” music that entranced the younger generation. Younger females frequently went braless. Surfing was "in", but somewhat frowned upon by the older generation. Marijuana was abundant but reserved mostly to those less than 25. Young people bemoaned their parent’s ignorance in consuming alcohol. They pointed out that alcohol to brain cells, caused liver problems, and lead to a hangover. The youth had discovered wonder substances, especially "pot", that did not kill brain cells, was harmless to the body and brought about no hangover the next morning.

Peace signs were abundant among the youth. The same gestures their parents had used as signs of victory following World War II were now criticized by the older generation's as "unpatriotic.”

Fathers were "hip" if they wore leisure suits and sported sideburns. Mothers were "cool" if they allowed their children to "do their own thing.”

"Dressing down" was "in" for everyone. The same was true of the environment. Bicycles were rediscovered. Wealth was not flaunted. That was "uncool.”

Pierced bodies or males wearing earrings were unheard of. Tattoos were a sign of military service or that one had served time in a juvenile institution or prison.

The Beach Boys, Bob Dylan, Sonny and Cher, Bob Dylan, The Mama's and the Papas, and Peter, Paul and Mary were popular. Jimmy Hendrix and Janis Joplin were also popular, and still alive.

The beach itself had a hedonistic “amusement park” atmosphere. The boardwalk along the beach was filled with people, but never overly crowded. Teenagers appeared to dominate. Characters abounded. The smell of marijuana permeated the air. Beer was drunk from bottles and cans. Other drugs were used even if not noticeable to the uneducated or uninitiated.

Traffic was light in those days. High-rises were unknown. I could easily find a free parking place at the beach or elsewhere.

Coffee was served in restaurants, not stands, for only 25 cents a cup. I could enjoy a Mexican dinner on a paper plate for 50 cents on Wednesday nights. A neighborhood theater had almost first-run movies for a dollar.

I felt a strong sense of community in Golden Beach in those days. Each major religious denomination had one church. A downtown area existed for shopping. I would recognize a neighbor in a supermarket, restaurant, or at church.

The community comprised approximately 37,500 inhabitants, primarily in the middle and upper-middle economic brackets, and almost entirely White Anglos. The average income was well above the nation at approximately $10,000. An average home sold for about $25,000. Golden Beach would grow in population and wealth as the years progressed. It was a noted tourist area that attracts many visitors, especially during the summer months. These aspects would become more pronounced.

Golden Beach was, and is, considered one of the more desirable places to live in the Greater San Diego area. My first reaction when I first came to Golden Beach, was "a lovely place to raise the family!" On the surface, so it appeared. I did not realize, then, that Golden Beach had the second highest rate of single parent households outside of Las Vegas. Over the next few years, this was to be the single most important factor in my research and the cold statistic that shaped the lives and behaviors those young people I came to know so well.

End Note

1. I refer to the community as "Golden Beach." This and other pseudonyms are used in this work in order to assure as complete anonymity as is possible to the subjects and others who would be affected. This is done on a consistent basis, including the use of pseudonyms for various references (census data, news reports, and so forth). Originally I used a pseudonym for the larger community of San Diego as well. However, over time, and gave my past affiliation with San Diego State University attempts to maintain that anonymity became fruitless.

Chapter 1

ORIGINS OF THE RESEARCH AND ORIGINS OF THE WALL GANG

THE INITIAL ESTABLISHMENT OF A RELATIONSHIP

I lived in Golden Beach for a year and a half before the initial opportunity for this research gradually unfolded. It began with an unplanned encounter.

In the fall of 1970, I was 31 and employed as a marketing representative for a large insurance company. I was also attending evening classes at a junior college in preparation for completing my bachelor's degree and entering graduate studies in sociology. I had developed a habit of studying at Billy's, a local restaurant. The opportunity stemmed from a chance meeting in the restaurant between me and a young man who was to become a key figure and an unofficial leader of the first group I would eventually study. Luke was then 16, attending Golden Beach High School and employed as a busboy in the restaurant. Luke was friendly and talkative. We soon discovered that I was also teaching some of his high school acquaintances in a youth program at St. Patrick's Catholic Church.

Luke, in a pattern I was to find characteristic of the group, did not long remain employed. However, I often saw him with a group of his friends along the beach. He would usually call me over, chat for a few minutes and introduce me to his companions. I began to notice a regularity in these companions. I soon learned the group was also noted by the restaurant manager, and by many other business people who, like me, were regular patrons. Members of the business community tended to look upon the group of long-haired, slovenly appearing youth as a "drug-using gang."

I had heard Luke mention his use of marijuana and, because I was somewhat familiar with the extent of marijuana use among Southern California youngsters from my church youth work, I was not particularly surprised to learn this. For some time, I had been extremely curious about the reason for the drug usage and its effects upon society. I had moved to California from my native state of Montana in 1966, just as the flower-children, hippie, drug phenomena had burst upon the scene and overwhelmed an unprepared populace. Although much of the way of life and mores of the new subculture were foreign to me, I was not totally unprepared to understand some of the values. My own youth was spent in a Franciscan high school seminary. My time in the Order of St. Francis of Assisi had instilled me with a spirit of tolerance for others and a philosophical position close to the "peace and love" concept verbalized by the movement. Much of this philosophy also had been expressed through my liberal political activity which included holding office in various county, state and national Young Democrat groups during the early 1960s.

These personal experiences seemed to add to the degree of prestige and acceptance I was granted by the group. At the same time, my 8-year insurance business career afforded me a similar acceptance among the businessmen who made the restaurant their informal headquarters. This acceptance offset many of their objections to my political beliefs. These peculiarities of my background were to contribute to the development of my unique opportunity and vantage point. They helped me achieve acceptance by and the ability to interact with the subjects of my study and to serve as an intermediary between them and the "straight" community.

My first experience as an intermediary occurred as the weather grew cooler and Luke and his companions sought the warmth of Billy's restaurant as a meeting and visiting place. The manager felt that he was losing money on the group's free coffee refills. Also, his business acquaintances and customers complained about the appearance of the youngsters. He therefore let it be known that they were no longer welcome in his establishment. In reaction, I argued that since he and his friends prided themselves on their activity in the Optimists service club, called "The Friend of Youth," they should prefer having the youth drinking coffee in Billy's restaurant rather than on the beach smoking pot. The ban was lifted. Since the group knew of my intercession, this was an important step in gaining their confidence.

A short time after this incident, I was invited to the home of Bob, one of the group, who was providing a small dinner for Luke, Tony and their dates prior to the Junior Prom. Within a half hour, the "small dinner" grew to a large pot party of more than 30 youngsters. This was my first opportunity to witness such an event. While I declined an offer to participate in the smoking, I was shown how to separate stems and seeds and portion of the marijuana which provided the best "high." They demonstrated to me how to roll a "joint." I also observed the progressive effects of the "weed." In fact, everyone became so "stoned" that they forgot to attend to the dinner. I saved the steaks from burning.

As the crowd of teenagers grew and the music and noise level increased, I felt it best to excuse myself along with the couples leaving for the prom. At this time, newspapers frequently had headlines, such as "Police Bust Large Drug Party in Golden Beach." To my astonishment, a police cruiser was parked outside the house as I exited. Luke had parked his car in front of a neighbor's driveway. The officers spoke a few words to Luke before allowing him and his party to leave for the prom. I realized that it might have taken only a matter of seconds for the police to have been at the door. I would have been the only adult present, which would have provided little to my defense as a nonparticipant. I remember starting the insurance company-owned automobiles and driving down the street and the cruiser seeming to follow me. I turned right at the next corner and the police car turned right as well. The same was true at the next corner when I made a left. Finally, after two blocks, I made a right turn, but the cruiser continued without making a turn.

The fear I experienced at that time would be recalled in my later observations of the group and cause me to proceed with caution when considering which of their activities to attend and under what circumstances. (In later years, I obtained a "Grant of Confidentiality" from the U.S. Department of Justice to conduct my research with freedom from such restraints.)

Following this event, I continued to meet the group casually and informally and became aware of those who were "regular" members of the group and those who were associated only occasionally with one or other member.

THE ROLE OF RESEARCHER IS INTRODUCED & THE GROUP BECOMES KNOWN AS A "GANG"

As summer approached, the group began to congregate regularly on the beach near a large motel. There is a sea wall at this location and the area was commonly referred to as "The Wall." The group became known as "The Wall Gang." Oddly enough, the group had actually moved to that location as a "hangout" and surfing spot to avoid others whom they labeled as "hard guys" who surfed in their earlier-preferred surfing area. "The Wall" was convenient for the "gang's" surfing interests and a local surf shop served as a message center and gathering place. Messages were sent and retrieved from a pay phone located nearby.

The gathering area also increased my contact with the gang, as it was situated at the end of the street where I lived. The amount of time I spent at the beach increased, along with my interactions with the gang. The stage was set for another step, a new level of acceptance of me by the group.

At that time, I resigned my junior executive position with the insurance company in order to pursue my academic career on a full-time basis. I also gave up my company car and purchased a small, more sporty model. In addition, I began to let my hair grow. Members of the group reacted almost immediately in a more open manner to me and expressed that my new image alleviated their fear that I might be a "narc" or undercover police officer.

I felt I had dispelled any fear that I was a "narc" and did not then realize how far I still had to go in overcoming the group's defenses. The new acceptance gave me sufficient confidence to use the group as my first test of a sociological theory. I was enrolled in a social problem course that summer. One evening, I completed an assigned reading, Becker's "On Becoming a Marijuana User[1]." I went to the wall to determine if the marijuana users with whom I was acquainted experienced the effects that Becker described. I was intrigued to hear such responses to my questions as:

> "Yeah, man, that's the way it happened to me. I didn't know I was high until this older dude started laughing at me."

> "The first time I smoked, I didn't get high, and, when I did, I though 'What's so great about this?'"

> "I was sitting on like this fucking high stool and started laughing. My brother like laughed at me and said, 'You're high man!'"

The gang was amazed that some "sociologist"said all this and had written such an accurate account of the step-by-step progression.

The next day I shared my "findings" in class. In an unforgettable moment, Dr. Dale Johnson of San Diego State University, called me to his desk after class, and gave me a most valuable piece of advice. He told me that if had a rapport with a group as it appeared, that I should begin researching them and writing down everything I observed. He said, "Someday, you might want to write a Master's thesis about them."

Little did I realize that the research would carry me to a doctoral dissertation, published papers and beyond to the present time.

The following term, I enrolled in a Juvenile Delinquency course offered by Dr. Robert Winslow. I asked him to guide my research. (Eventually, I would serve as his teaching assistant, he would direct my Master's Thesis and we would coauthor a text.[2])

I began my research as a "nonparticipant observer." By becoming a participant with the gang and involving myself in many of their interactions, I was able to increase my rapport and establish a confidence level with the group that allowed them to discuss their behavior with me freely and also act in their usual manner in my presence. However, by assuming the role of a "nonparticipant observer," as opposed to a "complete participant" in their deviant activities, it allowed me to avoid most of the moral, legal and ethical dilemmas inherent of studying deviant behavior without betraying my own values or objectivity. As I continued utilizing my role of a "nonparticipant observer," I utilized other methods of gathering information. In-depth interviews and numerous conversations were held with members of the group as well as with many of their friends, acquaintances, and family members. In addition, similar interviews and conversations were conducted with 31 young people of the same age range and similar socioeconomic background who live within the community but were not members of the gang. A more complete rationale for this will be presented in Chapter 4. I was able to refine this technique in years to come as will be described in that chapter.

As my relationship with the gang reached the stages of this formal study, I informed them of my intentions. Most members of the group were eager to participate and, in fact, felt honored, reasoning that if an objective person were to assess them and their marijuana use, the knowledge so obtained would justify their position in society as well as the use of marijuana. They were willing to share their pasts more fully, and they not only responded to my direct inquiries, but often pointed out matters which they felt might be of relevance to my research.

THE COMPLEMENTARY NATURE OF INTERVENTIONIST AND RESEARCHER ROLES

With the cooperation and information I appeared to be receiving, I felt I had no reason to doubt the completeness of my acceptance and the information. In hindsight, I did notice that a few of the members kept a certain distance in their relationship, but at that time, I attributed this to personality differences rather than to any doubts about my role. It took another event to help me break down the barriers still further, and to make me realize that my prior acceptance had been less than complete.

Matt had been one of the members who seemed somewhat reserved and distant to me. However, he and Luke and a friend of theirs, Laura, dropped by my apartment just to visit. Matt seemed very curious about me and the books that lined my shelves. Later, he would tell me that he thought I might have the answers to their behavior and his own self understanding. The following Saturday, on Labor Day weekend, 18-year-old Matt was arrested on the beach for possession of marijuana, then a felony. Matt was being held in the county jail, his arraignment scheduled for after the holiday. His parents' initial response was rejection and refusal of assistance. Upon learning of his plight at noon on Sunday, I contacted a law firm with which I was acquainted. The firm arranged to have Matt released on his own recognizance late that afternoon. In order that Matt might make a more favorable impression at his court appearance, as well as provide the now-homeless youth with some means of support, I persuaded the restaurant manager to give Matt a temporary job.

As might have been expected, my relationship and rapport with Matt strengthened. What initially amazed me, however, was that I found my role with the gang vastly redefined. I became privy to a flood of information from the youngsters and witness to a host of situations from which I had previously been excluded. I realized that which I was now hearing, seeing and experiencing was more characteristic of the true personality of the members. In addition, I was afforded access to information that would be quite incriminating in the hands of an officer of the law. I recall the reply of Tom, one of the members of the group to a nonmember who was reluctant to talk about drug dealing in my presence. The nonmember nodded toward me and stated, "He might be a narc." Tom replied, "Narcs put people in jail, not get them out!"

Increasingly I perceived that my relationship with the gang had taken on a new dimension. They still recognized me as a "non moralizing" researcher, but I had a new, more personal role that seemed to combine being a father figure and an interventionist. These two views quite clearly complemented each other. The members of the gang regarded the increased cooperation they could offer me with my research as a form of unsolicited payment for my various interventions on their behalf. I found that my insights into their perspectives were enhanced as I represented their interests before school principals, probation officers, prospective employers and draft counselors. This allowed me a greater understanding of their behaviors, attitudes and background, patterns of employment and school attendance and performance. Of note here is that as the role developed, I found myself increasingly involved with members of the group in aiding them with their difficulties. There developed an increasing degree of acceptance and confidence by the gang members that allowed me to penetrate their protective "fronts" and "pat responses." This permitted me to obtain the kinds of "insider" information and the perspective of the actors that many social scientists have described as crucial to the study of deviancy and the building of theories.[3] These included drug use, drug dealings, personal difficulties and interpersonal conflicts.

ROLE CONFLICT AND RESOLUTION

While this increasing degree of involvement was beneficial to my research role, it became increasingly necessary for me to remind myself of the necessity to maintain objectivity. Remaining neutral is especially difficult, if not impossible, under certain circumstances. The members of the gang often expected me to take a position in keeping with their view of my values. Often they would subtly seek my rebuke or my counsel that they remain in school or on a job when they felt an emotion urge to "drop out" against their own better judgment. To refrain from demonstrating the expected concern would have betrayed my own values and emotions as well as jeopardized the level of confidence and rapport I had attained.

My role became further complicated when Matt was arrested a second time, seven weeks later. Matt immediately sought my aid. After his first arrest, Matt had moved into a garage with one of the local high school "drug pushers." When I used my personal funds as bail on the second set of charges and assumed responsibility for Matt, I could hardly allow him to return to his garage abode. Consequently, I had no alternative but to take him into my own home. Although assumed to be "temporary," this arrangement lasted for the better part of a year. My interactions took on a definite "father-son" pattern. For this reason, I decided not to maintain with Matt any semblance of a researcher role, and made a conscious effort to make our relationship as "rehabilitative" for him as possible.

However, I could not separate the roles completely. Matt had been one of the gang and maintained many of his contacts with the members. I had become acquainted with him in the course of my research, and we were constantly aware of and interested in the subject matter. The long-term result of my close relationship with Matt was probably an even greater insight into the aspects of his background, values and personality which he shared with other group members. In addition, I had an unusual opportunity to observe the social-psychological impact on Matt's drug use of such events as loss of employment, failure in a school exam or rejection by his parents.

Matt and Luke would remain key figures in my research and in my life. Later, I will describe more of my relationship with each of them, where they have been in succeeding years and what they are accomplishing today.

My role as a father figure became more significant as time progressed. I would come to realize the extreme significance of adequate father figures and inadequate father figures in the lives of these individuals as well as others.

End Notes

1. Howard S. Becker, *Outsiders,* NY: The Free Press, 1963.

2. Jeremiah Lowney, Robert W. Winslow and Virginia Winslow, *Deviant Reality: Alternative World Views,* Boston: Allyn and Bacon, 1981.

3. Howard A. Becker, *Outsiders,* NY: The Free Press, 1963; Jack Douglas, Observations of Deviance, NY: Random House, 1970; Jeremiah Lowney, Robert W. Winslow and Virginia Winslow, *Deviant Reality: Alternative World Views,* Boston: Allyn & Bacon, 1981, pp. 4-14; Jacqueline P. Wiseman, *Stations of the Lost: The Treatment of Skid Row Alcoholics,* Englewood Cliffs, NJ: Prentice-Hall, 1970; William F. Whyte, *Street Corner Society: The Social Structure of an Italian Slum*, Chicago: The University of Chicago Press, 1955.

Chapter 2

THE WALL GANG - 1971-72

LACK OF FORMAL GANG ORGANIZATION

By 1971, the loose and shifting membership of the Wall Gang consisted of 23 white youths, aged 17 to 19. To the casual observer, the group appeared to be a gang whose primary interest was surfing. As noted, their long hair and slovenly appearance had led many members of the adult community to classify them as a gang which used drugs extensively. The term "The Wall Gang" became accepted in the summer of 1971 both as a label used them and others, and a description of the location they frequented along a sea wall, convenient to surfing and surf shops. It became evident early in this research that the group more aptly fit Yablonsky's definition of a "near-group[1]." Roles were not defined. Membership was difficult to determine and there were many youths who were only peripheral members of the group. The main source of cohesiveness seemed to be in the pursuit of pleasure-surfing, parties, drugs and sex. Although several incidents arose that might have allowed the members to prove their solidarity, such as when "busts" were made or feared to be imminent, the response was "every man for himself."In the course of the research, I was to be called upon, not only in emergency situations to bail a youngster out of jail or help him find employment, but more frequently, to give day-to-day encouragement to continue working or remain in school. As some of the youths came to me as a surrogate father, it was evident they were attempting to learn a degree of self-control associated with the attainment of independence, adult responsibility and economic self-support. Most members of the group lacked the ability to persevere in matters that would affect their future. Eight of the 23 were high school dropouts. Of those who graduated from high school, only one of the seven who enrolled in a junior college continued, and this was on a part-time and sporadic basis. Most did not live with their parents. Still, only one held a job for the entire six-month period of the initial phase of this study. The usual pattern was to save a small amount of money, become bored with the job and call in sick, or simply not arrive for work when employment interfered with a party or other activity.

FAMILY BACKGROUND

A most striking feature of the group was the similarity of family background of the members. All but two of the youths were from households where the estimated family income exceeded twice the national median. The other two households could be considered middle-class, economically. Each had one parent and an approximate annual income equal to the national median.

Typically, both parents worked outside the home. Five of the fathers and stepfathers were connected with the United States Navy, either as career military officers or as civil service employees. Many others worked in the electronics industry.

The most significant characteristic of family background was the incidence of divorce. Twenty-one of the twenty-three members had divorced parents, and serious conflict existed between the parents in the remaining two homes. Several of the parents had been divorced more than once. The extreme case was that of Kevin. Kevin's mother had been divorced seven times; his father five times. Many of his stepparents had themselves been divorced. Kevin's case also illustrates a rather extreme example of the heavy use of alcohol by parents. Kevin closed one discussion with me saying, "I have to go home and 'babysit' my dad. He is just so drunk that he crawls along the floor. They have tried everything with him. He even went through an experiment with LSD once, but it didn't work."

From interviews with the youths and from contacts with their parents, it was learned that parents were generally materially indulgent and that they tried to avoid any knowledge of their sons' drug involvement.

When drug use did come to light, such as in the case of an arrest, a typical response was anger and rejection.

More About Matt

The discussion of his home situation was an extremely painful task for Matt, then 18, who was described in the previous chapter. In ordinary conversation, he referred to his stepbrothers as "brothers" and his stepfather as "Dad." Without additional probing, I would not have suspected these were other than blood relationships. I still recall, however, the tears in Matt's eyes when he first discussed these matters with me and stated, "I never really had a father!" He did not dislike his present stepfather, but repeatedly said, "He just doesn't care!"

Matt's true father was alleged to be a sadist whom his mother had divorced when Matt was two. Matt's mother remarried a year later. This man, his first stepfather, was an alcoholic, and a second divorce occurred when Matt was 10. Three years later, the present remarriage took place. Matt's two stepbrothers were incompatible with Matt's mother and each left home when he turned 18. One stepbrother introduced Matt to marijuana when he was 13.

The family resided in a very expensive home that was then listed for sale at $69,000. The parents owned property in Idaho, rental property in the beach area and several lots. They had recently purchased a $50,000 condominium overlooking the ocean. Both parents were civil service employees. Matt seldom went home for dinner because, “I have to sit in the kitchen with Cindy [Matt's 12-year-old sister] while they sit in the dining room and discuss all their investments.” When Matt was first arrested for possession of marijuana, he telephoned his home. His mother informed him they would not assist him and he could no longer live in their house. I was to learn of Matt's predicament the following day and came to his assistance through an attorney-friend

Shortly after I obtained Matt's release from jail, he and I met some of the gang members who asked Matt if he planned to attend a rock concert that evening. Matt turned toward me and said, "I think I'm on restriction. Am I on restriction, Jerry?"

Matt moved in with one of his friends, but returned to my home that evening for no apparent reason. He soon informed me that he had sold his remaining marijuana to a friend. I reacted with anger that he would be committing what was another felony with the memory of the jail so fresh in his mind. Matt replied, somewhat perplexed, "Well, couldn't you tell I was stoned when you opened the door?"

With further emotion, I informed him I was not aware that he had been using marijuana. He responded, "Oh, good! For a while, I was afraid you didn't care." Matt's reaction toward me seemed to indicate a desire for a "father figure" who would furnish not just assistance out of difficulty but a firm attitude of discipline that would help prevent future difficulty.

In the course of the time that Matt became my “foster son,” there were many other incidents that demonstrated Matt’s desire for a caring disciplinarian as well as a willingness to change his behavior. I placed a midnight curfew on Matt. He usually came home well before the curfew. However, if I appeared to be overly concerned about my own academic workload or about other youth, Matt would sometimes tell me after dinner that he "would see me in the morning." I learned that this was a signal for me to demonstrate my caring through firmness. We would usually exchange words, and often raise our voices. On those evenings, Matt appeared to have a stopwatch and turned the key in the door about 11:59 p.m. He never violated his curfew, but argued about it frequently.

I also insisted that Matt be home in time for dinner every night. He and Maria, his girlfriend, asked me about this one morning. I mentioned that my father had always insisted on our large family being present for the evening meal. Unfortunately, that same evening, I had an appointment and began dinner early. Matt came home and was upset and would not speak. This continued over the next two days, when I finally forced him to tell me what was wrong he said, "You told me that your Dad always made sure you were home for dinner, and the other night my brother and his wife invited me to eat at their house. I told them you were waiting for me and, then, when I got home, you were almost finished eating!"

I apologized to Matt for my insensitivity. He told me he was also upset because that afternoon he had told Mrs. Sullivan that she could call me about her son, Sean. Sean, was 16 and had been having a number of difficulties with the law and problems in school. Mrs. Sullivan did not know how to handle the situation. Matt told her I knew "everything about kids." I was amazed at Matt's confidence in me. He seemed to expect me to be the "perfect father." (My eventual involvement with Sean will be discussed in the next chapter.)

As Christmas approached, Matt brought a stocking from his mother's home and placed it over the heater. On Christmas Eve, I put a few small gifts in the stocking, including a chess set. I went to bed. When Matt came in, he found the presents and made sure I was awake. He sat on the sofa and began to cry. He told me he had never had gifts before at Christmas. He asked me to play chess with him. (In any game of skill, Matt usually triumphed over me!)

I was able to eventually help Matt obtain employment in construction and become a member of a labor union. As he demonstrated more responsibility and independence, I was forced to encourage him to become more independent and live on his own. He accepted this verbally and told me he wanted to be independent of me. However, it took more gentle prodding and effort to eventually live on his own. For some time, he relied on me for a ride to work in the morning and would accept frequent invitations to dinner. It was difficult for him initially. He appeared to rely on drugs and girlfriends, at times, to cope. Over time, he became more self-confident and noticeably more mature.

In later chapters, I will describe Matt's continued journey and eventually successes in life.

The Case of Pat

The complications of home life were dramatically brought to my attention by Pat. At the age of 17, Pat was enrolled in a local high school, but was frequently truant. He had been arrested twice for possession of marijuana, but was no longer on probation. He lived with his father and an older brother. His father frequently "disappeared" for several days at a time and Pat was in charge of groceries and the household budget. Pat's mother had been married several times and, at that time, lived some 20 miles from the beach community. Pat did not drive, but had received 17 traffic tickets, all for bicycle or pedestrian offenses. In July of 1971, Pat received a citation for crossing the street on a "Don't Walk" signal. I went to the sea wall that same afternoon and was greeted by Pat:

> "Hey, man! I need you to do something for me. It's easy. I just want you to go to traffic court with me and just tell 'em you're my step-dad."
>
> "But, I can't do that. Why not get your father to go?"
>
> "No! Are you crazy? He'd kill me! He'll throw me out of the house if he finds out I got another ticket. If he has to leave work again and go up there, I've had it. Please do it for me. Just say you're my step-dad. Nobody will know the difference. Hell! My Mom would marry you. She's married all kinds of cats. But she can't come. She lives too far away and can't come."

I told Pat I would not lie and urged him to tell his father. He reiterated that he would be thrown out of his home. This was verified by other members of the group. I agreed to visit the juvenile court with Pat prior to the hearing date to inquire what might be done. The probation officer informed us that Pat's mother could write a letter appointing me as "the responsible adult" to appear on Pat's behalf.

The full impact of Pat's attitude toward parents and adult society was demonstrated when another youth asked Pat about the ticket. Pat replied, "Jerry fixed it up for me so he's gonna be able to go with me. I am glad not all adults are fucked!"

This quote illustrates the attitudes that I was to find increasingly among the gang members. These included a feeling that adults, particularly fathers, "did not care," resulting in the need to reach out to me as a "father figure" on whom they could depend for intervention on their behalf and who would admonish them to take the necessary steps to avoid difficulties and solve their own future problems.

Distinguished by his outspoken nature, his assumption of a leadership role as well as by and his brillo-like hair shooting out from his head in all directions, Pat would become a key figure in the study over the next 30 years.

The Case of Chad

Chad was 17, one of three siblings. His father had abandoned the family when Chad was five. Chad resented this greatly. At the conclusion of a lengthy interview, I asked Chad what he would say to his father if he would meet him. Chad responded, "I beat the shit out of him for what he did to us and our mother!"

Chad rarely went home. At times, he lived with an older male who provided him with drugs, including cocaine, and used Chad as a "model" to photograph. Chad frequently missed school.

In 1972, Chad was excluded from the group for "ripping people off." I saw him at times in 1975, but he, too, was using heavier drugs, particularly cocaine and did not frequent the wall or most of Golden Beach. By 1996, Chad was homeless and lived on the beach near a restroom north of Golden Beach. (In 2001, Chad lived with a woman who "took care of him." He continued to use drugs and surf.)

The Case of Ty

Ty was 18 when I first met him. He was somewhat reluctantly accepted by the Wall Gang after completing a sentence in a juvenile facility for possession and sale of heroin. Ty was "clean" in 1971. Ty's father left his mother at a very early age. Ty's mother was extremely indulgent with Ty's early deviant activities and use of drugs. Ty used a variety of drugs beginning at the age of 10. When he was 14, Ty first used heroin. He became addicted and financed his addiction through the sale of drugs. Ty told me,

> I used to go down to Tijuana. I could buy enough smack to take care of me for a week and enough to sell to give me enough fixes for two more. I would put the smack in a balloon and swallow it. I could then just walk across the border. After I got back, all I had to do was wait until it passed when I took my next shit. Then I had the stuff and could sell what I had to and use the rest...
>
> My Mom didn't want me to get busted. She was afraid for me because I was on probation. I told her I was going to deal anyway. So she would drive me to my buyer. That way I wouldn't get busted!

Ty's mother appeared to fit what will be described as an "overprotective" mother in subsequent discussions of the McCord-Chein model or theory of drug abuse.

For a period of time in 1972, Ty lived in a small house with Pat and Chad. Within a year, he relapsed into his heroin addiction. He was excluded from the gang. I saw him at times. I never found him in a condition in which he was sufficiently coherent to carry on a conversation. Ty died in prison in 1997. No one was certain of the cause of death. Some said he was beaten by the staff or other inmates. Other thought he may have died of hepatitis which he had contracted several years earlier.

The cases of Kevin, Matt, Pat, Chad and Ty each illustrate situations of members of the group who had either no father at home, a stepfather with whom they did not relate, or a dysfunctional father. In 1996, David Popenoe's extensive study of the literature, *Life Without Father*, traces the implications of these situations for children and society.[2] The same implications were evident throughout my study. In addition, it became evident that the youth involved in the "gang" found the group to provide primary groups relationships and a form of "substitute family" for them.

RELATIONSHIPS WITH THE OPPOSITE SEX

Several members of the group seemed to have an affinity for female companions who were willing and able to "enable" them from accepting responsibility for their actions as well as support them financially. During the summer months, Arizona "chicks" who rented beach cottages by the month were considered prime catches. While not in their presence, members referred to these young women as "little miss rich bitches." Contacts often continued with such tourists after the summer months, even though the members of the group might be living with other "old ladies" during the remainder of the year. Such was the case with Pops.

The Case of Pops

Pops met Lois during the summer of 1970. She and several of her friends spent six weeks at the beach after their graduation from an Arizona high school. Whenever Pops needed money or drugs, Lois would provide them even if she had to phone her physician-father for additional funds. Lois continued to write to Pops during that autumn. He did not respond until his car broke down. He then told her he needed $125 to fix the automobile so he could visit her. Lois sent the money, but after Pops received the money, he moved in with Mary Lou, a native of the beach area, whose wealthy father was supporting her so long as she attended college. Pops drove her to the campus each morning and had the use of her sports car the remainder of the day. This lasted more than three months. Mary Lou described the end of the arrangement,

> I was really stupid! He never even thought of paying me for food! He would just use my car, have me take care of him including fixing his meals. He wouldn't even pick up after himself. A lot of times, I felt like telling him to get out. He was always just sitting on the beach, smoking my dope all day. Then, I found out he was running around with Joanne. I sure was stupid! He would even leave me home alone in the evenings, take my car and go out with his friends. Half the time Joanne was with him. I finally told him to get out or I would dump all his belongings on the sidewalk. Then, he gets sick! I was a sucker for that and started giving him all kind of sympathy, but, as soon as he thought he had me around his finger again, he got well. Finally, I just had to move back with my folks to get rid of him.

Pops was able to make similar living arrangements with other young women, and when Lois returned to the beach area the following summer, she forgave him and continued to pay his expenses and give him spending money.

The Case of Vick

Unlike most of the members of the Wall Gang, Vick's family was intact. However, his father, a successful anesthesiologist, appeared to be ashamed of his wife, a homely uneducated woman, who seldom left their expensive home. Vick's father was a strict, demanding authoritarian who considered Vick to be a "bum" and the "black sheep" of his five children. He was especially critical of Vick's inability to achieve more than average grades. Vick's mother felt that Vick was a "good boy." Vick was arrested three times in seven months for felony offenses, twice for possession of marijuana, once for grand larceny. To each arrest his father reacted with anger and rejection. However, his mother denied Vick's responsibility and repeatedly stated that her son, "Doesn't have a mean bone in his body."

Vick moved in and out of his family's home depending on his father's mood. When not living at home, he lived with Patti. Patti, with her money, supported Vick at these times, bailed him out of jail, and gave him funds upon request, all without expectation of repayment. In spite of this, Vick was disloyal to Patti and had sexual relations with a variety of other women. He made some tie attempt to conceal these activities from her, but when they did come to her attention Patti was quite conciliatory. In Vick's words, "Well, she knows that's the way I am."

THE USE OF DRUGS

A variety of mood-altering substances was used by the Wall Gang. Marijuana was the substance used most frequently and, during this period, was the center of the parties. In 1971, the parties averaged about 30-40 participants. These would grow in size substantially in succeeding years. However, most of the group were "stoned" a good portion of each day through all their activities. The average age of first use of marijuana was 12. The cost of marijuana was minimal, about eight to 10 dollars for a "four-finger" lid or bag (a plastic sandwich bag four fingers wide). Marijuana was shared freely. Some reported smoking it several times a day for years without any purchases or payments.

The group seemed willing to try most any substance to get "high." These included barbiturates (or "Reds"), amphetamines (or "Speed"), hallucinogens, such as mescaline, peyote, and, on rare occasions (when possible to afford the cost), cocaine. Only one member of the group, Ty, described previously, had used heroin by 1971. The use of heroin was forbidden by the group and Ty was tolerated because at the time he was not using heroin or other opiates. The group also frowned on "huffing" of paint, glue or other chemicals. By late summer, 1971, and, more so, in 1972, in spite of the earlier admonitions regarding alcohol, I noticed that when marijuana was not available, the group drank beer or other alcoholic beverages. However, the making of a good party involved the quality of the "pot" available rather than the amount of beer.

In Relating to the Opposite Sex

A discussion I had with Vick early in my research exemplifies the use of drugs and alcohol by members of the group in their relations with women. Vick was on his way to a party, and he informed me that he had to be "high" before he got there. I inquired why it was necessary to do this since there would be a variety of drugs and alcoholic beverages available at the party. He replied, "Yeah, but you know how it is. The chicks are already goin' to be there an' I can't talk to chicks unless I am at least a little high."

I learned that Vick's response reflected a common practice among the group. The group often confirmed this use of drugs to aid them in sexual relations. Frequently, they invited several young women with the expressed purpose of holding an "orgy." Though such strategies apparently never proved successful, the "plans" called for everyone to ingest relatively high doses of drugs or alcohol, and for a few "volunteers" from the group to "get naked." Supposedly, this would "turn on" the women, and an orgy would be the natural outcome.

One member of the group, Keith, claimed many sexual conquests, but maintained he had never had sexual relations without the use of marijuana, cocaine, or hallucinogens. He firmly believed that LSD has "aphrodisiac" qualities.

The Use of Drugs to Reduce Anxiety and Escape Responsibility

Throughout the course of the research, numerous occurrences were noted in which it appeared that the youths sought specific states of "highness" to reduce the discomfort of anxiety-provoking situations. Most of these situations could be conceived of as normal, everyday stresses and strains of late adolescence. Many such occurrences had to do with school or employment.

For example, one youth reduced his anxiety prior to a school exam by using marijuana. Thus, he was not able to prepare properly. When the exam was completed and he realized he had done poorly, he used more marijuana to reduce the consequent anxiety.

The Case of Julian

Julian had been unemployed for several weeks. He was without food and had received an eviction notice from his landlord for the nonpayment of rent. He sought my intercession one afternoon to obtain a job for him. The following morning, I telephoned him to recommend employers he might solicit. Julian could not remain on the phone as he informed me he had to leave the apartment to sell 13 "lids" of marijuana. However, he was not making a monetary profit. In turn for selling 13 lids, he could keep six for himself. The same afternoon, I saw him at the beach. He was hungry but he would not sell the marijuana. His first concern was not food, but sufficient marijuana to remain "high" and thus avoid the anxiety generated by his circumstances. This, and other incidents, appeared indicated that he and others used marijuana as an escape mechanism.

THE USE OF DRUGS BY GANG MEMBERS AS COMPARED TO OTHER YOUTHS

The 31 non-gang youths whom I formally interviewed could not be properly classified as a "control" group. At best, they (and numerous other young people with whom I came into contact during the study) represented a loose "comparison" group during this phase of the research. I asked questions of and interviewed as many youths from the community as were cooperative, within the limitations of time and other circumstances. I located them under a variety of conditions, e.g., through loose connections with the gang, informally at the beach and through church activities. Twelve of these youths were young women. They appeared to represent a fair cross-section of the 16- to 21-year-old population of the community.

It was not in the kinds of drugs used that the youths who were not members differed from "The Wall Gang." Rather, it was in the frequency and conditions of use between the two groups that showed wide variation. In the period between 1971 and 1972, I found only one young person in the community to interview who did not admit to the use of marijuana. There was also considerable experimentation with hallucinogens.

Non-gang members used marijuana or alcohol frequently at weekend parties. Gang members used these substances daily. Non-gang members did not use marijuana prior to or during school or work, or allow these substances to interfere with their studies or employment. Gang members did use marijuana at school and work. Non-gang members only rarely reported using drugs to help them in their relationships with the opposite sex or in obtaining sexual favors. Gang members used drugs for both purposes.

The groups differed in other ways as well. Non-gang members were more likely to come from stable home situations (only three divorces were reported among this group), and seemed to have "normal" relationships with their parents. They also appeared to have good relationships with the opposite sex, which were not based solely on either sexual or financial exploitation.

CONCLUSIONS

The findings of observational research do not lend themselves to rigorous and statistical analysis. They must be reported as accurately as possible and allowed to "speak for themselves." It is necessary for the researcher to sort out those facts and incidents that are deemed important, and report them along with a description of the context and his role in the interactions. Such is my intention herein.

Thus, I concluded my first report on the Wall Gang in 1972 with a description of the "ideal type" or "typical" Wall Gang member as follows:

> The evidence contained herein seems clear. The 'typical' Wall Gang member is an upper-middle-class late adolescent. He spends the majority of his years living with his mother and one or more stepfathers, who often uses alcohol excessively and rejects him. Although his parents provide for his physical needs, he senses a lack of love and concern. He has low self-esteem and a poor sex-identity. Having been introduced to marijuana and alcohol at a comparatively young age, he has learned that such substances can reduce the symptoms of his anxiety. He uses the same substances to relate to the opposite sex. He has found the companionship of youths with similar backgrounds and behavior patterns. He has spent his formative years using marijuana and other drugs. His companions reinforce his attitudes, particularly his negative

> attitudes toward parents and society. He is only sporadically employed and is unable to find work or educational interests that stimulate him. He blames others for his problems. He lacks a religious background, and seeks pleasure in the "moment" through sex and drugs. He feels increasing guilt and frustration, but in a cyclical pattern, he copes through increased hedonistic pursuits. He may use marijuana, alcohol or other drugs as a 'tranquilizer' and may avoid more serious difficulties or personality disorders by doing so. It must be noted, however, that his patterns and the contributing familial backgrounds are similar to those found by Isidor Chein[3] among heroin addicts. They further bear a resemblance to the model of alcoholism proposed by the McCords.[4] Some of the cases are relatively 'typical' while others represent extreme examples of common characteristics and situations.[5]

In some ways, during the early to mid-1970s, the above description fit some youth in Golden Beach other than members of the Wall Gang. Still others stood in sharp contrast. Longitudinal research allowed me to investigate the challenge one Wall Gang member, Les, put to me, "It is not what we are doing now that matters. It is what we will be like 20 years from now!" This would be my major challenge. My research would continue beyond 20 years. I would investigate the long term effects of family background and drug use on the lives of the Wall Gang as well as on the lives of others with similar backgrounds. However, to completely understand them it would be necessary for me to also understand those whose family background and lives appeared to be quite different. Finally, it would be necessary for me to examine the lives and backgrounds of females as well as males.

End Notes

1. Lewis Yablonsky, *Gangsters*, NY: New York University Press, 1997, pp. 191-194.
2. David Popenoe, *Life Without Father*, NY, The Free Press, 1996.
3. Isidor Chein, D. L. Gerard, R.S. Lee, and F. Rosenfeld, *The Road to H,* NY: Basic Books, 1964.

4. William McCord and Joan McCord, *Origins of Alcoholism*, Stanford: Stanford University Press, 1960.

5. Jeremiah Lowney, "The Wall Gang: A Study of Interpersonal Process and Deviance Among Twenty-Three Middle-Class Youths", *Adolescence*, Vol. XIX, No. 75 Fall 1984, p. 537.

Chapter 3

CHANGES OCCUR & TRENDS DEVELOP

I continued to remain in close contact with the group throughout the years. I completed my bachelor's degree in the summer of 1972, and my master's in the summer of 1973. I continued to maintain journals of the Wall Gang and made notations of other young people and parents, as well as the general trends in the area. In addition, I was employed part-time at a residential treatment facility for delinquent and emotionally disturbed teenagers. I was assigned to a girls' cottage. This gave me additional insight into young people and their difficulties. At the same time, I became interested in how background factors, including the family, might be similar or vary among females as well as males.

In late summer, 1973, I moved from San Diego to enter a doctoral program at the University of Kentucky. However, I visited Golden Beach over holidays and during the summer months over the next two and half years. In addition, members of the Wall Gang and others remained in contact with me by mail, and, at times by phone. During the final months of my doctoral courses, I renewed I resided at and taught in the Franciscan high school seminary from which I graduated. The Wall Gang and others admired my Franciscan ties. This was accentuated by the Franco Zeffirelli movie, "Brother Sun, Sister Moon."

What follows are descriptions of the trends during this period of time taken from my journals as well as from some of the correspondence I received from the young people in Golden Beach.

Some changes began to occur in Golden Beach in 1972 that affected the lives of those living there. As freeways were completed, the population increased, As people became more aware of the area's attractiveness, an influx of tourism occurred. Finding a parking space became more problematic. High-rise buildings were erected. This led to a counter-movement and various initiatives to limit height and density.

Some were trends that first became apparent as 1972 continued and developed over time. The rhetoric became somewhat more conservative. Symbols of the peace movement were less evident. Crime began to increase.

By 1974 a trend toward a renewed involvement in religion developed. This was particularly evident among the young, including the Wall Gang.

Various changes occurred in the drug subculture. The more expensive street drugs became more popular. Cocaine had been considered "a rich man's high." Its use was not condemned but was considered too expensive for the youngsters interviewed. By 1973, large amounts of cocaine entered the beach community. Several youths, most members of the Wall Gang, used and sold cocaine during that period. At about the same time, a "heroin epidemic" spread through the community. Two members of the gang, Keith and Vick, used this formerly condemned drug for several months with few apparent problems in overcoming withdrawal symptoms. Others, including Ty and Kramer, were less fortunate.

Alcohol, formerly condemned by young people, now became somewhat popular. It was found at the parties along with marijuana and other drugs. Attendance at the parties increased. However, at this time, the success of the parties was not measured by the number of kegs of beer. Rather, alcohol and other drugs combined with the presence of "cool people" made for a "good time." Obtaining or using alcoholic beverages had not been considered difficult prior to this time. It simply became more acceptable. Ironically, the reaction of police and parents to youthful drinking was one of relief. It implied to them that youngsters who drank alcohol were not using marijuana or other substances. More than once I viewed police officers smiling and condoning the behavior of young people found drinking beer on the boardwalk. Parents would often remark, "My son (or daughter) came home drunk last night. Thank God, he (she) is not using drugs!"

These trends of drug and alcohol use were found among the Wall Gang as well as among others. In prior years, many of these youth had used amphetamines ("Speed" or "Whites") and barbiturates ("Reds").

By the summer of 1972, the "verbal ethic" was that "Whites" and particularly "Reds"were dangerous. Earlier, I had been told by males and females that it was "unladylike" to drink a beer in public. Thus, young females, including the "surfer chicks" who tended to hang out with surfers, used "Reds" to "get a high" especially on the beach or at the wall. This norm dissipated as well. These changes seemed to occur as the result of negative effects that they had either experienced personally or became aware within their peer groups. The negative effects included symptoms of addiction and withdrawal, including life-threatening withdrawals and death.

THE WALL GANG - HIGHS AND LOWS

For a period during late 1972 and early 1973, It appeared that the Wall Gang was losing its cohesion. A few persons had been excluded. Others drifted away. I found it necessary to make decisions in regards to my interactions with the Wall Gang. As I walked along the beach, and visited with various members, I was cautious not to pass on information which would be the source of preserving their cohesion. The original number of 23 dwindled to 16 by late 1972. By midyear, 1973, the group remained stable at about 13. Eventually others would join them. As younger members were accepted into their territory, The entire group became known as "The Wall Crew." At times, the original group referred proudly to their identity as "The Wall Gang" as distinct from the younger members. In years to come, they would look back with nostalgia to the days of "The Old Wall Gang."

Deviant Activities

A variety of deviant activities were engaged in particularly by the Wall Gang. Many of these were associated with their drug use. They included drug dealing, some property crimes and miscellaneous activities that were associated with having "fun," particularly when uninhibited while under the influence of marijuana or other substances. It must be emphasized that the property crimes were not engaged in to purchase drugs. They were merely the activities of uninhibited, and frequently intoxicated, young people.

Some of the activities resulted in arrests. The vast majority were never brought to the attention of law enforcement. Indeed, throughout the research there is strong evidence that legal sanctions had little if any deterrent effect. Indeed, as will be shown, some police activity actually increased deviant activities.

Activities Directly Related to Drug Use

In addition to the use of drugs and the sale of drugs, other activities resulted from participation in the drug subculture.

One of these involved the sale of a variety of innocuous substances under the guise that these substances were drugs. The first time I observed this type of scam, Vick and Luke placed drops of water on blotter paper and went to the boardwalk to wait for sailors to ask them for drugs. (They frequently referred to sailors as "swabbies" who, among other things, were easy "marks" for such a scam.) When two sailors approached them, Luke told them they had some good "blotter acid." The sailors paid a dollar each for two "hits" of what they believed to be LSD. Vick and Luke used the two dollars to pay their entrance to a party that evening. What was amazing to me was the degree to which the scam succeeded apparently due to a "placebo effect." Later that evening, I observed the sailors who were "tripping out" and enjoying various hallucinations along the sea wall. On other occasions, individuals bought oregano from the spice section of a supermarket and sold it as marijuana. Once, Pat was asked by a female classmate at Golden Beach High School for marijuana. Pat told her he did not know where to find it. She continued to make requests of Pat. Finally, Pat cut and broke down compound from his wood shop class and sold it to her as "good pot." The young student later sought out Pat for more of the "pot" she and her friends had enjoyed smoking.

These types of scams were not without risks. I viewed three non-gang members sell oregano to two marines. The next day, the two marines and two others returned asking me and others if we knew where they could find those who had tricked them out of their money.

These scams were acceptable if perpetrated on sailors or those who were not "locals" (from Golden Beach). Other actions were "totally uncool" if the victims were from one's own group or territory. This was particularly the case if someone stole drugs or drug money from others. If this was suspected, the person was excluded from the subculture and, at times, physically assaulted.

Heroin Arrives in Force

A "heroin epidemic"occurred during 1974. The national press mentioned San Diego as one of the locations that were experiencing this phenomenon. Official records of the San Diego Police Department showed a substantial increase in arrests for heroin in 1974 compared to previous years among the middle and upper classes. The press attributed the increase to the return of Vietnam veterans. Golden Beach was a part of that pattern.

When I visited in the summer of 1974, several of the young people informed me they had smoked heroin. They had been told that a person would become addicted by smoking heroin. They did not seem to make the connection between smoking heroin and smoking the opium from which it was derived. They were aware that in other parts of the world thousands were addicted to opium. Most who tried this technique did not become addicted. However, two of the Wall Gang did experience difficulties from opiate use.

Julian had been drafted and served in Vietnam as a military police officer. The experience had a profound effect on him. He had smoked opium in Vietnam and used it intravenously in Germany. In Heidelberg, he ran a military automobile into a Heidelberg bus. He was discharged from the service with "codes." He used heroin for a brief period of time when he returned to Golden Beach, as he said, "And that was with Kramer." By the summer of 1974, it was obvious that Julian's drug problem involved alcohol. He told me "I answered eight of 10 questions (regarding alcohol use) in Time with a 'yes'."

Julian admitted drinking Bloody Marys in the morning and beer throughout the day. He also smoked marijuana and used cocaine, but felt he was an alcoholic. I told him about Alcoholics Anonymous. He declined such assistance. Julian was unemployed and not attending school. His sister, Mary Lou, refused to talk to him any longer.

Kramer, who had described his father as a "hopeless alcoholic" was now addicted to heroin. Luke and Julian took Kramer to the hospital after Kramer's roommate had a fight with them and told them he did not want Kramer to return. Kramer was not employed.

Activities "Just for Fun"

Wall Gang members developed some of their own unique behaviors. One was to beg from passing tourists by asking, "Can I have a dime to call my mother?" In a short span, this could be quite lucrative and the youth could buy dinner or go to a movie.

Surfing was the major source of recreation and a surfer's status was determined by how adept he was at surfing. (It is noteworthy that at this period neither females nor those more than 30 years of age were expected to surf.) To steal, or to borrow and not return another's surfboard was the strongest of all taboos. The group especially enjoyed "surfing naked" as a challenge and a way to entertain themselves while shocking others.

Sexual activity was frequently extensive as the group, and others, adopted the norms of the "Sexual Revolution" occurring in America. Throughout the summer of 1972, Wall Gang members Keith and Turk, engaged in a contest. They competed with each other to determine which of them could succeed in having sexual intercourse with females (or, as they called it "make the most chicks"). Each morning they would report to each other and their friends as to their success the prior evening. Keith won the contest, but Turk claimed it was only because of Keith's shoulder-length hair. "What else has he got," Turk complained, "All he got is his long, blond hair!"

One activity that was engaged in "for fun," but perhaps indicative of homophobia, was "gay bashing." The most dramatic series of this behavior occurred during the summer of 1973. Pat and Chad, sometimes accompanied by others, descended upon a restroom frequented by homosexuals on the beach. Each night they would await the arrival of homosexuals. The Wall Gang members would either lure them aside or attack them physically. They stated that they were trying to "clean up the beach from those cigarettes!"

Activities Involving Money or Property

Property crimes were infrequent, and, contrary to popular belief were not usually engaged in to purchase drugs. Rather, they were a part of general youthful deviance more likely to occur under the influence of drugs.

At times, members would engage in "dine and dash," a variety of schemes to eat in a restaurant and leave without paying for the meal. Many times, this involved taking the check into the restroom, tearing it in pieces and flushing it down the toilet before departing.

On one occasion, Turk was walking down the boardwalk in the early hours of the morning, and decided to take two lawn chairs from a doorstep. He was using marijuana at the time and was arrested for theft and possession of marijuana, a felony. He claimed he was just "having fun" and had intended to return the chairs. Turk's felony charge was reduced to a misdemeanor. He paid a fine and a brief unsupervised period of probation.

ARRESTS

Other arrests occurred during these years. Some of these resulted in more serious consequences.

Pops

Pops was a member of the Wall Gang. He was described previously regarding his relationship with the opposite sex and ability to seek out females who would "take care" of him. His father was a high-ranking U.S. Naval officer serving on a large aircraft carrier. As with other military parents in Golden Beach, Pops' father was frequently absent for long periods of time during Pops' formative years.

Pops was engaged in marijuana and cocaine. In 1974, Pops was 22 when a "friend" led him to "guy he said he 'knew." Pops later discovered the friend had met the person only one time. When Pops entered the room to complete the cocaine deal, eight agents were in the room who "whipped out guns." Pops was arrested. Pops' family was "supportive" and his father put up bail and hired the "best attorneys." Pops was sentenced to four months and served three. Pops wrote to me,

> I was taken to the county jail for the first six days. That was the worst part. There were fights all the time. Guys were constantly approaching me for sodomy. There were lots of drunks. They also used 'kick pack' for those on H or Reds. Every day they would have everyone there kicking those guys as a part of the routine. After, I was transferred to the county camp in the mountains to fight fires. It was not that bad but could fuck a guy's head up.

Pops was very frightened by the prospect of going to prison. He spoke of his fears and related stories of prison's horrors that he had heard in jail and at the county camp.

Pops had written to me from the camp. I interviewed him in July 1974, while he was on parole. He told me he had gotten parole by telling "them" he was going to go to school. In July, he told me he "might" go to night classes. He intended to leave town that week. He was living with coke dealers. He said, "I think the house is being watched."

Pops was very nervous as I visited with him at a sidewalk restaurant. A friend of his approached Pops and said, "A guy wants 55 (dollars)."

Pops said he had about half, or 23 dollars. Pops was embarrassed that I heard the conversation and said he was not "using that much" cocaine, but that it "would be nice to have some now." His friend left. It was obvious that even after his experiences of arrest and incarceration and the terms of his probation that could end in his imprisonment for the use of cocaine, Pops was still using cocaine and associating with dealers.

Pops felt he "should get away from the beach scene. I know too many dealers and users."

He told me that he continued to use pot but was trying to "stay away from cocaine." Pops and I exchanged addresses. Two months later, I received the following letter from Pops:

Dear Jerry,

Thank you for your wonderful letter. It was good that I got out of San Diego and I did cause I would probably have gotten in trouble sooner or later. And you said, I guess this past experience has been a help to me in the long run. It has helped me see the light and start thinking of my future.

I started school at Washington Technical Institute and majoring in marine science. It's a two-year degree program. When I graduate, I will receive an Associate Applied Science degree. I will be qualified as a marine technician and you get a variety of jobs. At least, I will always be near the ocean, to which I'm attracted greatly.

There are only five whites in my school of 2000, which is located in the heart of Washington, D.C.. Now I know how it feels to be a minority. I hope there are no problems. After all, I'm there to get an education and am sure they are to.

My brother and I drove to Cape Hatteras, North Carolina a couple of weekends ago to go surfing. The waves were small but really fun. Very warm water with offshore winds. I hope I get a chance to go to the beach more often. I really miss it.

I really think it's wonderful for you to be doing so much for your fellow man, teaching, counseling, and your youth work. I'm sure it will work out well. I wish there were more people who could put so much positive energy into their work.

The weather here sounds pretty much like yours, hot and humid. It should be getting cooler as the weeks go by. Our house is located south of Alexandria on Mount Vernon. George Washington originally owned all the property where we live. His original mansion and memorial with his plantation is only a quarter-mile from us.

Jerry, if you're ever in the area please contact me. My parents would like to meet you too!

Write again when you have the time.

Take care,

Pops

Pops remained in the East with his parents for some time. In the summer of 1975, he returned to Golden Beach. Once again, he became involved in cocaine and cocaine trafficking. A year later, he left Golden Beach permanently. When he remained away from Golden Beach, Pops was not involved with cocaine. His case is typical in some respects.

First, his arrest and incarceration did not immediately or directly deter Pops from using drugs or associating with drug dealers. However, it may have been a part of a pattern. Pops had lengthy separations from his father. The arrest allowed his father and mother to express their support for him. Following his arrest, trial and incarceration, Pops was reunited with his family when his father was stationed at the Pentagon.

Second, Pops' relocation to the Washington area illustrates what was to be a trend with many of the youth. That is, they felt that they had to leave Golden Beach and the "wall" to succeed. Over the years, "getting out of the beach" and "away from the wall" became a familiar refrain among those who "did well." Pops had the benefit of an intact, caring family and the opportunity to attend college. This was not so for everyone.

Sean

In Chapter 2, I mentioned Sean. Matt had recommended to his mother that I could help her understand and deal with Sean, then 16. Sean's family was upper middle-class. His parents were strong Catholics. At that time, Sean had been arrested for possession of marijuana. I spoke with Mrs. Sullivan but provided her with no "miracle solution." Sean's difficulties with the law continued. In 1973, age 19, Sean was arrested at the New Orleans airport. He, his girlfriend, Molly, and Shane were charged with possession of large amounts of cocaine for sale. Molly had asked Sean to help Shane deliver the cocaine to New Orleans. Matt agreed because Shane had been hospitable to him.

I spent the Christmas holidays in Golden Beach. Matt informed me of Sean's plight and asked me to contact, once again, Mrs. Sullivan. Mrs. Sullivan described to me what had occurred. As it turned out, I was returning to Kentucky by bus and had to change busses in New Orleans. Conveniently, a hearing on Sean's evidence was conducted the morning following my arrival in New Orleans. I sat in court amazed when I heard the degree to which the undercover narcotic agents were prepared for Sean and his companions' arrival. The agents surrounded Sean and his accomplices as they departed from the airport parking lot.

I met with Sean's court-appointed attorney following the hearing. The attorney kept in touch with me by mail.

Initially, Sean claimed the entire case was a conspiracy, that he had been selling drugs to government agents, who were getting it illegally. He stated, "When the heat came down they had to bust someone, so it was me! The evidence will show this . . . I am a good actor . . . I can sway a jury."

Several days later, I received a letter from Sean's mother who wrote me that Molly had returned to San Diego and "Molly was told by her attorney that Shane was going to put the blame on both herself and Sean and say that he (Shane) was merely the courier for them." A motion was filed to grant a dismissal of the charge against Shane, in turn for his testimony. Molly was urged by her attorney to "tell the truth." She signed a statement. At first, Sean was unaware of Molly's role in affirming his guilt and the manner in which she was freed and given two years' probation.

In late January 1974, Sean entered a plea of guilty to one count of his indictment, distribution of .138 grams of cocaine. With Sean's permission, the attorney asked me to talk with the Probation Department and provide any assistance I could that would help in Sean's sentencing.

Sean corresponded with me frequently during the next few months. He provided me with background material to provide me a basis for recommending probation. In addition, he expressed himself freely. Sean was very bright, articulate and creative. His rhetoric, opinions and description of his lifestyle reflect those held by many young people at that time - the days of the "youth subculture." The following are quotes from a very lengthy letter from Sean shortly after his plea:

> I had good relationships with my father, mother, brother, sister, grandmother. Which does good mean? Well, we had quite a few arguments about staying out late at night when I was 17. I moved out. After I lived away from home for a while I began to appreciate my relationships with my family . . .
>
> In high school I got average grades as I could easily see through the teaching system. From 9th grade on it was the same stuff all over again all through the 12th grade. Public school didn't really have much discipline. I had good relations with most of the teachers except for a hypocrite, history teacher. I did some reports on pollution and this teacher strongly disagreed with my facts, which were, true, up-to-date, facts. He himself was rich and owned many boats which were .

polluting the bay. He wouldn't admit to his boats polluting the bay. We got into arguments about it. He started cursing at me and when I cut him down without cursing he got outraged and send me to the office. Ever since then he didn't like me. I had pretty good relations with my classmates but because I had short hair and big ears people teased me a lot. It didn't bother me that much, only in my relationships with girls.

The biggest and best change was in the second semester, 12th grade, when I switched from a public to a private free school . . . The founder and maybe you'd call him a teacher, was more of a father figure to me than anything else . . . That is where I opened up with girls, you might say . . . And around February of 1972, we, the members of the free school, started working with kids in the Old Beach Community Free School. It was a good experience working with younger kids and not and filling their ears with a bunch of American way shit!

In ninth grade . . . I started using weed. Everybody was talking about it and I want to see just what they were talking about. For me I feel it did quite a bit of good as it opened me up to talking with a lot of people I wouldn't have normally talked to or done things with, Matt for one . . . I started using LSD in 1971 in the latter part of the year. It was a good learning experience and not at all like drug pamphlets described it. One beautiful thing about "tripping" is the closeness you can have with some friends especially female companions. I would describe it is more an aphrodisiac or love drug than hallucinogens. Ever since I had been living with Molly for a while, I couldn't eat any unless she would eat it with me so that our communication would be mutual. We could make love all day and all night while tripping. Molly left for a while and went to Chicago with this bisexual dude named Lance, the same dude who I came here to give the coke to. This was in February of 73 when she went to Chicago and I had a lot of women over to the ranch and had intercourse, both sexual and mental, with most of them. Everyone may think my pitfall has been drugs when reality it has been women. I've tried lots of drugs but always I knew exactly what I was using and where it came from. Every experience, with the exception of alcohol and Seconal, is recorded and remembered in my mind. If something's novelty wears out, you don't buy any more unless you're addicted. There is one thing I can truly say about my cocaine usage is that I was never hooked physiologically or psychologically on it, but used it in fairly large amounts when it was given to me. I never bought any cocaine the whole time I was using it. I never went out for the downer drugs (depressants).

Some of my interests, hobbies, sports and things - you already know . . . I like to read, you already know. I like plants, farming, the outdoors, animals, building things which are useful to people, music, paintings, handball, and basketball....I want a more or less permanent trade such as carpentry . . . I want to be able to make enough money to put it in a co-op with friends who want the same basic things out of life. We would hunt for land that we could share jointly. Such as in the mountain somewhere . . . Our basic things out of life would be the peace and quiet, common love and respect, healthy environment . . . being more or less self-sufficient, something we could all call our own. (My criminal record is:)

16 years' old. Possession of marijuana – released to parents.

16 years' old. Possession of marijuana – released to parents consent to a six-week group counseling course. No probation.

17 years' old. Hit and run, felony. $308 bond posted– never went to court - used an alias. Failed to prosecute.

18 years' old. It was three days after I turned 18. I didn't go and get a license yet. Driving without license. I was told to get license by the judge.

18 years' old. Arrested for under the influence of drugs and/or alcohol–Case was dismissed after I submitted to blood test and urinalysis. No drugs, no alcohol.

18 years' old. Was arrested for taking the friends horses home when an Animal Regulation Officer tried to take them, so I let them go and yelled loud so he couldn't catch them. He had me arrested for interfering with the duties of the public officer. He was mad at me because he couldn't catch my dog running in the road.-- fined $50.

18 years' old. Arrested for failure to appear in court on a traffic ticket. A suspended sentence.

18 years' old. Felony. Smuggling a controlled substance–Deferred prosecution for one year.

19 years' old. THIS ONE! ...

I have used a few drinks every now and then, a couple of joints before going to bed now and then. After this experience - or mind juggler, I'm sure I can avoid selling drugs. Anyhow it would be hard to sell drugs now with my record. People would be scared to deal with me. There wouldn't be any problems staying away from drug pushers. There isn't ready that much (about me) that needs changing and my life on the street . . .

If I was sentenced under the Youth Act. I probably wouldn't do but a year anyhow. That's not that long and if I could continue to learn more about carpentry I want to stay and finish my learning. . . . Most of my good friends use is a little weed or drink a little bit, But do not pressure anyone into going along with them. I could stay away from San Diego if I had to, but that's where Molly is living, that's where my parents live, that's where most of my moneymaking jobs an resources are . . . I don't really think I would need any counseling in prison if I had to go to school or work. I could probably help others in a group counseling situation, though.

Nothing really detrimental has happened to me since I have been in here. Of course I haven't been here that long and this is rough on me as some places could be. I just feel I would make it with any woman I saw when I got out. If I do make probation some women here have offered me a place to stay for a day or two. Ah-haw!

Your friend,

Sean

Sean continued to write and requested books to read. I mailed him a number of academic texts, mostly sociological theories and philosophy.

In February, I received the following letter from Sean:

Hi Jerry,

I hope you don't think I forgot about you just because I got some time. I got the Youth Act last Wed., Feb. 20th. The (judge?) recommended I be sent to California somewhere where I can finish my carpentry apprenticeship, The P.O. also recommended the five years probation, but the judge said he does not give probation on such a large amount of drugs. Shane got 12 plus three years. He got sentenced before me and if I had any false teeth, I'm sure I would have dropped them. The judge is very hard-nosed. There's a man in here with ten years for a bad $500 check. Hard?

Thanks for all the help you've given me. I'll write you when I get to the joint. I am just reading a lot and playing poker - making $. I can't wait to get out of this place. Will probably in another week or so. Talk to you soon. - maybe by phone if I get a little closer.

AFA

Sean

P.S. Keeping you in my prayers

Under the provision of the Youth Act, Sean was placed in prison for youthful federal offenders for an indeterminate amount of time, plus parole.

In April, Mrs. Sullivan wrote the following note to me:

Dear Jerry,

Thanks for the letter. I sent yours onto Doug, who is now in Colo. I had hoped he would be sent to Calif & was very disappointed when he was sent still a long way from home . . . I wrote his P.O. there in New Orleans & the judge and pleaded his case like you did but to no avail. You know, I really do not agree with this business of letting one person go "Scot free" like they did with Molly simply because she "sang" like a bird so to speak. Of course, she go two yrs probation but she really is as guilty as either Sean or Shane. She is not even writing Sean now, but I hope she will soon. He really is crazy about her.

He seems to have accepted his sentence, "like a man" although he is just a boy. I think that he and Shane received very stiff sentences when one considers what murderers get these days & look at Agnew! Rather unfair, I'd say.

Take care and have a happy Easter, Warm regards,

Mrs. Sullivan

Sean did not hear from Molly and eventually accepted her role. I received mail from Mrs. Sullivan three times and had talked to her by phone a number of more times. I had never spoken with or heard from Mr. Sullivan. Sean made no additional mention of him in our correspondence. As I continued to read Sean's letters, I sensed an increasing amount of the "prisonization effect" on him and an increasing sense of alienation. His first letter from Colorado was upbeat as the following excerpts demonstrate:

Hi Jerry,

Just sitting here facing the east waiting for the sun to come up here in Englewood, Colorado.

This isn't a bad place. We have a lot of group rapping and activities. We get to rap with girls every Tues. night and get dances once a month. It's a pretty strange trip I guess and I haven't really adjusted to seeing women around. It's just kind of torture to me because I feel like a tiger let loose with my tongue hanging out. Sorry I haven't written in a while but I've been kind of spaced out.

They took me off my Valium and the doctor is still griping at my high blood pressure.

A lot of things you've said to me to help me keep it together. Thanks and I'll return the favor someday for sure. Well I'm going to breakfast.

A.F.A.,

Sean

As the months passed, I heard from Sean less often. His notes were less lengthy and his mood more somber. The following September, Sean sent me another letter:

Jerry,

It's been a long time since I got up the ambition to write you or about anyone for that matter.

I heard you saw Matt and company in "Dago." In your letter you sounded as though you are keeping your goals pretty well together.

We've both got different trips, but I respect yours and you mine that just sort of understood, but sometimes we have to remind ourselves of that. Having little or no problems with mine here. I'm still playing the skitzzo trip here. I have to be one person for the committee and another to keep from going insane.

I feel as though I will be a great storyteller after get out of here. So many stories that I can't write about it in U.S. mail. Plenty of comedies, lots of tears. Plenty of tear jerkers! A master of body language. One glance says 1000 words, every picture tells the story. I will quit boring you with this. Deja vu!

How backwards this system is when it locks you up and deprives a person of his or her most basic needs and desires, sex. Then they expect you to get your shit together!

Take it easy,

A.F.A., Sean

Eventually Sean was transferred to a Federal prison in California. He kept some contact with Matt and me. Sean became increasingly "institutionalized." He was able to find as many drugs in prison as in Golden Beach. His spirit seemed to be sapped. His dreams of carpentry, his creativity and intellectual curiosity appeared to have dissipated. He was more alienated toward society than ever, but now in a more resigned, skeptical mode, free of his youthful defiance. He had learned many things in prison, most not favorable to society's goals. Matt's last contact with Sean was a year later. Sean was home on a weekend furlough. It disturbed Matt that Sean had become institutionalized. Matt said, "He seemed to get like it (prison)."

Sean's family moved from Golden Beach. Neither I nor Matt has heard from him in the past 26 years. However, once again, it did not appear that Sean's arrest and incarceration had changed any of his attitudes toward his use of alcohol or drugs.

Sean's story indicates the degree to which his early use of drugs, his uses of drugs to interact with young women and s to engage in sexual activity were a part of the milieus of the times. He talks of how "shy" he was around girls. He claims that drugs served as an "aphrodisiac" for him and his girlfriend. This pattern of usage was found in other young men. I would examine this pattern more systematically in the later phases of my research.

In addition, Matt's relationship with his parents, females and the addictive character of his relationships along with is use of drugs appear to fit the patterns of described by Peele in Love and Addiction. [1]

Chad and Vick

Chad, who had been excluded from the Wall Gang, was charged in July 1974 with assault. He claimed, "A faggot propositioned me. I beat the shit out of him!" He said the other person was "dropping the charges." The police continued prosecuting the case. Chad went to court and received probation. At this time, Chad was dealing marijuana and cocaine in substantial amounts. I noted in my journal, "looked bad and going down hill." As noted in the previous chapter, Chad is currently homeless.

Vick had also been arrested for possession of marijuana that summer and placed on probation. He continued to use drugs heavily, including LSD. He was unemployed but enrolled in college. His use of LSD may have led to "LSD-Psychosis" and other consequences for Vick within the next two years. These will be examined later in more depth.

POLICE ACTIONS AND INTERACTIONS

Overall, law enforcement response to drug use was immediate and uncompromising. Arrests were made upon any indication of possession of marijuana by an individual, often upon evidence that was later invalidated by the courts (as was the case with Matt).

The news media frequently reported mass arrests of teenagers at "pot parties" on the beach or in their homes. Juveniles were placed in Juvenile Hall, pending their initial hearing, and, if the charges were upheld, placed on probation. Adults were charged with a felony and court proceedings were initiated accordingly, even though most charges were eventually reduced to a misdemeanor. On the other hand, as was mentioned previously, juvenile alcohol use was all but ignored. If action was taken, juveniles were reprimanded and/or taken home to their parents.

Beach Patrols

During this period of time which included the Vietnam War era, police employed three methods to patrol the beach. The most frequent technique involved patrolling with a four-wheel vehicle on the beach. In the vehicle were both the San Diego police officer and a military police officer. These vehicles could be seen approaching. Typically deviant activities including drug use would cease long before the vehicle arrived at the scene. (At times, such as when Matt was first arrested, intoxication or involvement in sexual activities lessened one's attention or awareness of the approaching police vehicle.) I observed this several times.

A second technique was for the police to drive a cruiser along the boardwalk from one end to the other. This was utilized for many years especially after dark. I observed this as highly ineffective and quite comical at times. As soon as the police cruiser began to drive the boardwalk, teenagers on bicycles would race along for the next two or three miles warning everyone, "The pigs are coming! The pigs are coming!" Everyone who was subject to arrest would immediately cease their activities or would disappear in the alleys, called "courts," until the police had proceeded onward. These included those less than 18 violating curfews or consuming alcohol, those using or possessing drugs, those with unregistered bicycles and anyone with an outstanding warrant. Those who remained would greet the police with the words, "Good evening, officers!" or "How ya doing tonight, officer!" The police would cruise by and the deviant activities would resume.

An even more overt technique was the use of police helicopters. These were largely employed in 1972 prior to the Republican National Convention which had been scheduled for San Diego. (Eventually, the convention was moved because of both a scandal involving political financing and the fears of demonstrations.) It was widely believed in the beach area that the helicopters were being used to practice for the convention. During a warm weekend, typically a Saturday or Sunday, the helicopters hovered over a party on the beach. Those along the beach as well as those several blocks inland would see and hear the helicopter. The word would go forth, "Something's happening!" More police reinforcements would converge on the scene wearing hard helmets and moving into the crowd with batons. The crowd in the immediate vicinity felt trapped. In the meantime, the crowd attracted to the action grew larger and more unruly. I witnessed some scenes on these occasions, when the vast majority the crowd simply wanted to leave but were hemmed in by police officers. Twice I viewed someone from outside the party crowd threw a bottle at the police officers. Police then began to club those near them and haul them into police vehicles. Such incidents reinforced the image of police as "pigs." Only after many more incidents and several years did the police begin to adopt new and more effective techniques of community relations. For many years, I noted that certain police officers appeared very discriminating in stopping, questioning and/or arresting individuals. Blacks, Hispanics, younger males and those with longer hair or unkempt appearance tended to be the most frequent targets.

In addition to these overt police operations there were undercover officers at work. Within the young adult and teen subculture a reality existed that it would appear there were far more police undercover officers in the area than would have been possible. In spite of this and the cases exemplified by Pops and Sean, there appeared to be very little deterrent effect resulting from the shared belief that there were a multitude of undercover "narcs." This should be kept in mind in later chapters within the theoretical concept of "external" controls of human behavior.

THOSE WHO WERE "DOING WELL"

Some of the Wall Gang began to drift away from their peers. In 1974, Turk and Barbara were married in a church wedding. They went on a traditional honeymoon. Both were employed. Turk was a waiter in a “high class”restaurant, and had completed 40 credits at a community college. He continued to surf on weekends. Turk, like Pops, was an exception in that he came from an intact family. He told me, “I am just stoked on life!”

Frosty had married a year earlier. He rarely, if ever, came to the beach. He continued to hold a job and attend college.

Mo had sustained serious injuries in a motorcycle accident in 1972. After a great deal of therapy, he was able to regain complete use of his leg. By 1974, he was rarely seen in Golden Beach. He moved to the northern end of the county. He worked in a cannery and was enrolled in college.

By that same time, Matt had been employed in a well-paying civil service job as a metalworker. He lived with Rosie. Although he rarely saw his parents, he maintained contact with me. Matt remained ambivalent about his future. He wanted to find more meaningful employment. His contacts with the Wall Gang were rare and only with one or two of these, his former peers.

“PRAISE THE LORD! I’VE BEEN BORN AGAIN!”

In spite of the difficulties associated with drug use for some, and the increased stability of others, still others moved in the different direction. Six of the Old Wall Gang became active in religious groups in 1974. At the time, this was known as “The Jesus Movement.”

Pat, who had no religious background, an alcoholic father, and who was the loudest voice of the Wall Gang, declaring himself “Da Mayor of Da Beach!”, wrote to me in January 1975:

> Dear Jerry . . .
>
> Praise the Lord, guess who got saved? Yep, yours truly. Surprised? Yep, I been goin’ to Emanuel twice a week and this new church “Maranantha.” It’s as new church on Monday nights in the park. I’m stoked! I been doin’ pretty well at school too. It’s almost the end of the semester. I ‘m gettin’ an “A” in Spanish, a “B” or a “C” in psychology and I don’t know my other grades. I’m still surfin’. The water temperature is a cool 54 degrees: brrrrr. Oh, yeah, remember that $41.25? (Pat owed me). You told me to give it to the needy.

So I guess I'm gonna do it by puttin' it in the offering at Emanuel and Maranantha. I'm probably up to eight or 10 bucks, maybe, by now. How's that? Well I really don't have a whole lot more to write about so I'll close for now. However, I'll enclose my address so you can write to me when you can find the time.

So long for now, Praise God!

In March 1975, I received a letter from Anne. Anne was a "surfer chick" who hung out at the wall. She was from a strict Baptist family and remained true to her religious beliefs. The following are some excerpts,

Dear Jerry,

How are you doing? I have been meaning to write . . . I'm glad I waited because now I've got something to tell you which I'm sure will blow your mind, as it did mine . . . The beach crowd has really changed since you last were here. Pat already wrote and told you that he's a Christian, right! He's been slipping a bit but I'm sure he'll end up doing ok. I've been blowing it a lot but I am still into Church and Jesus. If you'd pray for us, we'd really appreciate it. All the other "beach" Christians are doing exceptionally well spiritually. Les is not the same person. He talks about Christ constantly and has really grown up. You won't have to give me away to him, however, we haven't been friends for about four months. We didn't even speak civilly to each other until a couple of weeks ago.

Julian, Luke, Turk and Leslie (Julian's girlfriend) all had birthdays last week so we had a couple of fun parties for them. Julian and I have been very close lately and he's getting interested in the end times and Christ's return, etc. He says he's going to "steal a pass to get into heaven 'cuz he's sure not going the other way!" Murray, who became a Christian in '72, has started going to Church with me and he really likes it. He rededicated his life to Christ a couple of weeks ago.

We have all been going to a church called Maranatha Chapel. It began last July with 15 people for Monday Night Bible Study and has grown to nearly 1,000. We have meetings every day except Wednesday and they are fantastic. Many people have become Christians thru this ministry.

The Church is an out branch of Calvary Chapel and is nondenominational. All that we are taught is direct from the Bible and it is really neat. The emphasis is on worshiping God in spirit and truth.

Much of the service is music and we often sing for an hour before the message begins.

My family situation has not improved since we last talked. I love my family but I really feel like I need to "go independent." My Mom does not like any of my friends and if she knew I was still seeing the old beach gang she'd definitely hit the roof . . .

Here's the mind-blowing news. Keith and I started going out together about three months ago, and last weekend he asked me to marry him. I hope I didn't make a mistake by saying yes - but I'll have to cut my trip short so I can come back here to get married . . . I don't know what to think, it was all quite unexpected but God's in control so I'm sure everything will work out alright.

I was thinking about you today, and felt like dropping you a line. I hope you're doing well there and are happy.

Your friend,

Anne

These and other messages heightened my desire to return to Golden Beach and begin my dissertation research. I not only wanted to explore the effect of these "instant conversions," but several other trends. Moreover, I wanted to examine a much larger and broader sample of youth in Golden Beach. I would seek to study in much more depth the relationship between drug use and such factors as family, sexuality, school, religion and the general milieus of Golden Beach itself. Having completed my doctoral courses and exams, I was prepared for a much more systematic research project. Eventually, I wanted to determine if the same factors affected females as they did males.

In time, I still wanted to answer Les' challenge, that is, what would they be like in twenty years?

End Note

1. Stanton Peele with Archie Brodsky. *Love and Addiction*, NY: Taplinger Publishing Co., 1975.

Chapter 4

A MORE SYSTEMATIC AND IN-DEPTH RESEARCH PROJECT BEGINS

As I progressed through my master's and doctoral studies, I became acquainted with a variety of sociological and social-psychological theories that would explain many of the patterns of behavior I had observed among members of the Wall Gang.

Likewise, in an era in sociology in which there was considerable debate between those who favored "quantitative" research methods and those who advocated "qualitative" or descriptive methods, I was required to be familiar with both. Quantitative methods are those that apply the same research techniques to human behavior as is applied to other sciences. Thus, surveys, experiments, content analysis and other methods of gathering facts which can be numbered or "quantified" for statistical analysis are employed. On the other hand, qualitative methodologists point to the uniqueness of each human action so one person's behavior in one situation cannot be compared in equal quantity to that of another person in another situation. Thus, the emphasis is upon understanding the meaning of each person's action. As a result, this school of thought advocates researches methods such as case histories, participant observation (or in this instance "non-participant observation") and ethnographies that describe patterns of human behavior. The results are described so that the behavior may be understood to the reader from the viewpoint of those being studied. Qualitative or descriptive findings tend to provide a more in-depth picture of human behaviors and interactions. Given the makeup of my dissertation committee, I would use elements of both quantitative and qualitative methods. The result was, no doubt, a deeper understanding than if only one or the other technique had been employed.

THEORIES

A variety of theories have been offered to explain delinquent and deviant behavior patterns. Some deal specifically with the use and/or abuse of drugs and alcohol. Most of these, directly or indirectly, appear to emphasize the very basic sociological concept, "socialization." Socialization is the process whereby individuals internalize their culture, including the values, norms and ways of thinking that characterize each culture, or subculture. Socialization takes place within "primary groups," that is, small, intimate groups, the most significant of which is family, followed by peers.

Thus, in explaining behavior which deviates from the values and norms of the culture, these theories emphasize the degree to which an individual was not properly socialized particularly during their early formative years.

Social Control Theories

The focus of social control theories is not only why some individuals deviate from the norms of society, but also why other individuals act according to those norms, that is, the effectiveness of group "controls." They seek to explain, for instance, why some juveniles in some areas of high rates of delinquency do not participate in delinquent behavior, or why some persons living in neighborhoods marked by access to and consumption of drugs have not become involved with drugs or become drug addicts.

Walter Reckless approaches social control in a broad context with emphasis upon the interaction of both social and psychological factors. Reckless terms his model "*containment theory*." According to Reckless, containment, or social control, has two major aspects, namely, *"external" containment* and *"internal" containment*. These have also been referred to as "outer" and "inner" controls or control mechanisms. External components of containment reside primarily in the family and other "supportive groups." These include reasonable limits and responsibilities for group members, an opportunity for the individual to achieve a status, cohesion among group members, and a sense of belonging or identification with the group. [1]

Internal containment consists of "self" components (perhaps similar to "conscience"). They include a favorable image of self; being inner-directed and goal-oriented; a high level of frustration tolerance; and strongly internalized morals and ethics.[2]

Reckless views these two systems of containment as "buffers" or "insulations" against "pressure, pull and pushes" to deviate. When both components are weak, an individual is "vulnerable" to deviant behavior. Greater strength in either or both components reduces this vulnerability correspondingly.[3] The components of the outer or external control may be seen to include mechanisms of control such as police, the judicial system, psychiatry and so on. Reckless pointed out that in modern, mobile, industrialized societies, "inner" containment is more important than such "outer" mechanisms, which are less effective. [4]

There have been several other attempts to delineate components of social control. Hirschi proposes a model that accentuates the link or "bond" between the individual and society. The components of this bond include *attachment* to the moral obligation or opinions of others, *commitment* toward conventional activities and resultant investment of time and energy in these activities, *involvement* in conventional activities placing one apart in time and place from deviant activities and *belief* in conventional activities. In sum, these elements explain not why some individuals deviate, but why others conform.[5]

Albert Cohen notes that social control includes not only the "manifest control structure," such as police, probation officers, judges and programs of prevention but efforts toward deterrence, reform, vengeance, justice, reparation and so on. He notes the increasing role of youth organizations, correctional institutions, treatment facilities, regulators and the like as agents of external social control in modern societies.[6]

Differential Association

Differential Association was originally developed by Edwin Sutherland, later expanded by Donald Cressey. This theory emphasizes the factors of learning and primary groups. It has been stated as a list of propositions, each of which is testable: 1) Deviant behavior is learned rather than inherited; 2) it is learned in interaction with other persons in a process of communication; 3) the principal part of the learning process occurs within intimate personal groups rather than through impersonal agencies such as movies and newspapers; 4) the learning includes: a) techniques of committing deviant acts, and b) the specific direction of motives, drives, rationalizations, and attitudes; 5) the specific direction of motives and drives is learned from definitions of the legal codes as favorable or unfavorable; 6) a person becomes deviant because of an excess of definitions favorable to violation of law over definitions unfavorable to violation of law; 7) differential associations may vary in frequency, duration, priority, and intensity; 8) this process involves all the mechanisms involved in other learning; and 9) deviant behavior is not explained by needs and values, since non-deviant behavior is an expression of the same needs and values.[7]

The basic process envisioned is that of learning rationalizations and techniques within primary groups. The definitions are those both favorable and unfavorable to deviance. This theory is rather explicit and direct, and does not require deal of additional explanation. In essence, it describes, the process of socialization.

Convergence of Differential Association Theory and Social Control Theories

In 1969, Harwin Voss pointed to the "theoretical convergence" of the containment model of Reckless and the Differential Association model of Sutherland. In a sample of delinquents and non-delinquents, Voss demonstrated that what Reckless emphasized was the product of the socialization process, that is, internal control, while Sutherland was emphasizing the process itself.

Overall, these theories emphasize the extreme importance of socialization as to whether an individual is more likely to conform or deviate from societal values in a given situation. Given the importance of family as the primary agent of socialization, the family ought to be examined first. Likewise, the peer group, the second most important agent of socialization, ought to be next examined. Finally, the question arises, as I asked myself regarding the Wall Gang, "If the family's influence in the socialization of an individual is less, does the peer group have a greater influence?"

A Psychodynamic Model Specific to Alcohol and Drug Use: McCord-Chein

There was considerable data available in the 1970s to indicate that users of drugs, including the drug alcohol, were predominantly male. In 1972, The National Commission on Marihuana and Drug Abuse reported that twice as many males as females had used marijuana and more than twice as many males as females continued to use alcohol.[8] John A. O'Donnell and John C. Ball noted that in the United States male heroin addicts outnumbered female addicts "four or five to one." [9] Robert Straus reported that a review of several studies indicates "greater use by men than by women (the range of variation among men was between 75 and 79 percent; while the range of variation among women was between 56 and 62 percent)."

Straus pointed out that "key findings" of another study indicated that 72 percent of American men had "at least one type of problem associated with drinking." [10] Recent data indicate the male-female gap is narrowing. However, use of drugs, including alcohol, by females has all but been ignored in research and scientific literature. As a result, many theories are male-centered.

One such set of theories has been termed *"psychodynamic"* theories. The term "psychodynamic" refers to the interaction of personality and social factors. In many ways, these theories and research findings could be seen as specific application of social control theories to alcoholism and drug addiction. When I was introduced to these theories and models, they seemed to explain the patterns of behavior by members of the Wall Gang.

Among the leading researchers in alcoholism were two sociologists, William and Joan McCord. A major study of heroin users by Isidore Chein and his colleagues pointed to a similar psychodynamic model. I would combine them in my research and to refer to them as the "McCord-Chein" model.

The McCords' model resulted from the personal histories of a delinquent study conducted in the 1930s and 1940s. The McCords conducted follow up studies in 1948 and 1956. In the later years, the McCords examined the cohort to determine which of the earlier delinquents had become alcoholics. Based on their results, the McCords developed a model that envisioned a "dependency" conflict" resulting from the erratic satisfaction of early dependency needs and a lack of adequate male role definition. Thus, the person struggles to become independent yet is pulled toward dependency. In their model the inadequately prepared male, with a weak masculine self-image, is faced with an exaggerated definition of the adult male role through the media and other social factors. The increased pressure for masculinity and independence brings about tension in its physical effects as well as in social-psychological definition as a symbol of aggressiveness, achievement and manliness.[11]

The study by Chein and his colleagues, *The Road to H: Narcotics, Delinquency and Social Policy*, pointed to a similar psychodynamic process among heroin addicts as that advanced by the McCords for alcoholism. Among groups of addicts and controls from areas of high availability of heroin, Chein found family factors, particularly the absence of an adequate father figure, the most distinguishing set of characteristics between the two groups.[12] Chein sees the resulting offspring as weak in masculine identity and without "inner restraints."[13]

Combining the McCords and Chein findings, I refer to one model, as the *McCord-Chein model.* The major elements of the McCord-Chein model would be expected in the following temporal sequence:

1) The absence of an adequate father-figure combined with an overprotective mother.

2) Inadequate socialization in and preparation for the male role.

3) A perception of one's inability to assume societal expectations of the adult male role.

4) A dependency conflict or what is termed an *independence-dependence struggle.*

5) Sexual difficulties.

6) Tensions or psychological discomforts.

7) Societal definitions that drugs/alcohol would both reduce these tensions and strengthen one's male sexual identity (that is, to feel like and become a "real man").

8) The use of drugs, including alcohol, to reduce these tensions.

9) Drug addiction/alcoholism.

The above sequence of steps is necessary in the McCord-Chein model.

As has been noted, this model appeared in some ways to have value in explaining my earlier study of the Wall Gang. The same could be said of Differential Association and the broader social control theories.

Other theories, such as labeling theory, alienation and youth subculture explanations, were explored but had little if any broad explanatory power.

My next step was to develop a research design to adequately examine these theories as they might apply among a larger and more diverse sample of young people.

Methodology

I planned to continue to utilize the qualitative method of "nonparticipant" observation in order to, once again, overcome the methodological problems inherent in the relationship between persons defined as deviant and those defined as normal. As Howard Becker has noted, deviants are "outsiders" to the rest of society and the researcher must overcome the barriers constructed by deviants as a protection from punishment.[14] As a result, the researcher must find the subjects of his study, and, thereafter, establish a rapport and confidence that will encourage them to discuss their behavior with him freely and also allow them to interact in their usual manner in his presence.

One result of the barriers between normals and deviants is the tendency for deviants, when questioned by normals, to reply with a set of "pat responses."[15] Often these "fronts" or "pat responses" tend to conform with the stereotypes that normals hold. It is thus the position of various researchers of deviant behavior that official records, survey techniques and interviews lacking in rapport are inadequate tools to penetrate these "fronts" and may only arrive at a fragmentary or distorted knowledge of the phenomenon under consideration.[16]

This rationale guided my research at each stage, from planning, to locating the subjects, establishing rapport, observing, interviewing and through the analysis of the data itself. My aim was to obtain the actors' perspective. It was necessary, therefore, to reach a level of acceptance which would penetrate as many false barriers as possible. Thus, the study mainly employed what is referred to as "non-participant observation." This called for me to become involved with the subjects in many interactions without becoming a participant in the deviance, or drug usage, itself. Thus, many of the legal, ethical and moral decisions referred to by William Whyte [17] and Jerome Skolnick [18] were overcome. This methodology as opposed to becoming a "complete" participant observer was especially important in my situation in which I, a 36-year-old, was researching drug use and other activities among young people. In order to proceed with my research, I obtained the "Grant of Confidentiality" from the U.S. Department of Justice, Drug Enforcement Administration, mentioned in Chapter 1. This entitled me to attend parties, view drug deals, ask questions that provided me knowledge of "the nature, incidence, prevalence and patterns of youthful drug abuse . . . " and " . . . not be compelled in any Federal, State, or local civil, criminal, administrative, legislative, or other proceeding to identify the subjects of such research." (See Appendix A for the complete wording of this document.)

It was incumbent upon me, the researcher, however, to reflect upon my own involvement, assess objectively what impact I might be having upon the interactions, and report my role as objectively as possible for others to assess. This methodology and role will be more completely detailed as the next chapter unfolds.

I also utilized quantitative, or what are often referred to as "objective," techniques. The presentation of such statistical information will be made in a more conventional fashion. The manner in which this information was gathered from in-depth interviews will also be described. The complementary nature of the combination of these "qualitative" and "quantitative" techniques and the resulting enhancement of the research will become more evident in succeeding chapters.

End Notes

1. Walter C. Reckless, "Containment Theory," in Barry Krisberg and James Austin (eds.), *The Children of Ishmael: Critical Perspectives on Juvenile Justice,* Palo Alto, Ca.: Mayfield Publishing, 1978, pp. 187-189.

2. Ibid., p. 189.

3. Ibid., pp. 189-191.

4. Ibid., p. 190.

5. Travis Hirschi, *Causes of Delinquency*, Berkeley: University of California Press, 1969.

6. Albert K. Cohen, *Deviance and Control*, Englewood Cliffs, NJ: Prentice-Hall, Inc., 1966, pp. 39-40.

7. Edwin Sutherland, *Principles of Criminology*, Philadelphia: J.B. Lippincott, 1960, chap. 4.

8. National Commission on Marihuana and Drug Abuse. *Marihuana: A Signal of Misunderstanding.* First Report, 1972.

9. John A. O'Donnell and John C. Ball, (eds.) *Narcotic Addiction,* NY: Harper and Row, 1966.

10. Robert Straus, "Alcohol and Alcoholism," in *Contemporary Social Problems,* 3rd ed. Edited by Robert K. Merton and Robert Nisbet. NY: Harcourt Brace Jovanovich, 1971.

11. William McCord and Joan McCord, with Jon Gudeman, *Origins of Alcoholism, Stanford,* Ca.: Stanford University Press, 1960.

12. Isidor Chein, et al., *The Road to H: Narcotics, Delinquency, and Social Policy*, NY: Basic Books, 1964.

13. Isidor Chein, "Narcotic Use Among Juveniles," in John A. O'Donnell and John C. Ball, (eds.), *Narcotic Addiction*, p. 135.

14. Howard S. Becker, *The Outsiders*, NY: The Free Press, 1963.

15. Robert Straus, *Escape From Custody*, NY: Harper and Row, 1974.

16. Howard A. Becker, *Outsiders*, NY: The Free Press, 1963; Jack Douglas, *Observations of Deviance*, NY: Random House, 1970; Jacqueline P. Wiseman, *Stations of the Lost: The Treatment of Skid Row Alcoholics*, Englewood Cliffs, NJ: Prentice-Hall, 1970; William F. Whyte, *Street Corner Society: The Social Structure of an Italian Slum,* Chicago: The University of Chicago Press, 1955.

17. William F. Whyte, *Street Corner Society*: The Social Structure of an Italian Slum, Chicago: The University of Chicago Press, 1955.

18. Jerome H. Skolnick, *Justice Without Trial*, NY: John Wiley and Sons, 1967.

Chapter 5

DETAILS OF METHODOLOGY OR "HOW CAN WE ACCEPT WHAT YOU SAY?"

FOREWORD

Many authors choose to put most details of their methodology in an appendix. I will refer the reader to the appendix for some scientific details and to reference the forms and other material utilized. However, based on the nature of my research and my past experiences when I have presented my findings, I have learned that many people are intrigued with the details of my methodology itself. Some have asked about the objectivity of my observations and findings. Questions such as, "How did you know they were being honest?", "How did you make ethical decisions?", " How did you know you were being accepted?" and "How did our presence affect how they acted?" These are very valid and important issues which I hope to address in this chapter. Moreover, I hope that students of sociology will benefit from the details of my research experience. I pray that they will be inspired to take advantage of the opportunities they encounter. The continued sociological understanding of human behavior and human problems is in their hands.

To some extent, I set aside the continuing stories of Matt, Luke, Pat, Keith, Vick and others in this chapter. Nevertheless, I will mention the role which they played in helping me enlist new subjects for my research and in facilitating my acceptance among younger members of the youth subculture in Golden Beach. The stories of the above members of the Old Wall Gang will play a prominent part in later chapters.

In order for the scientist to conduct research and/or test theories, there are three requirements. First is a "laboratory" setting. Laboratories are the settings for most research in the natural sciences, such as biology and chemistry. The setting or "laboratory" for sociologists is the everyday world of human interaction. Second, a "sample" of subjects for the research is necessary. The subjects must consist of individuals who would adequately reflect the subject matter under consideration. The final requirement in all sciences is to measure or observe the subjects in the research setting. In this chapter, I will describe why Golden Beach made a suitable "lab" for this research. Next, I will describe the criteria and method I used to select the research subjects. Finally, I will describe the methods I employed to gather and analyze the data.

THE SETTING OF THE RESEARCH

I returned to Golden Beach on June 1, 1975. The nation had changed. Richard Nixon had resigned and Gerald Ford was President of the United States. The Vietnam era was coming to a close. The Peace Movement had become passe'. A "Jesus Movement" was taking place. Janis Joplin and Jimmy Hendrix had died of drug overdoses. Word was out that "Speed Kills" and some became aware that LSD could lead to flashbacks and psychosis. Alcohol increased in popularity among the young, but there was not a corresponding decrease in the use of marijuana. The Beach Boys remained popular but were fading. Simon and Garfunkel were being replaced by Lynyrd Skynyrd, Rod Stewart, and Fleetwood Mac. "Hard rock" had pushed aside the "mellow" music and folk songs of the late sixties and early seventies.

Golden Beach was affected by all of these trends as well. Some Old Wall Gang members who spoke the "love and peace" language five years earlier were now Vietnam Veterans. Julian decried the consideration of pardoning of the "draft dodgers" who fled to Canada. Pat and others had tried the "Jesus Movement." Members of the group were showing signs of alcohol problems. Attitudes were changing about barbiturates, amphetamine and some hallucinogens. They enjoyed the new rock music but waxed nostalgically about the Beach Boys to younger members who had joined them.

The beach itself was becoming increasingly crowded. Parking spaces became more difficult to locate. The pub that had sole one dollar Mexican plates had been torn down and several other establishments were displayed by large condominiums. A popular drive-in restaurant was replaced by an upscale restaurant and bar. The local movie theater was destined to be demolished for offices.

Census data indicated that Golden Beach had grown to 37,840 residents. Of these 93 percent were white, 2 percent of Spanish Heritage, and 1 percent black. The average family size in Golden Beach stood at 2.28, compared with 2.8 for the San Diego metropolitan area, and 3.46 for U.S. urban areas. Median family income was $11,588 compared to the U.S. and San Diego medians of $10,196 and $10,166 respectively.[1] Golden Beach was increasing in population and becoming more upper-middle class and white with fewer members in each household.

Other data indicated that households in San Diego and Golden Beach were not as stable as those in most of the country. Golden Beach had 11.6 percent of females over the age of 14 who were presently either divorced or separated, compared to 9.7 percent in all of San Diego, and 7.5 percent in other U.S. urban areas. In San Diego 24 percent of females over the age of 14 were known to have been ever divorced, compared to 14.4 percent for U.S. urban areas. Female heads of household composed 14.4 percent of Golden Beach households, compared to 13.5 percent in San Diego and 12.3 percent of U.S. urban areas.[2] In San Diego County in 1960, there were 42 divorces for every 100 marriages. By 1970 this figure rose to 60 divorces for every 100 marriages, and by 1976, the year I began this phase of my research, to 101 divorces for every 100 marriages. [3] This was the first year that divorced had exceed marriages in the county since statistics had been recorded.

It was obvious that I had chosen a worthy setting to study the effects of divorce and lack of a father on young people. The next question is whether or not the area was an appropriate setting to study drug use.

The common, everyday perception of residents of Golden Beach was that the community had an exceedingly high rate of drug use. The most common view, held by most adults in the community, was that Golden Beach was a "crisis" area. They believed that drug use in Golden Beach was substantially above other areas of San Diego, of California, and of the nation. I recorded 13 replies, similar to the following, during my first six weeks in the field, to inquiries of lay adults as to my purpose in coming to Golden Beach, "To study drug abuse? Well, you sure picked the right place. This is it!"

Many of the young people I encountered expressed skepticism that I would locate any subjects for my study who had never used marijuana.

It seems likely that these perspectives had been influenced by the visibility of drug use at the boardwalk area of the beach. Anyone who would walk the boardwalk during the summer months was likely to see and smell marijuana several times within a distance of one mile. One might notice that marijuana was mainly being used by young people. On warm days a substantial number of young people were drinking beer and other alcoholic beverages. I witnessed drug transactions, drug use and drug-related activities in my role as a nonparticipant observer. Nevertheless, I did not see evidence of marijuana, alcohol or other drugs being used in public places outside of the beach and boardwalk areas of Golden Beach.

I found a variety of perspectives among employees of official agencies. Their perspectives appeared to be influenced by their positions and the goals of the organizations they represented.

Phil Wilcox, the boys' vice-principal at Golden Beach High School, had a realistic view, "You shouldn't ask me that question. I am sure that I am the last one that would know. I know they probably have their lookouts, watching for me if I approach the boys' room or wherever they are doing that sort of thing."

The school district did not record data regarding suspensions and expulsions from individual schools. A drug education and a counseling program were administered by the school district. A counselor, at the district level, stated that he felt marijuana and alcohol were used "universally" by teenagers. He also felt that the use of amphetamines and barbiturates among young people was decreasing and that Golden Beach did not differ from other areas, in these respects.

The drug counselor assigned to Golden Beach High School rendered similar opinions regarding the use of marijuana and alcohol. However, his perspective regarding the use of other drugs was similar to the views often recorded as expressed by Golden Beach youths, themselves. He stated, "Kids in Golden Beach have other things to do, like surfing, and so on. This cuts down on the boredom, so they don't use pills and as much other stuff as kids in the other areas, further inland."

I interviewed the police officer who was assigned to the junior high and senior high schools, two Golden Beach patrolmen and the lieutenant in charge of the juvenile division of the San Diego Police Department. All of them felt that marijuana and alcohol were being used by large numbers of teenagers. They each mentioned that "pills" were being used by fewer people than in previous years and that cocaine was becoming popular among those youths in their early 20s. The arrest records for the department and the division reflect the trends mentioned by police personnel.[4] The police officers agreed, uniformly, that the beach areas were areas of "high-use." Each officer stated that there was considerable alcohol use by Golden Beach youth. Nevertheless, the degree of use was sometimes exaggerated due to the visibility of use at particular areas of the beach, by residents and nonresident alike. The extent of use of other drugs was more difficult to assess, but there appeared to be a consensus that the use of sedatives and stimulants was declining at the time of the study, compared to previous periods. Considerable amounts of cocaine were available during the same period of time. The field observations were consistent with these assessments.

The question remains as to the comparability of the use of marijuana and alcohol among Golden Beach youths with the use by youths elsewhere. A review of research at that time indicated that the extent of marijuana and alcohol use among Golden Beach youth was comparable to trends across the United States and to other metropolitan areas. Research sponsored by the National Institute on Alcohol Abuse and Alcoholism in 1975 and 1976 found that 73.8 percent of the high school students, between 13 and 18 years of age, had drank alcohol two or three times a week, or more; those who lived in metropolitan areas drank more than those in non metropolitan areas; and students in the western states had the nation's highest percentage of heavy drinkers (12.8 percent). Among young men between 20 and 30 years of age, 55 percent had used marijuana. Further, to arrive at comparable data for San Diego, one must take into account that residents of cities of a similar size, between 500,000 and 999,000 in population, were found to use marijuana at as even higher rate, 58 percent [5]

Overall, the facts would indicate that Golden Beach would allow me a most opportune setting in which to research drug use among young people. Golden Beach would be my "laboratory."

PERSONAL FACTORS THAT AFFECTED THE RESEARCH

My prior background in Golden Beach and my prior contacts were the most valuable resource at my disposal to conduct my research. My rapport with these individuals (hereafter referred to as the "Old Wall Gang") provided me a basis for using a "snowball" technique to research younger members of the entire group now known as the "wall crew." (The "snowball" technique is one in which the research utilizes rapport and acceptance by one individual or group to gain acceptance with others, and so on.) I also utilized these and other, older members of the drug subculture, to enhance my rapport with younger members who frequented areas other than the wall. The older contacts proved to be my most valuable assets.

In addition, my service in youth ministry at St. Patrick's Catholic Church provided me with ready-made contacts with other young people. For the most part, these young people were not as heavily involved with drugs. Likewise, I had established various social relationships with various families with teen-age sons and daughters. These provided subjects for the research in a "snowball" effect as well.

In order to insure objectivity, however, I did not include in the sample, those with whom I had previous, extensive interactions. While I collected data regarding as many of the Old Wall Gang members as were available, I used this only for comparison and longitudinal purposes.

I also eliminated from the research those youths whom I had counseled or for whom I had provided any extensive advice. Unfortunately, this may have eliminated a small, though unique, segment of the high-school age population. However, as with the Old Wall Gang, I continued my contacts with these youth and recorded my observations and conversation with them in my daily journals. Some of these would eventually become extremely important. One group that will be described later, I refer to them as the "Trio."

Prior to my return to Golden Beach, I had renewed my contacts with the Franciscan Order. On my return, I reestablished my relationships in youth ministry at St. Patrick's. I originally feared that this role might hinder my research. I, therefore, emphasized that I was not moralizing. Apparently such fears were unfounded. This role served to help my role as a researcher. I was, first of all, more accepted and trusted than ever among the adult community. I was able to make much-needed contacts with those youths who used drugs infrequently or not at all, through various church groups and families respected by the community. Moreover, the users, especially the heavy users, did not appear to be the least concerned that I might be moralizing, once they were convinced I was not the stereotype of what many of them conceived an "adult" to be. Rather, they accepted me, it appeared, even more because of my church affiliations. They expected me to be honest and trustworthy. The youths appeared to view me as also rejecting many societal values for Christian principles. They took my obvious financial struggles as proof of the same. They often told me that I was "different" from other church people, and several youths who were not Catholics stated that I was also "different" from other Catholics. I was once introduced as, "the only Catholic I ever liked," by a member of the Old Wall Gang. I tried to emphasize a non-moralistic approach by requesting all of the youths to act as normally as possible in my presence, for the sake of the research. This appeared to be accepted, in its fullest degree, only after occasions of my non-interference. Some youths were initially hesitant when I became aware of or observed their drug use, language patterns or sexual activities. They appeared to relax and behave in a more regular pattern once an initial incident had occurred and I did not react to it. In many instances, it was obvious that interactions had taken place between diverse groups and that I had gained a reputation of being "cool," someone to whom they could "tell anything," and one who respected their confidences.

My former activities were interpreted during introductions, and so on, as indicative that I was someone who "studies and helps kids." More will be said regarding these dual functions, shortly. Only two subjects ever mentioned that they interpreted my past volunteer service as part of a college internship with the San Diego Probation Department to mean I was "kinda like a probation officer." After I had gained a great deal of information regarding these youths, respected their confidentiality and reacted toward them with patterns of personal acceptance, the youths shared their earlier doubts with me. Moreover, their view of the role of probation officers was less that of "police officers" and more that of moralizing counselors.

Although my past interactions with the adult community allowed me a certain freedom of movement that I might not have otherwise enjoyed, I was also forced to limit my activity with them during the course of the research. It was necessary for me to emphasize my rapport with the youth subculture and to protect this rapport by avoiding many adult interactions. Although the adults accepted my insistence upon confidentiality, I soon learned that the youths were suspicious of any interactions I had with persons of authority, including parents. Many decisions had to be made accordingly. I avoided all contacts with law enforcement and probation personnel until the final weeks of the study. I postponed my contacts with school officials until the final days of my stay. On some occasions, I had to limit public activity with parents, friends of parents and other adult acquaintances. If possible, I explained these reasons to my adults friends in advance.

A final factor that affected my return to Golden Beach was my changed physical appearance. I had purposely grown longer hair and a full beard. I wore clothing that was compatible with the casual scene I was observing (for instance, on warm summer days, cut off jeans and sandals.). This appearance apparently afforded me a far greater initial acceptance than a man of 36 years would have been otherwise accorded. However, I believe its impact was primarily confined to initial impressions and among circles where I was relatively unknown. As I became known to individuals as a person, my physical appearance became less important. During the course of the research, I observed a trend of shorter hairstyles among some young people in the area. My physical appearance appeared to hinder my interactions with adults who met me initially or by whom my work was unknown. (One close friend would introduce me to others with an apology for my appearance and an explanation as to why I "looked like a bum.") During the first two months of the research, I purposely walked along a one-mile stretch of the boardwalk that overlapped into Sand Beach, just south of Golden Beach. I kept count that not once, in either direction, was I not asked to either buy or sell drugs. This is of special interest because when I would ask those involved with drugs what a "narc" would look like, they would respond, "He would be about in his 30's, have long hair and a beard, and he would be hanging out in Sand Beach."

At a later point, I will describe the continued development of my role in greater detail. Thus far, I trust that I have provided a sufficient background to allow others to appraise the methodology through its various stages.

THE STAGES OF THE RESEARCH PROJECT

I conducted this project, the dissertation phase of my research, from June 1, 1975, to February 13, 1976. There were specific stages to the project even though there was some overlap in the specific time frames. Some subjects were at one stage within the project while others were at another stage. Essentially, I tried to adhere to an overall pattern for each subject.

The Introduction Stage

The introduction stage covered the period from arrival in Golden Beach, on June 1, 1975, to the end of the first complete week of the schools' summer vacation, June 20, 1975. During this period, I became settled in a centrally located apartment, visited former acquaintances, and informed adults and juveniles of the reason for my return. I asked the cooperation of these individuals.

I particularly sought out subjects of my previous research and other young people with whom I was acquainted. I requested that they introduce me to various elements of the youthful subculture. I was immediately invited to parties and activities which surrounded graduation and the closing of the school year.

As potential subjects were introduced to me, I merely socialized with them and answered any of their questions. During this stage, I did not request anyone to become a subject of the research.

I attempted to familiarize myself with the milieu and any changes that had taken place since my last visit. I planned this initial stage so that I would be able to be on the beach as groups began to form for the summer months.

On my arrival, I immediately began to keep a daily journal of my activities. I noted anything that might be of later research interest. I usually kept this journal in my automobile during my rounds. I made margin notes each time I returned to the automobile. Before retiring, I would fill in these notes more completely. This led to a pattern of sitting in Billy's restaurant for several hours, each evening. The subjects became aware of my patterns. When they wished to speak with me or wished to relay information to me, they sought me in the restaurant.

By the end of my stay, I had completed eight notebooks, covering a total of 836 pages. I kept the notebooks divided into two sections. The front section contained observations and information pertaining to the theoretical frameworks under consideration. The entries were recorded according to their dates. The back section was devoted to methodological issues and notes regarding specific findings as they unfolded. I used code names and initials and I protected the notebooks in order to insure the confidentiality of the material. (The subjects eventually became aware of my sensitivity regarding the journals and this appeared to further enhance my rapport with them.)

The Acceptance Stage

During the next stage I continued fit into the "scene" and began to ask questions regarding drugs and potential subjects. I made several decisions regarding which individuals would constitute a representative sample during this time. I attempted to spend as many hours as possible, both during the day and during the evening hours with diverse elements of the youth subculture.

I sought, particularly, to become acquainted with as many young people as possible who were beyond the expected bounds of the "snowball" technique I was employing. Thus, I sought youths who did not frequent the area of the wall, non-surfers, non-Catholics, and some youths who did not reside in Golden Beach but visited it almost daily. I asked background information in a casual manner and noted the peer groups with whom the youths interacted.

I purposefully selected the sample in order to obtain as much depth and breadth of understanding as possible. I intended the sample to contain some bias that could contradict the major theories being considered. Therefore, I sought out individuals who presented contrasts. For instance, I became acquainted with individuals who used drugs heavily but appeared to be the product of stable, intact homes and others who used drugs infrequently but were the products of unstable or broken homes. I also attempted to become acquainted with non-surfers who used drugs heavily and surfers who used drugs infrequently.

This stage of the research was prolonged somewhat until I had received a "Grant of Confidentiality" from the United States Department of Justice (See Appendix A). This grant arrived on July 14, 1975. I was then confident that I could request individuals to participate in the research and know that they would be protected from any legal prosecution resulting from my knowledge of their activities. This procedure was in accordance with the approval of the Committee on the Investigation of Human Subjects of the University of Kentucky.

The Sample, Formal Consents and Initial Interviews

Seventy-two subjects were selected for and consented to participate in the project. Only two young men who were asked to participate refused to do so. Later, both expressed regret in that they were not a part of the project. Between July 14, 1975, and August 1, 1975, fifty-five of the subjects signed their consent. I conducted an initial interview with each subject immediately after I obtained his signed consent. Twelve others became "official" subjects during the month of August. Five subjects were chosen at a later point in time. Two of these were selected to replace two of the "Trio" with whom I had previous counseling contact. Three others, who were classified as "non-users, "were chosen later in the project, The delay was due to the difficulty I found when I attempted to locate non-users. Most of the youths with whom I had previous contact made statements, such as, "You will never find any guys that are non-users around here!" Initially, I avoided selection of subjects from the Catholic youth group to fill the category to minimize any bias in the findings. By late November, however, it became obvious that I would not otherwise be able to locate many non-users. The youth group was, itself, a gathering point for those less likely to be involved in the drug subculture. I asked three youths whom I had met at the youth group to participate. The three were selected carefully. One of the three was an agnostic. One was chosen because he was the one son of three in his family who appeared to be least similar to other non-users in the sample. The third was active in the youth group but associated with athletes who attended parties regularly.

I selected the subjects on the basis that they were males, from 14 to 21 years of age, and either a resident of Golden Beach or a nonresident who made Golden Beach the center of his recreational activities. I chose 12 subjects from four families to study individual differences within the same family, as follows:

(1) Four brothers from the Gilroy family, ages 16, 17, 18 and 20. They were the four sons of Mrs. Mary Gilroy, a divorced single-parent. Three of her sons used drugs either infrequently or not at all. The eldest son had used drugs frequently but his use appeared to have declined somewhat in the preceding months.

(2) Four brothers from the intact Jones family. I chose this family as a comparison with the Gilroy family. The Jones sons were aged 16, 19, 20 and 21. The three eldest sons had become heavy users of drugs. At the time, two of these were fluctuating in the patterns of drug use. The youngest was a non-user.

(3) Two brothers from the Dunn family. Like the Gilroy family, the Dunn family was headed by a single female parent. The youngest son was 14, whom I believed would provide a contrast with his 16-year-old brother. The 14-year-old was a non-user at the beginning of the project, but became a heavy user, like his brother, about midway during the research.

(4) Two brothers from the Roe family. These sons, ages 16 and 17, lived with their father and stepmother. Both used drugs frequently.

In addition, I selected 18-year-old Gil, of the intact Bayer family. Gil had a 17-year-old brother, Morris. Morris was one of the "trio" who had been eliminated from the study because of my previous interactions. He used drugs frequently. Gil rarely used any drugs. (In later years, the twists and turns in the lives of Gil and Morris would be very important to the longitudinal research. Likewise, each of the five families and the trio would prove to be very significant to the study.)

The sample of 72 consisted of mostly white, mostly upper-middle class males. This reflected the demography of the community. Only a few minorities were included. One subject was Japanese-American, and one had a Japanese mother and an Anglo father. One was Mexican-American. Another was half Mexican and half American Indian. Mrs. Mary Gilroy, the mother of the four sons in the study, was Mexican-American. Her former husband was Anglo.

I usually made a formal request for someone to participate and conducted his initial interview at the beach. This took between five and 10 minutes for each subject.

All but a few of the subjects had anticipated the request. Many seemed anxious to participate.

I followed the following procedure to obtain subjects' consents and conduct the initial interview:

1) I established an initial rapport with the individual during at least three interactions. When I gained sufficient rapport, I approached him to ask him to become a participant.

2) I explained the purpose of the project and described the manner in which the research would be carried out. I emphasized the confidential nature of the information that I would gather. I asked the person to act in his usual manner during the rather lengthy period of my research.

3) If the person agreed to be in the study, I had him read the letter granting me confidentiality by the Department of Justice. I further explained the meaning of the letter in terms he could understand.

4) I asked each potential subject to read a written explanation of the project. (Appendix B)

5) I then asked the subject was asked to sign a statement that I had fully explained the research project to him and that he fully understood the same. (Appendix C)

6) In privacy, I conducted a brief initial interview with the subject. The information was then recorded in "The Basic Data and Information Sheet." (Appendix D) The initial interview covered basic demographic information, in order that I could control the developing sample for over representation of any single segment. This sheet also provided the necessary information to locate the subject for a final interview. I recorded the data regarding the subject's initial use of each kind of drug and his current frequency of use of each such drug.

(7) I thanked the person and reminded him to act as normal as possible in my presence, and asked him to relay any information pertinent to me.

I should point out that a few young men and many young women expressed disappointment because they were not asked to be subjects. I explained to the males (usually not asked due to an over-sufficient number of subjects in the "heavy-user" category) that I could not include everyone. I told them I was interested in their lives and any information they could give me, and that I would be observing them as well. I explained to the females that most of the theories, and most of the problems, surrounding drug and alcohol use were confined to males. I informed them that science builds upon existing theories and previous research (without being specific). I further told them that it would be difficult for a man, age 36, to properly research young girls. However, I informed them that, even though they could not be official subjects, I was also interested in female drug use and in all young people. (As the project progressed, females were one of my most valuable sources of information regarding male subjects. As will be explained, in 1978 the next phase of the overall research, I obtained a sample of females in a similar procedure.)

I had designed the research design anticipating that I could obtain a minimum of 15 subjects within each of three categories by degree of drug use. I initially established the categories as "heavy users," "moderate users" and "non-users." Still, the nature of the research required that I be flexible and take into account the realities of the setting. I found that the original categories met a reasonable fit with the continuum of drug involvement in Golden Beach. On the other hand, certain subtleties were missing. Thus, I decided it was more feasible to make some refinements. I decided that "moderate user" was too broad and did not reflect the difference between "regular" moderate users, and "light" moderate users. With this in mind, I revised the categories to "heavy users," "regular users," "light users" and "non-users."

I defined "use" as the ingestion of marijuana and/or other drugs, [6] excluding alcohol, by those under the age of 21, and the use alcohol by those males by those under the age of 18. This reflected the legal distinction made by most states in 1975.

The final sample included seventy-two (2) subjects, as follows:

1) *Thirty-one (31) heavy users* who used any of the substances at least four times a week. Twenty-two (22) of these were daily heavy users who used substances one or more times.

2) *Eleven (11) regular users* who used any of the substances less than four times a week, but more than twice a month. Eight of these subjects were "heavy users" when the research began but their use decreased by the time of the final interview.

3) *Twenty-two (22) light users* who used any such substance twice a month or less.

4) *Seven (7) non-users* who had never used marijuana and/or other drugs, including alcohol, or whose use had been restricted to experimental use. Experimental use referred only marijuana and/or alcohol and only in those cases in which the use took place at least one year prior to the initial contact by the researcher, and involved no more than 10 such occasions.

Members of the "Old Wall Gang" were not included as "subjects" in the above categories and, thus, do not appear in the quantitative data comparing the various categories.

There were many other "non-subjects," males or females in Golden Beach under the age of 25, whom I observed and interacted with throughout this phase of the research.

Given the nature of the subject matter under consideration and the age group to which it was necessarily directed, the difficulties in obtaining a random sample that could have qualified for statistical generalization and representativeness would appear to be formidable. A school sample, for instance, would have excluded dropouts, truants and those youths detained by law enforcement officials. Likewise, many of the subjects in this project informed me that they (particularly the heavy users) often lied during surveys taken within the schools, The youths felt they were coerced into participation and doubted the confidentiality of such studies. It would appear that the present sample, although limited in some ways, provides the opportunity for greater rapport, honesty and response verification.

Observations and Gathering of Data

I observed and gathered data during the entire course of the project. However, observations and data-gathering received my almost total attention from July 1, 1975, when the majority of the subjects had been chosen, until November 7, 1975, when I began the final interviews. My pattern of observing differed between the summer months from the school year. I concentrated my efforts at the beach during the summer months. Heavier users were the ones most available for study at this time. As school began, the youths frequented a wider range of locations. Those who were less involved in drugs became the more accessible to me. I maintained contacts with all subjects at various times during the research. I made special efforts to locate a subject if had not interacted with him for any appreciable length of time.

I wrote regular, daily entries in the journals about each interaction or observation. Additionally, I made notations regarding non-subjects and any data that might have beared upon the research. I focused on information that pertained to the theories. I maintained separate notes regarding news items which might have an impact upon the research.

As I stated earlier, I also kept separate notes regarding methodological issues and any questionable effect of my involvement or the research may have had upon the subjects and their behavior.

Since the journals became voluminous, I developed a system of reference. I placed stars in the margin according to the potential importance of each item was perceived. The number of stars ranged from one to five, depending on whether I determined an item was "somewhat important," "important," "definitely important," "very important-don't forget" or "of utmost importance." Further, the initials and code names of the subjects were underlined in order to facilitate locating a description of their activities at a later date. During this phase, I made note of attitudes as well patterns of behavior. If I noticed a potential pattern, I gave it additional attention to determine how many other youths behaved in a similar manner, had a similar background experience or held similar attitudes. As patterns and processes became obvious, I recorded them in the journal with a large, marginal notation referring to the theory that had explanatory potential in relation to them. Certain patterns emerged that appeared to be indicators of other factors, such as family life, alienation form school and so on. I utilized these indicators to compose the questions for the final interview, the focus of the next stage. As a result I could measure the frequency of patterns among all subjects in a more objective manner. Likewise, I used many terms during the interview that reflected the contextual meaning of the language spoken by the subjects. I included terms, such as "uppers," "downers," "pot," "busted," and "having sex with a chick" in place of more technical terms. These terms became familiar to me through my earlier observations and interactions.

As the depth of my rapport increased, I was able to ask questions of increasing degree of sensitivity.

I took every opportunity to observe the subjects, and interact with them in as many phases of their lives as possible. I made a minimum of two visits to the beach each day through the summer. On each visit, I walked the length of Golden Beach. The subjects tended to interact with each other in various groups at specific locations on the beach. Thus, it was easy to locate them. At most times, the groups on the beach were made up of peers with similar drug patterns.

During the summer months, I visited the beach most evenings. These visits usually extended into the early morning hours. I changed my patterns at nighttime so that I could observe areas of the beach where the most activity appeared to be taking place. I spend the majority of my night "shifts" at the boardwalk area in Golden Beach and Sand Beach (south of Golden Beach and sometimes referred to as "low life" by residents of Golden Beach). On many evenings I had to forego these visits, or postpone them for a few hours, in order to attend some of the many parties occurring inland.

When school was in session, I paid a morning visit to the surfing areas, and an evening visit to the boardwalk area. I found these visits sufficient to observe the beach activities.

I attended a wide variety of functions in order to observe and to immerse myself in the totality of the Golden Beach youth subculture. During the course of the research, I attended: 55 parties, three picnics, two rock concerts, seven football games, eight basketball games, six softball games, a soccer game, four dances, three movies, 21 meetings of church youth groups (representing three denominations), and a funeral.

Eventually, I would meet one or both parents of 33 subjects. I communicated with three others by telephone. I was invited to the homes of 23 subjects. Five families (covering 11 subjects) invited me to their homes for dinner.

I visited the Golden Beach Junior High School twice, and spent the better part of 14 school days at Golden Beach High School. I limited my visits to the schools to the latter part of the research, after I had completed the final interviews and my rapport was at its maximum. This lessened any doubts as to my purposes or that I would betray any confidences to school authorities.

The research progressed in a "cumulative" fashion. As I became known and trusted, I became more involved with my subjects. Each degree of involvement brought with it increased rapport and further involvement. At each step, more, and richer, information was gained. In addition, both the nature of my involvement and the manner in which the subjects interacted with me, in themselves, became data. These types of data were extremely fruitful in gaining insights to differences and similarities among the subjects.

My involvement and rapport developed at differing rates from individual to another and from one group to another. There was some indication that younger subjects and non-subjects had greater initial skepticism. Contrary to what some might expect to be the case, those individuals who were the most directly involved in the drug subculture were the most likely to give me total acceptance once I had been accepted by their group. The group's acceptance appeared to be almost entirely dependent on assurances that I maintained confidentiality. On the other hand, those youths, who were often classified as "soshes," (social climbers or elites) or "jocks" (those involved in athletics) were more likely to accept me on an individual basis. They seemed to seek a greater protection of their individual reputations. Their acceptance was, more likely, to be based upon how I would react to them, once they shared parts of their lives with me. They had less concern that I would discuss these matters with parents or authority figures.

I will discuss my involvement with the subjects and an assessment of its impact at a later point. At this point, however, I should mention some my involvements with the young people, particularly those without that did not have a father at home. I found myself teaching subjects how to drive, helping four subjects and one non-subject obtain their drivers' licenses, helping subjects complete job application forms, driving subjects to prospective employment sites and telling them how to present themselves, aiding subjects in registering for and arranging their college class schedules, arranging bail for a subject, visiting the parents of one subject while the parents were confined in a mental health facility and providing rides for subjects to their places of employ, to school and to sports activities

Many of the above activities are those often associated with the role of a father or father figure. I was, therefore, continuously reminded of what it meant to a young man not to have the presence of an adequate father figure in his everyday life. In recent years, many of these individuals, now mature men, have told me how significant both my "non-moralizing" stance and my role as a father figure was to them at that period in their lives. Their statements as to the degree of this impact have both amazed and humbled me.

On many occasions, I questioned my involvement and often reminded the youths that I was attempting to conduct "neutral" research. I told them that it was necessary that I not affect interactions too greatly. The youths readily accepted these explanations when they were tied to confidentiality, or to any deviant or illegal activity. As to those things which they viewed as "good" or "beneficial" to them and which they realized were also esteemed in my value system, any refusal of assistance was deemed to be a sign of a lack of caring or laziness on my part. They fully accepted, for instance, the fact that I could not tell them the location of a party because such information could affect the size of and interactions at such a party. They also accepted the fact that I could not aid anyone in drug transactions, even though they were aware that I had knowledge of a wide variety of sources and markets for drugs. The denial of this type of information appeared to enhance the subjects' confidence in me, even when they tested my tenacity. On the other hand, when I appeared overly neutral or uninvolved, they were quick to point out to me that, if I was interested in young people, I should be doing something about it. A frequent, more subtle, tactic to remind me of the manner in which I was being perceived was for the young person to mimic a robot and chant, in a nasal, staccato tone, "I am here only to observe. I am only to observe and not to act in any other manner."

At other times, subjects would remind me with a firm, "You are always asking questions! Let's do something else!"

Thus, I had to be constantly aware of my involvement, its effect and the manner in which I was being perceived. Many decisions had to be made accordingly. However, the degree of involvement was not solely a matter of unilateral choice.

SIGNIFICANT EVENTS IN GAINING ACCEPTANCE.

Various events contributed to my rapport and acceptance among my subjects. I will attempt to outline those that I have determined to be the most significant in a developing chain of occurrences. Likewise, I will relate their observed impact on the research.

1) The initial introduction by older members of the "Wall Gang."

No single factor was more important in my gaining acceptance with the drug and surfing subcultures than my previous contacts with the subjects of my earlier research. This strongly influenced my initial entrance and the immediate manner in which many subjects reacted toward me. The influence of two of the older "generation" of the wall group was obvious to me. They were Pat, the "mayor" of the beach, and Luke, who was my initial contact with the Old Wall Gang.

The strongest initial influence was made by Pat. Pat frequented the wall area more, perhaps, than any other individual. He initially proclaimed to the younger surfers that I was "a nice guy, " and they had "missed something" by not knowing me a few years earlier. He informed them that I had helped him and that they "had better" cooperate with me. This occurred on the third day after I had returned to Golden Beach. The 17-to-21-year-old age group of surfers immediately accepted me, and began to converse with me.

The influence of Denny was also noticeable. Denny was a friend of Leo, a 17-year-old. Leo dealt marijuana and was reticent to answer many of my questions even though he had been assured of my confidence by Pat. Denny observed this. One evening, he called Leo over to the area where we were standing. Denny then gave Leo a lengthy discourse regarding my relationship with the older group. He concluded with the words: "Jerry was kinda our daddy." Leo's attitude toward me, and his openness in my presence changed, positively, from that point onward. He fully discussed all matters regarding drug transactions in my presence and even assured his customers that I was "cool." I was unaware of what other descriptions of me were given in my absence. However, the feedback that I received was to the effect that I was a "nice guy" who would help others. This set the tone for further interactions.

Initially, there were signs that the 13-to-16- year-old age group (semi-affectionately called "rats" by older surfers) remained highly skeptical and feared that I might be a "narc." Their conversations often ceased when I approached. I had learned their names from the older surfers. When I greeted two rats by name, their shock could not have been more obvious if I had displayed a badge and handcuffs.

Sixteen-year-old Art helped me to overcome this skepticism, but I was not to realize the part he had played until some months later.

2) Acceptance by some rats helps spread the word.

Art was recognized as one of the most accomplished surfers in the area. Thus, he had considerable esteem among his peers. He approached me only gradually and, initially, somewhat erratically. He would ask me a question or two and then dart away, as if testing the safety of the situation. As the days passed, he appeared to feel more comfortable in my presence. I asked him as many questions as possible about surfing to put him at ease. He asked me about my research and my vocation as a sociologist.

Art was frequently at the beach late at night. He drank large quantities of alcohol on those occasions. Twice, I expressed my concern regarding his ability to arrive home safely. I learned that he had not been eating a proper diet because his mother's alimony check had not arrived. One evening, I insisted on sharing my dinner with him. During the course of the meal, he revealed many facets of his life to me. He particularly spoke of his anxiety surrounding a pending two-month visit to his father's home. Art left a few days later, for the eastern United States.

At approximately this point in time, late June, I noted in my journal that I had apparently been accepted by the "rats." The first indication I noted was one which involved Norman Dunn and Nelson, two 16-year-olds. They walked up to me and, bluntly asked, "Can you help us get jobs?" Neither of these youths had spoken to me previously.

My rapport with the "rats" continued to build. I had not realized the part Art played until September, when Nelson told me, "I remember when you first came. Everyone thought you had to be a narc, or somethin', an' Art used to tell everybody, 'Jest give him a chance, and he'll help you.' Now everybody knows you"

On July 3, 1975, I had made notes in my journal that I was being accepted by the youths, but that I realized I had not yet reached the required level of trust I felt necessary. I likened the situation to a similar state during the earlier research of the Old Wall Gang, prior to my assistance in getting Matt out of jail.

Bill Jones and I had established a good rapport with each other. He was 20 years of age. He was a close friend of Pat and accepted me very willingly. He managed a small beach rental alongside the wall area. This was called the "shed." This became a gathering place for the wall crew. The surfers often changed clothes inside the small shed and stored their surfboards there. Thus, Bill was a central figure within the group.

On July 5, 1975, Bill, Leo and two girls were arrested for possession of marijuana. Bill was the only adult among the four. He was taken to jail. Bill's parents inquired regarding his status. They were told, by jail personnel, that he would not be arraigned until the holiday weekend was completed. I had previous experience with the process of the local criminal justice system, and was able to have bail set and a bond posted within a few hours.

The incident not only strengthened my ties with Bill and his three brothers (also subjects), it brought me within his home to meet his parents, and, above all, dispelled remaining suspicions regarding my role. I sensed that those who frequented the wall area had removed from their minds any doubt that I might be associated with any law enforcement program.

The subjects confirmed this. The following words were expressed by Rusty, aged 17, in late August,

> It wasn't until you helped Bill out that I was sure about you. You know, I saw these other guys telling you everything, an' I thought to myself, 'You know, that guy could be a nark, an' just doin' these things to get in.' The guys were all sayin' they knew you and what not, but I wasn't sure, so I kinda held off when you were around. Then, after you bailed Jones out, I figured you must be ok.

The rapport that I had achieved was built upon and branched-out to other areas of the drug subculture. Separate mechanisms, however, had to operate to gain acceptance by those youths who were not members of the drug subculture.

3) Participation in their activities aids acceptance by "soshes" and "jocks."

As mentioned earlier, acceptance by the "sosh" and "jock" groups was, typically, on an individual basis. Nevertheless, there were certain group interactions that aided the process. Certain interactions at the group level increased my contact with the individuals. The greatest acceptance among these segments of young people came about as I displayed interest in their activities.

I noticed a stronger acceptance after I began to attend the weekly football games of Golden Beach High School. Fortuitously, the football team gathered, prior to each game, in Billy's restaurant where I wrote my notes. Seven members of the varsity squad were subjects of the research. They did not fully accept my statements that I had other reasons to be in the restaurant, each week, at that hour. They were pleased that I observed them in the restaurant and at their games. They expressed the importance of their role, as research subjects, to other players and to the coaches. As the weeks passed, I became acquainted with the entire team and coaching staff. Each week, I discussed the games with them. I was invited to an increasing number of the parties that followed the football games. Individually, they approached me with a variety of questions, and became increasingly open to mine.

I gained similar rapport when I began to attend other school and sports activities. This was strengthened by my support in additional ways, such as participating in fund-raising activities.

When I initially attended church youth group meetings, I was treated courteously, but as an "adult outsider." As I began to participate in the activities of these groups, at the level of the youths involved (rather than as an adult authority), the youths reacted accordingly. Over time, they behaved comfortably in my presence. Again, apparently as word spread that I was someone they could talk to freely, they approached me, individually, and barriers dissipated.

4) Acceptance during the final stage of the research.

During the final phase of the project, I realized that I had reached a new level of rapport. First, my level of acceptance increased after I had completed the final interviews. The subjects responded positively to me because I continued to interact with them. Many said they were impressed that I continued to accept them in spite what they had shared in the interview. They appeared to be impressed by this because I no longer had the need of information from them, and, perhaps what was more important, because I had not reacted to their self-revelations in a moralizing, or rejecting, fashion. Second, the youths seemed to react to the fact that I had apparently been loyal to my promises of confidentiality during my interactions and interviews with parents, police, probation officers and school authorities. There was an initial hesitancy evident among young people when they first saw me interacting with these "authority figures." However, they were impressed when they did not suffer retribution. They interacted with me with renewed candor.

INDICATORS OF RAPPORT, ACCEPTANCE AND "NORMAL" BEHAVIOR.

It is worthy to point out the bases for my determinations of what constituted "normal" behavior, and, thus, adequate levels of acceptance and rapport. By doing so, it is possible to permit a more proper assessment of the objectivity and validity of the findings, and to increase confidence in them.

I based many of my determinations upon experiential or "subjective" knowledge. I had advance knowledge of what would constitute "normal" behavior in the given setting. However, there were many objective indicators that I looked for, or relied upon, during the field research. These included,

1) The sharing of information regarding the purchase of drugs.

This is particularly noticeable if the information is given in advance of such a purchase. It is less risky to share past information than information about future transactions. Subjects, and others, would not share this information with someone whom they did not trust, particularly if they suspected the person of being an undercover, narcotics' agent. This information was shared freely with me.

2) The sharing of information that the subject is engaged in the sale of drugs.

This information is particularly valuable if the person tells the sources of the drugs he is selling, his prices, and his knowledge of impending deliveries. Such information gives assurance, not only that the person does not doubt the researcher's confidence as regards law enforcement, but that he trusts the researcher will not relay the information to other dealers and users. The lack of strict confidentiality could not only endanger the person's legal status, but, also decrease his profits and cause certain drugs to be less available to him. I was privy to this information, particularly after I aided Bill Jones after his arrest.

3) The volunteering of information even when it is unsolicited.

If one is within the drug subculture, there are times when less-common substances become available in the area. There are also occasions in which information is shared only with a few close friends. I recall several occasions when individuals expressed a desire to "show me" something which they felt I may not have seen previously. I was shown, for instance, peyote, hashish oil, cocaine, certain types of marijuana and devices employed in the use of drugs. At other times, I was told that someone had "ripped-off," or "burned" others, or had been "ripped-off" by others. Moreover, I was requested not to inform others within the subculture. (At times, the individuals involved did not wish to suffer the embarrassment of having their peers know that they had been "taken." At other times, the individuals did not want others to know that they had stolen, or that they had sold one substance, such as alfalfa, as something more valuable, such as marijuana.) Often, the individuals who shared this type of information could have been in physical danger if I did not maintain utmost confidentiality.

4) The manner in which I was introduced by subjects to other persons.

If a subject was not willing to introduce me to his friends and acquaintances, without being asked to do so, it was evident that I had not gained a great deal of rapport with that subject. On the other hand, if a subject was eager to introduce me to others, and, especially, if he added a comment, such as, "You can tell him anything," or, "He's all right; he's cool." I knew I was adequately accepted by that subject.

5) The use of vulgar language in my presence.

Young males, particularly when females are not present, often curse, use vulgarities, or joke regarding sexual matters (sometimes referred to as "locker-room talk"). The matter-of-fact use of such conversation, with no apologies to me, was an indication, particularly among church youth-group members, that they were not perceiving me in a moralizing role.

6) The sharing of feelings with me and the solicitation of my advice.

This was not confined to the drug subculture. In fact, it appeared that the heavier drug users found it somewhat difficult to express their feelings. A sign of rapport was that an individual related to me in the manner of a close friend. Naturally, this was mitigated by my age and position. Subjects often asked me about their feelings toward girls, my opinions of girls feelings toward them and the manner in which they should pursue the courtship rituals. Many of these feelings and concerns, which might seem trivial to some adults, are quite painful for adolescent males, and quite private.

7) The manner in which I was treated as a regular friend.

A great deal of this rapport was noted within particular groups. Several of the wall crew learned that I had been called, "Looney," by Matt. I overheard one tell another, "Call Jerry, 'Looney;' he digs it." The nickname caught on among the other members.

8) The lessening of "tests" of confidentiality.

As youths became comfortable with my role and gained trust in me, they were less likely to test me. For instance, there were fewer instances in which I was asked if someone was subject of my research or the time and location of parties. Most such inquiries appeared to be a test to determine if I would reveal information. The less I gave information about others, the more confident subjects were that I would not reveal facts about them.

9) Direct statements, by subjects, of the rapport I had achieved.

Some individuals made direct testimonies regarding the degree of acceptance I had achieved. In early July, Floyd discussed my research and remarked, "You are really lucky; the way people trust you." After his interview, Martin stated, "Remember, Lowney, you are known for your confidentiality. Don't tell anyone."

In spite of the indications of acceptance, there were times for me to remind the subjects to behave naturally. Many youths felt uncomfortable the first time I met them at a party, particularly if they were drinking alcohol or smoking marijuana. Even though they had informed me of these activities during their initial interview, a number of subjects displayed initial embarrassment. I would react neutrally and ask that they continue their activities. The embarrassment typically vanished soon afterwards.

One such instance occurred in the parking lot of the high school prior to a dance. I knew of the activities that took place there. I arrived in my car.

As I left the car and was crossing the door, Ron, a member of the football team, noticed me. He began to hide the six packs of beer which he had apparently just begun to use. He then looked at me and stated, "Oh, shit! I'm gonna do it anyway. You told us to act normal." I smiled and verified his statement. On subsequent occasions, when Ron was observed drinking alcohol, he displayed no hesitancy at my presence.

SOME DECISIONS REGARDING INVOLVEMENT.

My involvement with the subjects was considerable. It was, therefore, necessary to make continuous decisions about possible effects of my involvement. The decisions centered on both scientific and ethical issues. The decisions were made after considering the following four questions, which I asked myself:

1) Is your involvement effecting the findings of the research in a manner that would not occur if you were not present or involved?

2) If an effect is occurring, are you able to assess the effect so that you have certainty as to what the result might be, were you not present or involved?

3) Are you disturbing the subjects in a manner in which you do not have a right to disturb them? If you are causing any disturbing effects, can you rectify the situation prior to your departure?

4) By not acting or becoming involved, are you, as a responsible adult, causing disturbances to your subjects and/or others that are not justified by the scientific knowledge that is gained?

Few issues are clear cut, and effects may often go undetected. Only constant vigilance and reflection provide a maximum assurance. To give an example, I will describe the subtleties involving one set of circumstances.

During the early part of summer, the police began a "crackdown" on activities on the boardwalk at the border of Golden Beach and Sand Beach. I was anxious to follow the police activity and study the results upon those who frequented the area. Thus, I began to arrive at the beach early in the evening to observe the number of times and the number of officers involved, the hour of each "raid" and the number of arrests that were made. Likewise, I noted the number of youths who left the area when the police arrived, the number who returned after the police had dispersed and, eventually, the number who arrived to watch the police activity itself.

During the first week of the increased police activity, the surfers at the wall area continued to remain there during the evening, as would have been their normal pattern. I soon realized, however, that they felt exceedingly uncomfortable at the mere presence of police officers. Further, I noticed that they moved physically closer to me each time the police arrived. I decided during the second week that they were seeking security, in me, from the police. This, first of all, meant that they were behaving other than they would have otherwise due to my presence. Additionally, the sense of "security" they had was a false one. I could not have prevented their arrest if they were engaged in any illegal activity. Therefore, I made a decision, based on scientific and ethical grounds. I decided to avoid that area of the beach, until later each evening. I relied on informants to describe to me what had occurred earlier. Almost immediately, the youths from the wall area noticed my absence. They asked where I had been the first morning following the change in my pattern. Within three days, they had, for the most part, abandoned the area after sunset. This had a major impact upon a wide variety of activities, during the remainder of the research.

On other occasions, it was necessary for me to involve myself on ethical grounds. Two such occasions involved youths who were drunk at parties. One evening, I found it necessary to struggle with a subject in order to obtain the keys of his car. The youth was insisting on driving himself and his companions to their homes. Another time, a subject, who was known for his belligerency when he was intoxicated, had been involved in two fights before I arrived at a party. The subject was bloodied and preparing for another fight. I appeared to be the only person who could reason with him. The host was quite relieved after I cajoled the young man into accompanying me to a restaurant for food and coffee. In each of these circumstances, the ethical issues outweighed research considerations.

In other instances, I was unable to completely change my research activity even though I noticed its impact. At times, it was necessary for me to downplay my activity to lessen the impact. For instance, the rats were particularly susceptible to my activities. They were often jealous of any attention that I gave other groups. Rats were often jealous of each other if I appeared to give particular attention to any one of them. In these circumstances, I attempted to conceal my activity as best possible.

One effect upon the rats, came as a result of my research focus toward sports activities. They soon learned that I was attending football games each Friday evening. Before the football season had begun, I had been attending many of the parties the "rats" attended on Friday evenings. They began to ask, on Saturday mornings, where I had been the night before. Initially, they responded to my replies by mocking the "football grunts," and by downplaying the Golden Beach High School team. As the season progressed, however, and they overheard me discussing the results of games with the ·team's fans, they began to demand my attention toward their own sports activity. I realized this when they began to bring a football to the beach. Among surfers, such activity had previously been unheard of. The moment I would arrive, Chuck Roe or Norm Dunn would toss the ball in my direction. Chuck later asked if he could attend a game with me. Norm attended his first high school basketball game with me.

I could not refrain from my research activity, even though it was having this somewhat minor effect upon these younger subjects. Finally, I decided the effect that was occurring was having no immediate or appreciable effect upon the main, dependent variable in the research, drug use. Moreover, the effects on the subjects appeared to be either neutral or positive subjects. Thus, I ceased to concern myself about this factor, and allowed myself to act with my natural enthusiasm about sports, when in the presence of Chuck and Norm.

The two young Rats, Chuck Roe and Norm Dunn, eventually forced me to make other decisions.

Increasingly, the pair demanded my attention and involvement in many facets of their lives. More than any of the other subjects, I had to remind them that I was attempting to conduct research and had to remain somewhat detached and objective. At the same time, I found myself becoming increasingly fond of them. On some occasions, when I attempted to turn my attention elsewhere, their jealousy spilled over into hostility. One evening, because I was focused on members of the Golden Beach basketball team, they threw eggs at my car as I was heading for a game. On another occasion, they tried to let the air from my tires.

I finally decided that the best manner to handle the situation was to conduct their final interviews as early as possible. I explained to them that, if I could complete my research regarding them, I could "close their files," and not worry about becoming involved with them. They both consented. While there were some apparently psychological denials operating during their interviews, the responses were as objective and as honest as one might expect. I then allowed myself to become increasingly involved with Chuck Roe and Norm Dunn. I helped them look for jobs, allowed them to drive my car as preparation for passing their drivers' exams and even placed them on "restriction," for having stolen from their employer. (The restricted them from the use of my car.) I ceased to hide my values regarding persons and property in their presence. I continued to not "moralize" them regarding drug use. Still, I did not refrain from informing them of the dangers associated with particular drugs.

The result of the increased involvement was, not less information, but more information. Chuck and Norm more open about their activities and our involvement led to further insights. I was able to observe how these subjects reacted in variety of circumstances. I soon learned, for instance, how differently they acted separately than with each other, and differently, still, when among other peers. I was able to meet the parents of both youths, study interactions in the families (each had a brother in the project), and observe their reactions to my own emotions and actions, including the restriction. (Chuck had never been on restriction before, and bragged to older youths that I had placed him on a restriction.) Finally, both youths began to increase the information they gave me regarding activities that they felt would be of research interest to me. Shortly before I departed from Golden Beach, Chuck clarified several things he had told me earlier in order that I would be assured of his final truthfulness. Norm became more forthright and direct in later years in describing my role and interactions as a father figure.

I have mentioned that I made a decision not to share most information among or between subjects. This decision encompassed many interactions and had, overall, positive effects on the research. I continuously avoided creating interactions that I was observing. This increased the confidence the subjects and others had in me. In turn, the amount of information to which I was privy also increased. This assisted me further so that I was able to possess information from several different sources. Thus, I had more information than any one of the individuals who were involved in a given interaction. Accordingly, I was allowed a view that was somewhat "transcendent" of what was occurring. In addition, I was able to avoid many ethical problems regarding possible research effects upon subjects and non-subjects.

I made another broad decision regarding my knowledge about drugs and their effects. It became obvious that the young people perceived me to be knowledgeable about drugs. I was often asked questions about these matters. The dilemma arose as to what effect anything I said about drugs would have on the research, on the one hand, and the effect of my refusal to answer such questions upon my rapport with the youths, on the other. I decided to answer any questions as openly and honestly as possible but without moralizing or volunteering additional information.

Most of these questions concerned the chemical and physiological aspects of drugs. I found the youths quite knowledgeable in their own right. Usually, the issues rased were those which involved conflicting scientific data. I usually prefaced my remarks with, "As far as it is known . . . " I separated this from, "What is not known, for certain . . . " I attempted to remain as factual as possible, and, if necessary, consulted references to obtain a complete answer.

It is difficult to assess the effects of such information. There were only three occasions when I felt the information was being asked in order to make an immediate decision regarding the use of a particular substance. The questions were raised by non-subjects. Two occasions illustrate the differential responses to the same information.

In August, a 5-,12-and 13-year-old, asked me about the effects of LSD. I strongly suspected that they were contemplating either buying or using the substance. I, factually, told them how little definite information was available. I informed them that little was known as to how the substance brought about the reactions it does and that it was not certain why some severe, adverse effects have, apparently, occurred. I explained to them that it was uncertain if adverse effects resulted from impurities within many of the hallucinogens which are not manufactured under FDA supervision, or if the effects came about because of distorted perceptions of realities during the hallucinating experience. Somewhat prophetically, I stated, "You could take some acid now, walk down the boardwalk and see the cops. Ordinarily, that might scare you, but under the acid you might flip out, and nobody would know for certain what had happened."

The youths departed. The following week, I learned that they had purchased LSD after our conversation. They had used it and walked approximately 100 feet into the waiting arms of two policemen. After a pursuit and interrogation, they were placed under arrest. Fortunately, no adverse reactions were reported. They described the incident later and said, "We should have listened to you!"

In September, an older18-and 19-year-old group asked me the similar questions, under a similar set of circumstances. I provided them with a similar response. About a month later, I asked one of the group if they had been considering using LSD, at the time, and what their decision had been. The youth replied, "Yeah, we were kinda thinking about it, but what you said about maybe impurities goin' to your brain made us decide not to."

The third occasion involved a group of 12-to-14 -year-old. The youths had earlier ingested Quaalude (a brand name for "methaqualone," Rorer,

Inc.). Several youths had taken the substance. Some had used the drug in combination with alcohol. I was asked, by each of the three yours separately, what the effects of the drug were. I showed each of them the cautions and interactions described in the *Physicians' Desk Reference*. In the reference book, rather strong warnings are given. The warnings contain specific reference to the interactional effects of alcohol and Quaalude.[7]

This was the only situation that I was able to trace which had some effect beyond the individuals to whom it was rendered. I received feedback from other youths, in the same age-bracket, who had developed negative attitudes toward Quaalude. All of this occurred in the later stages of the research. They did not affect responses during the interviews. Those youths who initially inquired regarding the effects of Quaalude had not enjoyed their experiences with the drug and, quite probably, would not have used the substance again.

If I was not present, the youths may have inquired and received similar, factual information elsewhere. Thus, the overall impact of my interaction may have been quite minimal.

POSSIBLE CONFOUNDING EFFECTS OF THE RESEARCH.

The introduction of any research situation is bound to have effects upon the subjects. In some types of research, various control groups and "post test" techniques have been utilized to assess the effects of such research. The contamination possibilities in qualitative research are largely judged by the researcher based on the objective criteria available.

The following are my analyses of several of the possible effects my presence and involvement may have brought about.

1) My presence as a "stabilizing" figure reduced a degree of uncertainty and tension among the subjects. This could have reduced their involvement in drugs.

There is no doubt that my presence was often a stabilizing effect at parties, at the beach and in a variety of other situations. The youths gradually came to expect my presence. A sense of uneasiness existed when I was not present at some of these functions. This did not appear to reduce the amounts or kinds of drugs they consumed. I did not detect a noticeable decrease even in those situations in which youths such as Bill Jones, Norm Dunn and Chuck Roe became more heavily involved with me, and relied upon me as a stable adult or father figure.

One incident, involving 17-year-old Eric, demonstrates these points still further. Eric, a junior in high school, was anticipating an early diploma by passing a proficiency exam which allowed California youths to leave high school after their 16th birthday. Eric received word that he had failed the exam. He left school in midday and looked for me at the beach. As I consoled Eric and tried to boost his morale, Mel rode up on a bicycle. Mel asked if we had completed our conversation. Eric responded affirmatively. Mel then said to Eric, "Good, let's go smoke some good Columbo I just got." Eric agreed, stating that he "needed some," at that moment.

The incident indicates that even though Eric and I had a close relationship and Eric had used the relationship to help dissipate his frustration and anger, the impact was not sufficient to cause him to depart from learned and established patterns of coping, aided by his peer.

2) The creation of deviance by the research or the risk that the research itself increased the use of drugs by the subjects.

I found none of this "secondary effect," whatsoever. I observed no occasions when the subjects used substances because I was present. No subjects either began to use drugs or increased their use of drugs in a manner that indicated the research had an effect on their behavior. Likewise, no subjects appeared to have ceased or decreased their use of drugs because of the research.

3) Subjects behaving in a manner unlike their normal or usual pattern due to the effect of the research and/or the researcher.

To a considerable degree, I have dealt with this issue. On the other hand, it would be fallacious to assume that the subjects behaved exactly as they would have if I was not present. Over time, I believe I achieved satisfactory rapport so that the findings were not appreciably altered. There were, for instance, no reports of subjects behaving in a manner differently than when I was present from informants who were present for a particular activity and I was not.

4) The effect of the values of the researcher upon the deviant behavior being studied.

I never found any indication that the subjects' drug use decreased their drug use because I abstained. When I was asked, I stated my belief that I did not see the use of alcohol and marijuana as morally wrong, but that I did not enjoy the feeling. Further, I would state that I could not conduct research and be objective if I was inebriated or in an intoxicated state.

On the other hand, my values regarding such things as employment and sports may have had some impact on the subjects with whom I interacted. None of this was sufficient to alter any of the conclusions.

Likewise, it is possible that my value for educational achievement influenced the subjects to some degree. The subjects knew that I was completing my doctoral studies, that I had taught at San Diego State University and that I was conducting the research to obtain my doctorate. This led to many conversations regarding the subjects' educational goals. They seemed most eager to inform me of their grades. One subject admitted that he avoided me when he was truant even though I had chided him about his truancy. I felt that two subjects may have been less likely to be truant because I in Golden Beach and would have become aware of their truancy. These were limited and minor effects, however, and appeared to have no effect upon the subjects' overall patters of drug use.

POSITIVE EFFECTS OF THE RESEARCHER'S INVOLVEMENT.

Any minor confounding effects were strongly outweighed by the major benefits of the research methodology (including my presence and involvement as a researcher). At the time, I assessed the major, positive results, as follows,

1) Honesty.

Several factors contributed to the honesty of the subjects' replies. The most obvious and far-reaching factor was the overall level of rapport and acceptance that I achieved. Additionally, my presence, my involvement and my potential knowledge served as checks upon the responses of the subjects. For instance, if a subject was not honest regarding his use of drugs, I would have been in a position to later learn the truth by observing him at parties and in discussions with others in the subculture. The subjects, however, were aware of my patterns and my knowledge. Thus, they did not make any attempts to conceal their patterns from me.

2) Depth.

The involvement, the rapport and the length of the study allowed me to penetrate areas that otherwise might have been inaccessible. This was of particular consequence when a number of subjects shared intimate details of their lives with me. The sharing occurred, most often, during the final interviews. Had the previous degree of rapport not been attained, the subjects would have probably been less willing to discuss the more sensitive aspects of their lives. My involvement also allowed them to discuss such subjects as relationships with the opposite sex, sexual problems and family difficulties during the observational stage.

3) Insights.

Through involvement and interaction with subjects and non-subjects, I became aware of the importance of many factors and the part they played in the use, and non-use, of drugs. (Sports, for instance, were an aspect whose importance I had originally seriously underestimated.) The manner in which other factors influenced their use of drugs became evident as I observed them more closely. Examples include family life, employment-seeking activities, behavior at school and church functions and so on. Understanding these interactions and relationships among life situations continued to be of value to me when I analyzed all of the data. Because I was familiar with the subjects and aware of their backgrounds, I was frequently reminded of what control factors within the data might be of substantive importance.

4) The overall amount of information.

The rapport, acceptance and involvement in a variety of situations contributed to the entire volume of the information that I was able to record.

5) The ability to locate and specify effects of the research.

My complete involvement in the research situation allowed me to assess the impact of each stage of the research upon the subjects. For instance, many of the youths mentioned that they had gained insights into their behavior after I had completed their interviews. They attributed this to my continuous probes during the interview to locate the temporal sequence of events. Many of the youths thanked me as they left the interview. I followed up these individuals and attempted to determine if the interview had affected their drug use. I found no one who had decreased his consumption of drugs because of new insights. However, if I had not been in the situation originally, I might not have thought to analyze this possibility.

6) The opportunity for continued long term contacts.

My rapport and friendship with the young people allowed to remain in contact with most of them over a period of years. Our continued relationship has permitted the longitudinal research to occur.

A Personal Note.

Before I proceed, I must be honest and report some of my own emotions as a result of my observations and interactions with the young people. My stress increased because it was necessary for me to control my emotions and remain objective and non-moralizing. I found this to be increasingly difficult given the amount of information to which I was privy and the more I cared for the young people taking part in the research. On September 9, 1975, I was having a particularly "bad day." I witnessed the wall crew taking increasing risks with drugs and dealing in drugs, men in their 30s luring teen-age girls with acid and heroin and increasing late-night violence occurring along the boardwalk.

I wrote in my journal,

> I'll have to make decisions. How far to go? How late to stay out along the wall? What questions to ask (heroin and dealing?) Also my emotions – Not to give as much attention to Art, Mike, Leo, and Bill. Today I felt very bad as I saw Bill, Rusty, and Pat head for the shed to smoke a joint. I want this research to be complete so I can let my own values and concern for them come out - to use my talents and knowledge without enabling them. I need to avoid any of this and not moralize in my research. God, is it hard?! Everyone thinks it's the easiest job in the world. If they only knew! Look at the young kids and the older, and the older yet. Is that where they are headed? They have little to fall back on - friends? Family? (Not much for most). They don't allow religion to enter their lives – Gets worse each moment away from reality into drugs and booze –So many of them! What's happening? Does anybody give a damn? – including priests, etc.?

I could not share these emotions with my subjects. For me, this emotional drain was probably the most difficult aspect of the entire project.

The Final Interviews

I conducted the final interviews between November 7, 1975, and January 6, 1976. I administered a pretest of the interview to a one of the Old Wall Gang. In addition, to the 72 subjects of this phase of the research, 13 members of the "Wall Gang" were interviewed. The latter group was representative of a somewhat different era. They were interviewed for both comparison and longitudinal purposes. Other than as specifically noted, their responses were not included in the statistical analysis.

The interviews lasted approximately an hour-and-a-quarter to two hours. I asked questions in an open-ended fashion to allow for a maximum of spontaneity and depth. When a subject did not elaborate to an open-ended question, such as, "What did you miss by not having a father?", I named specific choices, such as, "Did you miss discipline? Someone to talk to?" And so on.

I contacted each of the young men either in person or by telephone and asked when they could be interviewed.

The interviews were ordinarily conducted in my apartment. Due to mitigating circumstances, two subjects were interviewed in their homes, and two in automobiles. The setting in the apartment was private and confidential. The subject was welcomed upon his arrival, offered a soft drink and asked to be seated on one sofa. I sat on another sofa at an angle to him. I used a tape recorder. I placed it outside of the subject's immediate view with the microphone between us. I began by informing the youth that, if he did not wish me to record the interview or any portion of the interview, the tape recorder could be turned off. Only three persons, one a member of the Old Wall Gang, asked that the interview not be taped. Five subjects, during the course of their interviews, requested that the recorder be shut off during a particular response. Three of these requests were to the item, "Do your Mom and Dad ever fight or have arguments? Or, Did they before the divorce?" The remaining two subjects requested that the recorder be off for responses regarding sexual activity and drug trafficking, respectively. The other interviewees displayed no concern regarding the recorder. They were further assured that their names were not used on the tape and that I could be able to locate a particular tape by a code list that was stored separate from the tapes.

At the conclusion of each interview, I asked the subject not to reveal any of the questions to others. I explained that, in order to remain scientific, each question had to be responded to with the same degree of forethought by each subject.

I attempted to interview those subjects within particular peer groups, or who were known to interact frequently, in the shortest period of time possible. This was done to minimize the chance of revelation of any of the items to a subject prior to his interview. I was aware of only one instance in which a question was known by subjects prior to their interview. Two subjects, both of whom frequented the wall area, learned from another that I had asked, "What would you do if you found out your best friend was a homosexual?" Paul came to me and whispered in my ear that his response to the item was, "I'd kill him!" I traced the source of the leak. The person was told that it this the only item he revealed to others. Fortunately, there were only two members of the wall crew who had not yet been interviewed. I interviewed Paul and the other subject immediately. I asked that they respond to the item as if they had first heard of it. Upon reflection, both admitted that their responses would have been less violent than their original reaction. The rapport I had achieved was evident during the interviews. The subjects appeared to be quite relaxed and open. In concluding the interview, I asked "Do you have anything else to say or ask?" This prompted several subjects to bring up other topics and to seek my advice regarding their personal lives.

Many subjects lingered. They were intrigued by my books and the field of sociology. They asked questions about the research and the process d of preparing a dissertation.

During the interviews, three subjects requested information about professional counseling. I directed two of them to sources that were available, without cost, through San Diego County. The third subject, Jim, will be described in detail in a later chapter.

I reviewed the responses for internal consistency and verification with other information. I detected no appreciable inconsistencies. One subject "forgot" to tell me during his initial interview that he had once used LSD. He freely volunteered the information in the more lengthy, final interview. Another subject revealed, during the final interview, that he had once used marijuana experimentally. He admitted that he had not known me well enough, during his initial interview, to share the information with me.

Wrap-up and Departure

From January 7, to February 12, 1976, I undertook a final stage of the field research. During this time, I gathered census, police, probation, school, economic and other statistical information. In addition, I interviewed school and law enforcement personnel in their offices. I interviewed Mrs. Mary Gilroy (the divorced mother of four of the subjects) in my apartment. Her interview was most extensive, lasting more than two hours.

During this period, I spent four days on the Golden Beach High School campus.

It was important to prepare my subjects for my departure, during these final weeks. I continuously referred to the departure in order that the subjects would be reminded. I was cautious not to cease the activities I had been engaged in, such as attending sports, school and church events, in order that the youths would not feel as though I had only been interested in them as research subjects and not as persons. I made an effort to contact in person as many as possible to thank them for their assistance and to say, "Good-bye." Those whom I did not contact in person, I called by phone. I contacted and gave similar messages to the young people who were not officially subjects but with whom I had many interactions. In order to reach as many young people as possible, I composed a letter in which I informed everyone that I was preparing to depart. I thanked everyone who had participated in my research in any way. I delivered copies of the letter to the junior and senior high schools to place on their bulletin boards. I also gave a copy to leaders in the groups that might not otherwise see the letter. A copy was mailed to the local newspaper. The newspaper did not print the letter, but contacted me for an interview. I consented to the interview, but maintained caution in my wording and emphasized the importance of building up the self-image of the youths, rather than contributing to a group label of, "delinquents," or "drug users."

The youths, typically, greeted the news of my departure with pleas for me to remain and/or requests that I return. I attempted to explain the necessity for me to complete my dissertation at the University of Kentucky, and described the lack of job prospects in the San Diego area. I promised that I would return for vacations in the beach area when it was possible for me to do so.

I was treated to dinner by several individuals in Golden Beach prior to my departure. The Catholic youth group, Drop-In, honored me with an evening of prayers and a Mass offered for my intentions. One of the subjects and his girlfriend baked a large cake and presented it to me on behalf of the group. Several of the youths visited my apartment the evening before and the morning of my departure to wish me well. Up to the present time, I continue to maintain contact with many of them. Those who had appeared to most rely upon me as a stabilizing influence, have been the most likely to maintain their contacts. In 1976, I did not fully realize the degree to which many viewed me in this light and who felt that, in the long run, my values may have influenced some of their life decisions. This will be described and some of their correspondence will be presented in succeeding chapters.

PRESENTATION OF THE DATA

The findings of this phase of the research are presented in the next four chapters. Both qualitative and quantitative data are analyzed. The two types of data complement and enhance each other.

Most of the qualitative findings are based on journal notes and observations made during the field research. I selected the descriptive, qualitative data that provided the best possible insights into the everyday life of the subjects. In most instances, I chose the quote or an occurrence because I judged it to be most typical. In other instances, I selected the most extreme case which provided the greatest insight. Many subjects tended to be more verbal than others and were more likely to be quoted. However, I have exercised care so that quotes represent, not one isolated point of view of a single subject, but those that reflect, as best as possible a typical perspective.

The direct analysis of the theories was based on quantified data from the final interviews. This statistical analysis was supplemented by responses to open-ended questions as well as by other qualitative data from conversations and observations recorded in my daily journals.

End Notes

1. Statistics are derived from the *1970 United States Census* and the *1975 United States Special Census.*

2. Statistics are derived from the *1970 United States Census.*

3. Data gathered from the San Diego County Recorder's Office and the San Diego County Marriage Reconciliation Office.

.4. *San Diego Department Annual Reports*, 1970-1974, and *San Diego Juvenile Division Quarterly Reports*, 1970-1975.

5. Research Triangle Institute. "Some Sobering Statistics About Teenage Drinking," *Hypotenuse*, February, 1976., John A. O'Donnell, Harwin L. Voss, Richard R. Clayton, Gerald T. Slatin and G. W. Room, *Young Men and Drugs: A Nationwide Survey.* Research Monograph Series 5. Rockville, Maryland: National Institute on Drug Abuse, 1976.

6. Other drugs included those substances, the use of possession of which were illegal, per se, or illegal under the circumstances of their use. This definition included the ingestion of most hallucinogens, drugs for which a physician's prescription was ordinarily required, cocaine, heroin and other opiates. Likewise, it included the inhalation of fumes from volatile substances, such as glue, paint and gasoline. The use of tobacco was not included even though use of tobacco was illegal for juveniles in California. These laws were rarely enforced. (Given the changes in laws and law enforcement during the 1990s and 2000s, I would have included tobacco.) Minor, over-the-counter stimulants, and those containing caffeine were not included but blatant misuses of these substances were included under the definition. For example, the use of codeine tables, prescribed for a sprained ankle, and later used with alcohol in order to experience a euphoric sensation, was considered as, "use of other drugs."

7. *The Physicians' Desk Reference: To Pharmaceutical Specialties and Biologicals,* 26th Ed. Oradell, NJ: Medical Economics, Inc., 1972, p. 1172.

Chapter 6

EVERYDAY LIFE IN THE GOLDEN BEACH DRUG SUBCULTURE 1975-76

FOREWORD

This chapter presents an overall view of the drug subculture in Golden Beach, from June 1975, to February 1976. I use the term "drug subculture" to describe those who are most involved with drugs in their everyday life as opposed to the broader term "youth subculture" which includes all the youth of Golden Beach.

The everyday life of young people varied by season, time of day and degree of involvement within the drug subculture. The subculture itself developed and changed over time.

The Old Wall Gang was not immune to change. By 1975, various members of the group as well as the group itself made changes in their behavior. There are insights to be gained by comparing Old Wall Gang with youths with similar background. In 1976, the age range of the younger group was approximately the same as that of the Old Wall Gang during 1970 and 1971 when I first began to study them.

In order to understand the drug subculture, it is well to know the degrees to which various individuals became involved in the subculture. Some were more involved than others. Drugs were pervasive in their lives. Parties, rock concerts and other activities were essential aspects of the drug subculture in 1975 and 1976. They are described as well.

CHANGES IN GOLDEN BEACH THAT AFFECTED THE DRUG SUBCULTURE

There were some gradual changes within law enforcement agencies which began in 1973 and continued into 1975. Stories of mass arrests gradually disappeared from the headlines. I heard several reports of policemen who used their discretion by not arresting individuals possessing small amounts of marijuana. The juvenile probation department no longer recommended probation or incarceration for first, and many times, second drug offenses. Instead, the department initiated a program of counseling for the juveniles and their parents. Many adult offenders were not prosecuted by the district attorney. Other adult first time drug offenders were "diverted" into a six-week counseling program.

A new vice-principal, Mr. Phil Wilcox, was assigned to Golden Beach High School during the academic year of 1972-73. He was trusted by the students and he portrayed a less authoritarian stance regarding disciplinary measures than his predecessor. Dress and hair codes at Golden Beach High School were relaxed. An increasing interest in sports and school activities was evident.

Parents became increasingly aware of the extent of marijuana use among young people. They were less apt to be shocked when they learned that their sons or daughters used marijuana. On the other hand, parents began to develop a growing awareness of the increased use of alcohol among those less than 21 years of age.

As the Vietnam War and the military draft ended, young people were less likely to complain that they were alienated from American society. Although skepticism of politicians remained high during the Watergate revelations, the scandal did not appear to affect attitudes toward other social institutions.

As described earlier, a religious revival, or "Jesus Movement," was taking place. When individuals joined these movements, they appeared to decrease or cease using drugs and alcohol.

THE WALL GANG 1975-1976

Seventeen of the Old Wall Gang members were observed or contacted during this period. Pops, as described earlier, completed his sentence and moved to Virginia in August 1975. Ty was usually under the influence of heroin and sedatives. I was unable to interview Ty due to his lack of coherency and lifestyle. Roger, a third member of the group, was not in the area, but I was able to contact him by mail. I administered the final interview in person to 13 of the original 23 members. I obtained Information from others regarding the remaining seven individuals. The information that I obtained revealed no substantial difference in current patterns of the seven from those of the 16 whose patterns were verifiable.

How many had been "saved?"

When I arrived in Golden Beach, in June 1975, I was anxious to meet members of the Old Wall Gang and see how they had changed. My first interest was the effect of the newly converted "Christians." Between the time of Pat's and Anne's letters of late spring and my arrival in June, the initial enthusiasm for the "Jesus Movement" among the new "Christians" had been dampened considerably. I located Pat on the first day of my visit at the wall. Pat informed me that he had given up on the "church thing." He stated, "It didn't work out for me, man. I tried it and it was ok. I like those Christian guys and all, but it is not for me. I did quit using pot. I drink beer. Pray for me, Jerry, that I can quit drinking, will ya?"

I found that the newly-converted, including Pat and Keith, had experienced an initial emotional "high" from attending the charismatic church services, but, when this emotionalism had worn off, they simply returned to their former ways. Indeed, Keith was no longer dating Anne, let alone considering marriage. Keith was heavily involved in dealing cocaine. All but one of the other six who had experienced a dramatic "conversion" no longer attended services. They were using alcohol and/or other drugs, and engaging in other deviant activities. Les was an exception. Les was the son of a former minister who had divorced his wife and abandoned his family. Les renewed his religious fervor and continued to avoid drugs.

On the other hand, the Old Wall Gang members had made new friends and renewed other acquaintances through their Christian connection. Some of their new friends joined the group and became a part of the new "wall crew." They included all four of Jones' family and 19-year-old Carl. Each of them had been active in the Baptist Church with their parents. They continued to accept Christian beliefs and attended some services. However, except for 16-year-old Larry Jones, they did not put their beliefs into practice. They engaged in sexual activities rather freely and were heavy users of alcohol, marijuana, and, to some degree, other drugs.

I attended services at the fundamentalist chapel the first Wednesday after my return. The church group had leased a large hall in a neighboring community. The congregation consisted of several hundred 18-to-25 year-old males and females. They were led by a reformed drug user in his mid 20s. He spoke of his days in the surfer-drug subculture. The minister told of his former misguided ways A loud rock band provided musical accompaniments. Emotions were heightened through the preaching of the "coming end time.". The preacher then selected passages from the Bible, particularly the prophets and the apocalyptic writings, to confirm that the current conflicts in the Holy Land were evidence that the end time was at hand. The congregation appeared to be mesmerized by his preaching and several proclaimed they "accepted Jesus Christ as their personal Savior." I was accompanied by 19-year-old Toby. Toby had recently arrived in the beach area. He was heavily involved in drugs. During the service, Toby stood and waved his arms along with the others and professed his "salvation." Toby thanked me for taking him. When we returned to the beach, he joined a group of pot-smokers and spent the night with a 18-year-old girl he had met two days earlier.

In the long run, I determined that what was actually occurring was a true "revival" - a revival of the individual's earlier religious practices and beliefs. Youths who had strong religious backgrounds were returning to religious services. They chose services that were similar to those in the faith in which they had been raised. Thus, those from a fundamentalist tradition were attracted to the newer, more "in" fundamentalist services that appealed to youth. Likewise, those whose families were grounded in the more mainline Protestant denominations or Catholics were attending services and programs aimed at youth. Typically, they participated in youth programs at a church of their own religious tradition or one with similar beliefs and practices. Specifically. I found that the youth programs at the Golden Beach Lutheran and Presbyterian churches, though small, were attracting younger siblings whose older brothers and sisters had ceased to attend church services. The trend was most evident at St. Patrick's Catholic parish. St. Patrick's utilized the former Baptist property to enhance and renew their youth ministry program. Fr. O'Malley and Sr. Blase directed the youth with a "team" of high school student leaders and advisors. The team met on Sunday evenings to plan activities. The major focus of the week was a Wednesday evening "Drop-In." (The term was a play on words of the earlier "hippie" "drop out" ethic.) Each Wednesday evening, 70-130 teens would gather for activities. These included breaking into small groups to share feelings and concerns, creating artwork and dramatic presentations which reflected lessons in living. The evening concluded with a folk Mass. Fr. O'Malley presided while seated on the floor in the midst of the entire group. He used a small two-foot high table as an altar. The young leaders read scriptures and provided guitar and other music as background. Communion was shared from one to another while still seated on the floor. The crowds grew over the next several months. Although many who were not Catholic attended, most of them remained active for only a brief period of time. Many Catholics whose parents no longer practiced their religion attended occasionally.

Members of the Old Wall Gang and the larger wall crew floated into and out of the various religious settings. It appeared that religion in itself did not lead to any immediate and permanent conversion from drug use and other deviant activities. However, the churches' efforts to reach young people in terms of music, services, settings and various activities that were meaningful to them ameliorated some degree of drug use. In addition, they provided healthy outlets for those who did not wish to partake in the "party scene." The degree of this was most effective, however, when the young person had been socialized within their family according to the values that were commiserate with the same or similar religious beliefs.

Marriage, Education and Employment

Three members of the Old Wall Gang had married. Two of these had divorced within the first year of their marriages. Five had "steady" girlfriends with whom they had developed a relationship for at least six months. All five lived with females. Three lived with their girlfriends, and two with girlfriends of others. The latter two maintained what they said were Platonic relationships with their roommates. In four of the five relationships, the males appeared to depend upon the females for strength in certain areas of their lives. For instance, the four depended upon their female roommates to waken them for work. Three of these females showed strong tendencies to "baby" their boyfriends and encourage certain dependencies. Despite the various living arrangements and unchanged moral standards, there was less sexual promiscuity than in previous years. In interviews, six of the Old Wall Gang members stated that they had greater confidence in their own masculinity. Likewise, they were less fearful of homosexuality than five years earlier.

The members of the group remained very ambivalent regarding education. They expressed a desire to either complete high school, if they had not done so, or to return to college. In most instances, these desires were not carried out by actions to accomplish their goals. Of the six who had dropped out of a regular high school program, only one, Beaver, had completed the requirements to receive a "general education diploma" from the State of California. However, Beaver's lifestyle differed from other members of the Old Wall Gang. Beaver no longer used drugs other than alcohol. He attended church services regularly. Beaver was employed for more than one year and had a steady girlfriend for four years.

The eleven who had graduated from high school had entered college. All, but two, enrolled in a community college. However, only four were continuing their college education. Those who were not currently enrolled in college indicated that their college experiences were less alienating than their high school experiences had been. They desired to return to college. The desire to receive a college degree, in most instances, did not appear to match assessments as to abilities, talents and areas of the individuals' interests. Rather, the desire appeared to have been instilled by societal standards of goal attainment, status and prestige. These conflicting and ambivalent values appeared to further complicate the individuals' search for employment and pursuit of a career.

An example, in extreme form, is that of Pat, then 21-years-old. Pat had begun five semesters at the community college, but completed classes in only one of the semesters. He sought employment, however, that would not interfere with attendance at college. During several months of the study, he was employed in a position, working for low hourly wages, in the late evenings. Pat and the other employees had to phone their employer late each afternoon to see if they were to work that evening. The employment was erratic and Pat was often discouraged. He was having difficulties with the few courses in which he was enrolled. In late October, Pat dropped all of his courses and, a few weeks later, was fired from his job. Pat anticipated his return to college the following semester and again sought employment compatible with school hours. In the meantime, opportunities were open for him to receive federally funded training in metal construction which could have led to employment with a large shipbuilder at a rather substantial salary. Pat refused to pursue this opportunity because it would interfere with college classes. I asked Pat if it might not be better for him to have a career without a college degree, which, in the long-run, was perhaps more lucrative. Pat replied, "Hell no, man! Who's gonna look at you if you don't have a college degree? No one is gonna come paddlin' up to you on a surfboard and ask you to be president of I.B.M. if you don't have a college degree?"

Pat did not appear to have a realistic view the rewards of a college education or, in his words, becoming "president of I.B.M."

It should be remembered that Pat's father was an extreme alcoholic. He, like others, was lacking in parental advice and support that might have provided him with more direction.

Although most of the other members of the Old Wall Gang had been raised in upper-middle class homes, they lacked parental guidance regarding educational attainment. Moreover, their absent fathers were not responsible for their college expenses or other support after their sons turned 18.

The employment patterns of the Old Wall Gang continued to follow a rather unsteady course, similar to that which had existed during previous years. Individuals gained and lost jobs, worked for rather low salaries and were frequently dissatisfied with the positions they currently held. Mo was pleased with his career as a cook-chef. Vick was moderately satisfied with his position as a waiter in an expensive restaurant. Frosty was somewhat satisfied with his current position as a delivery driver but did not intend to remain in that position indefinitely. Matt, had been my "foster son" had remained with one employer longer than any of the Old Wall Gang members. He was also the highest-paid of the group. He, essentially, achieved his goal of employment in an occupation that was meaningful for him. Matt, then 22, was employed as a metalworker at a naval base under U.S. Civil Service. He had been working at the base for more than three years. It is interesting to contrast his opportunities with others, including those open to Pat. Matt had obtained employment as a common laborer when he lived with me. I used certain contacts to obtain work for him that both made him eligible for union membership and gave him needed experience. In addition, his mother and stepfather were civil service employees who understood the processes involved in obtaining government employment. He utilized this base to obtain metalwork training and employment. He received a promotion to metalworking two years earlier. Matt was somewhat dissatisfied with his work. He believed there was waste and a lack of productivity within the civil service system. However, he was reluctant to change employers during a period of high unemployment because he felt fulfilled in the fruits of his labor.

The inconsistent patterns of employment and educational behaviors might be viewed as fitting what has been described as "amotivational syndrome" found among marijuana users. Erich Goode has described its effect on users,

> Users become apathetic, become ineffective in achieving conventional goals - even goals they themselves valued prior to use - find themselves unable to carry out long-range plans, have difficulty in concentrating, and begin to do poorly in school. There is a dropping away of the will to succeed, a lack of interest in achievement, a life characterized by lethargy, sloth, and languor.[1]

I viewed these behavior patterns among Old Wall Gang from 1970 to 1976. I found a similar pattern among the younger heavy users in Golden Beach during 1975 and 1976. The question arises whether or not the "amotivational syndrome" is totally a result of the use of marijuana. There are many other situational and background characteristics, including "life chances," which could produce a lethargic personality or a sense of low self-esteem. The resulting personality characters could, in turn, preclude a high level of academic and educational performance. A variety of authors have commented on this syndrome.[2]

The examples of Pat and Matt provide some indication of the complexity of the discussion. Moreover, the long-term results of the research eventually provided additional insights.

Drug Involvement

The "heroin epidemic" had passed. Ty, a "former" member of the group, was now excluded because of his heroin addiction. In previous years, three individuals had injected opiates intravenously. One of these had also injected stimulants intravenously. Another had injected cocaine intravenously, but had never used any form of opiates. Some of those who rejected the intravenous use of opiates smoked marijuana cigarettes which had been laced with heroin. Julian smoked "opium goo" on cigarettes in Vietnam. Otherwise, except for Ty, opiate use was brief and experimental. However, several members began to use cocaine on a somewhat regular basis.

In the past, several members of the group had experiment with sedatives. The group now strongly condemned sedatives as dangerous. The same ethic was passed on to younger males who began to frequent the wall area.

By 1976, the use of drugs among the Old Wall Gang was limited to alcohol, marijuana and cocaine. They made exceptions for the instrumental use of stimulants in work or academic situations. Two individuals who were enrolled in four-year colleges told me that they used stimulants during final examinations. Four others had limited their use of stimulants to employment situations (for the most part, as restaurant employees). Thus, a total of six of the thirteen individuals who had ever used stimulants, did so to function to perform their roles in life. The remaining seven individuals, who had used stimulants for one-to-six month periods earlier in their lives, no longer used them and they condemned those who did.

I identified three individuals who had serious drinking problems. They admitted to their problems both in our interactions and in their formal interviews. All three had employment difficulties resulting from their alcohol consumption patterns.

Mo and Beaver continued to hold steady jobs. Increasingly, they began to lose contact with the group.

Group cohesion increased among those who remained in the area. Luke, Pat, Julian, Vick and Les were at the wall on a daily basis. The wall remained a meeting place and message center. Those who moved from San Diego became more integrated into the larger society. Their involvement in the drug subculture declined.

To summarize, the Old Wall Gang members remained only marginally integrated into the larger society. This was true in spite of their more conservative attitudes including an absence of verbal defiance against "the establishment." In January 1976, their drug patterns were mainly confined to marijuana, alcohol and cocaine. Use of stimulants was confined to utilitarian purposes. Based on my observations over the six-year period, it appeared that the group cohesion and certain drug-use ethics were interacting factors. When some persons moved away from the group and to another area of the country, they were likely to decrease their overall drug use. On the other hand, if a member used heroin or stimulants, particularly if he used the drugs intravenously, he was excluded from the group. Once excluded, if the person remained in the general area, he was more likely to become even more involved with opiates and stimulants. It was increasingly clear to me that alcohol was becoming the drug that posed the most serious consequences for the Old Wall Gang.

THE WALL "CREW," 1975 - 1976

As the number of members in the older group declined, a younger group of youthful surfers began to frequent the wall area. By the summer of 1975, they exhibited some patterns which were quite similar to those of the Old Wall Gang during their high school years. The young group differed in other ways. They became integrated with the Old Wall Gang members and the entire group began to refer to themselves as the "wall crew."

The opportunity to study both similarities and differences between the older and younger members proved to be an important benefit to the longitudinal nature of my research. I found that a major consequence of the interactions among the wall crew was the process of socialization. This allowed the older generation to give "feedback" to young members about the dangers of certain drugs. The process will later be described in more detail.

The wall crew was, by far, the most cohesive of any group on the beach. Nevertheless, the younger members were not as close-knit as the Old Wall Gang was five years earlier. Perhaps, an indication of this was their use of the term "crew," rather than "gang," to describe themselves. Although their membership fluctuated considerably, the wall "crew" was larger than the Old Wall Gang had been. I estimated that between 35 and 40 young men, between the ages of 14 and 21, could have been considered members of the wall "crew." (Twenty-seven became research subjects). When they were not at the wall, the younger members tended to socialize in smaller groups of three to five. The older group all attended parties and other functions together. The younger members arrived with three or four of their closest friends. Even though almost all of them attended the same parties and other functions, they usually interacted within the smaller circle of their peers during the activities.

Many interactions at the wall were governed by "generational" distinctions. While the wall "generations" overlapped considerably, they were grouped by age with approximately four-year intervals. The original "wall" generation, preceded the "Wall Gang," and currently ranged in age from 25 to 29 years. The "Wall Gang," ranged in age from 21 to 25 years. The next, succeeding generation ranged in age from 17 to 21 years. As noted previously, those 16 and under were called the "rats." The rats had the lowest status in the pecking order of the wall crew. Further, the rats resented, and often harassed, younger, 12-and-13-year-old surfers, who attempted to surf in waters near the wall.

The wall crew was distinguished by their degree of involvement in and commitment to surfing. This influenced most other interactions as well as the social structure of the group. Status was largely defined by one's ability to surf. The exclusive nature of the group was influenced, in part, by their desire to maintain uncrowded waters that were safe and desirable for surfing. Order and standards of cleanliness were enforced to facilitate surfing and comfort in beach attire. The wall itself was located close to parking and was convenient for changing clothes and storing surfboards. The nature of surfing and the manner in which it pervaded the lives of its adherents increased the occasions for them to interact.

Their interactions resulted in common mannerisms, speech patterns and "surfer" language. In addition, although they were of different "generations," the wall crew members had similar family backgrounds. They tended to relate to females in the similar ways. They had similar patterns of school attendance and of drug use. Indeed, members of the older generations of surfers and some non-surfers attributed a causal connection to the relationship between surfing and drug use. It would appear that the relationship was actually one of peer influence rather than any "causal" attribute inherent to surfing. For some, the term "surfer" conveyed a lifestyle that included both surfing and frequent drug use. Other Golden Beach youth simply "surfed," without being labeled as a "surfer" or accepting the label as part of their identity. In 1970, all of the older wall generation were heavy users of drugs. In 1975, of 27 wall "crew" subjects, 19 were heavy users, three were regular users, four were light users and one was a non-user. When I asked surfers if they saw any similarities between the feelings they experienced when surfing and when "high," a majority replied negatively. Those who said there were similarities believed the similarities included a sense of being alone and free from others, or simply that "both are fun."

The older wall generations socialized the younger members regarding acceptable and unacceptable behaviors. This was most obvious in their interactions with the rats. Most of the socialization was devoted to teaching younger males the norms regarding surfing and beach "manners," including the deference paid to older surfers. However, the older members spoke of the similarity in family backgrounds of many of the younger members to their own. They consciously endeavored to teach and discipline the rats in other ways as well. The older youths urged these rats to remain in school, to seek employment and not to steal. On one occasion, several older members called the police to report the continued truancy of the rats. Pat and Vick lead the effort to make the police report. Pat and Vick were the two individuals who were most likely to be truant a few years earlier.

The socialization included teaching the younger generation about drug use. The older generations frowned anyone who introduced younger people to any new drugs. Still, they accepted the fact that young members used of marijuana, alcohol and, to some degree, cocaine. Some took considerable advantage of the rats' contacts with other drug users. They used the rats' contacts to sell marijuana to other high school students. Frequently, those over the age of 21 purchased alcohol for the rats. The expected fee for each alcohol purchase was one can of beer for each six-pack of beer purchased, or a six-pack for each case of beer purchased. However, the older members strongly enforced their norms about other drugs upon the younger members. They did not tell those younger members of their own past deviations from these norms. At times, they told me that they sometimes felt "like hypocrites," but, "it's good for the 'rats'." This socialization appeared to be quite effective. The younger group confined their use of hallucinogens to the patterns currently acceptable among older members of the wall crew. One norm was that hallucinogens ought to be used only rarely and on "special occasions" (such as the 4th of July, birthdays, and New Year's Eve). Following the current norms of the older members, none of the younger wall crew used opiates, stimulants or barbiturates. The use of these "heavy drugs" and the use of hypodermic needles were more strongly condemned among the younger group than had been the case among the Old Wall Gang. After they had used Quaalude, a few of the rats were shocked to learn that Quaalude was a sedative and similar to barbiturates ("reds"). As a result, they did not share their lapse with the older group members for fear of being sanctioned.

The derision of barbiturates and the protection of the younger members from association with users of "harder" drugs was also evident in their scorn expressed toward a group of "hard guys" who frequented the area adjacent to the wall. This group was labeled "red freaks" by two older members and the reference became accepted by entire wall crew. This occurred in spite of the fact that there was no evidence that the individuals, so labeled, had ever used barbiturates. Pat explained this to me, "Look, a 'red freak' is someone who is dirty and would use any kind of drug. He jest wouldn't care, man. Whatever was available, he'd use. We don't like them dirtying-up the place. Why don't the cops do something about them? We don't want anyone associating with them."

On several occasions, rats were reminded of this. They were criticized if they rode their bicycles through a group of the "red freaks," or if they responded to a "red freak" who asked the time of day. Silence and obvious exclusion greeted any individual who appeared to fit the stereotype of a "red freak" and dared to enter the territory of the wall crew.

Perhaps, these socializing mechanisms were effective because they were not only spoken, but also practiced by the older members. On the other hand, when older members deviated from the norms, the "rats" ridiculed them. The day after one incident, a 13-year-old said to me, "Did you hear him? We weren't that drunk, an' he was sitting there drinking a six-pack when he told us that, if he saw us that way again, he'd punch us in the nose."

I found such comments and the entire process of socialization taking place most interesting. The rats usually mimicked comments and attitudes of the older members of the wall crew. Nevertheless, when older members violated their own norms, the rats said their actions were like the "hypocritical behavior" of their parents.

It was obvious that feedback occurred between the generations. There was a perception among the younger generations that the failings of the older drug users resulted from their "elders'"current and past drug use. The dangers of prolonged hallucinogen use were reinforced by reports that individuals who appeared to have some mental defects "burned their brains out on acid." (None of these reports were substantiated.) The sloven appearance of others was characterized as resulting from use of heroin or barbiturates. Younger members frequently made remarks to me regarding older users, typified by the following:

> *Nelson*: "Look at Les! I think he is an alcoholic. He isn't even working!"
>
> *Sol*: "I don't wanna be like Pat. He's gonna be sittin' here at the wall, drinkin' beer 20 years from now."

> *Nelson*: "The reason we won't turn out like them older guys is 'cause we haven't used acid like they did in the old days, and we are not dropping out of school, like they did."

While there was some evidence that similar feedback mechanisms were operating among others in the drug subculture, they were not as pronounced as those within the more cohesive wall group. Likewise, socialization was not as effective or as evident as that between wall generations.

Overall, it appeared that the wall crew was meeting the needs of the younger rats just as had the "Wall Gang" met the needs of a previous generation. These cohesive peer groups provided intimacy, structure and discipline that seemed to be lacking within their homes. The patterns indicate support for Sutherland's Differential Association theory. They obviously point to positive peer and "older generational" influences as well as negatives influence. A casual observer would likely be unaware of the positive influences.

Before proceeding to a description of the overall drug subculture, certain other trends should be noted regarding the wall crew. There was a trend for increasingly conservative attitudes to be expressed by the group, both intra-generationally and inter-generationally. The Old Wall Gang members became slightly more conservative in their opinions regarding politics and morality. However, each successive younger generation appeared to be increasingly extreme in their conservative attitudes. Nevertheless, their behaviors did not always match their attitudes regarding the "work ethic" or "law and order." Several expressed moral guilt about their sexual activities and their use of drugs. The guilt did not appear to translate into behavioral changes, at least at that point in time.

There were many expressions of racial, ethnic and religious prejudice by members of the wall crew. The attitudes appeared to reflect those of their parents and peers.

None of these attitudes were evident, five years earlier, in the "anti-establishment," "flower-children" generation of the old "Wall Gang."

THE OVERALL DRUG SUBCULTURE, 1975-1976

Foreword.

The "Glossary of Terms" (Appendix E) may be of assistance in understanding the totality of the picture that is portrayed in this section.

It should be reemphasized that limitations of time and space required selectivity in choosing those features of the scene that best provide a background sketch for the reader. I have exercised my best professional judgment in determining what characteristics are essential.

Elements of Involvement.

Involvement in the drug subculture in Golden Beach was a matter of degree and relativity, rather than one of clear-cut membership. Table 1 shows data from interviews of all 72 subjects.

The data indicate that involvement in the drug subculture was related to the grade level when initial drug use occurred, to the kinds of drugs used, selling drugs and growing marijuana. I used grade level in school, rather than age, because I found that grade level was how the subjects categorized their life histories. In addition, there was little discrepancy within the sample between the grade-level they had attained and the grade-level expected for a corresponding age.

Initial use of marijuana and initial use of alcohol were closely related. There was some indication, however, that marijuana was the first drug used by most subjects. Typically, alcohol was used after the initial use of marijuana and the use of other drugs followed. This progression was most evident among heavy users.

The data suggest that the degree of involvement in the drug subculture was associated with early use of drugs as measured by grade level.

A second element of involvement in the drug subculture was "the use of other drugs"(other than marijuana and alcohol). I chose the use of "other drugs" to reflect the realities of the drug subculture in Golden Beach. The use of marijuana and/or alcohol reveals nothing more than is evident in the categories of degree of drug use alone. Moreover, there was a near-perfect correlation between the use of marijuana and the use of alcohol. (The younger generation did not make the distinction between "anti-establishment" marijuana and "establishment" alcohol as had the Old Wall Gang.) In addition, by 1975, the two substances were used, more often than not, on the same occasion. On the other hand, for a person to use drugs other than these "ordinary" drugs reflected a decision to become more deeply involved in the drug subculture. The data in the table reflect this reality. Except in the four cases of sniffing glue or paint, use of all other substances followed a continuum from heavy users to non-users.

TABLE 1

ELEMENTS OF INVOLVEMENT IN THE DRUG SUBCULTURE BY DEGREE OF DRUG USE

	Heavy Users	Regular Users	Light Users	Non-Users	All Subjects
Median Grade Level of Initial Use					
Marijuana	7th	9th	9th	9th	8th
Alcohol	8th	9th	9th	9th	8th
Other Drugs	9th	11th	9th	n/a	10th
Percent Using Other Drugs					
Hallucinogens	77%	27%	13%	0	42%
Stimulants	52%	27%	9%	0	29%
Sedatives	52%	9%	9%	0	26%
Cocaine	74%	18%	17%	0	40%
Opiates	16%	9%	4%	0	10%
Glue/Paint	10%	0	14%	0	6%
Percent Who Sold Drugs					
Light, Only Marijuana	58%	27%	9%	0	24%
Heavy, Only Marijuana	16%	0	13%	0	11%
Marijuana and Other	16%	18%	0	0	18%
Percent Who Grew Marijuana	74%	46%	26%	0	47%

The use of substances other than marijuana and alcohol corresponded to current ethic regarding these substances. Although hallucinogens were the "other" drugs most often reported, their use was confined to an initial experimental use, or on an infrequent "special occasion" basis. Cocaine was reported to have been used by the next largest number of subjects. Cocaine became increasingly available during the study and was generally regarded as a safe substance (although 15 of the 29 subjects who had used cocaine believed it was addictive, physically or psychologically). Its use appeared to be only mitigated by its expensive price ($40 to $90 a teaspoon in 1976). The use of stimulants was largely confined to employment circumstances (mostly by restaurant employees). Otherwise, stimulants, sedatives and opium were limited to one or two occasions, each, by the subjects who had used them. The only exceptions to this were three subjects who had used stimulants and sedatives extensively before they resided in Golden Beach.

Three subjects had used heroin. Each had used intravenous methods of injecting both stimulants and heroin during a period of their lives. Only one of the three used heroin and stimulants during the previous year.

A third element of involvement in the drug subculture, shown in the table, was selling drugs, or "dealing." Again, involvement in drug dealing follows the pattern of the other elements.

The table also shows degrees of selling drugs. "Light, Only Marijuana" refers to the practice, within the subculture, (not fully regarded as "dealing") of either acting as a go-between for a "dealer" and one's "friends" or taking advantage of an offer to "go in" with one or more peers toward the purchase of a kilo of marijuana. In the latter instances, the portion, not used by the individual, himself, was sold to a few, close friends. Only minimal profit, if any, was sought or gained through such transactions. The usual payment for acting as a "go-between" was the right to "pinch" a portion of marijuana for oneself. A fair "pinch" from a "lid" (about one ounce) of marijuana was not expected to exceed the amount necessary to make three or four "joints" (marijuana cigarettes).

"Heavy, Marijuana Only" refers to transactions involving a kilo, or more, of marijuana. Such transactions were usually conducted with the intended purpose of acquiring a profit. In following the economics of more than 50 cases of this type of dealing, involving both subjects and non-subjects, I concluded that there were very few instances, in which less than two kilos were involved, which resulted in any clear profit. Operating expenses including personal use, free samples, discounts for friends and being "burnt" (having one's marijuana stolen or having delivered the marijuana to a bad credit risk) all cut into the large profits. The dealers downplayed these costs to their peers. The substantially larger transactions, involving many kilos were far more lucrative (I witnessed several, ranging from 10 kilos to 500 kilos). The marijuana in these transactions was sold by the kilo and a quick turnover was considered the key to success, both financially and in reducing the risk of arrest. Those individuals who engaged in these, larger transactions were likely to deal in other drugs. They are included in the "Marijuana and Other" category in the table. The "connections" for cocaine, hashish, opium, heroin and large amounts of sedatives, stimulants and hallucinogens were frequently the same connections as those for large amounts of marijuana. This degree of dealing was separate from dealing between peers. The dealers tended to be secretive of their activities and avoided close, personal relationships within the subculture.

In order to illustrate the progressive nature of dealing, I include an interview with Keith, who was then 22. Keith, was the member of the Old Wall Gang who had been taken part in the "contest" to have sexual intercourse with the most females a few years earlier. He was mentioned in Anne's letter as her prospective husband. Keith asked that the tape recorder be turned off at this point in his interview. I have reconstructed his words from my notes. Keith began using marijuana at the age of 12. He was in the 7th grade. He had used many kinds of drugs. Except for his drug transactions, Keith was currently unemployed. During most of our interactions during 1975, he was under the influence of cocaine. I scheduled the interview early in the morning in order that I could waken him and interview him before he was under the influence of any drug. Many portions of Keith's story were verifiable. Through the years, he had confided in me regarding many matters with no sign of serious exaggeration or untruthfulness. I chose his story because of his description of the details of his progressive involvement in drug dealing. Moreover, I had confidence in its veracity.

> I began selling pot when I was 14. At first, I just dealt in lids Then I began to deal kilos. I guess I began because I knew where it was where I could get it. When I was 17, I made my first big deal. I made $500 on that. I turned over 500 keys (kilos), in one deal. It was for the same people I had been getting the other stuff form, earlier. It was when I began working that I got my big break. Oh, yeah, in the meantime, I dealt to a lot of things. I dealt in hash for the same people when I was younger. The most

I sold, at one time, for profit, was a pound. I sold a lot just for friendship. Let's see, then, I sold a lot of acid (LSD) I sold hits by the thousands. I would buy them for 25 cents and sell them for a dollar, or a dollar and a half, a piece, depending on the quantity someone bought. I was still 17, then, too. I had a job then just for spending money. I dealt uppers . . . that was kinda just small to help people when I was using them. The first time I dealt coke was when I was 17. I lost my shirt on it the first couple of times. I give away too much for a period. I was dealing with the same people as with the pot.

I progressed as I began to meet different people. When I was 18 or 19, I met more high-society-type people. They could afford to have it in quarter ounces, and I could buy them (the quarter ounces), and, if I didn't tote cocaine, I could make $200 to $210. If I did tote, I would go in on a whole ounce and break-even. There were seven grams in a quarter-ounce, so I could sell five, to make the bucks and have two left over to tote. If you cut it (dilute cocaine) right, you have three grams to play around with. When I was 22, when I made the next step. I started dealing in pounds. A pound costs about $1500. I deal in one-a-month, about. Then, I break them into ounces or sell pounds, sometimes. Usually I make eight-hundred to a thousand a week. When a shipment comes in, the deal might be over in a day or in a week. I get a call an' go look at it, sample it, and see what he has to offer from ounces to pounds. These are different people that I met when I was working. They are very *incognito*. Financially, they are very well off. I only have to worry about three people. I have to deal with three of them. One calls me, and I call the two others.

I don't worry about getting busted. I can tell when the phone is being tapped. I don't intend to stay in it. I'd be cheating myself out of life. I don't know how long I'll stay in it. Right now, I have about $10,000, saved up. My goal is $100,000. I have the money and it is not in a bank, or in a safety deposit box; I have to worry about the IRS.

Pretty soon, I'll be leaving town for quite a while. I can't tell you when. I'll be going to South America on a big deal. I'll get a phone call. It could be in two days, or in two months.

Keith's progressive involvement in dealing was similar to the paths taken by others. Keith's advancement to higher-profits involving larger amounts of drugs was typical. (In a subsequent chapter, Keith's continuing story and his entrepreneurial skills will be seen in a new light).

There are a wide variety of reasons why others did not follow the entire course that Keith or other "big dealers" had followed. Two other members of the Old Wall Gang had reached a level of dealing in which they dealt in quarter-ounces of cocaine. Pops was arrested by undercover narcotics agents, served in a county honor camp and was currently on parole. Turk was frightened out of the drug trade when someone pulled a gun on him. Turk was robbed of several hundred dollars. It was his final drug transaction. Fears and paranoia about detection by law enforcement increased at each step. There was a corresponding decrease of trust in one's "business associates."As indicated in Table 1, various individuals were at various steps in the process at the time of their interviews. To the degree to which they had progressed, their steps were similar to those taken by Keith. The key element in becoming a successful dealer was having contacts to obtain drugs. There were no problems, whatsoever, in locating customers.

The final element of involvement in the drug subculture, shown in the table, was that of "growing marijuana." In the eyes of the law, this was regarded as more serious than trafficking. But, this was not the perspective of those involved in the drug subculture. Most were unaware of the harsh penalties for cultivation of marijuana. Moreover, the penalties were not a deterrent to those who were aware. Successful cultivation was rather rare. Many plants died. Many others were discovered by parents or other authority figures and destroyed. The greatest risk appeared to be the "rip-off," having the plants or leaves stolen. Because most plants were raised at home and required sunlight, eventually, they had to be transplanted outdoors. I was able to trace some of the "rip-offs." I noted two major forms of "ripping-off." The first was by friends of the grower who knew the location of the plants and the owner's patterns of movement. The second was by youngsters, usually 11 to 13 years old, with early-morning paper routes. The paper boys purposely checked the yards of individuals whom they believed might be cultivating marijuana. (In fact, an early morning paper route was a source of a great deal of stealing. During the hours when the youths were free to move about and the neighborhood inhabitants were asleep, several "entrepreneurial" youths successfully stole car accessories and burglarized many homes.)

It was obvious that "free enterprise" and "the work ethic" were adequately serving this middle-class American drug subculture. In time, the entrepreneurial skills of many of the individuals became useful for more legitimate enterprises.

To summarize, the four elements which reflected degree of involvement in the drug subculture were early initial use of drugs, use of a variety of drugs (particularly substances other than marijuana and alcohol), drug trafficking and cultivation of marijuana.

Pervasiveness of Drug Use in the Daily Lives of Heavy Users

The interview schedule contained a number of items derived from my observations of and familiarity with the drug subculture. The items covered a variety of events in the daily lives of young people and a several rationales for using "pot, booze or other drugs," as follows,

> Before school?, During school?, Before going to a sports event? , Before participating in sports?, During a sports event?, Before a movie?, Before or during a dance?, Before a date or going out with a girl?, Been high or drunk while driving a car or motorcycle?, To have sex or turn yourself on or get loosened-up?, To turn her on, or get her loosened-up?, To enjoy sex more?, To sleep?, Before church?, To relate better to others?, To eat (enjoy it more)?, When There was nothing better to do?, Just to 'have fun'?, To be accepted?, Just to get your mind off things for a while?, When you should have been doing something else?."

I asked each interviewee to respond, "never," "once," "a few times," or "frequently," according to the frequency with which he used any drug under for each purpose or each circumstance. The questions were not originally designed to constitute a scale. For illustrative purposes, however, I weighted each response to each item on a scale from "0" to "3." I then calculated a total score for each respondent. The results are shown below in Table 2.

TABLE 2

PERVASIVENESS OF DRUG USE IN DAILY LIVES BASED ON TWENTY-ONE INTERVIEW QUESTIONS

	Heavy Users	Regular Users	Light Users	Non-Users
Mean Score	41	28	18	3
Range	27 - 55	13 - 46	4 - 41	0 - 8

The numbers indicate that the ''pervasiveness of drug use'' scores, by mean and range, were directly associated with degree of drug use. The mean score of the heavy users was 41, yet the score of the non-users was only 3. The highest score was 55 out of a possible 63.

To further illustrate the meaning of the items in the everyday life of a heavy user, I constructed the following description of an "ideal type." The individual does not exist in reality, but his patterns are an "ideal type" or composite of those individuals who closely approximated this extreme. I call the person "Smokie." The following is a pattern of his day,

> Smokie arises each weekday at 7:00 a.m. After a shower and a bowl of cold cereal, he leaves his home, at 7:30 a.m., to meet his friend, Puff, in the canyon. Puff and Smokie smoke two joints before he arrives at the school for their 8:00 a.m. class. Smokie is stoned, during his first two classes. At 10:00 a.m., the effects of the pot are beginning to wear off. He requests and receives a pass to the boys' room. He meets his buddies there and they smoke a joint together. He returns to his classes. At 11:30, his lunch break begins. He can easily cross the street to the parking lot since school officials do not check to see if students leave campus early. He heads for Doobie's van where he knows many of his buddies will be congregating. They share two joints. Smokie enjoys lunch more when he is stoned. Pot helps him get the munchies (a craving for food following use of marijuana). After he eats his lunch, he shares the last of a roach (the butt of a marijuana cigarette) that Doobie offered him, and he heads back to the campus. His next class is history, so he "turns himself off" and waits for the final period, his physical education class. In the locker room, Puff offers Smokie a few drags on another joint. Smokie feels better and less self-conscious in his gym shorts when he is stoned. He cuts class early and heads home. Some of his friends are out for football and remain at school. A few others work after school. Smokie is bored and does not know what to do with himself. He wants to get "in" with Don across the street who, he heard, has some good contacts for hash. Smokie sees the dude in his garage. He takes his stash (supply) of pot and goes across the street to offer the dude some. They roll some of Smokie's pot into joints. Later, the dude invites Smokie to try some of his hash. They "mellow out" and listen to music. They purposely smoke another joint before Smokie leaves in order that they will be able to "munch-out" at dinner. Smokie's mother will be home from work so he tries his best to "maintain." Smokie calls Puff after dinner. They discuss whether they should eat some peyote and see the latest surf flick, or go to the football game. They decide to go to the game. Smokie enjoys another joint as he drives to Puff's. He and Puff have another before

> going into the stadium. After the game, they go to the school parking lot where they anticipate that the usual ‘‘partying” will take place before the post game dance. Puff's older brother buys them some beer. They drink a six-pack with their classmates, and share in the joints that are being passed around. A lot of groups are sipping bottles of sweet wine. At about 10:30 p.m., the groups begin to break up and guys begin to enter the dance. Smokie looks for Liz. He's got the courage, now, to ask her to dance, because he's "high." They dance. He asks her if she would like a ride home. He lets Puff know, and he and Liz leave the dance together. As he starts the car, he asks Liz if she would like to try some of his stash. She expresses consent. He drives to a hillside park, thinking to himself that if he can get Liz stoned she'd be a lot easier to "make" and, when he's stoned, he enjoys sex more. Smokie rolls two extra-large joints. They smoke the joints and Liz passively accepts his sexual advances in the backseat. He takes her home at 2:00 a.m. He goes behind his house to have one last joint before going to bed. He likes to have a joint to help him to sleep and not to worry about things while laying in bed.

Each of the circumstances in the above drama was reported and/or observed numerous times during the research. Though Smokie does not exist, many heavy users repeated similar patterns on a day-to-day basis.

The skeptic may wonder why parents, school officials or teachers did not recognize Smokie's condition. Like Smokie, the most members of the drug subculture attempted to"maintain," or, perform in a manner so that others will not suspect their drug-induced state. (They were usually quite successful). To act otherwise, or to draw attention to oneself or to the group was considered "uncool" or unacceptable. This ability was particularly essential when encountered by law enforcement personnel or when greeted by one's parents at the end of an evening. The unacceptability of not being able to "maintain," in the drug subculture, appeared to be similar to the anti-social behavior, in adult society, of not being able to "function" after consuming a "normal" amount of alcohol.

Smokie's story and the underlying data illustrate a pattern that may reflect the previously described "amotivational syndrome" associated with marijuana use. The behavior of the heavy users of drugs among the 14-to-21-year-old subjects was similar to that of the Old Wall Gang members.

Hazards of Involvement in The Drug Subculture

There were certain inherent hazards associated with participation in the drug subculture. These hazards were directly related to the illegal nature of the activity itself. Some hazards involved direct confrontation with the legal system. Other hazards were indirectly related to the illegal nature of one's activities. The civil and criminal protections were unavailable to those engaged in the drug commerce. The subculture attempted to control and govern these functions with its own set of norms and sanctions. However, the imposition of sanctions was typically inadequate. An examination of some major hazards follows.

"Getting Busted"

The risks of being arrested were considerably less for participants in the Golden Beach drug subculture compared to their counterparts in previous years. If arrested, the youth were subjected to far milder consequences than in earlier periods. Nevertheless, avoidance of entanglement in the criminal justice system remained a part of the day-to-day reality and excitement of the drug scene. The relaxed enforcement policies appeared to be responsible for some lessening of alienation toward symbols of adult society and a certain openness about drug use.

Many youths admitted that the secretive nature of their activities was a large part of the "fun" involved in drug use. To illustrate, I present the reactions of some youths to a discussion regarding the legalization of marijuana. It was suggested to the group that the substance might someday be decriminalized. The group consensus was that, if such action were taken, the use of marijuana "wouldn't be any fun." When someone stated the possibility that marijuana cigarettes might eventually be manufactured and packaged, Eric, 17, became very upset. He stated,

> Oh, shit, man! That would ruin everything! I mean, like that's half the fun! You know, hiding some place and rolling your own and making sure no one is coming. I mean, that's the thing that makes it all fun! I'd probably quit if they did that. It wouldn't be any fun anymore, at all!

To some degree, police and probation officers indicated that they, too, sought a middle-ground in the "cops-and-robbers" game. All of the officials I interviewed acknowledged the widespread use of marijuana and alcohol by teen-agers and their inability to affect a substantial reduction. Their attitudes and policies reflected their attempts to "keep a lid" on the situation. A typical attitude was expressed by one police officer on the Golden Beach beat,

> Look, we know it is going on all over. What we don't like is the open defiance--the younger kids, especially seem to do that--you know, just openly defying the law, sitting on the boardwalk, smoking pot, just defying someone to do something about it. That's what I don't like, because that shows they have no respect for the law. I do something about that because they have to learn. But we know kids are going to smoke pot and we know that they are going to have parties and get drunk. What we have to do is to protect them and others, to keep them away from the hard stuff by concentrating on the traffickers and to keep them from killing themselves or someone else in a car.

Those in the drug subculture continuously devised new methods of avoiding arrest. It appeared that both sides in the "game" developed a new offense as quickly as their opponent responded with a revised defense.

In late June, the wall crew told me how they had found a "safe" haven for smoking marijuana. It was located, nearby, on the bay. I was assured, by them, that "no one" ever came there and "the cops would never bother" them. On June 27, 1975, Bill Jones described to me how he stored his "stash" inside his right sock. Bill stated,

> If the cops do frisk you, they pad you down on the way down and they never feel the inside of your right ankle. They're right-handed, so, if they do feel inside your ankles there, they'll search your left one.

On July 5, 1975, Leo and Bill were arrested at the "safe" bay location. Bill was charged with possession of marijuana. The police had searched him and found a marijuana cigarette inside of his right sock.

A brief notation of each case and its outcome illustrate the differential manner in which cases were handled by type of offense and the status of the offender, as follows:

1) Two juveniles, Norm Dunn, 16, and Morris Bayer, 17, were arrested for possession of alcohol and shoplifting. They had stolen the alcohol from a liquor store. They were read the Miranda warning, handcuffed and placed

in the backseat of a police car. The police officers talked to them and released them a half-hour later.

2) Leo, 17, an "emancipated" juvenile, was arrested twice for possession of marijuana. Because Leo was legally "emancipated" from his parents, both cases were eventually transferred to adult court. Leo's charges were combined in the final court proceedings. His attorney negotiated a guilty plea in return for reduction of both offenses to misdemeanors, a fine and sentencing under the "diversion" program, which consisted of six one-hour group counseling sessions.

3) Hap, 19, was placed under arrest twice for "being a minor in possession of alcohol." On the first occasion, Hap felt he had been "framed." He maintained that he had just finished drinking a canned soft drink, was about to leave the area, and was placed under arrest by a police officer who had picked up an empty beer can. Hap claimed that the officer then accused him of discarding it. Hap was jailed until the following morning when the charges were withdrawn. (He was upset that his mother had paid a fee to a bondsman not realizing that her son's charges were being dropped.) Three months later, Hap was again placed under arrest, in my presence, for the same offense. Taking advantage of a momentary diversion of the officers' attention, Hap fled and outran the officers. He told me that he had "evened the score" for his first arrest.

4) As described earlier, Bill Jones, 20, was arrested for possession of marijuana with Leo. I bailed Bill from jail and he reimbursed me for the bondsman's fee. His parents hired an attorney. The charges were dropped at the time of his arraignment, and Bill paid the attorney s fee of $75.00 to his parents. His only previous offense had been an unpaid traffic warrant, for which he spent three days in the county jail.

5) Andy, 17, was arrested for possession of marijuana. He was taken to his home in handcuffs and released to the custody of his parents. No charges were filed. Andy had no previous offenses.

6) Lee, 19, was arrested twice. He had a lengthy juvenile record of drug and property offenses and had been incarcerated in the county's juvenile honor camp for three months. In August, Lee was arrested for possession of marijuana. He was unable to afford an attorney, argued with the judge during his court proceedings, pleaded guilty and was fined $50. He was arrested in September for purchasing alcohol under the age of 21. He appeared before the same judge and was sentenced to 30 days in the county jail.

The patterns exemplified in the above cases are consistent with other cases involving non-subjects, recorded during the project. The case of Lee is somewhat unusual because he had a lengthy prior record and displayed a negative attitude to the judge. The overall pattern stated by officials was that they regarded alcohol offenses as the least serious offense, marijuana as somewhat more serious and other drugs the most serious. In addition, juveniles less than 18 were treated with a greater degree of leniency and informality than others. The final disposition was often influenced by the social status of the juvenile's family (as admitted by probation officers) and his prior record. I observed a number of occasions in which the police simply gave a verbal warning to a person in possession of marijuana. Alcohol offenses were typically ignored unless citizens had complained directly to the police.

During the summer months, citizen complaints led to a series of "dragnets," or "crackdowns"on illegal activity along the boardwalk. These "dragnets"resulted in Hap's two arrests. Lee's second arrest was, indirectly, a result of citizen complaints. Lee was apprehended purchasing alcohol in a liquor store. Other businessmen in the area complained to police that the store was the major source of the large amounts of alcohol being consumed on the boardwalk. Undercover agents had "staked out" the store the evening of Lee's arrest.

On July 1, 1975, the governor of California signed into law legislation that reduced the possession of less than an ounce of marijuana, for personal use, from a felony to a misdemeanor. The law provided that the charge was to be handled by a "ticketed" citation, similar to that issued for minor traffic violations. The individual so charged could contest the allegation or pay a relatively small fine by mail. The law became effective on January 1, 1976. The changes did not change the juvenile codes. The effective date of the legislation was too late in this period of the field research for me to assess its immediate impact. However, in the long term, marijuana use decreased. The decrease came about after the legislation went into effect. This was followed by even more lenient practices by police. In my observations covering the next twenty-six years, I never once witnessed a police officer writing a marijuana "citation" as mandated under the 1975 legislation. I observed many situations in which marijuana was being used in plain sight or smell of police officers.

Conditions of the illegal market.

The criminal penalties for drug use forced those in the drug subculture to utilize their own illegal market. This posed additional hazards. These included increased costs, consumer fraud and lack of regulation of market transactions. The increased cost of alcoholic beverages for juveniles appeared to be standardized so that one can of beer was given to the provider of a per six-pack and a six-pack was given in for each case of beer. In those, relatively few, instances in which juveniles requested adults to purchase wines and spirits, the juveniles reimbursed the adults with an amount of money sufficient to purchase a small quantity of beer for themselves.

A DRAMATIC ILLUSTRATION

The market price of marijuana and other substances fluctuated according to their availability. One particular set of circumstances allowed me to trace the market conditions as they were dramatically affected by law enforcement.

At the time of my arrival in Golden Beach in June 1975, the current market price for "commercial" (standard, Mexican-grown) marijuana was from $10 to $12 a "lid" (approximately one ounce). The substance was plentiful and readily available. Some "Oaxacan" marijuana was also available. The Oaxacan marijuana was considered to be a more potent and was a preferred variety. (Its name was derived from the Mexican state where it was grown.) Despite its reputed potency, very few young people purchased Oaxacan. In addition, some expensive "Thai Sticks," were available. Dealers complained that they were "stuck" with their oversupply of Thai Sticks. Most buyers purchased the less-expensive "commercial" marijuana.

On July 12, 1975, the local press reported that a federal grand jury had indicted 36 persons in San Diego, Tijuana and Mexico City. The indictments, reportedly, culminated more than two years of undercover law enforcement activity. The marijuana "ring" had been involved in transactions of "tons of marijuana" each month according to the *San Diego Tribune*, July 12, 1975.[3] There were more indictments and arrests during November and December 1975 and in January 1976.

Within a two-week period following the initial indictments, the supply of marijuana in Golden Beach decreased dramatically. Those in the drug subculture called this "drought" the worst they had experienced. The"drought" lasted until early October 1975 when large shipments of marijuana arrived in the area. By that time, the market conditions had changed from what they had been in June and early July.

During August and September, "commercial" marijuana was practically unavailable. Increasing amounts of Oaxacan and Thai Sticks were available, but at prices ranging from $20 to $35 per "lid." Other "brands" began to appear, also at inflated prices. These included "Columbian" (grown in Columbia, South America) at prices ranging from $25 to $40 per lid, "Maui" (grown on the island of Maui, Hawaii) at prices ranging from $20 to $50 per lid and "homegrown" (fresh marijuana, grown within the United States or recently in Mexico) at prices ranging from $11 to $20. All of these price-ranges were considerably higher than the prices for similar kinds of "pre-drought"marijuana. In addition, the margin of profit was greater for each of these items than on regular, "commercial" marijuana. Thus, the dealers increased their profit and "bottom line" due to the drought. I realized that most persons who wished to purchase marijuana at the higher prices were able to find a plentiful supply. From my observations and inquiries (counting the number of times I detected the smell of marijuana on the boardwalk, asking subjects how much they had smoked each day, and so on) the amount of marijuana being smoked had not decreased substantially, if at all. This was particularly obvious among the heavy users, most of whom continued to remain "high" during the majority of their day.

Moreover, the "drought" brought about permanent increases in the price of marijuana and changed in the habits of marijuana users. Following the end of the drought, in October 1975, to my departure in February 1976, the price of "commercial" marijuana remained at the "inflated" range of $12 to $16 per lid. However, many of the heavy users who had become accustomed to smoking the "better" varieties told me that they no longer experienced the same "high" from "commercial" marijuana. They continued to use the more expensive varieties. Three heavy users from three different peer groups told me that these changes resulted from their increased physical tolerance for marijuana. Two other heavy users, each of whom was present during one or the other of the above conversations, held a contrasting opinion. They believed that people who began to use the "better varieties" had merely developed a "taste preference" for the higher-priced brands. Chuck Roe described his experience, "It's kinda like driving a compact car and then getting a big Cadillac. Once you get used to the

Caddy, you wonder how you ever managed with that little car, bouncing around on the road, so you stick with bigger cars."

While some issues in the debate of "increased physical tolerance" may not be resolved, the series of events I witnessed point to an interesting latent function of effective law enforcement in the various "wars on drugs." An indirect effect of this particularly successful battle in the "war" may have been the use of more expensive (and probably more potent) marijuana in Golden Beach. In addition, "consumers" began a trend that was to continue into the 21st century, a preference for higher quality and far more expensive varieties of marijuana. The price increases have vastly exceeded the inflation rate in the United States.

Consumer Fraud

I found "consumer fraud" to be widespread among drug traffickers. "Consumer fraud" is used to describe the practice of selling or receiving one substance for the price of another, purported substance. In the subculture, this was recognized as a form of "being burned" (being taken advantage of for money). Purchasers of illegal substances were ready victims of "consumer fraud" and had no legal remedy. Within the Golden Beach drug subculture, there were limited methods of controlling fraud. These were based primarily upon the value of a "good" reputation to a drug dealer. This was highly ineffective, however, in transactions involving "outsiders." To deal with "outsiders" was itself a violation of an ethic of the subculture, "never deal with a stranger." (The clearest evidence that this oft-spoken norm was not always practiced comes from my own experience. As I mentioned earlier, from June 1 to August 1, 1975, I was asked to either buy or sell marijuana every time I walked the length of the boardwalk. I was a stranger to everyone who made a request.)

A few instances of "consumer fraud" are illustrative.

The first case involved Albert, a 18-year-old subject, and Mario, a 19-year-old non-subject. They approached me on the beach on a Friday evening in late July. Mario was very upset. They asked me to smell a "baggie" of "homegrown" marijuana Mario had purchased from a "red freak" for $15. They asked my opinion regarding the substance. I told them that it did not seem to be marijuana. We asked two dealers who were standing nearby for their opinion. The dealers also doubted the authenticity of the substance. They each expressed an opinion that it was alfalfa. Mario made the purchase on the boardwalk an hour earlier. The person who made the sale allowed

Mario to smoke a "sample," supposedly taken from the baggie. The sample appeared to be of good quality. A cigarette, rolled later from the substance in the baggie, did not. Mario was incensed, but acknowledged that he had little recourse to regain his money. The dealer had been an "outsider."

The following evening, I again met Albert and Mario on the boardwalk. They and two others were conversing with me when two sailors approached. Mario asked the sailors if they wished to purchase some marijuana. He and the sailors stepped into an alley. Mario returned a few moments later to inform us he had regained his $15. He had allowed the sailors to smoke a marijuana cigarette and, then, sold them the baggie of alfalfa. He seemed to be sure that the sailors would not attempt to return to harm him because they were "outsiders" to the community.

About one month later, the above scene was replayed in all its essential details. The script was the same but there was a different cast of characters.

A second type of "consumer fraud" was reported by 14-year-old Lonnie, a subject, who had made kilos of alfalfa into bricks, placed marijuana on the top of each brick, and sold them as "good deals" to nonresidents of Golden Beach for $225 each.

Other examples I observed were selling "commercial" marijuana as "Oaxacan," stimulants (mainly amphetamines) as LSD, paper as LSD and stimulants as THC. In addition, I was able to trace much of the cocaine that had originated with Keith through "cuts" (dilutions) as it passed hands four times. The final result was a product one-eighth as potent as the original, sold at an average price greater than four-times what Keith had paid for a similar amount. At each step, each dealer had told his customer that his product was "pure" and "uncut." Only at the final step did customers complain to their dealer that what they had purchased was mostly "flour." The final dealer was Toby who admitted to me he had used some flour and a large quantity of "baby powder" to cut the cocaine.

In each of these instances, the consumers had no legal recourse to correct the fraud or to prevent those committing the fraud from continuing their activities. There was no "Better Business Bureau" or "Consumer's Union" to monitor the illegal drug market.

In a similar manner, who had drugs, or drug-related money, stolen from them were usually prevented from seeking legal protection for their "properties." I recorded numerous instances of drug "rip-off's." A substantial majority of these cases involved rather small quantities, and, often unknown to the person whose drugs were taken, the culprit had been a "close" friend or family member. In some instances, however, substantial amounts of drugs and/or money were involved, and the relationships were more distant.

A few typical cases provide examples.

Eighteen-year-old Dennis, a subject, was a close friend of another 18-year-old, Ralph, a non-subject. Ralph dealt heavily in a variety of drugs and Dennis assisted him in many of these deals. The transactions were usually conducted in Ralph's apartment. One November afternoon, Dennis brought two acquaintances to Ralph's apartment in order that they could buy a "lid" of Columbian marijuana from Ralph. On the way, Dennis mentioned that he and Ralph planned to attend a party that evening. The transaction took place so that the two customers became aware of the location within the apartment where Ralph stored the marijuana. When Ralph returned from the party, late that evening, more than $300 worth of marijuana was missing. He and Dennis suspected the pair. They had been made aware of Ralph's absence and the location of the missing marijuana. No recourse or proof existed. Ralph suffered a "business loss.''

Martin Dunn, 14,told me about a situation involving his older brother, Norm Dunn, 16, and Lou, 17. Martin said, "I didn't take Norm's pot. Lou did. Norm thinks I did, but, you see, I got insurance. If Norm picks on me, Lou will protect me and beat up Norm. Besides, Lou has to give me some of the pot so I won't tell Norm that he (Lou) took it."

In the above situation, Norm had neither a legal recourse nor a familial recourse (that is, by informing his mother) because of the nature of the illegal "goods" involved.

The largest drug-related "rip-off" I recorded in my daily journal involved three non-subjects. All three were residents of Golden Beach. Emil, 21, managed a family business. He had several hundred dollars in his savings account. Sam, 20, attended college. Emil told Sam that he was acquainted with a person who had contacts to purchase kilos of marijuana at very reasonable prices. Arrangements were made for Emil to invest $450 for the purchase of three kilos. They invited John, also 20 years-old, to finance the purchase of a fourth kilo for an additional $150. Emil assured his two young entrepreneur friends that his acquaintance was "safe" and reliable. The transaction was scheduled to take place at a distant San Diego location. The seller was to deal through Emil. The seller met the trio at his van. He allowed Emil and Sam to enter. Emil sampled the marijuana. The seller then asked Sam and John to leave during the completion of the transaction. Emil rode in the van with the seller and the marijuana. He informed the seller that he had the $600. At that point, Emil was assaulted by the seller, robbed of the $600 and pushed from the van. In this instance, Emil had made guarantees to Sam and John regarding the soundness of his original proposition. He raised the money to repay. No one saw the reputed seller again. Sam told me that he believed that the "seller" was a "junkie." Though the participants in this and previously described incidents were not pleased with their misfortunes, they accepted them as known risks of their participation in drug use and/or drug trafficking.

THEFT AND VIOLENCE

I compiled a considerable amount of evidence about theft and violence from observations, interactions and interviews. I discovered that the patterns which I found did not always match those portrayed in the media.

Theft

During their interviews, I asked each subject, if he had stolen, in what amounts, and during what period of his life. On the one hand, the responses indicated that those who were more heavily involved in drug use were more likely to have *ever* been involved in stealing. On the other hand, what might seem surprising is that most, 21, subjects began stealing *prior* to their initial drug use. A smaller number, 17, began stealing *after* their initial drug use. Moreover, there were no particular trends evident between degree of drug use and a *continued* pattern of theft. Indeed, 44 percent of the light users admitted that, at the time of the interview, they continued to steal on a regular basis compared with only 33 percent of the heavy users.

These data are consistent with my own observations and reports. Most of the stealing that occurred took place during the persons' junior high school years. Excitement was a major incentive for most. There were very few utilitarian thefts. None of those who reported a regular pattern of theft did so for the purpose of obtaining drugs. Two individuals had been and continued to be engaged in rather extensive utilitarian theft. Both began to steal and shoplift prior to their initial use of drugs. Neither used addictive drugs. Both bragged that they were proficient "thieves." Even though they each had been arrested several times for property crimes, they had no intention to cease their activities. One of these, Chuck Roe, was eventually sentenced to prison. The details will be reported in a later chapter.

Violence

In 1975 and 1976, there was a minimal amount of physical violence in Golden Beach. I observed a few fist fights and threats of fist fights during parties. In each instance, the subjects were under the influence of alcohol. The disturbances did not involve one group against another and most potential fights were broken up by friends of the likely participants.

At times, threats of physical violence were made, but these were usually a part of loud, drunken, "machismo" behavior. The threats lacked substance and were not followed by any action.

In Sand Beach, I witnessed two knife fights in which two individuals were wounded. I heard reports of several others fights that occurred in Sand Beach. Those involved were not residents of either Sand Beach or Golden Beach. When I was able to trace a rationale for the fights, I found that the disputes typically resulted from drug trafficking and/or relations with females. Two of the attacks occurred among the "red freaks." Several members of the wall crew witnessed one of these. The word of the fight increased the disdain of the wall crew toward "red freaks."

In later years, the reports of violence and threats of violence increased in Golden Beach. These were usually related to drug trafficking in which large sums of money were at stake. In many instances, the participants were under the influence of cocaine or highly addictive drugs.

I studied the mood changes under the influence of drugs. Most persons became increasingly passive under the influence of all drugs, including alcohol. Marijuana appeared to have an immediate pacifying effect. Several subjects, however, responded aggressively under the influence of alcohol. This was particularly true of two subjects, whose behavior under the influence of alcohol was subject to erratic change. I found it difficult to separate mood changes resulting from alcohol and those resulting from marijuana because the two were so frequently used together. The reactions to hallucinogens were extremely varied and erratic. Many of the substances, sold as "psychedelic mushrooms" or peyote, were actually LSD and/or strychnine. Likewise, what was claimed to be LSD often turned out to be strychnine and/or amphetamine. I was unable to make generalizations about other drugs because my observations were limited. In addition, the persons who used other substances were under the influence of alcohol and/or marijuana when they used them.

In general the level of violence did not fit the stereotypical picture most Americans had of the drug subculture. Many of my friends and family were concerned about my safety when I was doing my research. I felt quite safe. I knew how to behave in situations that did arise and, if someone had tired to harm me, I had many friends nearby who would have immediately come to my rescue.

PARTIES

Those most involved in the drug subculture were the most likely to attend parties. There was a considerable amount of alcohol and marijuana at most parties. Nevertheless, there were differences between the types of parties, those who attended particular parties and the activities that took place.

Parties were more frequent during the summer months than during the school year. Parties were usually held on weekends. Many occurred when word spread that someone's parents were going to be absent over the weekend. Many times, the "host" did not consent to the party or his/her consent came very reluctantly. During the early evening, large numbers of his friends and classmates simply arrived at the house much to the "host's" surprise. There were frequent rumors of upcoming parties which never occurred. Some rumors were entirely false. Others were based on a false assumption that someone's parents were gone for the weekend. At other times, a young person left his home so that he/she would not be pressured into a party at his parents' home. Many homes and furnishings were damaged during parties. Frequently, make-up and jewelry were stolen from the bedroom or master bath.

Based on my observations, the attendance varied by degree of drug use as follows,

1) Heavy users attended nearly all parties they were able to locate. They frequently moved from one affair to another, in the same evening, seeking the greatest amount of "action."

2) Regular users reserved most of their partying activities to weekend evenings. They attended some parties to which they were not specifically invited, but only if they were assured that many of their acquaintances would be present. They also moved from one affair to another, but not as frequently as the heavy users.

3) Light users rarely attended parties to which they were not specifically invited. They did not move from one function to another unless they were required to do so in order to make a "social appearance" at each. They

attended parties with less frequency than heavy or regular users. They rarely attended a party on an evening preceding a school or work day.

4) Non-users rarely attended any parties and were somewhat unaware of the existence of most of these affairs. They were uninvited, not due to their social unacceptability, but because others were aware of their preferences. They did not attend parties if they knew alcohol or other drugs were going to be available.

Most parties were held in the home and/or backyard of the host. The number in attendance varied greatly, from twenty to more than 1,000. The parties were usually held in the evening, but some began in the afternoon and extended into the late-night or early morning hours. Some parties attracted a rather limited age-group, but the larger affairs were attended by those from early teens to those in their middle to late 20s.

The ingredients that were defined as constituting a "good" party included:

1) The size of the crowd attending relative to the space available. Too few or too many participants were considered undesirable.

2) The number of females present. The higher the proportion of females, the more successful the party.

3) The number of kegs of beer that were available. The more beer, the better the party. Parties were advertised as "one-kegger," "two-kegger," and so on, up to "10"and "15-keggers." (I rarely heard individuals consider the relative number of expected participants compared with the amount of beer to be provided. When the beer supply had been depleted [often early in the evening] complaints were voiced at the party, but only a few foresighted individuals anticipated this occurrence by bringing an "extra" personal supply.)

4) The presence of a band or bands. There was some form of music at most affairs, but the presence of a live band was considered to be an added attraction.

Parties were held for a variety of reasons, such as birthdays, housewarmings, holidays, school vacations and so on. Many were primarily money raising affairs. Most hosts attempted unsuccessfully to limit the attendance. Word of an impending party appeared to spread like a wildfire throughout the schools and at the beach. A few hosts stationed friends at the entrances to regulate incoming traffic. There were no age limits. If attendance was limited, the limitation was based on the degree of relationships with the host.

The majority of the parties were not chaperoned. In some instances, an anxious mother greeted guests in the kitchen and attempted to direct traffic. In a very few instances, two parents were present. When parents were present, their supervision was limited.

Police usually ignored the activities. When they did take action, it was due to extenuating circumstances. Police ordinarily did not act until after 10:00 p.m., the curfew hour in San Diego for juveniles. A high-ranking officer told me the police did not like to initiate action unless traffic was being interfered with or they had received complaints regarding the noise. He further stated that they did not wish to make arrests unless a citizen was willing to sign a formal complaint and testify in court. This policy was evident in the patterns of police action in the field. The initial police contact consisted of an officer arriving at the location and asking to see the host. The officer appeared to be oblivious to illegal activity which was taking place, such as juveniles in possession of alcohol or the use of marijuana. The host was informed that neighbors had complained, or that traffic problems were being created, and so on. The host was told that if the noise could not be kept down or if the guests did not remain on the premises, it would become necessary to disperse the guests. Most hosts cooperated and asked their guests and/or the band to comply. If it was necessary for the police to make a second visit, the host was informed that, unless he or she could keep matters under control, the host would be subject to arrest. If they did achieve cooperation within a reasonable length of time thereafter, the police returned with backups and asked the crowd to disperse. Only those participants who were not cooperating were placed under arrest. Typically, this action was not necessary. The youths knew of the police patterns and appeared to cooperate. At times, the party was moved to another location. I observed only two occasions when the police confiscated the kegs of beer.

There was marijuana at most parties, but it was smoked within small groups and, usually, at a location that was somewhat removed from other activities. The most common locations were garages (often rebuilt into "small houses" for sibling use) and adjacent alleys. In the course of an evening, most of those attending an affair took part in the marijuana smoking, one or more times. The use of other drugs was not common during parties. On some occasions, however, participants arrived at a party under the influence of drugs other than marijuana and alcohol. (In subsequent years, cocaine would change the nature and focus of parties.)

Some parties were money raising affairs. Publicity was optimized to maximize profit. Most bands felt the experience and exposure which they received were ample compensation for playing. Thus, the investment was minimal. The young entrepreneurs invested in the kegs of beer (approximately $22.00 each), some paper cups, a hand stamp and ink pad. (There were, however, "hidden" costs in property damages often discovered after the party.) The price of admission was either $1.00 or $2.00 per person. Often, females were admitted free, or at a discount, to encourage an increased attendance of males. The person's hand was stamped on admission. The guest was then free to enter and leave the premises at will and drink as much beer as was available. (Many times, as stated earlier, foresighted individuals brought additional supplies for their use.) These money-raising affairs tended to be the largest parties and the most likely to come to the attention of the police. I was able to obtain estimates of the profits of three such affairs. One grossed more than $1,000. (This was the largest party I observed). Another grossed more than $600. The third party lost about $35, due to what its hosts termed, "poor publicity." Again, the subculture seemed to have adopted the "free-enterprise" techniques of the larger society.

On rare occasions, parties were run as "scams." The scams were usually hosted by older individuals in their middle to late 20s. For instance, the individuals would advertise that a large number of kegs would be available. However, the host or hosts would purchase only one or two kegs. The fee was collected from several hundreds of individuals. The music was turned up. Then one of the hosts would secretly call the police to complain. If necessary, a second complaint was lodged. The police would arrive and break up the party. The host or hosts made healthy profits from the purchase of one or two kegs. I appeared to be the only one, outside of those hosting the party, that was of the scams.

For the most part, socializing at parties was minimal. It usually was limited to the same group of friends with whom one had arrived and/or interacted with frequently. Many young men said they attended the parties to meet young women with whom they could have sex. Occasionally, some sexual activity occurred in a bedroom. This was rare and was more likely to occur if the male had cocaine to share with the female (referred to as "coke and poke.") A very small number of males and females paired off and left the party together. The amount of sexual bragging the next day far exceeded the realities that had taken place. Dancing was also minimal. It was typical only at those parties at which light users were in a majority.

The main activities consisted of drinking beer and smoking marijuana while listening to the music (the volume of which usually prohibited a great deal of conversation and socializing). Food was served at only five of the parties I attended. All of these parties were hosted by either light users or non-users. Many youths spoke freely of not eating beforehand so that the food would not interfere with the anticipated effects of the alcohol they intended to consume.

In order to present a more complete picture of parties, and a contrast between participants at two types of parties, I have chosen two entries from my daily journal. The first example is more typical than the second. Although the first party, Albert's, was smaller than most, I chose it because of the wide variety of participant-subjects present. The participants were residents of Golden Beach and Diamond Heights. No band was present. The mother remained in the "main house" while most activities took place in the backyard and a "little house" in the rear. The host had attempted to achieve some limitation upon attendance and spoke of maintaining "law and order." In that respect, the affair was atypical, even though his efforts were unsuccessful. The party was hosted by Albert, 18, a regular user.

ALBERT'S PARTY

Daily Journal, August 1, 1975, 8:00 p.m. to 1:00 a.m.

The party was in a home estimated to cost $75,000+ (considerably more expensive than the average Golden Beach home in 1975). Albert had "law and order"arranged. In the small house in the rear, he had his stereo well-guarded. The speakers were extended into the yard (so as not to face neighbors' houses). Football 'jocks' were guarding doors and gates and not allowing people to go to the back-end of the yard (and disturb the neighbors.)

There were four kegs. Approximately 100 people present, two males to each female.

Subjects present. = 19. There are no non-users present.

Two light users:

Sam, 17, arrives at 10:00 p.m.--Does not drink. His older brother, 21, is there and does not drink. Sam is also with Kent.

Kent, 15, does not drink but wants to see a fight between Reed 17 and Roger, 17. (Roger later became a subject, was not contacted until after the party.) Kent is friendly to me and makes a point of coming over to say 'Good-bye,' about 11:00 p.m.

Two regular users:

Jack, 17. He says John, 18, a light user, is out with Betty and Paul, 17, a non-user, and Mary. Jack arrives early and is drunk. He tells me that Skip's, l4, a heavy user, Mom died. John was at home with Skip's sister, Joannie, last night. Jack waits until he is sober to drive John's motorcycle home. He began drinking at 5:00 p.m.

Albert, 18. It is his party. He appears to irritate people by his 'police' tactics.

Fifteen heavy users:

Norm Dunn, 15. Drunk. He talks about getting a job. He is upset about Skip's Mom. He leaves at 10:00 p.m. and returns about midnight. He had smoked pot. He says he went to see Nelson, 16, a heavy user, at the Roe's, house, and Nelson wasn't there. He gets to parties by telling his Mom he is spending the night with Nelson.

Chuck, 16. He does not drink much. He wants to see a fight. He asks me about a job.

Bill Jones, 20. He is with Theresa. He smokes pot and drinks a lot. They neck.

Max, 16. He drinks and helps with the tap.

Frank, 18. Tells me how he got some 'bad acid,' 'yellow microdot,' on the boardwalk (He says he knew the person he bought from). It turned out to be speed. He says, 'I'll never touch it again!' He drinks beer. He had been drinking rum earlier. He also smokes pot.

Bart Roe, 17. He smoked pot and leaves early with Dean, 18.

Dean, 18. He smoked pot and leaves early. Bill Jones says, 'They always do.'

Leo, 18. Smoked pot and drank beer. He tells me how he worked at an amusement park two days and showed up late. He had words with his boss. He feels upset and says he doesn't 'fit in.' He wants to go back east. He is drunk. Drives home?

Paul, 16. Very upset earlier. His sister had sold a two-barrel shotgun that his Dad (deceased) had left him. He asked for it several times and she told him before he left for the party, 'I sold it for $25.' She thought her ex-boyfriend had bullets for it and was going to kill her. Paul asked her to repeat this. She did and he decked her - very hard, and left her on the front porch. He thinks she's 'crazy' and wonders if he can get the gun back. He's worried about getting into trouble with the law because of assaulting her. He almost gets into a fight with Roger. Roger was not supposed to let people in or out the gate. Then, Paul gets friendly with Roger and tells him all about his sister, the inheritance and the gun. Roger shakes his head--like 'talking to a drunk.' Bill and I have a hard time getting Paul out of the party. I take his keys and drive his car to the wall. He then gets into it (a fight) and almost punches two 'red freaks' who called Rusty, 17, another heavy user, a 'surfer faggot.' Then he takes off for something to eat on a bike. His car was still there (at the wall) at 2:00 a.m. Bill Jones reports that Paul is 'always loud,' but 'last year or so he's getting more feisty.' --Anger in him about the inheritance???

Sol, 16. Drinks and smokes pot. He is with an older friend who knows Jack from church. He also knew Skip's Mom.

Nelson, 16. He is happy about his job. Drinking and smoking pot. Says Rick, 16, wants me to help him find a job.

Dennis, 18. He is with Bob Holt, 18, a heavy user, and Bill Holt, 16, also a heavy user. Very drunk! (All 3). Dennis says he would like to fight, 'but I can't fight. I got a bad left arm.' Bob has vodka in one hand, and a beer in the other. His brother, Bill, is passed-out. He drank several beers, two shots of whiskey, and two of vodka. He also smoked some Columbian pot. (Lots of talk tonight about Columbian).

Andy, 17. (on LSD???) Only there a few minutes. He lives around the corner. He works Tuesdays and Thursdays as an office-boy, and Wednesday as a gardener. He has to leave to get up at 5:30 for a paper route. He noticed I had just trimmed my moustache. I said, (suspecting LSD) 'How come you always notice such little things?' He split.

Al, 16. He is with a girl (name?) He just got back from camping so he could go on daily trips with her and her family. He maintains well (drinks some). He gets a bang out of how many people I know at the party.

Eric, 17. He is with Bridget. He tells me that: a) He is going to get some mescaline tomorrow. (I later learn it is from Bob Holt. He lives near the Holt's), b) He and Bridget are both upset about Skip's Mom, c) When I asked, 'Why did you quit drinking beer?' (He is drinking water from one of the cups.) he tells me it was because of what is happening at home--both his parents are alcoholics. (The mystery is now solved!)

Most of the pot-smoking was in the little house and in the corners of the yard. A few Diamond Heights people came about 11:00 p.m. Many peer groups were represented, jocks, church, wall crew, upper beach, etc.

Five or six said there were 'too many people.' Eric felt it was too much of a sosh party. This was the most socializing I have seen at a party, but still mainly within their own groups. No dancing. One-third of the crowd eventually are girls. More than usual.

I heard lots of comments regarding hash (Bill Jones), Columbian, and mescaline.

As I left the party, despite the obvious drunken 14-year-olds, Albert's mother asked if I had smelled pot at the beginning of the evening (I did and a lot was going on in the little house then). She was apparently horrified at this. I tell her that I can't break any confidences. I was in a hurry to get the keys away from Paul and couldn't talk long. I only met Albert's Dad for a second.

Paul, 16 says Leo, 18, a heavy user has a keg and will have a party tomorrow night.

Beer lasted until past midnight. Only 20 or 30 people were there when I left, circa 1:00 a.m.

(Albert's mother later complained of missing cosmetics, trampled flowers and broken furniture.)

Melissa's Party

A second example does not involve the drug subculture. Rather I use it to compare and contrast it to Albert's and similar parties. Everyone in attendance at this, Melissa's party, were either non-users or light users. It was an extreme case. Indeed, it was atypical by the very fact that most of those in attendance rarely attended parties. Melissa, the host, was preparing to move to the eastern seaboard with her family. Her father was a U.S. Navy Officer. Those invited were her friends from the Catholic youth group, Drop-In.

Daily Journal, July 16, 1976, 7:30 p.m. to 10:00 p.m.

Party at Melissa's for St. Patrick's "regulars."
Present:

Reed Gilroy, 17,subject, a non-user.
John Gilroy, 18, a subject, a light user.
Mark, 16, a subject, a light user.
Betty, 17, a non-subject, a non-user.
Mary, 16, non-subject, a non-user.
Rita, 16, a non-subject, use?
Cherrie, 16, a non-subject, use?
Ron, 17, a subject, a regular user.
Ken, 16, a subject, a non-user.
Phil, 16, a subject, a non-user.

Tony, 17, a non-subject, a light-user.
Laura, 17, a non-subject, a non-user.
Kathy, 16, a non-subject, use?

Both of the parents are home, but try to appear unobtrusive, except when serving the food or directing people to towels and the bathroom. The younger children are urged to play in one of their rooms, but they catch the eye and attention of the older girls (especially Betty).

They swim a lot. They don't play music because the next-door neighbor is also having a party and they do not want to interfere. (Mothers' orders!) The parents greet each of the guests as they arrive.

There is a lot of food, fresh strawberries, chips, dips, cold cuts and root beer.

Tony tells me that he never goes to the beach. He stays home. He talks a lot about baseball, but is quiet.

Ken, 16, is still the clown. He keeps getting thrown into the pool with his clothes on.

Most jokes are a test of 'see how far we can go' regarding sex. Lots of double-meaning by the guys when the girls are present. Suggestive, but not direct. Lots of giggling.

Betty, 17, and Reed Gilroy, 17, are very close all evening. She sits on his lap, etc.

Lots of horseplay in the pool. Splashing water. Throwing the ball. Pushing others in, etc.

The girls 'cat-on' (gossip about negatively) the party next door. It is much larger with Christmas tree lights, music, and so on.

Betty and Ken, 16, both talk with others about attending the First Baptist Church and hearing stories about Catholics 'worshiping the Blessed Virgin' and being superstitious about scapulars, etc.

The house is across the street from the border of Diamond Heights. It is very expensive. It has a large, kidney-shaped pool, an outdoor gas-barbecue, and other amenities. There is a lot of talk about what everyone is going to do this summer and next school year. The boys keep talking about sports and the girls begin to talk between themselves to change the subject.

Everyone leaves at about the same time, 11:00 p.m. Most are making plans to meet at the beach tomorrow. Melissa's mother reappears to bid farewell. All thank her.

The size of the above gathering was much smaller than that at Albert's party, and Albert's party was smaller than most. The ratio of females to males was about even, six females and seven males. The participants were homogenous in age, ranging from 16 to 18, as well as religion (only two were not Catholics). These factors and the lack of loud music may have contributed to the greater degree of socializing and conversation that took place at this party in comparison to Albert's party. However, sociability was a normal trait among those present.

It was evident that there had been much more adult participation in planning the second party. Albert had arranged most of his party on his own, including the keg, the guards at the entrances and the opportunities for smoking marijuana. In fact, Albert told his parents he was going to have party. When they objected, he threatened them with the fact that if he could not have the party at home, he would have a larger party elsewhere with less supervision. Eventually, he dictated the terms of the party.

The sounds coming from the larger party next door to Melissa's may have dampened the spirits of the youths. However, they appeared to enjoy themselves, particularly in the pool activities. They appreciated being guests and remained orderly and mannerly throughout. I saw no evidence of drugs and no one spoke about alcohol or drugs.

ROCK CONCERTS

Rock concerts had become an integral part of the drug subculture. They had deposed the "folk concerts" of the 1950s and early 1960s. Rock concerts and parties had also replaced traditional high school and college dances. Indeed, one-on-one dating, dances and proms had all but disappeared by the early 1970s. By 1976, it seemed that they might be making a slight. However, rock concerts were still the "in" thing, the "cool happening" to be a part of.

I observed two rock concerts. The larger one had been discussed weeks in advance on the beach and at parties. It was held outdoors at San Diego City Stadium, Sunday, August 31, 1975. It featured Loggins and Messina, Fleetwood Mac, Lynyrd Skynyrd and Rod Stewart. My companion escorts were Nelson, 16, and Sol, 15. We met many other subjects throughout the day. Nelson and Sol had given me some advice in advance. They warned me that it would be cool in the morning, then warm up, and turn cool again after sunset. I was prepared for the weather change. I did not adequately prepare to be hydrated. Others were bringing coolers of beer and other beverages in plastic containers. I brought water and soft drinks in cans. My escorts told me we had to be there "early" to get good seats. We arrived at 9:45 a.m., fifteen minutes after the gates opened. Nelson and Sol had not informed me that metal and glass containers were prohibited. My beverages were confiscated upon entering. The following my entries for that day,

Daily Journal, August 31, 1975

CONCERT (50,000 present)

8:45 - I go to the wall. Pat and Bill Jones are there. Bill says there is a party at Joe's. 'Most of your subjects are going to be there.' I tell him about the concert. He responds, 'You?!'

Chuck Roe, and Norm Dunn are there. Norm says, 'You know how it is when you are a working man.' They can't go. Sol shows up. Alex, 14, says he can't afford to go.

9:00 a.m. - I leave for the concert. I arrive at 9:45 (gates opened at 9:30 a.m.. The concert begins at 12:00 p.m. (Crowd Control!) Everyone dashes for field position. There are lots of blankets, coolers (No bottles or cans are allowed.) My five cans of pop and iced tea are confiscated. Lots of booze around!

Nelson packed sandwiches, 7-Up, and lemonade (plus about 10 joints).

Lots of lawn chairs and beach chairs. People use flags to locate their friends. There are also balloons (one has about 75 yards of string), frisbees, fireworks (each time crowd yells, 'Yeah!') People are tossed in the air and caught in sleeping bags. Some build human pyramids

Many roll joints, sell joints, and sell 'coke.' The people behind us 'do coke,' using a paper dollar and a mirror. One person asks, 'Will you cut up some if I pay $5?' Across the aisle, others are selling. Others come by and ask if we know where they can buy.

Joints pass freely - whether or not one knew, the AROMA would tell. As I stand, one guy passes a joint to me to pass to a girl. She passes it back to me to give to him. (They intended for me to smoke it too.) She leaves with him. I see this repeated many times on the field. I was offered lots of joints, and some "sips." People are surprised I don't partake.

The crowd is receptive to anything! They stand, cheer, etc. at everything.

As sun comes out at noon, shirts and pants come off. There are lots of shorts and bikinis. I go to the men's room. It is invaded by females. There were long lines to the ladies' rooms so they took over two of the men's rooms.

1:30 p.m. 1st group, Lynyrd Skynyrd, play. (Nelson and others tell me the next group will be more "mellow") My ears ring and I feel dizzy from the heat and the noise. Lynyard Skynyrd plays until 2:15. There is a half hour break.

3:00 p.m. Fleetwood Mac plays. They are even louder. The crowd goes into a frenzy to their beat, clapping hands above their heads, some down on their knees.

3:55. Another break for 55 minutes.

4:50. Loggins and Messina play. The crowd responds, especially to the country and 1950s rock and rolls songs. Also, Indian-type beats.

5:40. Another break for 50 minutes.

6:45. A burlesque type of music for the entrance of Rod Stewart. He plays until 8:20 p.m. Large string section. People ask if he is a 'fag.' Lots of gyrations, a wild outfit and large cape. He dances with the mike. He ends with 'Old Song,' 'Twist,' and other Rock and Roll songs.

We moved to the far end of the stadium. There are all kinds of dancing going on, singles, couples, chorus line style, and some with 15 to 20 people in a circle.

7:00 p.m., As the sun goes down, people put their clothes back on.

There are lots of hawkers of posters, t-shirts, candy apples = 50 cents, hot dogs = 60 cents, drinks = 35 cents or 60 cents.

I see one group from Diamond Heights. I see J.B. catch a joint yet he does not join in smoking it.

I see Toby, 19; Chuck Roe, 16; Eric, 17 and Al, 16. Also, (the 'trio') several times - Morris Bayer, 17; Rich, 17, and Grant, 17. At times Marlene is with them. Lois is also there. She gets up on the stage. Rick is there from Billy's. There are lots of other Golden Beach people. None from Lime St.! No Jocks. Most those of college age dance guys with girls on their shoulders.

Lots of suntan oil. Constant milling around. I move up front toward the stage. There are only about 10 people older than 25 or 30. Almost no children. Only a few are younger than high school.

At 3:00 p.m. I walk around the balcony. I see:

1) Ladies in men's room

2) Three passed out, two friends try to help. Drunk or? In the field more people are standing than passed out.

3) One group tries to jump over the barbed wire fence. The ushers charge them. One hurts his knee but he might have gotten away.

4) I have to stand aside - I was almost puked on.

5) There is Lots of trash, beer cans (especially outside with cups, plastic bottles, etc.)

The ushers are young. They wear white t-shirts with emblems and dark pants. There are no police in view except for security guards at the entrance.

At about 6:30 p.m. two or three cops are on the City college balcony with field glasses (I used Nelson's glasses to see them) One is on his back with his feet propped up studying the crowd at the concert. Others just watch with field glasses.

At the beginning of the concert, a local d.j. 'Tomcat Kelly' of KCBQ thanks the crowd and describes the next concert. Nelson and Sol paid $8.50 for the Elton John concert.

Nelson, Sol and I meet Brian, a nonsmoker, who has only 'experimented' with pot once with Nelson. Nelson wants to smoke, but Sol has just disappeared. Brian does not want to smoke pot again. Nelson says, 'It is no fun alone.' He smokes one joint per hour. He tells me, 'Music and stuff are better when you're stoned. I don't feel like a beer. I am getting sick.'

I see why they have breaks . . . lots of equipment. There are several moving vans and fork lifts. The 'stars' pull up in back in black limousines. (This stirs the crowd.) I count 160 plus speakers.

I compare the event. The atmosphere is not 100% like a concert I attended two nights earlier but there are similarities. I went to the concert with two adults. The San Diego Symphony played the 1812 Overture with cannons, fireworks, etc. at SDSU featuring Andre Kastelantez. There were booze and picnic on the lawn prior to that concert. So this concert was not unlike that concert in some ways.

Or

Like a football game, there were large crowds who rushed for tickets and seats. Booze is usually at the games, but most adults are not aware of the pot and other drugs the kids are using. At both there are males with bare chests, and so on. However, most who are "high" try to "maintain" at the games. Although many do not smoke or drink at games, there are a few fights. For instance, Butch and Arlo almost got in a fight over his 'coke' friends at the last game.

I also noted the 'controls' by the staff at the concert. There are various 'rituals' in concerts like there are at games and other events. I recall the 1960s and the divisions that existed then between the adults and youths. Now Elvis has become "institutionalized." The same was true with Frank Sinatra's crowds and, maybe, Rudy Vallee. ???? Is it the same here?

11:00 p.m. I drive back to the beach. I 'cruise' the beach area. It is very busy. It looks like there are a lot of tourists here, but they are quiet. I do not see anyone I know. There are a lot of fires in the fire rings. I head to Billy's to write this up.

The next day in the *San Diego Union*[4] there was no mention of the concert or the 50,000 young people who attended.

The description of the concert needs no further explanation.

THE "TRIO"

This is an appropriate point for me to describe the "trio" in more detail. I have referred to them several times. I did not include them in the sample or the final interview. I had decided that my previous interactions with them might contaminate that data. (They felt somewhat "left out" because of this decision, but accepted my explanation.) Nevertheless, I continued to interact with them and wrote about them in my journal.

The trio consisted of Morris Bayer, Rich and Trent. All three were 17, seniors at Golden Beach High School. I became acquainted with Morris Bayer when he was 11. I was a close friend of his parents. Morris was one of eight children. Mrs. Rita Bayer was a prominent member of St. Patrick's parish. Her husband was a biology professor. All of the children were "stand outs" academically, socially and athletically, except Morris. The sibling who stood the most and whose status affected Morris the most was Gil Bayer. Gil was a year older than Morris. He was student body president in junior high school, captain of the soccer team, a captain of the football team and an outstanding student. Morris was not involved in student politics. He had not participated in school sports. Hc was a "B" student. The other children rarely, if ever, had trouble with the law. Morris had been stopped and/or arrested a number of times. Some of the other Bayer children had smoked marijuana or drank beer. Morris was the only one who had ever been caught.

Each time Morris was caught and in some sort of difficulty, his family, especially his mother referred to him as "Dumbshit!"

Morris had confided in me for many years. Most people were unaware that Morris' father was a functional alcoholic. Morris was disturbed by his father's drinking behavior.

At about the age of 13, Morris introduced me to Rich and Trent. The three would frequently stop by my apartment. They told me all the minor "naughty" things in which they had been engaged. They seemed to want me to tell them what not to do. Many of their acts were simply mischievous. They began smoking cigarettes. At times, they were involved in minor shoplifting. Eventually, they advanced to other more serious acts.

On one occasion, they dropped by to visit me. They had a bottle of barbiturates. They had obtained them from Grant, a youth their own age. Grant came from a wealthy family in the northern part of the county. I discussed the matter with them and convinced them that the best thing would be to flush the drugs down the toilet which we did. (I realized they came to see me to be "convinced" of this course.) I also advised them to stay clear of Grant.

The trio began to use marijuana regularly, and eventually entered the party scene. Mrs. Bayer informed Trent's grandmother of this, but the grandmother, who frequently had charge of Trent, would not enforce the restriction.

I learned that both Rich and Trent had difficulties at home. Once, all three youngsters received poor report cards in junior high school. Morris' father was very upset and put him on restriction. Grant's father yelled at him briefly. And, as Trent said to me in the presence of the other two, "Rich's Dad didn't do anything and that's the worst of all! *He didn't care!*"

Eventually Trent's parents divorced.

During the next several years, arrests and "trouble" became more frequent. The three became increasingly involved in the drug subculture. Morris separated himself from Rich and Trent somewhat. Rich and Trent associated more frequently with Grant. A few years later, Rich stole Morris' surfboard. This created an additional rift.

In 1975, Morris Bayer got a break. His brother, Gil, had graduated form high school and went to Mexico for a semester to practice soccer. Morris did not have to live in his brother's shadow. He went out for football. He ran only one play a game. His role was to tackle the kicker of the opposing team immediately after the kickoff. This boosted Morris' self-esteem. It allowed him to be a part of a new peer group.

I introduce Morris Bayer, Rich and Trent, at this point, as appropriate to the discussion of the Golden Beach drug subculture. In subsequent chapters, I will describe the events in each of their lives which made their stories so significant.

IN CLOSING

In this chapter, I have described the drug subculture as it existed in Golden Beach during 1975 and 1976. I have detailed various elements and patterns of behavior which were common within that subculture.

The drug subculture, however, represented only one aspect of the everyday life of young people in Golden Beach. The totality of the youthful subculture will be discussed in the next chapter.

End Notes

1. Erich Goode, *Drugs in American Society*, 4th ed. NY: McGraw-Hill, 1993. p. 202.

2. James A. Inciardi, *The War on Drugs: Heroin, Cocaine, Crime and Public Policy*, Palo Alto, Ca.: Mayfield, 1986; Lloyd D. Johnston, *Drugs and American Youth*, Ann Arbor, Mi.: Institute for Survey Research, 1973; William H. McGlothlin and Louis J. West, "The Marijuana Problem: An Overview", *American Journal of Psychiatry*, 125 (September): pp. 370-375.

3. *San Diego Tribune*, Tuesday, June 12, 1975, page B-l.

4. *San Diego Union*, Monday, Sept. 1, 1975.

Chapter 7

WHERE ARE YOUR CHILDREN, TODAY AND TONIGHT? THE LIFE WORLD OF GOLDEN BEACH YOUTH, 1975-76

The daily lives of the young people varied between summer and the school year. Likewise, their patterns of behavior varied between the daylight hours and late evening and night time hours.

THE BEACH, SUMMER DAYS, 1975

A substantial portion of Golden Beach youth spent a majority of their free time at the beach during the warm, summer afternoons. Most of the young people frequented specific areas of the beach where they would join their closest peers. Consequently, the composition of groups was remarkably stable. The patterns of drug use within these groups were consistent. Moreover, I found an overall pattern. As I proceeded from a northern point on the beach to the southern border of Golden Beach, the wall area, I noticed an increased amount of drug use. Some indications of this pattern were the number of times I smelled or saw marijuana, by the number of times I saw individuals drinking beer and the number of empty beer cans I counted on the beach in each area.

Sixty-two of the 72 subjects were at the beach most days. Given the patterns of drug use on the beach it was not surprising to discover a consistent pattern so that those who were heavy users were at the southern area of the beach and light and non-users were more likely to be at the northern area, as follows,

The Wall area:

Heavy users 19; regular users 2; light users 4; non-users 1.

Lime Ave:

Heavy users 1; regular users 1: light users 8; non-users 1.

Main St:

Heavy users 0; regular users 0; light users 1; non-users 1.

Wellspring St:

Heavy users 0; regular users 4; right users 4; non-users 4.

Old St:

Heavy Users 2; regular users 0; light users 0; non-users 0.

Ten "cruisers" varied their activity from one place to another. Two were heavy users, one was a regular user, five were light users, and two were non-users.

The only group which was divided equally among the three categories of drug users was the "Wellspring Street" group. This group had many subgroups, or sub-cliques. No one in the group was a heavy user. The only notable exception to the south-north pattern was found at Old Street. Old Street, like the wall area, was a surfing location. Both were frequented by heavy users of drugs.

I made an effort to observe each group at each location twice each day during the summer months. I varied the times of my observations to avoid any confounding effects.

The following were the patterns of behavior within each group and differences between groups:

1) Patterns of drug use.

Drug use, most notably marijuana and alcohol, was almost completely uninhibited at the wall and Old Street locations. The only limiting factors were the precautions taken to avoid detection by law enforcement officials. Although I observed arrests at both locations, other users said that those who were arrested were "stupid" or "careless" because the locations afforded a direct view of any approaching police officers. Beer and marijuana were used by juveniles quite openly in view of passing tourists and other adults.

The other three locations were not as well situated to avoid police detection. However, this was not the sole deterrent to drug use. The groups themselves applied strong informal sanctions to anyone drinking alcohol or using drugs. This was particularly true at the Wellspring location. I never witnessed the use of marijuana at Wellspring Street during the daytime. On two occasions, individuals joked about "pot." The frowns and silence in response were indicative of the group's disapproval. On two other occasions, young people drank beer in the area. On one afternoon, members of one of the subgroups at Wellspring Street purchased a six-pack of beer. They began to consume it at the fringe of the area. Others, particularly the females, made remarks that those who wanted to drink beer should go elsewhere. The second occasion involved a "cruiser" who entered the group carrying a can of beer. Again, the group made subtle disapproving remarks. The individual understood the message and departed. Occasionally, beer was consumed by a few individuals at the Lime Avenue and at Main Street. Marijuana use was infrequent at these two locations during the daytime. When it was used, it was smoked by persons who did not regularly frequent those areas. Although some disapproval was expressed, the sanctions were not as strong or as effective as those at Wellspring Street.

2) Relationships between the sexes.

The ratio of males to females at the wall area, on any typical summer day, was approximately 10 males for every one female. Three of the wall crew members had steady girlfriends who were often found waiting for their boyfriends to return from surfing or some other activity. When boyfriends and girlfriends were together, one of two extremes of behavior was exhibited. They were likely to be engaged in heavy petting and necking, or they totally ignored each other. Ignoring each other was usually a result of frequent jealousies, disagreements and quarrels. A few other females came to the wall area to "hang out." Many times, they appeared to be seeking males to "turn them on to" marijuana and/or alcohol. These females were regarded by the group as "skuzzy" (undesirable and promiscuous). For the most part, the wall crew ignored them.

The small group who frequented Old Street consisted entirely of males and there was little, if any, interaction between the sexes. There were, typically, an equal number of males and females at the Lime Avenue location. However, the age-composition of the group was such that the average age of the females was somewhat younger than that of the males. The males were composed of a younger "generation" from 12 to 15 years of age, and an older "generation," from 16 to 18 years of age. The members of the younger group were Golden Beach residents and a majority of the older group were residents of an adjacent community, Alta Mesa. The females ranged in age from 12 to 16 years. Most Interactions were within the group, rather than one-to-one, and spanned both generations and sexes.

There were a few one-to-one relationships that developed between some of the older males and the females. Some necking resulted. A few of the younger males and females would "go with each other." However, these younger individuals seemed to change relationships, often with great emotional expression, as frequently as the tides.

A similar situation existed at Main Street. The pattern of this group was somewhat less consistent. The group was composed of nonresidents of Golden Beach. There was an overall comradery that also precluded one-to-one relationships. Females slightly outnumbered males.

There were usually two males for every three males at Wellspring Street. The group was structured by age and by gender relationships. There were three main subgroups. They usually spread their beach towels in patterns so that each subgroup was 20 to 50 feet from each of the other subgroups. The subgroups were organized according to the academic year in high school. In turn, each subgroup was divided into unattached males, unattached females, and those males and females who were "going together." Certain activities were reserved to males and others to females. Male-female interactions involved various stages of the courting process. There was considerable discussion about when to ask someone for a date, how to determine the extent to which one was attracted to another, when someone should "go steady," and so on. As a relationship developed, the couples spent more of their hours at the beach with their towels adjacent to each other's, and, eventually, engaged in necking. Male-female contacts were not seen as disruptive to the group activities. It was expected that couples would separate to participate in group activities with members of their own sex.

3) Topics of conversations.

The topics of conversation also revealed various patterns and differences. Very little conversation took place at the Old Street and wall areas. Conversation was engaged in more frequently at Lime Avenue and Main Street. The greatest amount of conversation and social interaction took place among the Wellspring Street group.

Conversation at Old Street and the wall area dealt with surfing, drugs, sex and upcoming parties. Politics and sports were rarely mentioned.

Topics of conversation at Lime Avenue and Main Street were y centered around employment, sports, politics, families and the previous evening's activities.

The main topics of conversation at Wellspring Street involved sports, politics, school, dating and various social functions (the functions were usually school or church activities).

The manner in which sex was discussed in conversations also varied. At the wall and at Old Street, sexual bragging and references to past and anticipated sexual intercourse was discussed in vulgar and explicit terms. These matters were only briefly and jokingly mentioned, in "forbidden" tones, at the other, three locations, even when females were not present.

There were differences in the manner in which homosexual topics were handled. Homosexuality was frequently condemned, unequivocally, at the Wall and Old Street locations and among the "younger generation" at Lime Avenue. The terms "faggot" and "queer" were used to taunt each other and to scorn anyone whom they found offensive. Homosexuality was rarely mentioned by the "older generation" at Lime Avenue or among those who frequented the Main Street area or the Wellspring Street area. When the subject did surface, it was handled in a matter-of-fact manner. The term "gay" was used, rather than terms of derision. The youths within these three groups also appeared to be comfortable with jokes regarding homosexuality, even when such humor was self-directed. For instance, the young males would imitate a stereotyped homosexual speech and mannerism to tell another youth that they "liked" his new haircut, but not to tell their girlfriends.

4) Types of recreation.

There were differences between the groups in the types of recreation in which they took part at the beach. Outside of surfing, there was little physical activity at the wall or at Old Street. The only major exception was some volleyball activity at the wall area. Surfers ordinarily entered and left the water singly, and the choice to surf at a particular time was mainly an independent decision.

The amount of surfing at Lime Avenue was relatively minor. The main water activity for them, however, and for virtually all of the youths at Main Street and Wellspring Street, was body-surfing. The decision to body-surf at a particular time was decided by the entire group or several members. Often, individuals pleaded with others to enter the water with them because they disliked body-surfing alone. Numerous other physical activities occupied the time of members of these groups. The groups were frequently innovative in devising new activities, such as a variety of "keep-away" and various water-fighting games. The Lime Avenue group set up a horseshoe-pitching game at the beginning of each day. Football was common among the males at Wellspring Street.

5) Amount of time spent at the beach.

Surfing was considered to be best during the early morning and immediately prior to sunset. Consequently, it was not surprising for those at the wall and Old Street locations to be at the beach during those times. However, they usually remained at the beach during most of the day (and often into the night). Some of them went home for meals. Many bought food at nearby stores and consumed it on the beach. In some cases, the young people did have a parent at home and/or there was no food at home for them to eat.

The youths who frequented the other three areas of the beach typically arrived at the beach during the late morning or early afternoon and departed in mid or late evening. As a group, the Wellspring Street youths spent the least number of hours at the beach. They departed, almost in unison, at some undetermined cue, between 4:00 and 5:00 p.m.

I observed many other young people at the beach who were not subjects of my research. For the most part, the patterns exhibited by the groups who frequented the wall and Old Street areas were typical of other heavy users. The pattern of the Wellspring Street group was typical of the other extreme, the non-users. The patterns of regular and light users were best exemplified by the Lime Avenue and Main Street groups.

Given these patterns, there was evidence that each peer-groups exerted considerable control over the public use of drugs, as well as the overall degree of drug use. This should be considered, along with the earlier-described socialization and feedback mechanisms operating "generationally" at the wall, to assess the effect of peer groups in maintaining social control.

It addition, it appears that the groups consisting of heavy-users were less traditional in their sexual relationships. They differed, also, in the manner in which heterosexual and homosexual activity was discussed. The non-users appeared to be the most traditional in their sexual relationships and attitudes. The light users and the regular users appeared to lie somewhere in-between.

Differences in adherence to traditional behavioral patterns were also evidenced in other areas of conversation and activity as well.

This section described the beach activities during the daylight hours of the summer months 1975. The following section describes the activities that occurred in the same general areas, during the hours after sunset.

THE BEACH, AFTER DARK, THE SUMMER OF 1975

Introductory Notes.

For a more complete understanding of this section, it is helpful to know certain background material. The most significant background information is that concerning: the "red freaks," and the police "dragnets" which occurred during the summer of 1975. These events were interrelated with and affected other developments.

"The Red Freaks."

As has been mentioned earlier, the term "red freak" was somewhat of a misnomer. I found no evidence that the "members" of this "group" were engaged in any substantial use of "reds," or barbiturates. The term "group" is also less than appropriate because many of the so-called "red freaks" had little or no interaction with each other. I found that those who were labeled as "red freaks" were unaware that they had been so labeled or that the label even existed.

What then constituted a "red freak?" Or the group of "red freaks?" Among the youth of Golden Beach and Sand Beach who frequented the beach after dark, the label was applied to fit the stereotype of a person who frequented the area at the border of Golden Beach and Sand Beach, was "dirty" in personal hygiene and in conforming to "beach manners" about trash disposal, used "hard" drugs, was violent, a "criminal" who had probably "done time" and who lived Sand Beach or an area reputed to have high rates of crime and/or a high percent of racial minorities.

It was difficult for me to research the individuals who were labeled as "red freaks."[1] The members of the group fluctuated from day to day. Nevertheless, I made some qualified generalizations. As best as I could determine, most "red freaks" were individuals who were: less than 35 years of age, nonresidents or temporary residents of either Sand Beach or Golden Beach, and had been involved in the drug subculture elsewhere. The persons discovered the area through contacts with others who had been there or, often, by chance.

There was some evidence that inland residents of San Diego scheduled occasional "happenings" at the location. However, most of the "red freaks" seemed to have found the location due to the convenience of nearby parking, the proximity of the location to the ocean, the proximity of a large liquor store and the size of the crowd at the location during the evening hours.

I followed three cases of teenagers from other states who were initially frightened by the "red freaks" and attempted to socialize with the wall crew. Due to the exclusiveness of the wall crew, the outsiders eventually joined the "red freaks."

Most of those who frequented the location did so for limited periods of time. Some individuals were observed only once. Others spent a weekend. Others were on a two or three-week vacation. A few had rented an apartment or motel room for a month or more. I observed others who came and went from time to time. An exception to this transient pattern was "Midget," a short, usually very drunk, male in his 30s. Midget was known as a "character." He was very loud and, at times, he appeared obnoxious to passers-by. Perhaps, Midget contributed to the overall stereotype of the group.

I became acquainted with some "red freaks" with varying degrees of rapport. One, Lee, remained in Golden Beach and became a subject of my research. Another gave me a complete history of his life in June 1975. I followed his activities for four years before he left San Diego.

I observed a wide variety of drugs including heroin at the location. However, the stereotype did not fit the group as a whole. Their day-to-day drug use centered on marijuana and alcohol. They appeared to drink considerable amounts of alcohol, particularly wine. The loud behavior of some while under the influence of alcohol created an exaggerated impression of the entire group. A number of violent acts occurred while individuals were under the influence of alcohol, and these, too, tended to be exaggerated in subsequent accounts.

A majority of those whom I interviewed on an informal basis had been in contact with the criminal justice system, usually as juveniles. Most of the charges involved drugs and/or burglaries.

Their manner of dress, rather than their personal hygiene, appeared to be the source of their "dirty" reputation. A few arrived in the area after long-distance hitchhiking and lacked the comfort of a warm shower. However, it appeared that many of the impressions others had of them were a result of their lack of participation in water activities. They did not ordinarily surf or swim. They were not usually attired in bathing suits. The males typically dressed in blue jeans, boots and a long-sleeved shirt. The females typically wore a blouse, pants and sandals.

In general, the group appeared to be made up of individuals of a much lower socioeconomic background than the average Golden Beach youth, but there were some individuals who apparently had upper-middle class backgrounds. At any given time, there were a relatively small number of blacks and Hispanics in the group.

The number of individuals at the location varied considerably, and depended largely on the inland temperature that day. Greater numbers were present on weekend evenings than on weekday evenings. These numbers began to increase as the summer progressed. I observed more than 200 at the location on some late evenings in mid-July.

The size of the crowd, the noise they generated and the habits of some (particularly the breaking of glass containers by those under the influence of alcohol) resulted in citizen complaints. The police responded to the complaints. This led to a change of patterns of behavior at the beach during evening and late-night hours. The interactions between the citizens, the police, the red freaks and the wall crew and other Golden Beach "regulars" were very revealing.

Police "dragnets" and "crackdowns."

The San Diego Police Department had a policy, for many years, of increasing patrols at the beach during holiday weekends and summers months. The complaints of citizens, spearheaded by motel owners in the immediate vicinity of the Golden Beach-Sand Beach border, forced the department to increase the number, frequency and manpower of these patrols.

The situation was ironic both in its inception and its net result. Many of the motel owners who initiated the complaints both directly to the department and through the Sand Beach Town Council were those who rented out low-cost, older units. Many of their tenants were the "red freaks" that appeared on the beach at dusk. In addition, the motel taxes were used by the San Diego Visitors and Convention Bureau to propagandize the benefits of vacationing in the San Diego climate and at her beaches. I spoke to many of the "red freaks" who come to the area as a direct or indirect result of such advertising.

The results of the increased law enforcement activity in the area increased the number of "red freaks" and solidified their territorial rights at the doorstep of the motel whose owners had been most active in demanding police action. There was a decrease in the number of older, wealthier tourists in the area during evening hours, and a decrease in number of youthful Golden Beach residents in the area each evening.

The patrols began to increase during late June. Initially, the pattern of activity involved the appearance of two patrol cars at the wall area at dusk. The officers appeared to take minimal action at this time. Four or five cars, including a four-wheel drive beach vehicle, would arrive from three or four directions, within a half-hour prior to the 10 p.m. curfew. Arrests for various offenses followed.

Initially, the officers concentrated directly on the "red freaks." The wall crew had been accustomed to remaining at the beach, following their sunset surfing, until late night or early morning. They and the "red freaks" had, for years, respected an invisible boundary-line down the middle of the street at this location. Members of neither group crossed this line unless it was necessary to do so to reach a destination beyond the others' territory. As the arrests began, the wall crew stayed behind this line, joined by other Golden Beach residents, and cheered the actions of the police. Many comments were made, such as those by Pat, "I'm gonna write those cops a letter congratulating them. It's about time someone cleaned up this beach!"

Gradually, the officers expanded the dragnets and began to check the identifications and activities of everyone. Golden Beach youths, instead of arriving in time for the "festivities," began to avoid the police actions. At this stage, I made the research decision, described earlier, to not be present in the area during the early part of the evening. The wall crew vanished from their territory, in the evenings, except for an occasional visit to meet or locate another of their group. When they vacated their territory for the evening hours, the "red freaks" invaded it.

Although the wall crew changed their location in the evenings, they did not reduce their use of drugs. They planned an increasing number of parties and gathered, increasingly, at the homes and apartments of members who did not live with their parents.

Other residents and nonresidents modified their activities when the police increased their patrols. Adults, including tourists, who had previously walked the boardwalk at dusk, all but disappeared. The same was true of many young people who previously came to the area to ride their bicycles or engage in other non-drug-related activities. These youths told me that they were uncomfortable with the presence of the police on the boardwalk and that "the 'red freaks' were getting too thick." Still other youths, who had come to the beach in order to use drugs, simply moved further north and south beyond the area of the police activity. They smoked marijuana and drank alcohol feeling they were relatively immune from police detection.

The motel owners continued to complain as the number of "red freaks" increased. It appeared that police activities signaled the location as a place for "action" to those were looking for excitement. As word of the increased opportunity for excitement spread inland, the numbers and the activities of the "red freaks" steadily increased.

The police responded to the increased pressures of the community by varying their patterns. They increased their patrols. They began to patrol the length of the boardwalk on foot, to vary the times of their arrivals, and to unexpectedly have a second patrol immediately follow the first. With each variation, a few unsuspecting youths would be arrested. However, most of those, who were in possession of marijuana and alcohol, or, who were in violation of curfew laws, appeared to be boundless in their ingenuity to adjust to each new variation and avoid arrest. The prevailing atmosphere among the youths at the beach during these evenings appeared to be that of excitement and challenge as they played a "cops-and-robbers" game.

The police appeared to perform professionally in most of their interactions. However, by the time they approached an area and asked for identifications, juveniles in possession of alcoholic substances or in violation of curfew laws had departed. When the police left an area, the juveniles, the alcohol and the marijuana reappeared.

As the summer progressed, the number of arrests decreased. On several occasions, I would witness an officer detain someone, only to see the same person on the boardwalk a short time later. I was informed that the police took the person to a nearby parking lot, talked to him and released him. In the closing stage of the research, I asked police officers about this policy. One beat officer told me, "What you have to do is pick out the loud-mouth, the troublemaker, early in the evening. If you move in and get him out of there and away from the area, you'll save yourself a lot of trouble the rest of the night."

A lieutenant in the juvenile division said, "What's the use? In most cases, all we can do, if we want to take action, is to take him to the (juvenile) hall. The probation department won't keep him on a status offense so they call the parents. The parents come and get him and he's back down on the beach before we are finished filling out the papers on him."

The cycle of police activity, increased "red freak" activity, continued complaints by property owners, increased police activity and so on, continued through July and August, and into September. After Labor Day and the opening of the school year, the activities began to decline. However, by February 1976, the "red freaks" remained active during the evening hours, even though their numbers had diminished considerably. The wall "crew" had not yet regained their territory. This would not change for several years thereafter.

One evening in September, a number of the wall crew members lingered in the area after dusk. A photographer took a picture. The following Sunday, the front page of the local newspaper carried the headline, "Beach Area Residents Fed Up With Hooligans: Police Catch the Heat." Beneath the caption was a picture of the wall area. The only person in the photo who was identifiable was Barry, a member of the wall crew. Barry did not smoke marijuana. He rarely used alcohol and attended church regularly. Barry's father owned a large motel at the location. The wall crew was incensed, even though the story mentioned, "Police say the beach regulars do not cause trouble, but people from outlying areas who always seem to find a party at the beach, or a place to start one."[2]

The wall crew modified their activities and did not remain in the area after dusk. The newspaper account was followed by a continued decrease in the number of adults from the community in the area at sunset.

The San Diego Police Department kept a record of this police beat, covering the period from July 1, through December 1975. The data showed that only 50 of 210 arrests during this period involved residents of Golden Beach or Sand Beach.

Police officials were aware that their actions were counterproductive, but told me that public pressure had precipitated their response. The lieutenant, whom I interviewed in early February, was scheduled to meet the motel owners of the community shortly after our visit. The motel owners remained dissatisfied with the situation.

The Young People Who Frequented the Beach After Dark

My observations of young people after dark revealed very different patterns from those during daylight hours. Those who frequented the boardwalk in the evening were almost all heavy users of drugs. I regularly observed and interacted with 34 subjects after dark. Of these, 27 were heavy users, five were regular users and only two were light users. The vast majority of those who were at the beach during these hours were at the wall (24 of the 34). Four subjects tended to "hang out" in Sand Beach at Blount Court. Two frequented Old Street. Three "cruisers" moved from group to group along the boardwalk, often on bicycles. Lee interacted with his own "red freak" group.

After the police crackdowns and "dragnets," these patterns changed. The areas near Lime Avenue, Wellspring Street and Main Street were quiet after dark, except for an occasional activity organized by families, churches or other organizations.

The Blount Court group consisted of a varying number of males, most of whom either had never surfed or limited their surfing during recent years. When they did surf, they did so at Old Street or locations other than the wall area. They did not feel comfortable interacting with the wall crew. The core of this group had attended Catholic parochial schools. They called themselves, "the Catholic boys." Their only other distinction seemed to be the fact that most of them had been active and successful in sports until their first year of high school. They no longer participated in team sports. Blount Court was located in Sand Beach. The group chose this location because of the police activity further north in Golden Beach.

The median age of nighttime habitues of the beach was considerably higher than in the daytime. Still, there were a rather substantial number of very young males and females along the beach at all hours. This was so in spite of the curfew laws, the increased police activity and the publicity about the nature of the activities which took place after dark. I observed unchaperoned youngsters, some as young as 10 and 11 years, present on the boardwalk as late as 2 a.m. There were two groups of 12-and-13year-old youngsters (from six to eight in each) regularly on the boardwalk after midnight.

The youngest youths appeared to be lacking supervision or discipline at home. The following is a conversation I witnessed and overheard at approximately 1:30 a.m. in July 1975,

> *Youth #1*: Where is Tony?
>
> *Youth #2*: Tony is home. His old man is fucked! He won't let Tony out after 10 o'clock.
>
> *Youth #3*: That is just 'cuz his Dad cares. I wish my Dad cared. I can do anything I want.
>
> *Youth #1*: My old lady tries to make me do things, but she can't. I just tell her to get fucked. She can't do anything.

I overheard a number of similar exchanges. What was said lends considerable support to social control theory. Likewise, they provide additional insights into the quantitative data that will be presented in the following chapter.

The sex ratio during the hours after dark was approximately nine males for every one female. The females, unlike the males, were not typically residents of Golden Beach or Sand Beach.

Activities at The Beach After Dark.

There was little variety in the activities during the evening and early morning hours. The most frequent activity included drinking beer and smoking marijuana while sitting along the wall. The young men faced the boardwalk and frequently greeted passers-by, especially females.

The most common stated-goal of this nighttime activity was to have sexual intercourse with a female whom, it was anticipated, the young male would meet during the evening. The intended "modus operandi"consisted of greeting females as they walked along the boardwalk, asking them if they would like to "smoke a joint" or "drink a beer," engaging the females in conversation, smoking more marijuana and/or drinking more alcohol with them, pairing-off with one female, suggesting that they depart to a convenient home or apartment to enjoy more drugs and, finally, engaging in sexual intercourse at the home or apartment. From all my observations and reports, the goal was very rarely accomplished. Many females seemed to walk the boardwalk without stopping, but apparently enjoying the attention they were receiving. A lesser number stopped and drank or smoked marijuana with one or more groups of males. Fewer still, lingered more than the length of time it took to smoke one joint of marijuana or drink one beer. The percentage of these who later joined the males elsewhere appeared to be quite minimal. I recorded only three cases during the entire period of the research in which a subject may have met a female with whom he later had sexual intercourse following this late night ritual along the boardwalk

The majority of the conversations among the males dealt with this topic or with tales of past sexual accomplishments. "Machismo" language regarding sex and violence was extensive when the youths were in the presence of their peers. Two subjects, who were extreme in their language and in their statements to their peers about making sexual conquests, confided to me privately that they were experiencing difficulties in achieving a sexual climax. The discussions with me took place during the summer after their peers had left for home.

Another common activity involved the purchase and sale of drugs. This included "beer runs" (having an overage individual purchase a supply of alcoholic beverages). A large number of drug transactions, usually involving small amounts ("for personal use"), took place on the boardwalk. Although drug transactions transpired at all hours, most took place after dark.

Many times, word of various parties would spread along the boardwalk and individuals moved back and forth between these parties and the boardwalk.

Evening Activities at Locations Other Than the Beach.

I found it somewhat more difficult to observe individuals who were not at the beach in the nighttime hours during the summer. I frequently relied on information from young people during the daytime about their activities the previous evening. Based on the available information, the following appeared to be common patterns of the other groups.

As has been stated, when members of the wall crew were not at the beach in the evening, they gathered at homes, and often organized small parties. They invited females to these gatherings. It appeared that they had a considerably higher "success" rate in obtaining sexual favors from females at these small parties than they did at the beach. The sexual activity was usually in private, and followed a considerable degree of drug consumption by both participants.

The subjects who comprised the Lime Avenue, Main Street and Wellspring Street groups during the daytime hours engaged in a wide variety of activities during the evenings. They participated in softball, baseball and summer basketball programs. They visited and dated girlfriends. They attended movies, bowled or gathered in groups at an ice cream parlor. Some evenings were spent at homes watching television. Those who worked in the daytime or attended morning summer-school classes limited most of their social activities to the weekends. Occasionally, a few attended parties or went to the beach at night. However, as a whole, the groups appeared to be unaware of the nighttime activities on the beach. They became aware of the deviant activities as a result of media publicity surrounding the police dragnets.

Some Concluding Remarks

The activities of the police during the summer months permitted me to make observations that pertain to social control theories. The presence of underage youngsters and their activities at the beach may fit the McCord-Chein model as well as social control theories. The differences in activities that were engaged in by various groups of young people, according to their degree of involvement with drugs, points to the very clear distinctions that existed within the youthful subculture. These will be examined in greater detail later in this chapter and in subsequent chapters.

The summer months were somewhat unique and the activities of young people varied somewhat from those of the school year. The patterns of youthful behavior in Golden Beach during the school year are described in the next section.

GOLDEN BEACH YOUTH DURING THE SCHOOL YEAR

Introduction.

All but 11 of the 72 subjects were enrolled in school at some time during the study. The beach-centered tourist base of Golden Beach affected the patterns of daily activity of most young people. Thus, there was considerable variation in their patterns between the summer and non summer months. This section describes the patterns during the school year. A description of the patterns on weekdays is followed by a description of the patterns on weekend, days and evenings.

For the most part, the behavioral patterns of non-users and light users were similar. Heavy users were typically quite distinct in their activities when compared with others. Regular users held a middle ground, in some instances reflecting patterns of light and non-users, and, in others, reflecting those of the heavy users. Because the patterns were, to a large extent, dependent upon the school (school functions and the school schedule), and because the regular users were active, as a rule, in many activities related to school (particularly in sports activities), their patterns normally followed those of the light and non-users. On the other hand, regular users were distinct in their behavior patterns directly related to drug use. Because of these similarities and differences, I have divided the descriptions in this section according to heavy users and the other three categories.

Heavy users.

During the school year, the most obvious pattern that distinguished the heavy users from others was the frequency with which they were absent from school. The pattern of school truancy was consistent among heavy users at all levels of education, including the seven heavy users who were enrolled in college. Those who attended college often expressed their satisfaction with college as compared to high school, but, as had been their pattern in high school, they frequently missed classes or entire days of school. Although the pattern of truancy among the heavy users varied somewhat, relative to weather conditions and the size of the waves, it was not confined to surfers.

Junior and senior high students employed numerous methods to get around the schools' attendance offices' rather elaborate system to prevent truancy. The schools' systems were ineffective if parents were uncooperative or if parents were not at home when the attendance office phoned. The boys' vice principal of Golden Beach High School, Phil Wilcox, was aware of the parents' involvements. Mr. Wilcox stated,

> You'd be surprised how often the parents will lie, or even just tell you they are letting the kid go somewhere . . . We can't get every parent with a truant youngster by phone every day. The gals try to concentrate on those with the most frequent patterns first. The census card has a place on it for phone numbers at work, but most parents can't or don't want to be bothered at work unless it is a real emergency. Sometimes you call them at work and you get a response, like, 'What are you bothering me for about a silly, little matter like that?'

The police on patrol in the beach areas rarely extended themselves to deal with truancies even though there were many youngsters, obviously of school age, at the beach each day. The lieutenant, in charge of the juvenile division, explained the policy,

> Now we're being saddled with this 'status-offenders' bit and the probation department won't and can't do anything about truancy. The parents usually don't care . . . If the officer sees a kid in an area where he might cause trouble, and it is during school hours, he is liable to stop him and inquire. If it is a nice day, the kind of a day that the officer might have

> taken off on when he was a kid himself, and the kid is at the beach, chances are that the officer won't do anything.

Many of the heavy users in high school left the school grounds early. Some would leave the campus for an hour or more and return later in the day. They said that they did this because they were dissatisfied with a particular teacher or because they believed a particular subject was unimportant.

When truant, the youths spent most of their time at the beach. Many surfed, early in the day, then smoked marijuana and ate a restaurant meal (often with their school lunch money). In the afternoons they surfed, sunbathed on the beach, smoked marijuana, and, frequently, drank beer.

The heavy users had definite patterns on the days they attended school. They, typically, began the day by smoking one or two joints of marijuana. They smoked marijuana at the home of a friend whose parent(s) had departed for work earlier, or at a convenient, unobtrusive location on the way to school. At school, some smoked in the restrooms, but most waited until their lunch period. At that time, junior high students headed for a nearby handball court, or an alley, to smoke marijuana. Senior high students went to cars on the parking lot. They smoked marijuana in a car, and then ate their lunches, either in the car or in the cafeteria area.

The junior high students completed their school day at 3:30 p.m. Senior high students completed the formal school day no later than 2:20 p.m. After school, the students, typically, went to their homes or the homes of friends, whose parents(s) were not present. Frequently, they smoked again after school.

Depending upon the weather, the typical heavy user went to the beach for a part of the late afternoon or early evening. Some surfed during this part of the day. Otherwise, the hours before dinner were spent within the individual's immediate neighborhood. Homes in which parents were not present were favorite locations to gather. It was considered enjoyable to smoke marijuana in order that dinner would satisfy their "munchies."

The heavy users varied in their activities in the evenings during the school year. At times, there were parties on week nights in which most participated. They seemed to experience a great deal of boredom at this point in their day. Many drank beer and/or smoked marijuana in the late evening. (Some used marijuana to help them sleep.) They were not usually engaged in school, church, or other organization functions. They typically retired early on week nights during the school year.

Regular, Light and Non-users.

Truancy was infrequent among those in the other three categories. Nevertheless, some few regular users skipped school on a few occasions. Likewise, the regular users tended to smoke marijuana before school with some frequency, though not daily. They were even less likely to smoke marijuana on late afternoons or evenings during the week. There was considerable evidence from conversations with regular users and in their observed patterns of drug use that participation in extracurricular school activities, particularly sports, was a factor that limited their drug use. This appeared to be only slightly related to the physical effects of the drugs upon athletic performance. Such effects were usually taken into account only in decisions whether to use drugs immediately preceding a competitive event. Nevertheless, participants did not wish to end their participation in sports by taking the risk of being apprehended using drugs at school. A more practical matter involved attendance at school. In order to participate in sports, the student had to be present in school that day and, to remain on the team, he had to attend the daily practices. This decreased their likelihood of being truant or departing from school early, and, in turn, the opportunity to use drugs. Likewise, attendance at practices during the mid to late afternoon hours further limited the occasions to use drugs. Finally, some attention to homework was required in order to maintain satisfactory grades to remain in school and be able to participate in extracurricular activities.

Related to the above were the opportunities for regular users to be influenced by peers who were less likely to use drugs. Many regular users, who might have otherwise been heavy users, were involved in peer activities (many directly or indirectly related to sports activities, such as, decorating homecoming floats, planning banquets and so on) with light and non-users.

Individuals in all three categories, in addition to attending school regularly, were involved in a variety of organized, extracurricular activities during afternoon and evening hours. During the evening hours they did homework, participated in school or church-related functions, visited girlfriends and watched television.

WEEKENDS DURING THE SCHOOL YEAR - DAYTIME HOURS

Heavy users.

The daytime activities of heavy users during the school year on weekends were similar to those of the summer months. They were typically at the beach. They surfed a great deal. As the study progressed, I noticed a slight increase in the number of Sunday afternoon parties. On these occasions there was an increased amount of alcohol consumed. This trend may have been the result of temporary circumstances. (Southern California was undergoing unusually warm weather and a prolonged dry spell. Some entrepreneurs scheduled Sunday afternoon "keggers" for several successive weeks.)

Regular, light and non-users.

Those in the three other categories were involved in a wide variety of activities. The activities were centered around home, church, and school.

These youth were involved with their families in a number of ways during weekends. These included working around the house, visiting relatives and participating in family picnics and dinners. They typically attended church on Sunday and were involved in other church-related functions during other parts of the weekends, such as money-raising activities, youth retreats in the mountains and church-sponsored breakfasts and picnics. The youths in these groups were busy with athletics and other extracurricular and curricular school activities during the weekends. On Saturdays, they participated in car washes, made preparations for school dances, attended committee meetings and so on. Sunday afternoon and evening were usually reserved to complete more extensive homework assignments and papers. In most of these activities, the individuals were likely to be associating with members of the opposite sex. Some daytime dating also took place on weekends.

WEEKENDS DURING THE SCHOOL YEAR - EVENINGS

Heavy users.

The evening hours of the heavy users did not vary appreciably at this time of year. Their weekends were comparable to their weekend hours during other months. Parties were standard activities on Fridays and Saturdays. Occasionally a few heavy users attended a school athletic event or a dance, but these took second priority to the many parties that were held.

For the most part, nighttime activity on weekends at the beach had decreased. A few lingering "red freaks," remained. Others used the boardwalk area to meet their friends before and after parties.

Regular, light and non-users

Regular and light users, and non-users, spent their weekend evenings, typically, at school-related activities, primarily sports events and school-sponsored dances. The patterns of the regular users resembled those of the heavy users except that they attended parties after school, sports and other functions. Before they entered dances, they spent a considerable amount of time in the parking lot, drinking beer and smoking marijuana.

The light and non-users frequently attended church-sponsored social activities on weekend evenings. They ordinarily returned home immediately after the event unless they had plans to gather as a group at an ice cream parlor or restaurant.

Concluding Remarks and an Example

As was the case in previous sections, this section has pointed to the differences between the various categories of drug use, especially between the heavy users and the other three categories. There appeared to be a totality of patterns that were related to degree of drug use or non-use. The degree of drug use or non-use was related to the degree of involvement with family, church, school and school-related activities, including participation in sports. As a result, there were differences in the interactions and manner of relationships between male and female peers.

To provide an example which would encompass as many of these elements of possible, I have selected a set of passages from my daily journal. These entries were chosen because they covered a Friday, Saturday and Sunday that included daytime and evening activities. During this period, I was able to observe activities at school and outside of school. Because my observations were concentrated somewhat on school and church functions, the notes do not adequately portray the typical patterns of truancy and weekend parties. These have been covered elsewhere and the activities of the heavy users are referred to in my entries. With these qualifications, the notes appear to have an adequate balance and reflect rather typical patterns.

The notes begin the day of my first visit to Golden Beach High School. Some entries have been edited in the interest of conserving time and space. In keeping with the purpose nature of the example, whenever possible I provide the age and the category of drug use of each individual. Some of the individuals in the example were not subjects of the research. In most instances I knew their degree of drug use based on my previous interactions with them. I repeat the age and category of each person more than once. However, if the individual has been described several times, I avoid repetition of this information.

Daily Journal, Friday, January 16, 1976

It is hot! In the 80s!

10:00 a.m. I go to the wall. Pat, the 22-year-old mainstay of the Old Wall Gang is there along with other members of the wall crew including Carl, 18, and Jeff, 19, both heavy users. Bill Jones, 20 and Dave, 20, go to the shed and sit on the wall to smoke a joint. Bill is skipping classes today.

Golden Beach High School - 10:30 a.m. to 12:30 p.m.

I arrive at Golden Beach High School. First, I go to the admittance office. Norm Dunn, 16, a heavy user, brought a forged note today. He skipped yesterday. Next, I go to the office of Mr. Phil Wilcox, the vice-president. He is occupied. I make an appointment for Monday. I go to the office of Alvin Coser, the school drug counselor. He is not in his office. I visit with Officer Clark, the San Diego Police Officer assigned to Golden Beach High School. He says that he "drops by" once a week.

I decided to check with some of the kids. I talk to Eric, Vick, Al, Theresa, Morris Bayer, and others. They are all heavy users but none of them ever heard of Officer Clark!

Vick, 16, a heavy user, tells me how they get around absence procedures. He goes to roll call and then skips the next class.

Later, Bart Roe, 17, and Eric, 17, both heavy users, leave campus early. I see them about 1:00 p.m. at the beach

I see Karl, 15, and Don, 15. Karl is a regular user and Don is a heavy user. They say, 'No more skipping for us!'

The kids I talk to agree (a consensus) that pot is smoked:

1) In bathrooms (They say this is for hard guys and is dangerous). I check the boys' room. There are butts on the floors and 'hash oil' (is) written on the walls.

2) In cars in parking lots. It is illegal, to go to parking lots, especially during lunch hours. The kids say, 'Teachers try to bust us all the time.' I see several heavy users head that way later. Afterwards, Norm Dunn, Chuck Roe and the other rats appear stoned.

3) Some leave in cars and go to Linda McNeeley Park or other places during lunch hours.

4) Some go down to the creek near the school.

I was only asked once (after 2 hrs) if I was a 'student' and if I had a 'visitor's pass'. Wilcox gave me an ok earlier.

On a main bulletin board is a large poster, about .20" x 30", reading,

'*MR. DOOBIE SAYS,* (a drawing of a marijuana cigarette shaped man was placed here)

'HIGH! COME BONG WITH ME! JOIN THE BONG-A-MONTH CLUB NOW.''

(Note to the reader: "doobie" is a subculture term for a marijuana cigarette. "Bong" is a bamboo pipe used to smoke marijuana or hashish. The term "high" refers to the euphoric feeling under the influence of marijuana and/or other drugs.)

I confirmed three times that the poster has been up for a week. (The kids tell me, 'Don't you tell them what it means!')

When I talk with Ken, 16, a non-user, he discusses the 'Hamburger-eating contest' (They're meeting at Hot Dog King tonight and win prizes. They call it 'skarf and barf.') Eric, 16, says: 'I'm in the bong-eating contest. It's beforehand, comes first.' (Laughs)

I note that I know at least 10 percent of all the kids in Golden Beach High School.

The first reaction to me from the kids is usually, 'What are you doing here?' They often gathered in groups around me. They also talk to me individually to me including Rick, 16, a non-user; Vick, 16, a heavy user; and Woody, 14, a regular user. Others ask for help. Nelson, 16, a heavy user, asks where he can get a SAT book to study. Others discuss SAT exams. Willie, 17, a light user, did well, but not exceptionally well. He's concerned about not receiving a university basketball scholarship. Steve, 17, a light user, is waiting for his scores. Louise, 17, a non-user, says, 'I did not do well.' Eric, 17, a heavy user, is waiting for his proficiency exam to get out of school. He does not go to classes. He writes papers. He is writing a science fiction story.

I go to the lunchroom. Most of those eating are 'jocks.' One table is occupied by basketball players: Ernie, 16, The Smith brothers, 17, and Zane, 17. The Smith brothers challenge the others to an arm-wrestling contest. Football and basketball players challenge each other. A group of black "jocks," including Vince and Hank, sit at a separate table. Another table is occupied only by Chicanos. I sit at a table with junior varsity soccer players: Nelson, 16, a regular user; Rick, 16, light user, and several others. Rick gives Nelson the answers to history homework. Nelson asks about the SAT. They all wear Golden Beach soccer t-shirts. They invite me to go to the class to hear their 'dingy' history teacher. I decline stating that I was not invited by teacher. Mark Gilroy, 16, a non-user, joins us. They all ask me to come to their soccer game tonight (several times). Cliff, 17, a non-user sees me later and asks me to come.

Willie, 17, a light user, says he always sees me at the basketball games and appreciates the support.

The soccer players point out that the posters on the lunchroom walls support the basketball team, but have no mention of soccer. Nelson says, 'Look at all the soccer posters!' The basketball posters read: 'Dump 'em, David,' and 'Murder 'em, Mulcahy,' and so on. Zane, 17, a light user comes by the table to ask me if I'll be at the basketball game tonight. Others, not on the team, ask or just say, 'See you there.'

I go outside during lunch period to observe. Luke, 16, a light user, wants to show me around the campus. Woody, 14, a light user, is with his friends but leaves them to talk to me on the side, alone. He is upset. He tells me his Dad still stays on the road all the time. His brother is giving his mother a hard time and wants to move in with his Dad after the divorce. His grandpa and grandma are moving back east. He feels this is good because they fight with his Mom a lot and go out in the street and 'yell and everything.' (He seems to be hurting a lot.)

Terry Jones, 16, a non-user, is 'getting a "B" in history' (He considers this very poor.)

Norm, Chuck, and Luke come back from the parking lot. They sit on the bench outside the lunch room. They look very stoned. They avoid me. (Are they embarrassed?) They did not expect me to be at the school. Nelson says Norm would be good 'If he'd get away from Chuck. Then he'd get on the football team . . . ,'

I see Ken, 16, a non-user, several times in different places. The same is true regarding Stephen, 15, a heavy user, Andy, 17, a heavy user, and Reed Gilroy, 17, a non-use. They all serve on ASB (The Associated

Student Body) and are working on activities, contacting people during lunch hours, and so on.

Other "jocks" hang out together. They also spend time with their girlfriends. Zane, Ron, 17, a regular user, Roger, 17, and Frosty, 18, regular users, ask about my research and talk about the football season.

Rich, 17, and Trent, 17, heavy users (two of the trio!) show up at the end of lunch period. (Were they smoking pot in the parking lot?) They have on heavy jackets (it's in the 80's). Their jackets are open and they are bare chested underneath. (Machismo?) Rich says, 'If Mr. Wilcox catches us, we're bustedl'

After the lunch period, I see Marie, 16, a heavy user. She is working in a garden. She says, 'Better than going to a biology lecture' She does it one day a week. Steve, 17 and Louise, 17, both heavy users, end their school day at 12:30 p.m. They are going to the beach.

Bart Roe, 17, a heavy user, leaves on a motorcycle. Earlier he was with Dorothy, 17, a heavy user. Eric says Bart, 'Comes here to party.' Later, Al, 16, a heavy user, says, 'Bart is here, physically. Yesterday he realized in the 5th period that he had lost his jacket and gloves in the shop during the 1st period!' (He had been using psychedelic mushrooms.)

Theresa, 17, a heavy user, Liz, 17 and a girl from St.Patrick's are waiting outside P.E. They took a test today. Ned, 17, a non-user, had been running an assembly in the auditorium during the lunch hours. They had a rock group. He's disappointed that more did not show up. Students ate outside or in the cafeteria.

I notice that soshes do not stay in groups. They mostly seem to be running around the campus.

Al, 16, a heavy user, is sitting outside a classroom with his shirt off, writing a paper. He says he didn't smoke any pot from Christmas Eve until two days ago and had played soccer 'excellently' until then. Then he bought a half a lid with Ed, 16, a regular user, and smoked it. And, then, he says, 'and yesterday I did lousy!' I'm going to sell it back or give it to somebody . . . Ed has been hanging around with Travis and getting some good Columbian and getting stoned three or four times a week.' (Jim, in his interview, blamed Al's pressure for his smoking pot. Is it because Al is in sports and not with him? And now only Travis?)

Some kids, like Woody, thought that the last bathroom (where pot is smoked) was a 'legal' smoking area

I asked several kids if they would trust Alvin Coser, the drug counselor and tell him the things they have told me. They responded,

Nelson, 'No!'

Rick, 'No. That program may be successful elsewhere but not here!'

Eric, 'Yer. kiddin'!?'

(All three are heavy users.)

I saw 24 out of 36 subject who are enrolled at Golden Beach H.S..

Ruthie, 17, a heavy user, is outside with a group of hard looking girls waiting for a friend to get out of school.

1:00 p.m. to 5:00 p.m. at the beach.

Scene: hot and a lot of people around.

I see Albert, 18, a regular user. He is sunbathing. He only worked two and a half hours today. He is skipping school. He's looking for a job with Don's father. He wants to make money to go skiing. He does not plan to go back to school.

He tells me about other ways to 'beat the system' in order to skip school, 'All you have to do is get a blue slip, saying, 'he is excused at (for a whole day)' or, if you go to one class and skip the rest, have it read, 'From 9:00 a.m. to 2:20 p.m.' Anyone can get one in the morning and sign it themselves or have a girlfriend sign, but if you do that too often it gets hairy. Seniors always get blue slips because they don't call the seniors' homes. If you're outstanding and so on, you can get one. I did about one time every two weeks . . . The school likes blue slips because they get money from the district for them, but they don't get it if you are not excused.'

I see Kevin, 15, a light user. He was in Mr. Wilcox's office today because he went to the dentist and did not have a blue slip. He was excused, When I tell him that I am to see Mr. Wilcox on Monday, he says to me, 'Tell me what he says about ditching.' Kevin still drinks at parties.

Pat and Jeff, of the wall crew, feel they are getting a run around when applying for jobs at the shipbuilding company. They always say, 'Come back later.'

At 6:00 p.m., Rusty, 18, a heavy user comes by my apartment to see me. He's straight (not under the influence of any drug) and fairly calm. We talk about him and why this 'gay' thing came up. He admits of nothing, but Herb talks of his 'mothering' of Herb and the emotional attachment. He says everything is coming in on him at once. He owes money. His car is broke. He has final exams. He blames it all on Herb,. 'I knew from the first that he lied. Then I became attached in helping ways. One night he used junk.'

I asked if he had any homosexual feelings. He says, 'NO! At least not expressed . . . Maybe I was misinterpreted when I gave him (Herb) the surfboard for Christmas. He acted kinda, like warm toward me'

He admits he uses pot to get away from things. 'But my body is so used to it, it just keeps going.'

Rusty leaves before 7:00 p.m. He said he is going to 'have a few beers.' He is going to meet some friends tonight. He does not have any money.

7:30 p.m. to 12 midnight -
Basketball game, Hamburger-eating contest and the beach

I go to the basketball game As I arrive at the parking lot, Paul, 17, a heavy user, rides by on his bike and blows pot in my face. (Teasing). As I get out of my car, a guy in the car next to mine and offers me a joint. He's smoking it in one hand and drinking a beer in the other as he drove up. I have seen him but do not know his name.

Paul asks Mario to 'smoke a doobie.' When Mario arrives with his girlfriend, Mario lets the girl go into the game (she's a cheerleader) and he joins Paul to smoke the joint.

As I enter the building, Morris Bayer, 17, a heavy user, borrows $5.00 to get into the game. He did not go home for supper. He is very stoned. In the stands, I hear Ben, 16, a regular user, call Morris a "doper" when Morris walks (very obviously stoned) across the floor.

Brendan, 15, a non-user, is with Linda. It seems things are moving along for him. They join Pete, 16, a non-user, and some of the 'jocks.' Terry Jones, 16, a light user, wants to call his Mom for a ride home. I tell him I am going to the hamburger earing contest. He wants to go. I take him. He never went to a game before because he didn't have the money for an ASB card at the beginning of the school ear. He talks about his brothers, Pete, a regular user, and Bill, 20, a heavy user. Pete is allowed to drive the car because he paid the insurance. Bill and Terry are not allowed to drive

Golden Beach wins the game, 72-61. It is a packed house, a big rivalry with Diamond Heights. Golden Beach is now: 4 - 0 League, 16 - 4 overall.

Vick, 16, a heavy user, and Phil, 17, a light user, say they did poorly in wrestling last night.

Today, the junior varsity soccer game ended in a tie. Paul, Rick, Jeff and Nelson all ask me to come to their game Tuesday. I promise to be there.

I count the number of subjects by category at the basketball game. There are 22 subjects at the game, two of the 31 heavy users , five of the 11 regular users, eight of the 20 light users and all seven of the non-users. The only ones who appear to be stoned are the two heavy users, Paul and Vick.

There were 14 Golden Beach H.S. students who are subjects but were not at the game. Ten of these are heavy users, one is a regular user and one is a light user. Two other was light users were working this evening. ALL NON-USERS WERE AT THE GAME!

This is the first basketball game Terry Jones has been to in his life. Earlier in the year he went to his first football game.

Roger 17, a light user, tells me there is to be a party tonight on the bay. Others told me earlier that they had not heard of any. Roger's information proved to be false.

Hamburger Eating Contest.

The contest is held at a drive-through restaurant. All the subjects who were at the basketball game are present, except the Gilroys, Reed and Mark, and Paul (They went to the bay to find the party).

There are 200 cheering "fans." Five girls and five guys are contestants. They were chosen at a half-time drawing during the basketball game. They are to eat as many hamburgers as they can in 15 minutes. Sarah, a cheerleader, won the girls' contest. She ate three and a half hamburgers. Brendan,15, a non-user, is the only subject who is a contestant. He ate four and a half hamburgers, but one of the Smith's brothers won in the guys' contest by consuming four and three-quarter hamburgers.

Mr. Wilcox, the vice-president, Mr. Cohen, the ASB advisor and one of the coaches were present. The students say that Mr. Wilcox goes to all games, and other activities. He appears to relate well.

Midnight at the beach.

The beach is very quiet. Only a few 'red freaks.' There is no sign of a party on the bay. I got to Billy's to write up my notes.

Saturday, January 17, 1976

I see Dr. Bayer (Morris' Father) at the restaurant in the morning. He says that he and his wife came home last night, and saw Morris about midnight. He did not know Morris had not eaten dinner. He says Morris was eating and 'looked like he had a couple of beers.'

I go to the beach. It is very hot - in the 80s. There are large, excellent waves. It is crowded. There are lots of bikes on the boardwalk, many people in the water and on the sand. I go to the wall and walk north to Old Street.

Mike, 18, a heavy user, comes up to me. He says he has to talk to me 'a lot' if I'm leaving soon. He has a new girlfriend, but doesn't want any of the wall crew to know. (They'd tease him.) He says, 'I'm head-over-heels for her.'

Walter, 13, another heavy user, tells me about a 'rat' party at Copper St. last night. The cops showed up at 9:00 p.m. The party was in the recreation room of a large condominium. Walter took a beer and ran when he saw the cops. Skip, 14, a heavy user, 'grabbed a whole six-pack and took off'. In addition to the 'rats,' Alex, 14, a light user, was present. Walter wants to talk to me more. He and Kevin, 15, a light user, are together. They want to come to St. Patrick's tonight to see the play because Doc, 14, a heavy user, is in it. Slick, 21, a heavy user, gives Walter a beer.

I see Bob, 13, and Phil, 13, both heavy users. They were at the party last night. They were also at Mark's, 13, a heavy user, when the bust occurred. There was pot there. The cops showed up because a couple of runaways were supposed to be there. Mark was sentenced to a work crew because it was his 5th offense. The eight others were suspended from school for the rest of the day. They were all ditching school when the police came. Bob ditched yesterday. A girl writes notes for him. 'They only call home if you do it all the time.' Phil says he does not have to worry, 'No one is home because my folks are at work when they call.'

Bill Jones had a fight with Theresa, last night. They are together again. Bill is stoned. The only 'jocks' I see at the beach are Ben, 16, a regular user, and Luke, 16, a light user. There is lots of pot around. I smell it eight times. There are some juveniles drinking beer.

The whole wall crew is around the area except for Norm Dunn and some of the older guys. Pat is at someone's house. Norm is out hunting.

Floyd, 19, a light user, says he got into a welding program through the San Diego Community College. He hopes to get Hap, 19, a light user, into the same program. He's very happy.

Dean, 18, a heavy user, says Pat was on the Bayside drinking vodka Thursday. Dean is the third person since Thursday to say Pat is 'an alkie.'

Chuck Roe called about some jobs advertised in the paper. They told him to call back later. He says, 'I got stoned and didn't.' He and Paul, another heavy user, seem jealous when I talk to Walter. They keep hitting me to get my attention. Chuck is ignoring Joyce, 16, a regular user. She has asked him to a dance, a party and to play tennis. He told her, 'Yeah, sometime.'

Arnold, 22, a non-user, tells me his brother used to hang out at the wall five years ago and used a lot of acid. Now, his brother is back east and has, 'been saved.' Arnold is back in law school. He says he sees the surfer lifestyle as a temptation. He leaves to go to study.

Skip, 14, a light user, has a bunch of joints in his pocket. He says it is easier to smoke pot at Diamond Heights Junior High than at Golden Beach Junior High. (He was expelled from Golden Beach Junior High and transferred to Diamond Heights.). He also says it is easier to get away with "a lot of things"' there.

Slick keeps giving more beer to Walter. Bart Roe, 17, a heavy user, is looking for a scale to weigh cocaine to sell. I leave the wall at 1:00 p.m. at the wall. Every one of the crew is drinking beer. Some are smoking pot as I leave.

St. Patrick's Coffee House

At 7:30 p.m. I go to the Coffee House sponsored by the Drop-In group at St. Patrick's.

The kids worked all afternoon on their own, getting the stage ready, lights and tables set up and taking care of other details.

There are lots of people, including two large families, the Gilroy's and the Kramer's. John Gilroy, 18, a light user, got a permanent (hairstyle). Reed 17, and Louise, 17, light users, came to watch.

There are eight subjects participating, four non-users, three light users and one regular user. The four non-users, Reed Gilroy, Brendan, Ken, and Ned do well. Reed is the M.C. He provides lots of humor. Brendan does a lot of ad-libbing in play. Ken ad-libs as well. Ken does a very good job with his reading. The three light users, Mark Gilroy, Phil and Luke, also do well. Mark is praised for organizing things and runs the lights. Phil does a great reading about himself. He gives me the original copy. Luke plays bongo drums in the orchestra. Ron, the only regular user participating, runs the sound system and directs a slide show.

One heavy user, Doc, is supposed to perform. The other participants were prepared for his act, 'Confessions of a Teen-ager', but it had to be canceled because Doc did not show. (I learned the next day Doc, Walter and Steve, all 13-and-14-year-old, bought LSD and 'took a trip' tonight.)

Two other regular and 3 heavy users who are members of the youth group did not show. The evening's skits, readings, songs and poems were written by the kids. They also did the art work. The theme was 'Self-expression and Creativity in the Acts of the Apostles.'

Sr. Basil and Mrs. Gilroy remark how much Mark Gilroy, Phil and Lee Kramer have matured this year. (I notice that the same holds true for Reed Gilroy and Ron). (Note: I think about this and compare their maturity with that of Mike and Carl earlier at the wall. They don't want others to know about their girlfriends because they'll be teased by the wall crew. Perhaps, the maturity of a junior high age-level?)

Brendan is still not sure about Linda being his girlfriend, 'I can't talk now.' He has to do a six to eight minute report Monday about 'Teachers violating students' civil rights.'

After the clean up organized by Mark Gilroy, Ron, 17, a regular user, and Luke, 16, a light user, Brendan and Ned, 17, both non-users, are going out with three girls. They are discussing whether to go bowling, miniature golf or to Bud's Ice Cream Parlor. Brendan has only one dollar and does not want to spend much.

I go to the beach. Most of the wall crew is at the party in Alta Vista. I see Albert, 18, a regular user, and Paul, 16, a heavy user. I ask if other parties around. They went to two, one by Coast Oil Station and one on

Silver and Hall Streets. They could not get into either party. They say the people there are 'weird.'

Later, Paul told me that after I left that they had, 'Chased a faggot. Boy, was he scared! We saw him up the Gold Avenue head and took off after him.'

The boardwalk is like summer. Lots of 'red freaks' by the motel. The only ones I recognize are Todd, 14, a heavy user, from Texas and a few junior high-age girls. There are lots of people, pot and booze. Many guys trying to pick-up 'chicks'. There are many fires on beach and large groups around the fires.

At 11:00 p.m., I go to Billy's restaurant to write my journal. Les, 21, of the Old Wall Gang but now a non-user, and Pete Jones, 21, a regular user, come in. They had been to a Baptist Coffee House in Turf Beach. Les tells me that the preacher, 'Kicks people out of the church and won't let them come back if they disturb things.' They had a folk singer tonight. There were lots of young people in their early 20s.

Les tells me that an old girlfriend of Milt, 23, of the Old Wall Gang, is going to be at the wall tomorrow. He asks me, 'She says she is not a junkie 'cause she only shoots-up two times a week. Is that right?' I try to clarify the meaning of addiction for him.

Sunday, January 18, 1976

It is Super Bowl Sunday. The beach is very quiet. It was sunny earlier. The fog came in about 1:00 p.m. Now it is cold.

Paul tries to watch the game on TV at Murphy's Motel dining room but is kicked out. Later, they refuse to allow Rusty to sit on the patio and eat his lunch from a brown bag. Bill and Pete Jones and Barry eat lunch on the patio.

Skip, 14, refuses to drink coffee. 'I just killed two six-packs of beer and don't want to hurt the effect.' He talks again how much easier it is at Diamond Heights Junior High. He is going to work at his sister's today. He has to earn $10 to pay the court fee for his bicycle violation.

Steve, 17, a light user, and Louise, 17, a light user, are at Lime Avenue. Louise says Sr. Basil is too strict so she does not go to Drop In. I ask about Alvin Coser, the drug counselor. Steve say, 'I'd never trust him like I do you!' (He shakes his head and makes a facial 'disgust' look.) He seems to indicate he has been to see Alvin Coser, but does not want to talk with Louise present.

Bill Jones tells me that some of the 12 -and -13-year-old rats have been eating acid. He doesn't like it. He thinks someone should 'talk' to them. Later, Pete Jones tells me Bill Jones did not go to church today but left the house to "smoke-out" with Eric instead.

I leave the beach about 2:00 p.m. It is colder and quiet. (Everybody watching Super Bowl?)

Comments regarding the example.

Although the above set of journal entries encompassed less than a three-day span, they provide evidence of some of the patterns that have been mentioned regarding drug use, recreation, entertainment, church, school, sports and relationships with both males and females. There are stark contrasts evident between the heavy users and others, especially the light and non-users.

The notes provide an indication of the manner in which a great deal of the observational data developed and were recorded. Some entries seem inconsequential. Some of these were significant at later dates (or when they were compared to earlier entries). Some, such as the use of marijuana in the school parking lot and Mr. Wilcox's lack of familiarity with the terms used in the sign on the bulletin board, required follow-up. (For instance, during my interview with Mr. Wilcox, the vice-principal, he mentioned that he would "surely like to find out" what the terms "doobie" and "bong" meant.)

The entries also provide some insights into my relationship with the subjects and some consequences of this (such as jealousy). The description of these interactions provides further insights into the youthful subculture, adolescent concerns and so on. In regard to "adolescent concerns," it is worthy to note the youths' reactions to me which resulted from my attendance at their athletic events. Their appreciation was far more important to the subjects than I had initially imagined. Likewise, several of the youths, immediately told me of their accomplishments and concerns regarding school (grades, SAT exams, papers and so on). I viewed this as an effect of an adult male entering their world, and, to varying degrees, their identification with me as a partial "father figure."

A final related point deserves comment. There was a distinct contrast between the attention given those who had participated in activities such as sports and the "coffee house," and those youths who did not participate in these or other activities. The nonparticipants, typically heavy users, did not receive the positive attention that resulted from athletic or other accomplishments. They were treated differently. For instance, some of these heavy users were not allowed to remain in Murphy's Motel dining room or patio on Sunday during the Super Bowl. The heavy user, the nonparticipant in school and church functions, had generally negative feedback from society. No doubt this affected his or her self image. The typical light or non-user was bolstered by his sense of accomplishment and by the positive feedback he or she received for participation in these activities.

In the next section I provide additional insights regarding the interaction of adult society and the youth subculture. I follow this with some conclusions regarding how the findings of this qualitative research may fit the major theoretical frameworks under consideration.

INTERACTIONS BETWEEN THE ADULT WORLD AND THE YOUTH SUBCULTURE

Compared to five years earlier the responses of adults to youthful behavior had mellowed considerably. In the early 1970s, a national commission had called marijuana "a signal of misunderstanding,"[3] In 1975 and 1976, marijuana continued to divide the generations, but its use no longer evoked the strong reactions from adults that were prevalent during the teen-age years of the "Old Wall Gang." Its symbolic link with the Vietnam War and draft protesters had disappeared. Fewer adults, particularly professionals dealing with juveniles, regarded marijuana as physically addictive. It was no longer assumed that those who used marijuana engaged in other criminal behavior. The parents of a few subjects had used marijuana. I encountered many other adults who had experimented with marijuana but never discussed their experience with their children. Other "symbols," such as dress and hairstyles, were less likely to create inter-generational feuds.

Still, marijuana remained a matter that stirred emotional reactions by most adults. Youths were uncomfortable in sharing their views of or experiences with marijuana with most of adults. In turn, most segments of the adult society reacted more strongly toward juvenile marijuana use than toward juvenile alcohol use. They seemed to be somewhat aware of the extent of marijuana use among juveniles, but preferred not to have to deal directly with this reality. During this time, I learned how many symbols of drug use were very obvious to anyone familiar with the subculture yet were not the least apparent to other in the "straight" society. (An example was the "Mr. Doobie...Come Bong With Me" poster on the bulletin board at Golden Beach High School.) Nevertheless, I saw instances when adults ignored obvious indications of drugs. This was particularly apparent if the signals were associated with their own sons or daughters. (For instance, cigarette papers, paraphernalia, empty beer cans and the arrest of close friends for possession of drugs.) Many adults expressed their fears, admitting that they felt uninformed as how to deal with a situation and confused by conflicting information about drugs.

These overall attitudes, and resulting actions or inactions, interacted with contrasting attitudes and actions of the youth in Golden Beach.

In addition to the attitudes related to the use of marijuana and other drugs, there were other aspects of adult society that interacted with and affected the lives of young people. I have organized them according to three levels of society. The first, and primary, level is the family. The second level includes the secondary agents of society, particularly the school, police and probation officials. The third and final level is the general society itself.

1) The family

My direct observations of family interactions were limited. However, I was able to observe patterns of behavior which directly or indirectly involved the family. The patterns of drug use were frequently related to the indirect results of broken homes and the lack of an adequate father figure. These indirect relationships dealt with some of the practical matters surrounding drug use and the opportunities to use drugs. A summary of these relationships and the manner in which they provided opportunities for youths to become involved in the drug subculture follows:

(1) Opportunities for a location to use drugs.

There were many patterns which were the result of the combination of father-absence and working mothers. These situations provided many opportunities for youths who wished to use drugs. The young people planned, in groups, to meet at those homes where no adults would be present, prior to and after school. The same situations affected the youths' patterns of truancy. The "latchkey syndrome" provided the opportunity for truancy by reducing the chances that the attendance authorities could contact a parent. Likewise, these homes were safe havens to spend the school day and use drugs while truant.

In many ways, these patterns were interactional and cumulative within some neighborhoods. In one two-square block area of lower Golden Beach, I was familiar with members of 14 families who had male siblings between the ages of 13 and 17. In 10 of these families the parents were divorced parents and no father was present. The youths established an entire network to facilitate drug use and truancy. The patterns were quite regular so that, in certain homes the youths used drugs before school, in other homes they used drugs after school, and, in still others they met to use drugs in the evening hours. One evening, 14-year-old Martin Dunn and, 13-year-old,

Chris, a non-subject, took me on a "tour" of the neighborhood and described their patterns to me. The tour ended at a nearby park where, Martin informed me, they smoked marijuana on Saturdays, "when our moms aren't working, *like they are supposed to be.*" Martin and his friend told me they felt the park was not as safe to smoke marijuana as their homes because of the increased likelihood of being detected by the police.

(2) Opportunities for late-evening activities.

The situation of a broken home, combined with father-absence, had other indirect results which came about through the dating patterns of the divorced mother. There were, first of all, the opportunities to use the home for drug use and other purposes, on those evenings when the mother was dating. Maternal dating patterns, however, were not confined to single evenings. Many of the mothers, some quite regularly, spent entire weekends out of town with boyfriends. The weekend trips were usually known in advance by her children and others. These weekends provided opportunities for parties. Alcohol and other drugs were used at the parties. Sexual activities took place as well. In addition, the youth whose parent was away for a weekend was more or less free to set his or her own hours to frequent the boardwalk or other locations.

Two cases illustrate that these opportunities were related indirectly, rather than directly, to the broken-home syndrome. The cases each involved youths from intact homes. The subjects were light users. Each subject attended church regularly and was involved in sports and school activities. Nevertheless, the youths and their brothers seized the opportunity to enjoy their "freedom" while their parents were not at home.

The two cases occurred during the summer months. The parents and younger siblings, in each case, had left the area on vacation. In each case, the two eldest sons did not join the rest of the family on the vacation because they were attending summer school and/or were employed.

The first case is that of Phil. Phil, 17, and his 18-year-old brother awaited the opportunity, on a July weekend, to have "fun" while their parents were gone. I met Phil on the boardwalk the first evening his parents had left. He was amazed at what took place there. He had been unaware of the nighttime activities. He met Morris Bayer, the 17-year-old member of the "Trio" described previously. Phil was shocked to see Morris sitting on the wall smoking a hashish pipe in plain view of all. Phil's parents phoned that evening and were upset that neither of their sons was home. They phoned the next morning and informed their sons that they would be calling again that evening. The youths planned to be at home, but only at the hour of the scheduled call. Phil was out late again that evening. His brother was later disciplined after a neighbor informed the parents that the brother's girlfriend had apparently spent the night in the parents' home.

The second example is that of Alex. Alex was 14. He and his 16-year-old brother planned for the days when their parents and younger brother were to be on vacation. They held a large party. The party, as frequently happened, became larger and more out-of-control than the brothers had planned. The youths spent a day and a half attempting to place the house in sufficient order so that their parents would not suspect what had taken place. Apparently, they were successful.

The above two cases entailed exceptional circumstances for the youths involved. Other youths, primarily those whose mothers dated out-of-town men, had more frequent opportunities for such behavior and were able to plan and organize in a more regular fashion. If a mother was a single-parent, but did not leave her children without supervision and maintained control, the opportunities simply did not present themselves.

(3) Absence of discipline.

There were many indications that youths who did not have a father present were more likely to become involved in the drug subculture because they were relative free from disciplinary measures. Their presence at parties, their evenings spent along the boardwalk and their truancies were indications that their hours and activities were not closely supervised, regulated or controlled. The youths often expressed sentiments that they could "do as they wanted."

I will present quantitative data regarding the absence of discipline in Chapter 8. However, a case example may prove helpful at this point. The case is that of 17-year-old Art, a heavy user.

During June, Art was one of the last youths to leave the boardwalk each evening. He was usually inebriated each evening. In early July, Art told me a portion of his life history and his feelings regarding his parents' divorce,

> They thought it was best. Parents always know best! (Cynically) At first, I was stoked! I thought it would be neat getting rid of my old man and not having anyone telling me what to do all the time . . .
>
> Yes, I miss my Dad, and now things are different, but, when you are in 7th grade, you don't think of those things . . . *I don't ask my mother what to do. I tell her!*

I asked Art if he had missed the discipline of a father. He replied, "I guess. But it's too late now."

Art began to use marijuana shortly after the divorce. He began to use barbiturates, amphetamines and hallucinogens while in the seventh and eighth grade. He left Golden Beach for two months, during the summer of 1975, to spend the time with his father in a state in the eastern part of the country. During that period of time, his drug use was confined to "a few beers." Art reverted to his former patterns of drug use when he returned to Golden Beach at the end of the summer. One evening, he was at my apartment. He phoned his mother, giving her no explanation as to why he would not be home for dinner. I heard his final words in the conversation as he slammed down the phone, *"I'll be home when I want to!"*

This pattern frequently involved a divorced single mother who was unable to control her teen-aged son. This breakdown of discipline led the youth to activities and late night hours where drugs were available. Thus, the relationships between broken home, father-absence and use of drugs were not direct, but indirect, due to lack of discipline and increased opportunities to use drugs.

2) School, Police and Probation Officials.

As indicated earlier, school officials, police officers and administrators, and probation officers appeared to be aware of their inability to eliminate or substantially reduced the use of drugs among juveniles.

Interviews with representatives of each of these groups were consistent in responses that indicated, "marijuana is a given," and that "kids will always do some drinking." Their efforts toward eliminating drug "problems" were directed toward the control of substances other than marijuana and alcohol. However, they appeared to become increasingly aware of the extent of alcohol's "misuse" by juveniles, and increasingly spoke of the "teenage alcoholic."

As laws and policies regarding marijuana use became less stringent, there was less alienation among young people toward the school and law enforcement as symbols of society. However, this reduction in alienation did not appear to have an immediate effect on the extent of marijuana use among young people of Golden Beach.

The responses during interviews with the officials were consistent. They all agreed that disciplinary actions by them without the cooperation of parents were ineffective. The school officials and the police officers expressed sentiments that the "real" problems were in the home. They believed that broken homes contributed to most of the problems. They maintained, therefore, that there was nothing school or police could do to change matters. The probation officers, whose jobs included working with parents, expressed frustration. The following are examples of their comments.

> "I get so used to parents who don't even want their kids, I forget that it is not normal for parents not to love their kids. My mom pointed that out to me when I was talking to her last weekend."

> "By the time we get the kid, the home is so screwed up and the kid is so messed up from being batted around or let on his own, there's nothing we can do. It's frustrating!"

> "Most of the kids to get so far that they filed upon (in juvenile court) for pot or booze have to be pretty messed up. Our policy now is that you don't even file until the third offense, so the kid has to be doing quite a bit to get busted and turned over to us by that time. So, if he has a serious problem or drug problem, it is far gone by that time. And what are you going to do with him? The parents are usually alcoholics, too. Locking him up isn't going to solve the problem. It may dry him out for a while to keep him from hurting himself, but it doesn't get at the problem . . . The Family Service Bureau (the probation departments counseling unit) is worried about their statistics, their rate of success, so they can get more money. Well, they don't want drug problems or really bad family problems - that hurts their success ratio. They get to choose the cases they want to work with, so they pick the easier ones."

The drug counselors in the schools expressed similar sentiments. Alvin Coser, the counselor at Golden Beach High School, admitted that the youths who did come to see him were mostly females and that the problem was centered among males. He confirmed to me that he could not promise confidentiality to counselees in spite of what was termed the drug programs "no bust" policy. The youths, in turn, seemed to be aware of this. Consequently, they expressed extreme distrust in the drug counseling program. Mr. Coser attributed many of the drug "problems" to be symptoms of other problems that stemmed from home conditions. He mentioned that he was unable to deal significantly with "home problems."

3) The larger society.

The more general society, typified in Golden Beach by business, church and community leaders, appeared to cling closely to the attitudes described earlier. Their fears regarding marijuana lessened somewhat. They appeared to stereotype the "drug addict" or "marijuana user" according to physical appearance, "bad" family (economically), lack of participation in sports or church activities and so on. As best as I could determine, they usually were unaware of the true extent of youthful involvement with alcohol, marijuana and other drugs.

Because of these beliefs, the community was supportive of the earlier described activities, which they associated with light and non-users . The businessmen, for instance, through various programs and service organizations supported sports activities. The businessmen were inclined to hire youths who had been active in sports, school activities, or who had been recommended by other businessman. If the broken home was related to drug use, the heavy user had a further handicap. He was less likely to have a father, and thus friends of his father, to recommend him to business associates for employment

Fr. O'Malley, the priest in charge of the Catholic youth group, "Drop In," accepted of these beliefs. This young priest, who surfed and frequently rode his bicycle along the beach, had a favorable rapport with young people. Nevertheless, he once told me, "None of our kids ever use marijuana, I'm sure." On one occasion, I introduced him to Frank, a 18-year-old heavy user whose mother was active in church affairs. A few moments after the introduction, Fr. O'Malley remarked, "Now someone like Frank hangs around here (the wall), but wouldn't use drugs. Would he?" (I did not respond.)

At the beginning of each academic year, Fr. O'Malley and Sr. Basil chose the director and board of advisors for the youth group from those who had been the most active members during previous years. Unconsciously, they were choosing among those youngsters who were least likely to be heavily involved in the drug subculture. They mentioned that they sought a "school leader," someone who was involved in sports and in student government. They said, in this way, they did not have to train leaders, but were selecting youths who had already developed that capacity.

Fr. O'Malley often told me that the youth group was not of help to the "kind of kid" who had problems, "We're more geared to a certain type. I don't like the term, 'jock,' but, you know what I mean, someone who is involved and who has certain abilities to express himself and to socialize. The kind of kid like is at the wall just wouldn't be able to fit in here."

My observations confirmed what Fr. O'Malley stated, that, when surfers and/or heavy users attended the group's meetings, they did not "fit in."

Nevertheless, this was a further demonstration of the fact that the heavy user may have been tied to an increasing cycle of exclusion from society. This exclusion process was tied to the person's drug use, not directly, but indirectly because a lack of participation in other activities. Additionally, it may be that, having not participated in one activity, such as sports, drama or music, he felt uncomfortable in other activities, such as church youth groups, whose members were very involved in many varied activities.

These indirect exclusion mechanisms lend support to a broad interpretation of labeling theory.

Many of the patterns I have described fit within the frameworks of the major theories under consideration. That discussion follows.

THE PATTERNS OF BEHAVIOR AND THE THEORIES UNDER CONSIDERATION

In the previous chapter I described the drug subculture in Golden Beach during 1975 and 1976. In this chapter, I have traced many of the patterns of behavior and interactions within that subculture and how they contrasted with and were a part of other elements of the larger, youth subculture. Both of these chapters have relied upon "qualitative" observational data.

Qualitative data are particularly useful in locating processes and patterns of human interaction. This has been demonstrated. However, these data do not lend themselves to the testing of theory in the normal manner of quantified "hypothesis-testing." "Quantitative" data, which are employed more thoroughly in the subsequent chapters, lend themselves directly to this approach through the use of statistics. Nevertheless, the patterns and processes indicated by qualitative techniques do provide material to examine and determine to what extent they "fit" various theories.

This section examines some of the patterns described earlier and includes brief comments briefly about the "fit" or "match" with each of the major theories under consideration.

1) The McCord-Chein, Psychodynamic Model.

The McCord-Chein model assumes a sequence of facts that begin in early childhood. The model envisions a pattern of inadequate socialization in, and preparation for, the male role resulting from the lack of an adequate father figure and an overprotective mother. As a result, the young male has tensions and sexual difficulties. The person then seeks to alleviate his condition through the use of use alcohol and other drugs.[4]

The observational data was rather limited regarding family patterns of a "psychological" or "social-psychological" nature. Further, observation, at one point in time, does not lend itself well to obtaining information about events which occurred at another point in time. Due to the difficulty in gaining information regarding early childhood influences on the subjects, there was little evidence to indicate support, or lack of the same, for the early childhood factors inherent in the McCord-Chein model. There was evidence that the heavy users were affected by the absence of an adequate father figure in their lives. On the other hand, there was very little evidence about the negative effect of an "overprotective" mother. There were a few exceptions. One such exception was found in the case of Ty, the heroin addict, whose mother drove him to his drug deals. Another exception the case of Pops, who had served time for cocaine trafficking. In Pops' case there was no indication that his biological mother was "overprotective." Rather, Pops was able to strike up relationships with young women who would protect him and shield him from his responsibilities or consequences of his drug use.

Indeed, the more "practical" aspects of parenting, such as providing discipline, appeared to be more directly supportive of social control theories than of the McCord-Chein model.

Those aspects of the McCord-Chein model that deal with sex identity were supported by certain patterns that I observed. One of the most significant indicators was the heavy users' defensive reaction regarding their masculinity and regarding homosexuality. Indeed, there were many indications of homophobia, though some degree of this could be considered normal during early adolescence.

Additionally, there were patterns that indicated heavy users typically related to females as "sexual objects." They sought immediate sexual satisfaction without building and maintaining long-term relationships with females. This appeared to contrast with others who related to females on a day-to-day basis through involvement in a variety of circumstances, without the sole purpose of obtaining sexual satisfaction. They appeared to be more sexually mature and secure in their sexual identity.

There was some indication that the young men were not prepared to assume an "independent" role as adult male.

The observational data did not reveal the exact sequence of these factors. Did drug use follow, or precede, problems with sexual identity? Moreover, the question as to whether or not subjects' use of drugs was connected to the resultant tensions of their masculinity and struggle for independence remained unanswered.

Due to the inherent difficulties in attempting to validate family and sexual patterns from observational data alone, caution must be exercised before any theoretical "leap" is made. These issues were explored in greater detail during my final interviews. The results will be presented in the next chapter.

2) Social control theories.

Likewise, it was not possible to assess each aspect of internal control as stated in Reckless' "containment" theory.[5] However, the differences in behaviors between those at the extremes of use and non-use of drugs are apparent. The heavy users lack the inner control to refrain from drugs and sexual activities, even when they considered the activities morally wrong. This was particularly evident among at least one group of heavy users who openly expressed the greatest degree of conservative morality about drug use and sexual activity. They did not attempt to condone their behavior. (An example of this inner struggle was evident in a drawing by Bill Jones in which he depicted himself either as a "winner" or a "loser" in his fight with Satan. See Appendix F.)

Likewise, the heavy users exhibited patterns that demonstrated a lack of their ability to be inner-directed and goal-oriented regarding school and employment in sharp contrast to light and non-users. There was some evidence that the heavy users had lower levels of tolerance for frustration than others.

At the same time, external mechanisms of controls were ineffective. The police, probation officials and school administrators were admittedly unable to contain drug use and other deviant activities.

There appeared to be several patterns that fit other aspects of social control theories. These included the apparent difference in family disciplinary measures. When family control mechanisms were absent, the young people utilized the opportunities to use drugs, be truant, party, or frequent areas where drugs were available. This was all the more significant because the external control mechanisms, exercised by school and law enforcement personnel, were ineffective and were easily circumvented.

Moreover, what was most striking were the patterns of social control exerted by peers. The evidence that these controls were effective in regulating the types of drugs used, the manner and place of use and the degree of use provided strong support for social control theories.

Utilizing Hirschi's model of social control theory, the four major components of social control behavior were evident in the behavior of light and non-users.[6] The light and non-users appeared to be *bonded* with society, *attached* to the opinion of others, *committed* to willing to invest time and energy in conventional activities, *involved* in conventional activities that placed them apart from deviant activities, and *believed* in these conventional activities. Their behaviors were in sharp contrast to the heavy users whose attachment, commitment and involvement were directed toward drug use and other deviant activities.

Overall, the qualitative data provide considerable support for social control theories.

3) Differential Association.

Sutherland's Differential Association theory emphasizes that one learns deviant and non-deviant through interaction within primary groups.[7] Thus, the "peer control" patterns were equally compatible with Sutherland's Differential Association learning theory as with social control theories. Indeed, the numerous differential patterns of behavior described pointed to the frequency, duration and intensity of peer group interactions involving both techniques and rationalizations for various behaviors. For instance, light users associated with other light users and non-users at school, in sports activities, in church youth groups and so on. On the other hand, heavy users not only used drugs and partied together. They surfed together and skipped school together. The patterns of behavior among regular users, who stood between these two groups, gave some additional support for the theory. The behavior patterns of the regular users varied as they changed from one peer group to another. This was particularly apparent when they were influenced by their peers on athletic teams.

It was difficult to assess Sutherland's concept "priority" based on observations made during a brief time frame. Likewise, a "causal" connection is difficult to determine based solely upon current peer associations. Still, there were some indications that many peer relationships or "associations" were influenced by prior family interactions. Indeed, it was obvious that there were continuing interactional effects between family relationships and peer relationships. This was most evident in the encouragement from family members to participate in athletic and church activities. Subsequent accomplishments in athletics and church activities resulted in positive sanctions to continue the activities.

4) Differential Association and Social Control theories as alternative explanations to youth subculture theories.

Overall, the patterns observed did not support some youth subculture theories that were prevalent during the 1960s and1970s. The theories implied that drug use was a symptom of the alienation of most youth from American middle-class values.[8] There were substantial amounts of pleasure-seeking and hedonistic behavior among heavier drug users. On the other hand, heavy users did not tend to voice attitudes which justified their actions. Indeed, among the wall crew, there was some evidence to the contrary.

The patterns of truancy, use of drugs before and during the school day and involvement in school activities indicated that differences existed between degree of drug use and the subjects' relationship with school. There was no definitive indication that alienation or frustration preceded these patterns of behavior. Likewise, it was not clear whether or not lack of involvement in school preceded or followed initial use of drugs. Rather, it seemed that the relationship between involvement in the drug subculture and lack of involvement in school activities was interactive and cumulative. Social control theories appear to provide the most satisfactory explanation of these patterns of behavior .

The relationship between extracurricular involvements and sources of achievement in the larger society, such as obtaining employment, may have been a potential source of frustration with and alienation from the larger society by heavy users who were not involved in extracurricular activities. Nevertheless, initial drug use typically preceded the frustration .

Most members of the "Old Wall Gang" accepted the common belief that education was the key to economic success. Their lack of educational achievement was a source of frustration for many. However, their lack of achievement was often the result of drug use and lack of motivation. Moreover, many of their earlier sources of "alienation" (police patterns, the Vietnam War, and the military draft, for instance) had disappeared.

The longitudinal data provided the opportunity for me to examine the attitudes verbalized during the era of Vietnam and the "flower children" from those expressed by the same persons in the mid 1970s. It was evident that the association between drug use and the attitudes of alienation verbalized in 1970 and 1971 was likely the result of a historical accident. This was evident in the changing attitudes of the Old Wall Gang "generation" from 1970 to 1976. Though their attitudes and opinions became more conservative and conventional, they continued to be involved in the drug subculture. Likewise the younger "generation" in the drug subculture of the mid-1970s expressed views that would have been seen as incompatible with the rhetoric of the "the youth subculture" a few years earlier. The attitudes that were expressed and the changes in attitudes may be better explained by Sutherland's Differential Association theory.

5) Labeling Theory.

Labeling is sometimes called a theory, at other times, a "perspective." It does not seek to explain underlying "causes" of deviant behavior, but describes a process whereby individuals are labeled by others and adopt the label as a self-concept. The development of the self-concept is likely to result in increased deviance in what becomes a self-fulfilling prophecy.[9] Although labeling was not one of the three major theories under consideration, I was constantly aware of the degree of labeling that occurred. The original "Wall Gang" adopted the name given to them by others. The "red freaks" were never aware of the label used by others in reference to them and their conduct. A number of individuals had been arrested, but did not see themselves as "criminals" or "delinquents." School officials and older members of society frequently spoke of "those bums," "jocks," and "soshes." Individuals were treated differently by older adults depending on the perceptions of the adults. Indications were that immediate peer labeling and labeling within families was more effective than that from official or more distant others. Still, there were no indications at this point that labeling or the acceptance of a label resulted in drug use or an increased use of drugs.

Some Final Remarks.

As previously stated, the above comments do not imply "tests" of any theoretical frameworks or propositions derived therefrom. The next chapter presents quantitative data bearing directly upon the major theories under consideration.

The quantitative data were derived primarily from interviews. For the most part, the interview data agree with the observational data. As a result, the quantified data enhanced the picture by more clearly defining patterns and apparent differences between subjects and by providing information regarding events that were not readily accessible to observation.

Likewise, the quantitative data were supplemented by additional qualitative material. It is hoped that as complete a picture as possible results from the employment of both types of data.

End Notes

1. It was interesting that when I began to study the "red freaks" and was seen in their "territory," adjacent to the wall crew, members of the Old Wall Gang were most solicitous of my welfare. Pat, Luke and Bill Jones would observe what was taking place in apparent fear that I would be "jumped" or harmed in some way. They often cautioned me about those whom I was observing and the care I should exercise.

2. *San Diego Tribune*, September 28, 1975, 1-2A.

3. National Commission on Marihuana and Drug Abuse. *Drug Use in America: Problem in Perspective.* First Report. 1972.

4. See William McCord and Joan McCord, with Jon Gudeman, *Origins of Alcoholism*, Stanford, Ca.: Stanford University Press, 1960, and Isidor Chein, et al., *The Road to Narcotics, Delinquency and Social Policy*, NY: Basic Books, 1964.

5. Walter C. Reckless, "Containment Theory," in Barry Krisberg and James Austin (eds.), *The Children of Ishmael: Critical Perspectives on Juvenile Justice,* Palo Alto, Ca.: Mayfield Publishing, 1978, pp. 187-189.

6. Travis Hirschi, *Causes of Delinquency*, Berkeley: University of California Press, 1969.

7. Edwin Sutherland, *Principles of Criminology*, Englewood Cliffs, N.J.: Prentice-Hall, Inc., 1966.

8. See Jerome Himmelbach, Benjamin S. Brashears and John R. Rayfield, "Hedonists and Moralists: Contrasting Culture Among Green Mountain Town Youth," *A Vermont Youth Study*. Goodard College, 1962.; also Ernest A. Smith. *American Youth Culture: Group Life in Teenage Society.* Glencoe, Illinois: Free Press, 1962; and Paul Goodman. *Growing Up Absurd.* NY: Random House, 1956; Edgar Z. Friedenberg. *The Vanishing Adolescent.* Boston: Beacon Press, 1959.

9. See Howard S. Becker. The Outsiders. NY: The Free Press, 1955; Erving Goffman. *Asylums.* NY: Doubleday and Co., 1961; Kai T. Erickson. "Notes on the Sociology of Deviance," *Social Problems*, IX, Spring, 1962, pp. 307-314. Edwin M. Lemert. *Human Deviance: Social Problems and Social Control.* Englewood Cliffs, New Jersey: Prentice-Hall, 1967.

Chapter 8

THEORIES: FAMILY AND PEERS

INTRODUCTION

In this chapter, I present data regarding family, sexuality and peer influences. I analyze the findings according to the McCord-Chein model, Differential Association and social control theories. While I place considerable emphasis on quantitative data from the final interviews, I supplement that data with responses to open-ended questions and other material.

The lack of a random sample did not allow me to employ statistical "tests" to generalize beyond those who took part in the interviews. The lack of statistical generalization should not, however, be interpreted as a lack of "substantive significance." The strengths of the relationships are quite large in many instances. They lend a corresponding degree of weight to the findings. Unless otherwise noted, a total of 72 respondents replied to each item, 31 heavy users, 11 regular users, 23 regular users and seven non-users.

I have attempted to present the data in a manner that is readable, thorough and with as much brevity as the subject allows. Nevertheless, I include details regarding the manner in which each item was measured, coded and analyzed [1]

The tables show the percent differences between degrees of drug use and a number of factors related to the theories. The statistical techniques "gamma" and "Yule's 'Q'" were employed to measure the direction and degree of the relationship of these factors to the degree of drug use. Gamma and Q are similar. Gamma was used in those instances when the four categories of drug use are studies. Q was utilized in those instances in which the categories of drug use are collapsed from four to two resulting in a "two-by-two" table (for instance, when heavy and regular users are combined into one category and light and non-users are combined into another). The possible range of both gamma and Q is between -1.00 and o +1.00. A gamma or Q of -1.00 would indicate a 100% negative relationship between one variable and the other. A gamma or Q of +1.00 would indicate a 100% positive relationship between the two variables. For example, a Q of +1.00 would result if the rate of parental use of alcohol among heavy users and regular was 100% and parental use of alcohol was zero among light and non-users. In other words, there would be a perfect positive relationship between parental use of alcohol and degree of the siblings' drug use. Such perfect relationships are unheard of in most studies of human behavior. A gamma or Q of + or - .50 or higher would indicate a strong relationship.

THE FAMILY

Divorce, Conflict and Doubts About Parental Care.

Table 3 shows the results of responses to the interview questions that dealt with divorce, parental conflict and expression of doubts about parental care.

TABLE 3

RESPONSES TO ITEMS REGARDING FAMILY BY DEGREE OF DRUG USE

	Heavy Users	**Regular Users**	**Light Users**	**Non-Users**	*Gamma*
Parents Divorced	52%	45%	39%	29%	*.24*
Parental Conflict	74%	64%	43%	14%	*.56*
Divorced & Parental Conflict	88%	40%	56%	0	*.72*

The data indicate a relationship between divorce and drug use. The strength of the relationship (indicated by a gamma of .24) appeared to be somewhat weak. Divorce, by itself, did not explain a great deal of the difference in degrees of use and non-use. However, in this and other data one must keep in mind that I purposely chose seven individuals whose situations were counter to this anticipated relationship between drug use and divorce. I selected the four Gilroy sons because three were light or non-users raised in a single-parent household. I selected the four Jones siblings because three were heavy users from an intact two-parent family.

On the other hand, the relationship between parental conflict and degree of drug use was much stronger, a gamma of .56.

Moreover, when I examined the perception of parental conflict separately for the 32 subjects whose parents had divorced, gamma increased to a very strong .72.

My interactions with the subjects during the interviews shed more light on this. When I asked questions about parental conflict, three subjects requested that I temporarily turn off the tape recorder. They stressed how important confidentiality was to them when giving their responses to these questions. In addition, these three subjects and others showed signs of discomfort as they discussed the conflict between their mother and father. Some examples,

> "Oh, God! It was awful! They used to fight so much. I couldn't stand it. I would have nightmares and everything."

> "I remember, when we were little, an' my Mom and Dad used to come home when they had been out and he would start fightin' with her and me and Joe started crying once, an' my Mom came in and held us, so we'd stop cryin'."

> "Oh, it's a lot better now. Since they got a divorce, they get along a lot better now than they did before."

> "Yeah, they almost got a divorce once. An' it was all because of me. I was getting bad grades in school then, in sixth, an' it caused them to get into fights and they start yellin' at me and then at each other. Now, I'm doin' better. That's why I want to keep doin' good in school."

Several of the young people said that parental conflict usually occurred when their parents had been drinking. The most serious instances involved situations in which both parents had drinking problems. Seventeen-year-old Eric played down this aspect when I inquired about his parents, "Oh, yeah, they really get going at it sometimes. But it doesn't bother me. I jes' go out by the pool and sleep where I can't hear 'em yellin' at each other."

A few expressed their positive feelings toward the lessening of parental conflict following the divorce,

> "They don't fight as much as they used to. When I was in fifth and sixth grade, it was pretty bad. Now it's pretty good, even if my ol' man isn't everything he should be."

> "I don't know why they don't fight like they used to. For a while there it as pretty bad. I don't know what happened. I know it is a lot better around the house than it used to be."

For most, however, the breakup of the home was seen as negative, even when conflict had preceded it,

> "My last memory of my Dad is of him walking away and my Mom crying on the front porch. I'll never forget that!"

> "I guess it was best for them. Parents never ask the kids what they feel was best for them, do they?"

Three young men were undergoing considerable trauma at the time of the research because their parents had initiated divorce proceedings. For instance, 17-year-old Jack initially lost the social support of both his peer group and his family. For a period, immediately prior to the research, he would have been considered a heavy user. The following is his story as reconstructed from field notes,

> Oh, I never smoked pot except once and hardly ever drank before I went back east. I got there and started running around with a different crowd. We would skip school every day and go to this one kid's house and get drunk. I was really in bad shape and almost didn't graduate last year because of it. And, while all that was going on, was when my Dad left my Mom. He just took off and went to Florida. He never did tell me anything. That's what bothers me. The least he could do is tell me what was wrong. Everything was fine, one day, then . . .

At the time of our initial conversation, Jack did not see a connection to his family situation and his drinking patterns. Later, he told me that he had not wanted to admit to it, at first, but that he had been trying to "drown his sorrows." Nevertheless, he reverted to his earlier "light" use of marijuana and alcohol after he returned to Golden Beach and associated with his former peer group. Jack, like some others, was disturbed by the unexpected occurrence of the divorce. He had no prior indication of parental conflict.

There were several occasions when I observed young people along the beach or elsewhere at very late hours. I later learned that they had been avoiding their home due to the parental fighting that was taking place.

Taken together, divorce and parental conflict are strongly related to the degree of the subjects' drug use.

The final column in Table 3 demonstrates the strong relationship between the subjects' degree of drug use and their responses that their parents did not "care." Gamma was a strong .66.

I used "care," in this instance, to include more than the mere provision of physical necessities and protection from physical harm. Rather, it was meant to encompass these as part of an overall emotional concern for the total well-being of another person. It appeared the subjects understood this as the general meaning of the concept being considered.

I asked each subject, "Have you ever doubted that your parents care for you?"

I excluded any minor or incidental doubts, such as,

> Oh, yeah, a few times after I'd get a spanking when I was little, I guess so. When my older brother got to stay out all the time and I couldn't 'cuz I was younger

On the other hand, the types of responses that were coded as representing a "serious" doubt included,

> "Yes, after the divorce (subject was 13- years-old), my Mom used to go to San Francisco a lot and I would cry and beg her to stay. She'd always say, 'I'll be back on Monday.' Now, when I go to visit her and she wants me to stay longer, I remind her of that and tell her how much I used to want her to stay and she wouldn't. I guess I'll never forget that."

> "When I was in tenth grade, one night my Dad came in and told me, 'Get out!' I felt that he didn't like me. I left."

> "Yes, my Step-dad, when he would hang me and all my stepbrothers upside down on the bed, it was a bunk-bed, and beat us with a coat-hanger. He tried to make me cry and I would try not to cry. He was a Golden Glove boxer and would beat us with his fist sometimes, too, sometimes for nothing at all."

I analyzed the responses according to the life history of the individual to determine if the doubt began before or after initial drug use. In order to assess this relationship, I used only those instances of "serious" doubt about care by one parental figure or another (including stepparents) that occurred or began prior to the person's initial drug use.

In addition, there were indications that some subjects might have been in denial regarding the lack of parental care. In my field observations, I noted four heavy users who appeared to either have been neglected or been physically abused by their parents. However, during the interviews, none of the four reported doubts regarding parental care. Each case involved either severe physical beatings or neglect by not providing basic needs, such as food. The parents involved were defended by the subjects when I questioned them further. For examples,

> "I know my Dad loves me. He tells me so every time before he hits me in the jaw (with his fist). Then, afterwards, he always hugs me. (On one occasion, the father broke the subject's jaw.)"

> "Our Mom wants us to learn how to take care of ourselves so she feels, if we can get food and cook it for ourselves now, then we can take care of ourselves when we are older." (The parent had a substantial income, but frequently dated on evenings and for entire weekends, often leaving no food or grocery money with the children. This subject, Norm Dunn, then 16, would openly admit this as neglect when we met several years later.)

Overall, the evidence indicated a significant relationship between degree of drug use and divorce, parental conflict and doubts of parental care. These results are compatible with Differential Association theory, social control theories and the McCord-Chein model.

Father-absence and father-inadequacy.

Directly pertinent to the McCord-Chein model, and consistent with the other theories is the issue of an absent father, or the lack of an adequate father or father figure.

The first criterion of "father-absence" was defined as the absence of a father or a male perceived as a father figure for a majority of years between the subject's fourth birthday and his14th birthday. If a father or stepfather had not been present, I asked the son, "Is there anyone else who has been a father to you?" The most frequent substitute "father figure" mentioned was a coach. Others included counselors, clergy, older brothers and the father of a peer.

Table 4 shows the responses to questions that dealt with these individually as well as in combination with parental conflict.

TABLE 4

SUBJECTS' RESPONSES TO ITEMS REGARDING FATHER BY DEGREE OF DRUG USE

	Heavy Users	Regular Users	Light Users	Non-Users	*Gamma*
Father Absent	45%	18%	17%	14%	*.50*
Inadequate Father	55%	55%	13%	14%	*.59*
Either Absent or Inadequate Father	65%	55%	26%	14%	*.59*
Parental Conflict & Lack of an Adequate Father	55%	27%	13%	0	*.72*

The data show a moderate relationship between drug use and father-absence. There is little difference in the percentages for regular, light and non-users (18 percent, 17 percent and 14 percent, respectively) but the heavy users stand out. Forty-five percent of the heavy users in the sample did not have a father present during their formative years. Gamma is.50.

Table 4 shows the responses to questions that dealt with these individually as well as in combination with parental conflict.

The lack of a stronger relationship may indicate that although father-absence alone, like divorce alone, is associated with some degree of drug use other factors regarding fathers and father figures. Thus, I examined those situations in which the father was present but inadequate. I asked each subject, "When you think a father should be as a kind of ideal, but recognizing that no one is perfect, do you feel your Dad (or Step-Dad or other) measures up to that? That is, is he what your idea of a father should be? (If not, why not?)" Gamma rose to 59. The data show a stronger relationship for "inadequate" father than was the case for "absent" father. The heavy users and the regular users differ markedly from the light and non-users increased. However, when I examined the cases in which the father was *either absent or inadequate.* I found a substantial and consistent relationship with degree of drug use. The gamma of .59 is the same as for that of an "inadequate father" alone. Nevertheless, the consistency of the trend provides greater support to the theories under consideration.

Most subjects related the inadequacies of their fathers in a manner indicating physical or emotional weakness. These were often expressed in degrading terms such as,

> "He's a puss."

> "My Dad is the kinda guy that, if I tried to play catch with him,
> I'd have to teach him how."

Many of the comments contained sentiments deploring the fact that their father figure could not discipline them, that the mother was the "boss" in the home and that the father figure had either no interest or no ability in sports. Three youths felt their fathers were not "men" because of their weaknesses for alcohol. Seven indicated expressed that of their fathers were inadequate because they either had abandoned the family and/or did not provide adequate support following the separation.

In contrast, three subjects stated they did not feel their fathers were adequate because they were unable to express warmth or emotion. One 21-year-old stated,

> My Dad isn't too good at expressing his emotions. I just wish that he would have been able to, ya know, put his arm around me and me, physically, that he cared.

I asked those subjects who did not have a father present or expressed the inadequacy of their father figures, "What do you think you have missed by not having a father?"

Twenty-six subjects mentioned one or more aspects, as follows,

Discipline	16
Going Camping	14
Going to sports events	12
Learning to drive	3
Someone to talk to	14
Learning about girls and sex	8
Other	8

It is noteworthy that the aspect of the father's role the youths missed most was that of disciplinarian.

In addition to the interview responses, there were other elements of the role of father figure that add a depth if understanding I became aware of during my interactions with the subjects. The heavy users, placed pressure on me to interfere as disciplinarian with such remarks as, "Why don't you do something about that? Don't you care?" or by describing activity or behavior to me in such a manner as to draw my opinion, such as, "Would it be all right if I . . . ?" Or, "What would you think if I . . . ?" The light and non-users rarely, if ever, attempted to place me in the role of disciplinarian. Likewise, the heavy users were most likely to ask me to "get" them a job, as opposed to simply asking me if I knew of an employment opportunities. The heavy users were likely to ask me to "fix" them up with a girl, as opposed to the light and non-users who related to me as a "best friend" who could provide opinions of dating or relating to a particular female.

Finally, the data in Table 4 indicate a very strong and consistent relationship between degree of drug use and the combined effect of having both parental conflict and the lack of an adequate father figure. The strength of this relationship was reflected in the very large gamma, .73.

Overall, the data regarding the role of fathers and father figures lends strong support to the three major theoretical models under consideration. This is most pronounced when parental conflict is also considered.

Overprotective Mothers.

The next element of the McCord-Chein model I examined was the relationship between overprotective mother and degree of drug use. The role of the overprotective mother or mothering-figure is an essential component in the McCord-Chein model. It is not a component in the other theories.

I asked each subject, "Do you feel your Mom cares about you?" If affirmative, I asked, "Do you ever feel that she cares *too much?* I emphasized the words, "too much," so that the subject would understand the item as meant to indicate ' 'over caring" or ' 'overprotecting," rather than the expected and ordinary motherly care.[2]

The results showed a consistent, but rather weak relationship between perception of mothers as overprotective and degree of drug use. The percentage difference between the non-users and the heavy users was only 23 percent. A gamma of .32 was indicative of this weak association. In spite of the consistency of the trend and some observational data that indicated a few cases of "overprotective mothers" among sons whose drug use was at the extreme levels, the data do not lend strong support for this important element of the McCord-Chein model.

It may be that my questions were not phrased so as to measure degrees of overprotectiveness. On the other hand, it may be that the McCord-Chein model fits only extreme cases of an overprotection. (An example is the case of Ty, the young heroin addict whose mother was drove him to his drug deals.)

In addition, many youths volunteered their appreciation for the care and love of their mothers toward them. They were especially appreciative of the care by their mothers when their fathers were either absent or inadequate. Indeed, those with no father in the home, frequently expressed anger at their father for not providing sufficient alimony or child support for their financially strapped mothers. In general, the lack of maternal care appeared to be much more significant than an "over caring" or "overprotective" mother. This included doubts due to a lack of caring discipline.

Doubt regarding discipline as care and method of discipline.

Both the specific psychodynamic McCord-Chein model and the more general social control theories take into consideration the relationship of childhood discipline and subsequent deviant behavior. Likewise, childhood discipline is implied within Differential Association. The first element of discipline I examined was that of perception of parental discipline as a sign of caring. I initially determined who, if anyone, the subject perceived as disciplinarian(s) in his family. These included "mother," "father," "stepfather," "both" or "other." Next, I asked whether or not he felt the discipline was administered because the person(s) cared about him. If this evoked an affirmative response, I asked, "Have you ever doubted this?" and "When?"

If there had been an initial doubt that was later resolved, I did not code the response as "doubt regarding parental care" unless the doubt preceded the youth's initial drug use. Likewise, I did not record those responses that dealt with an immediate situation of being disciplined.

In addition, I asked, "How were you disciplined? Physically? Restrictions? Or what?"

If the respondent answered, "Physically," or "It was physical and other," I inquired further, "Was it ever severe?"

I recorded each affirmative response to the "severe" inquiry along with details as to how the discipline had been administered. I coded as "severe" only those instances of physical discipline in which the subject was treated medically either for the results of such discipline and/or during which the subject was physically bound during the administration of discipline. Seven cases met these criteria. Six of the cases were reported by heavy users (amounting to 14 percent of all heavy and regular users). Only one case was recorded among the light and non-users.

Twelve subjects, who lived at home and were under the age of 18, reported that they were never disciplined. Their responses were coded as, "Discipline absent." Eleven of the 12 subjects were heavy or regular users. The other subject was a light user. In each of these cases, the youth had been disciplined as a child, but discipline ended as the young male entered adolescence. The median grade level during which discipline ended was ninth grade. In all but two cases, a broken home had been involved, and, in all but four cases (two from the same family), no father figure was present in the home. Examples of these are,

> "No one disciplines me!"
>
> "My Mom used to try to, but she found out she can't tell me what to do."
>
> "Since the divorce, no one!"

Six of the 24 respondents who said that they were not disciplined stated that they had "missed discipline" because they did not have father figures in their homes.

Because the element of parental discipline was a critical element in the theories and because there appeared to be a variety of factors involved within discipline, I analyzed several items more thoroughly. I collapsed the four categories of degree of drug use into two. I placed heavy and regular users in one category, and light users and non-users in the other. Not only did this appear to reflect the similarities within and between the larger four categories, but it allowed for multiple controls and comparisons. Thus, I used Yule's Q, rather than gamma.

The results shown in Table 5 were striking. In every aspect of discipline or combination of discipline with other factors, there were strong differences between the heavy and regular users on the one hand, and the light and non-users on the other. Heavy and regular users tended to see discipline as care and missed discipline. They were more likely not to have a father at home and missed discipline. They were less likely to have been disciplined by a father or both parents. They were more likely to have been disciplined severely, to have been without discipline and, if disciplined, more likely to have experienced only physical discipline. They were less likely to have been disciplined physically in their earlier years and to have experienced other techniques of discipline, such as restrictions and curfews, as they grew older.

These results provide strong support for social control theories as well as Differential Association. Moreover, the role of a father as disciplinarian as opposed to that of a mother is consistent with the emphasis of the McCord-Chein model.The strong importance of family factors in the lives of the young males was evident. In was obvious that degree of drug abuse was related to divorce, conflict, an absent or inadequate father-figure, parental drug use, a lack of discipline and a lack of caring.

All of the results are consistent with the McCord-Chein model, as well as Differential Association and social control theories. However, a key element of the McCord-Chein model, the overprotective mother, had only a weak relationship to the subjects' drug use. The next section deals with the latter "stages" in the McCord-Chein model. The latter stages link factors of home life to alcoholism and/or drug addiction. The model envisions that the lack of an adequate father figure combined with an overprotective mother is likely to result in problems with sexual identity and sexual difficulties, an independence-dependence struggle and psychological tensions. Thus, it is theorized, the male attempts to alleviate his problems and tensions by using alcohol and other drugs.

TABLE 5

FACTORS REGARDING DISCIPLINE BY DEGREE OF SUBJECTS' DRUG USE

	Heavy & Regular Users (n = 42)	**Light & Non-users Regular Users (n = 30)**	*Yules's Q*
Saw Discipline As Care & Missed Discipline	43% (n = 28)	7% (n = 28)	*.81*
Father Absent & Missed Discipline	81% (n = 16)	40% (n = 5)	*.73*
Disciplined By Father or Both Parents	50%	83%	*-.67*
"Severe" Physical Discipline	14%	3%	*.66*
Discipline Absent	26%	3%	*.82*
Discipline Either Severe or Absent	40%	7%	*.81*
Physical Discipline Only	33%	10%	*.67*
"Other" Discipline Only	19%	10%	.36
Physical Discipline Earlier, Now "Other	29%	80%	*-.82*

SEXUAL IDENTITY AND SEXUAL PROBLEMS

There are inherent problems in any attempt to measure sexual difficulties and weaknesses.[3] These problems are increased when attempting to study adolescents. I chose questions for the interview schedule and asked them in a sequence that would allow openness of response, a minimum of uneasiness and a maximum flow in the interview. These items dealt with issues of both heterosexual and homosexual relationships.

In order to measure sexual problems stemming from heterosexual relations, I asked, "Have you ever worried about your sex life or had any troubles of this kind?"

If the subject asked for further direction, he was told, in a matter-of-fact tone, "I mean, have you ever worried about sex, had trouble keeping it hard, reaching a climax, or anything like that?"

The data shown in Table 6 indicate that the "heterosexual problems" reported were related to the subjects' degree of drug use. This was true regarding most individual types of problems as well as in the overall frequency of problems reported. Additionally, it should be noted that those problems that would seem to be most threatening to one's masculine identity are noticeably skewed toward the heavy users, namely: "Difficulty in maintaining an erection," "Difficulty in reaching climax," "Feared impotency" and "Afraid of girls."There were indications that some of the sexual difficulties were directly related to the effects of alcohol and other drugs consumed prior to the sexual activity. In fact, in two of the four cases in which the person reported difficulties in "maintaining an erection" and in one of the three reported cases of difficulties in "reaching a climax," the problem occurred while attempting sexual intercourse under the influence of substantial amounts of alcohol, a depressant. In these instances, the sequence is the opposite of that predicted by the McCord-Chein model. The temporal sequence of the McCord-Chein model envisions that the use of drugs is a result of experiencing sexual problems. It does not envision the problems occurring after (and perhaps as a result of) the use of drugs.

In order to measure fears and difficulties of a homosexual nature, I asked each subject, "Have you ever had a feeling or fear or an incident about homosexuality or some other guy that scared you?" The responses are shown in Table 7.

The data indicate that the more threatening problems were experienced by heavy drug users. It was predominantly heavy and regular users who

TABLE 6

HETEROSEXUAL FEARS, CONCERNS AND DIFFICULTIES BY DEGREE OF DRUG USE

Difficulty	Heavy Users	Regular Users	Light Users	Non-Users	All Subjects
Maintaining an Erection	13% (4)	0	0	0	6% (4)
Reaching Climax	10% (3)	0	0	0	4% (3)
Pregnancy Occurred	6% (2)	0	0	0	3% (2)
Ungrounded Fear of Pregnancy Occurring	6% (2)	0	0	0	3% (2)
Fear of Impotency	3% (1)	9% (1)	0	0	3% (2)
Afraid of Girls	6% (2)	9% (1)	0	0	4% (3)
Fear Not Attractive to Girls	6% (2)	9% (1)	9% (2)	14% (1)	8% (6)
Concerns of Sexual Performance	0	0	9% (2)	0	3% (2)
Other Fears or Guilt	0	0	9% (2)	0	3% (2)
TOTAL REPORTING ANY DIFFICULTY	42% (13)	27% (3)	26% (6)	14% (1)	32% (23)

reported they had been frightened by homosexual feelings, feared they were homosexuals, feared the presence of an obvious homosexual, had reacted reacted violently toward homosexuals without provocation, and/or had an incident involving homosexual physical contact. Nineteen of 26 of such instances were reported among the heavy user category alone.

Various types of homosexual incidents and fears were reported, such as the following:

> "Yeah, . . . Ya know, sometimes I have seen guys an' I have just thought, 'Well, maybe that would feel good,' or like I have more wondered what it would be like . . . When I got feelin's like that it scares me . . . You're the first person I ever told."

> "Yeah, I had a fear, and still do. There is so much around. I worry that I might become one . . . When I was 16, it was really bad. I thought my mind was slipping away. I would lay in bed and look at muscle magazines and felt I wanted to experience it. I would be scared when I thought about it later, the next morning. I guess it lasted 'til I was 18. I haven't had any of those feelin's since I have been on my own."

> "When we were little, we jes' started to fool around, I guess. You know, when our mothers were away. It was in fifth and sixth grade, and we would get naked. Then we started, you know, playing with each other. Then, this one guy, well, he was the first one that started, ya know, to, I guess, give some of us a blow job, or, at least, to suck it . . . We were young. It felt good, at first, so I guess we began to play around. We all tried it eventually . . . I never did kiss anyone, though, and I never did swallow it."

> "Oh, yeah, I used to be one of the 'Silver Street Raiders.' We used to go up there and kick shit out of those queers. Those queers! We used to beat the shit out of them, man! An', ya know, they still hang around that head!"

These responses give some support to the McCord-Chein model. Of six instances that involved direct homosexual fears, feelings or physical contact, and in which the subjects reported a temporal order, five were reported to have occurred prior to the subject's initial drug use. However, the number of instances reported were extremely small.

I used an additional, more covert, item to gauge homosexual fears that might not otherwise have been reported. The question was meant to determine the subject's reaction to a hypothetical situation, "What would

TABLE 7

HOMOSEXUAL FEARS, CONCERNS AND DIFFICULTIES BY DEGREE OF DRUG USE

	Heavy Users	**Regular Users**	**Light Users**	**Non-Users**	**All Subjects**
Homosexual Fear that Scare the Subject	13% (4)	0	0	0	6% (4)
Fear that I am a Homosexual	6% (2)	0	0	0	3% (2)
Fear When Homosexual Present	13% (4)	9% (1)	4% (1)	0	8% (6)
Unprovoked Violence Toward a Homosexual	13% (2)	27% (3)	4% (1)	0	11% (8)
Homosexual Incident Involving Physical Contact	16% (5)	9% (1)	4% (1)	0	10% (7)
Attempted Seduction by a Homosexual	32% (2)	36% (4)	30% (7)	43% (3)	33% (24)
Other	3% (1)	9% (1)	9% (2)	29% (1)	8% (6)
TOTAL REPORTING ANY CONCERN	45% (14)	73% (3)	52% (12)	71% (1)	54% (39)

you do if you found out your best friend was a homosexual? Just hypothetically, without tying it to any particular person."

I coded the responses according to increasing degrees of defensive reactions, namely: "Defensive reaction," and "Continue as friends" or "Non defensive reaction." There was only a moderate relationship between these responses and degree of drug use. The trend is inconsistent, with the greatest frequency of defensive reactions occurring among the regular users, 17 percentage points higher than that among the heavy users.

TABLE 8

HIGH SCHOOL AGE SUBJECTS' REACTIONS TO QUESTION REGARDING IF A BEST FRIEND WAS A HOMOSEXUAL BY DEGREE OF DRUG USE

	Heavy Users (n = 16)	Regular Users (n = 6)	Light Users (n = 14)	Non-Users (n = 7)	Total Percent (n = 42)
Defensive Reaction	87%	83%	50%	0	60%
Non-Defensive Reaction	13%	17%	50%	100%	40%

Gamma = .82

Older subjects were less defensive. They tended to be more accepting of homosexuality. At times, they responded in a manner similar to Gerald, "I used to be pretty hung-up on that, but now I realize they can't help it, so as long as he didn't bother me, I would probably continue to be his friend." On the other hand, the youngest subjects tended to the most defensive. Thus, when I examined the responses of only those of high school age, gamma rose to a very strong, positive .82. Eighty-seven percentage points separated the heavy users responded from the non-users, as shown in Table 8. Taking all the data into consideration, it appeared that there might be some support for the proposition that a weak male sexual identity and/or sexual problems were related to degrees of drug use. However, caution is urged. The data presented, thus far, did not take temporal sequence into consideration. The temporal sequence is implicit in the McCord-Chein model. Thus, although there were some associations between both sexual identity and sexual problems and degree of drug use, there was very little evidence to indicate that identity problems occurred prior to initial drug use. The reverse sequence was found in some instances. In addition, involvement in drug-related activities may have limited their participation in conventional activities, such as sports, that might have allowed them to feel more secure in their sexual identity. Continued drug use prior to or during sexual activity and in relating to the opposite sex during adolescence may have affected the normal development of their sexual identity. The qualitative findings raised this question. I explore the results of quantitative data in the next section.

Use of Drugs in Sexual Relations and Sexual Activity

In order to obtain information regarding initial sexual intercourse, I asked each subject a series of questions,

> "Have you ever had sex with a chick?"
> "What was your age or grade the first time?"
> "Was the first time satisfying?"
> "Did you have any guilt afterwards?"
> "Were you drunk or high?"

Fifty-seven of the seventy-two subjects had sexual intercourse at least once. The median grade-level of initial sexual intercourse for heavy and regular users was 9th grade. The median grade-level for light users was 11th grade. Only one of the seven non-users had engaged in sexual intercourse. He was in the 12th grade.

The responses to the other questions are shown in Table 9. There was no relationship between degree of drug use and perception of initial sexual experience as satisfying or followed by guilt. The very weak negative gammas are indicative of this. The gammas are skewed in the table, however, because there was only one non-user who had ever engaged in sexual intercourse. He found it unsatisfying and felt guilty afterward.

However, there was a very strong relationship between degree of drug use and being "drunk" or "high" during the initial sexual experience. The gamma is a very strong positive .84.

The fact that initial sexual activity occurred under the influence of drugs raises additional questions. The problems occurring during sexual activity may have resulted from the effects of the drugs. In addition, individuals with a weak masculine identity may have been more likely than others to use drugs for sexual performance

TABLE 9

REPORTS OF SUBJECTS REGARDING INITIAL SEXUAL INTERCOURSE BY DEGREE OF DRUG USE

	Heavy Users (n = 30)	**Regular Users** (n = 9)	**Light Users** (n = 17)	**Non-Users** (n = 1)	*Gamma*
Was Not Satisfying	37%	44%	47%	0	-.24
Felt Guilty Afterward	27%	44%	29%	100%	-.17
Was High or Drunk	73%	44%	14%	0	.84

In Chapter 6, I listed of items that I asked each subject who had ever used any drug to measure the pervasiveness of drug use in daily activities. Included in these items were two that measured drug use in situations involving relations with the opposite sex. They were "Before or during a dance?", and "Before a date?"

There was little variation in the responses of subjects who have ever used drugs before or during a dance. Ninety-five percent of all users had on one or the other occasion. There was greater variation in the responses to the question, "Before a date." A 51 percent difference separated the light users from the heavy users. Two above items measured the use of drugs in courting situations and non-sexual activities with females.

Three other items measured the use of drugs during, or for the purpose of engaging in sexual activity, namely, "To have sex - to turn yourself on?", "To have sex - to turn her on?" and "To enjoy sex more?"

There as very little between degree of drug use and the subjects' responses to, "To have sex-turn her on." A substantial, 77 percent, majority of those who had ever used drugs had used them at least once with this purpose in mind.

There was greater variation among responses to the items "To have sex - to turn yourself on" and "To enjoy sex more." The trends were consistent. There was a difference of 45 percent between the responses of the heavy users and the light users indicating that they had used drugs to "turn themselves on." Moreover, there was a 57 percent difference between heavy users and light users who admitted to use of drugs "to enjoy sex more." However, these substantial differences must be interpreted with caution given the greater likelihood of the heavy users to engage in sexual activity, to engage in sexual intercourse more frequently, and to be more likely to be under the influence of drugs at any given time. Consider these responses,

> "I don't do it for that reason, but it usually is there"
>
> "I am usually high." (This response was coded as "never, "indicating the respondent did not use drugs with the purpose of having sexual relations by "turning himself on or loosening himself up.")
>
> "You can't enjoy it (sex) more. You feel less, even though I am usually stoned." (Coded as "never.")

It should also be noted that some youths who never had sexual intercourse indicated they had used drugs with such a purpose in mind. (Apparently they were not successful.)

I measured the current frequency of sexual intercourse, by the question, "How often do you have sex now?" The median frequencies were two or three times a month among heavy users, one time every two months among regular users, one time a year among light users. The one light user who had sexual intercourse did so only once.

In summarize, those who used drugs most frequently were more likely to have experienced sexual problems and homosexual fears. They were more likely have engaged in sexual activity at an earlier age and do so more frequently. They were more likely to have used drugs in relating to females and as a part of sexual activities.

Evidence of an Independence-Dependence Struggle

The next step in the McCord-Chein model is an independence-dependence struggle within young males who are ill-prepared to assume the adult male role. I tested the struggle for independence by asking those subjects who were living with one or more parent, "Do you want to be on your own soon?";

Of the sixty-two subjects who responded, two-thirds (66 percent) expressed a desire to be on their own. Heavy and regular users were more likely to respond affirmatively (83 percent and 70 percent respectively). Only half of the light and non-users preferred to be on their own.

In order to compare the subjects' desire to be on their own with their perception of their capability of attaining this goal, each subject, "Do you feel you are prepared to be on your own financially?" and "Do you feel you are prepared to be on your own emotionally?"

The data show that the independence-dependence struggle was confined to the emotional rather than the financial realm. A gamma of -.76 indicated a strong negative relationship between feeling prepared emotionally and degree of drug use. All of the light or non-users felt emotionally prepared to be on their own. Seventy-one percent of the regular users and 60 percent of the heavy users felt they were emotionally prepared to be on their own. On the other hand, a low gamma of .11 indicated that there was virtually no relationship between financial preparedness and degrees of drug use own.

The Use of Drugs to Overcome "Bad" Feelings

The next issues considered were those that might be termed the "final stage" of the McCord-Chein model. According to the model, the final "result" of the struggle by the young male is the use of drugs to overcome the psychological discomforts, insecurities, inabilities and anxieties.

I chose two measurements as indicators of psychological discomfort. One, "Do you ever feel depressed?", was meant to measure a rather "normal" discomfort level, likely to be experienced to some degree by most everyone. The other, "Do you ever feel uncared for?" was meant to reflect a more extreme anxiety, the loss of social support or of being "uncared for." I coded the responses to the items as affirmative or negative.

Most subjects, 83 percent, responded affirmatively to the first question. There was no trend or direction in their responses as indicated by an extremely low gamma of .07.

On the other hand, there was a moderate relationship between feeling of anxiety, or not being cared for, and degree or drug use. Gamma was .51. However, most of the variation was accounted for by the large number of reports from heavy users (45 percent). Virtually no differences existed among the other three categories (regular users, 18 percent; light users, 17 percent; and non-users, 14 percent).

I decided that one additional question was necessary to establish whether or not those who had such feelings used drugs to overcome them. Each subject was asked, "Have you ever used alcohol, pot or other drugs to help you with any bad feelings or if you feel tense or nervous?"

TABLE 10

SUBJECTS REPORTING THE USE OF DRUGS TO OVERCOME "BAD" FEELINGS AMONG THOSE WHO REPORTED FEELINGS OF DEPRESSION OR ANXIETY BY DEGREE OF DRUG USE

	Heavy Users	**Regular Users**	**Light Users**	**Non-Users**	*Gamma*
Felt Depressed & Used Drugs to Relieve Depression	81% (26)	60% (6)	17% (3)	n/a	.79
Felt Uncared for &Used Drugs to Relieve Feelings	86% (14)	100% (4)	50% (2)	n/a	.56

As shown in Table10, among those who reported feelings of depression, there was a very strong positive relationship between the use of drugs to overcome "bad" feelings and degree of drug use. The relative strength and direction of this relationship are indicated by the positive gamma of .79. On the other hand, among the small number of subjects who reported feelings of being uncared for, there was only a moderate relationship between the use of drugs to overcome "bad" feelings and degree of drug use. The gamma of .56 must be interpreted with some caution because of the small number of subjects noted in the table.

The results indicated a rather strong association between the use of drugs to overcome feelings of psychological discomfort and degree of drug use. The trend was consistent and there were substantial percentage differences between each category of drug use (heavy users, 74 percent; regular users, 55 percent; and light users, 22 percent). The positive gamma of .70 is indicative of the strength and direction of this relationship.

Before I comment on an analysis of the data in support of the McCord-Chein model, I present the very unique case of Jim.

The Case of Jim

One case from the research so well illustrated possible links between home life, sexual difficulties and the use of drugs to overcome psychological difficulties related to the sexual difficulties that it compels reporting. I refer to him as "Jim." I use this fictitious name, which differs from the pseudonym used elsewhere, in order that his identity will be more fully protected. The case is unique. I do not claim that it illustrates any pattern. I present it in order to demonstrate the relationships that may exist elsewhere, in other forms. It would appear that the case closely fits the McCord-Chein model. Perhaps, it may point to a direction for future research. Given my involvement in the case, I narrate it entirely in the first person.

I became acquainted with Jim at the beginning of the research. He frequented the wall area, surfed, and did not seem particularly different from other members of the wall *"crew." In h*is initial interview, Jim stated that he used marijuana frequently since the seventh grade and had used alcohol with somewhat less frequency. He used hallucinogens but had not used sedatives or stimulants. Jim was 18 and had graduated from high school.

During the course of the research, I became increasingly acquainted with Jim, as I did with other subjects. Jim did not seem to be a subject who was particularly close to me on a personal basis. He appeared to be somewhat more anxious than others to inform me of his activities, particularly those surrounding drugs.

Jim's relationships with girls seemed to follow the pattern of others within his peer group.

I frequently observed Jim under the influence of marijuana and alcohol. During the course of the study, I noted he had increased already heavy drug use. He began to use some pills and hallucinogens, although infrequently.

Jim asked several times when I was going to begin my final interviews. Other subjects had also inquired, so no particular note was made of the matter. When the interviews began, Jim asked when I would interview him.

I was attempting to interview wall "crew" members in as close temporal proximity as possible, so I informed Jim that I would interview him on the following day.

I visited the wall area early the next afternoon. I had an interview scheduled and was to drive another subject from the wall to my apartment. Jim asked what time he could be interviewed. I told him that he should arrive at my apartment in about two hours.

During my interview with the other subject, Jim telephoned to ask if he could arrive early. The interview was nearing completion so I told Jim he could come by shortly thereafter. During his interview, Jim did not seem anxious although he asked that the tape recorder be turned off for the item and discussion regarding parental conflict. There had been a considerable amount of conflict between his parents. The interview shows that Jim's early life was spent without a father in his home. He had lived with relatives for some periods and regarded one such relative as a substitute father figure. His mother later remarried. Although some conflict existed in the home thereafter, Jim did not feel that his stepfather was inadequate and referred to him as "my Dad." All this occurred before Jim reached the age of nine. When Jim was in fifth grade, his mother had a severe mental breakdown. She suffered a setback when Jim was in seventh grade. Throughout the interview, and subsequently, Jim discounted any effect of his mother's mental illness on him. The remainder of the interview followed a rather typical pattern. Later, I would verify all of his responses, except those referring to homosexual incidents. During the interview, Jim had only referred to a few homosexual incidents, such as advances which had been made to him while he was hitchhiking or changing clothes at the beach. He seemed apologetic that he had never experienced any heterosexual relations until he was in the 11th grade.

When the interview was completed, Jim lingered. He told me that he had a problem and that he thought he knew the solution would be to tell someone but he was unable to discuss the matter. I sensed that Jim wished to tell me and, for a rather lengthy period of time, attempted various maneuvers to allow him to feel sufficiently comfortable to do so. Finally, Jim, with great initial discomfort, was able to discuss the matter with *me.*

Jim informed me that he had difficulty in urinating in public places and he believed he knew the reason. He believed that, if he could discuss the reason, the problem would be alleviated. Jim said that he first noticed the difficulty when he was in the seventh grade, and he was certain that it developed because of homosexual activities he had engaged in during the sixth and into the seventh grade. The activities involved "homosexual play" among a group of youngsters the same age as Jim. The activities had occurred on numerous occasions and Jim said he never connected this play as "queer" until a group of his seventh grade classmates were discussing "queers" in the boys' rest room at school." One of the boys, who had participated in the activities with Jim, said to the others, "Well, what would you guys think if Jim and I did those kinds of things?"

The remark was not taken seriously by the others, but Jim was frightened. He no longer took part in the homosexual activities. Shortly thereafter, he discovered that he was unable to urinate in restrooms when others were present or when they could hear if he was doing so. He recalled that the initial occasion occurred when a junior high school "jock" was in the school restroom with him. The problem grew steadily worse over the next several years. Jim had told no one. He had avoided public functions, ceased sports activities, declined opportunities to make lengthy trips and experienced extreme discomfort many times.

Jim had, however, one source of relief. He discovered that when he was inebriated or under the influence of marijuana he was able to urinate in the presence of others. What began to bother him, however, was that it was necessary for him to increase his intake of drugs to obtain the same effects. He had begun to use other drugs, hallucinogens and sedatives, intermittently. He expressed the fear that he might become an alcoholic and, several times, made the statement, "At least I haven't become a heroin addict."

Jim expressed relief at having narrated the history of these events to me. He appeared to be optimistic that, having done so, he would have solved his problem. I attempted to give him encouragement, but informed him of my professional limitations. Whenever I hinted that he might seek more professional, psychological help elsewhere, Jim reacted quickly. He would say words, such as, "No. I trust you. I don't want to talk to anyone else. I'm sure it'll be ok now that I've told you, anyway."

I told Jim that we should continue to have such talks in order that he could let me know how he was doing. He agreed that I could ask him when I met him and he would not be embarrassed if no one else was around. He indicated we would talk again at length.

In the meantime, I consulted with a priest, who was also a clinical psychologist. Jim was a Catholic but had ceased practicing his religion and going to confession after the first homosexual activity. The priest offered professional advice and said he would be willing to accept Jim's case at a downtown clinic where he practiced as a "doctor" without his Roman collar.

Jim informed me, a few days later, that he had urinated within hearing distance of others. He continued to tell me that he was making progress (but not uniformly) each time I inquired. He was unable to urinate when others were immediately present and he was not under the influence of any drug.

A few weeks later, Jim asked if we could talk again at length. I arranged an appointment. On this occasion, Jim told me that he had a girlfriend with whom he "was really in love." He felt that she was unlike other girls with whom he had sexual intercourse in order to "prove my masculinity." He informed me that he felt the relationship was genuine. Jim had spent the night with her, caressing and kissing her without having intercourse, because he wanted sexual intercourse to be "right." He was anxious to talk to me because he wanted to take a vacation with the girl and could not do so with his "handicap." He was unable to tell the girl.

I used this occasion to have Jim tell me more details of his sexual feelings and earlier homosexual relationships. I attempted to have him "talk it out." He appeared to be impressed that I was accepting, understanding and not "shocked." I also urged Jim to see someone else, informing him that I would soon be leaving Golden Beach. He agreed to this request and I told him of the priest's offer. I urged him to continue such consultation even after his "immediate problem" was solved. The conversation ended after Jim had burst into tears telling me that it was the first time in years that he had felt relaxed. He sobbed, "I really love her! I *want to get* rid of this!"

I attempted to reassure Jim and described relaxation techniques to him.

The following evening, my dinner was interrupted by a telephone call. Jim was phoning me from his place of employment. He exclaimed, "*I did it!* There was a guy standing in the room right next to me and everything! I had to call to tell you. I hadn't smoked a joint or had anything to drink or anything!"

I arranged for Jim's appointment with the priest-psychologist and accompanied him on his initial visit.

During the brief period following these events until my departure from Golden Beach, Jim no longer had difficulties in urination and continued to express his happiness and optimism. He did not, however, immediately change his drug patterns. Today, he is happily married and a successful businessman. He continues to express his profound appreciation to me.

The case of Jim is dramatic and unique. Ordinarily, there is no clear-cut evidence of psychological difficulties manifested by outward physical manifestations. Thus, relief of psychological discomfort by the use of drugs would not be as obvious to the users or to the researcher as was the case with Jim. It appears that several elements of the McCord-Chein model are present within this case including early parental conflict, father-absence, homosexual activity that resulted in psychological discomfort, and the use of drugs to relieve the discomfort. The connections within most of the data are considerably more tenuous than they are in the case of Jim. The weaknesses of such "links" will be discussed shortly.

Other points should be made regarding Jim's case. First, Jim did not admit to any homosexual activity or refer to his problem during the interview. He discussed it only after the interview had been completed. This points to the difficulty in obtaining this type of information in the best of research situations. Jim initially admitted the earlier homosexual activity and his problem only when he was faced with an immediate physical manifestation. He discussed it more fully during our second visit when the physical manifestations were impeding his continued relationship with a girl of whom he appeared to be quite fond. Second, when the immediate "problem" was relieved, Jim's use of drugs did not decrease. The best that might be inferred is that continued involvement with and progression into the use of different substances was, perhaps, slowed or prevented. By the time his psychological discomforts were dealt with professionally Jim had developed patterns and involvement in the drug subculture. Thus, for several years, he continued his heavy use of alcohol and marijuana. Today, he is drug-free, except for an occasional beer or wine with dinner.

AN EXAMINATION OF THE OVERALL DATA IN SUPPORT OF THE MCCORD-CHEIN MODEL

In the first section of this chapter, I described my analysis of various family factors which were compatible with the McCord-Chein model. The data generally indicated support for the model. An exception was the lack of support for the role of an "overprotective mother." In the next section, I analyzed various aspects of the latter stages of the model. The data indicated that there were relationships between degree of drug use and several other variables, namely, sexual difficulties, problems of sexual identity, an independence-dependence struggle and the use of drugs to overcome feelings of psychological discomfort.

However, I urged caution in the interpretation of the statistical relationships. Various temporal priorities and "connecting links" within the theoretical framework were unclear. Most responses indicated that problems in the family occurred prior to initial drug use. In other instances, the temporal sequence was unknown or in the reverse of the sequence predicted by the model. Examples were found in the relationship between drug use and both initial sexual intercourse and sexual problems. Initial sexual intercourse typically took place after the young male's initial drug use. Likewise, most sexual problems occurred after initial use of drugs.

Certain "connecting links" are critical to the McCord-Chein model. The first is the link between family socialization and sexual identity. The second is the link between sexual difficulties and the use of drugs to overcome feelings of psychological discomfort. It was felt that sexual difficulties might be an indication of problems with sexual identity.

I took additional steps to obtain an indication from the data that would support these links. I examined the variables which appeared to have the strongest relationship to degrees of drug use and appeared to be consistent with the model's logical sequence in combination with each other. Thus, I selected the variables "parental conflict," "lack of an inadequate father figure," "doubts of parental care," "heterosexual difficulty" and "use of drugs to overcome psychological discomforts." Based on each subject's responses to questions about these variables, I examined them with one another in a step-by-step correlation. Although there were correlations between them at each step, when I examined all of them together at the final step, only five subjects who would have fit the entire profile. That is, only five of the 31 heavy users out of 72 subjects responded affirmatively to the questions measuring each of these variables.

Given these considerations and the lack of ability to definitively establish the temporal sequence, the McCord-Chein model appears to be of limited value in explained degrees of drug use among the subjects of this research. Based on the data, it might be said that, at best, the model explains the pattern of only a few individuals. The extreme cases of Ty and Jim are obvious examples. However, the McCord-Chein model does not account for the remaining 83 percent (26) of the heavy users.

AN EXAMINATION OF THE SAME DATA IN SUPPORT OF SOCIAL CONTROL THEORIES

Up to this point, all of the data were consistent with social control explanations. These theories envision direct relationships between family background and deviant behavior, including drug use and sexual behavior. They allow for explanations of drug use that are free of the necessity to demonstrate the temporal sequence of family factors, struggles for independence, problems with sexual identity, psychological discomforts and the use of drugs to alleviate psychological discomforts.

Additionally, social control theories appear to be in greater conformity with the subjects' own perceptions as to why they use drugs. The subjects' use of drugs in order to relate with females, for sexual purposes and to overcome psychological discomforts were only a few items from a long list of reasons to and occasion for drug use. These same subjects used drugs to sleep, to enjoy food more, and before movies and school. Moreover, the question that was responded to with the greatest degree of affirmation was "Have you ever used pot, booze, or other drugs, just to 'have fun?'" The results were overwhelming. Ninety-three percent of all subjects who had ever used drugs did so to have fun, and used drugs most often for this sole purpose. This compares with only 51 percent of the users who had ever used drugs to overcome feelings of psychological discomfort, and 46 percent who had ever used drugs to enjoy sexual activity (which did not exclude "having fun"). It is quite probable that Differential Association as well as social control theories may provide better explanations for overall variation in drug use and non-use.

SOCIAL CONTROL AND DIFFERENTIAL ASSOCIATION THEORIES

Both social control theories and Differential Association emphasize the role of peer groups as well as the role of families. Social control theories emphasize the relationship between peer groups and ties to conventional activities. The major emphasis of Differential Association is that deviant behavior is learned in primary groups, including peer groups. In this section, I explore the relationships between family, peer groups and drug use.

Lack of communication and lack of an adequate father-figure.

Positive family-child communication is an essential component of Differential Association theory. Likewise, Hirschi saw it as critical in his analysis of social control, stating: "In the ideal control situation, parents are the centers of a communication network . . . "[4]

To the question, "Do you communicate well with your parents?", every non-user and all but three of the light users responded affirmatively, but a majority of the heavy users (61 percent) and regular users (55 percent) responded negatively. More significantly, when controlled for lack of an adequate father- figure, none of the non-users or light users stated that they lacked both an adequate father figure and parental communication as compared with 34 percent of the heavy and regular users.

Use of drugs and alcohol by parents.

If parent-child verbal communication is important, it is logical that parental behavior would be equally if not more important in influencing children's behavior. This aspect of socialization effect is compatible with social control frameworks, but, in some ways, is more directly related to Sutherland's Differential Association theory. Accordingly, I used a number of questions to determine drug and alcohol use by parents.

I asked each subject if he was aware if either of his parents used marijuana. Four subjects reported that their mothers had smoked marijuana and continued to do so. Six reported that their fathers had smoked marijuana and continued to do so. Two subjects reported that their fathers had "tried" marijuana. Two others said they were not certain but "thought" their fathers had used marijuana. Five subjects had smoked marijuana with one or the other of their parents. One son stated that his father was growing marijuana at his home. (The son did not live with his father.). The father of another had pleaded guilty to a charge of smuggling marijuana across the U.S. Mexican border. The amount of marijuana involved exceeded 100 kilos.

All but two of the above cases involved parents of heavy users. The other cases involved the mother of a regular user and the father of a light user.

There was little variation among both subjects and parents who had ever used alcohol. Sixty-five of the 72 subjects used alcohol. There were only ten subjects who reported that neither of their parents used alcohol. Of these, eight were from two families, the Jones Family and the Gilroy Family.

When "heavy use of alcohol" by son was compared with "heavy use of alcohol by either of parents," a different pattern emerged. Two-thirds of those who reported that one of their parents was a heavy user of alcohol were themselves heavy users of alcohol.

The patterns of behavior in response to alcoholic parents were not consistent. For example, two youths came from families in which both parents were alcoholics. One responded by renouncing all alcohol. He rarely used marijuana. The other youth had used alcohol and other drugs extensively.

Peer influences: Processes of introduction to and continued involvement with drugs.

Although, at the theoretical level, Differential Association places emphasis upon primary relationships and early socialization within the home, a considerable amount of research has concentrated upon the process of learning deviant behavior within peer groups. As I have described in previous chapters, there was a consistency within the qualitative findings that indicated home life and the family variables were related to drug use patterns among the subjects. I examined peer influences as well as the role played by families which affected peer relationships.

The first step was to establish the degree of relationship between current peer association and current degree of drug use. To measure this association, I asked two series of questions. Each question elicited either an affirmative or a negative response. The first series measured overall peer associations and situations which provided an opportunity to use marijuana or alcohol as follows,

"Do most of your friends smoke pot?"
"Is there pot at most of the parties you go to?"
"Is there beer at most of the parties you go to?"

The second series of questions dealt with "close" friends and their use of drugs, as follows,

"Do most of your close friends use pot?"

"Do most of your close friends drink beer?"
"Do most of your close friends use other drugs?"

The results in Table 11 show the percent of subjects who responded affirmatively to each item. The data indicate a very strong relationship between degree of drug use and peer association. The very large positive gammas in each instance are indicative of the strength and direction of these relationships. However, considerable caution is urged in the interpretation of these statistics. First, they reflect the peer associations at the time of the interview. Second, it must be pointed out that a great deal of sampling of the responses took place within peer groups and through "snowball" techniques whereby one friend introduced the researcher to another. Finally, gammas and relationships greater than .90 would suggest that one is measuring two indicators of the same phenomenon.Consideration of the observational data in previous chapters and the realities of the drug subculture would tend to confirm this.

Degree of drug use itself could be seen as a measure of involvement in the drug subculture. Likewise, the items, "Most friends use pot," "Most friends use beer," "Beer at most parties attended," and "Most friends use other drugs," could also be seen as measurements of involvement in that subculture. Each of these gammas is .95 or larger. In regard to "Pot at most parties attended," the gamma of .75 in the table appears low. However, when I eliminated those who did not attend parties, gamma increased to .85. Marijuana use at parties often took place quietly and in small groups removed from other activities. Thus, it was possible that the activity was not always observed by the other participants. This was confirmed by my field observations.

Only 69 percent of the subjects responded in the affirmative to the item, "Most close friends use pot." Because it indicates the elements of both quantity and proximity of peer association, it is, perhaps, the most valid indicator to determine the degree and type of peer association envisioned by Differential Association theory.

Nevertheless, neither the mere association with drug using peers nor opportunities to use marijuana or beer are not, by themselves, of extremely substantive significance. There were other issues to consider in the complex learning process envisioned by Differential Association, such as,

Was the process of drug use and peer association cyclical? That is, do peers introduce an individual to drugs? Then, does the individual use more drugs as he associates with others who use drugs? Does this 'secondary association' lead to still further drug involvement? To a deeper commitment to the drug subculture? And so forth?

I dealt with these issues separately.

TABLE 11

AFFIRMATIVE RESPONSES TO ITEMS INDICATING ASSOCIATION WITH DRUG-USING PEERS BY DEGREE OF DRUG USE

	Heavy Users	Regular Users	Light Users	Non-Users	All Subjects	*Gamma*
Most Friends Use Pot	100%	100%	70%	29%	83%	*.95*
Most Close Friends Use Pot	100%	73%	44%	14%	69%	*.80*
Pot at Most Parties	97%	100%	76%	20%	81%	*.75*
Most Friends Use Beer	100%	100%	78%	29%	86%	*.96*
Beer at Most Parties	100%	100%	91%	40%	88%	*.96*
Most Friends Use Other Drugs	77%	18%	0	0	35%	*.97*

The first issue I examined was that of introduction to drugs, the initial experience. I asked rather broad, open-ended questions, as follows,

> "What were the circumstances when you first used pot?"
> "What were the circumstances when you first used beer?"
> "What was the circumstance when you first used (each other drug indicated by name)?"

I coded the responses according to whether the individual was introduced to each substance by a peer of the same age or younger, by an individual a year or more older than the subject, and, if by older individual(s), whether such individual(s) was (were) an older sibling and/or peer(s) of an older sibling. These distinctions were made in order to categorize responses, such as,

> "Jes' some friends had it and I had always wanted to try it, so we did it together. That was Bill and Lonnie." (Peers)

> "My brothers were smokin' it, an' I found them in the garage one day. They got me to smoke it so I wouldn't be able to squeal on them." (Older siblings)

> "My sister and her boyfriend were drinking when my Mom was gone, and so they asked me if I wanted to have some, and I did." (Older sibling and sibling's peer)

> "Tony came over to look for Joe one day. I guess to smoke some pot. Anyway, Joe wasn't home so Tony asked me if I'd ever smoked. I told him, 'No.' So he says, 'Would you like to try it?' I figured, 'Why not?'"(Peer of an old sibling)

In many cases the subject had initially used a substance (typically alcohol) at a party. These were coded as "peers." I eliminated those responses indicating that the person first used alcohol within his home under parental supervision.

In most cases, peers had initially introduced the young male to a substance. However, I found a particular pattern. This pattern provided me with an opportunity to understand the manner in which each succeeding "generation" initially became involved with various drugs. Table 12 contains the data regarding the introduction of substances to subjects by older individuals. A substantial number of the youths were introduced to each kind of drug by older individuals. Further, a substantial number of these older individuals were either older siblings or peers of older siblings. In the case of marijuana, 28 of the 64 subjects who had used marijuana were introduced to it by an older person. Eighteen of these 28 subjects were introduced by an older sibling or the older sibling's peers. These 18 subjects made up 28 percent of all subjects who had used marijuana, and 64 percent of 28 subjects who had been introduced by an older person. Subjects were frequently initiated to "other drugs" by older persons but the older persons were less likely to be older siblings than was the case with marijuana. Only 30 percent of those who had used alcohol were introduced to it by older persons. The approximate number of years between the subject and the older person are shown in the table. There were no particular trends in the data by or substantial differences between various categories of drug use.

The interview data, shown in Table 12, quantify the patterns that I observed in my field research. Typically, a 12-or-13-year-old was introduced to marijuana by his older brother or an older group of youths at the beach. It seemed that the younger person was attempting to be accepted as "grown-up, "when he first used the substance. Shortly thereafter, the younger male youth would initiate his peers. The new, younger group of drug users would then utilize the contacts of the older group to obtain drugs. However, the pattern was not universal and there were norms prohibiting the practice of introducing younger individuals to drugs. These norms were violated frequently enough, however, to continue a cycle of increasingly younger individuals using marijuana and alcohol over time.

To determine the degree to which inner controls were breached by peer or sibling influence, each subject who had used marijuana was asked, "When you first smoked pot, you may have had some barrier against using it, because of drug education, your parents, or whatever, what made you break that barrier and go ahead and use pot?"

There were a wide variety of responses. The following are examples of some typical responses,

> "Other people were doing it. Curiosity, I guess. I thought, 'Why not?' And, I liked it."

> "Because my sister kept telling me to."

> "Well, pot kinda broke down barriers. You know, to get into the group. I was scared of it, but I did it to be cool."

"Because of my friends. I didn't want to seem different. If you don't, you're a square."

TABLE 12

INTRODUCTION TO DRUGS BY OLDER PERSONS, INCLUDING OLDER SIBLINGS, BY DEGREE OF DRUG USE

	Heavy Users	**Regular Users**	**Light Users**	**All Subjects**	**Median Number of Years Older**
Marijuana					
Any Older Person	52%	36%	35%	44%	2 years
Older Sibling &/or Sibling's Peers.	26%	27%	30%	28%	2 years
Alcohol					
Any Older Person	39%	18%	26%	30%	2 years
Older Sibling &/or Sibling's Peers.	16%	9%	17%	14%	1 year
Other Drugs					
Any Older Person	43%	20%	60%	46%	3 years
Older Sibling &/or Sibling's Peers.	*3%*	*0*	*40%*	*8%*	*2 years*

> "Oh, it was just me an' a friend, now with a crowd. The same as with as with beer. I guess we were kinda at that experimenting stage."

> "Peer pressure! I felt alienated because I wasn't using it. After, I didn't care if I was alienated. I didn't like it."

> "I was curious. Everyone else had been using it. It didn't seem to be hurting them any, so I didn't believe any of the stories about it."

> "There were no barriers! I just did it."

A considerable number of the subjects mentioned that some degree of peer influence in their initial decision to try marijuana. Forty-eight percent of all those who used marijuana indicated they had done so under peer influence. Thirty-one percent indicated a degree of curiosity was present in their initial decision. (It might be further argued that curiosity was, in itself, a product of peer influence. That is, the widespread use of marijuana among the youthful population and the subsequent attention paid to this phenomenon produced a desire within the person to experiment himself.) The remaining subjects said there had been no barrier to their initial use.

In order to trace the reaction of each subject to his initial use of marijuana and how such initial use affected later drug patterns, I asked each one was asked, "Did you get high the first time (you used marijuana)?" If a negative response was given, I asked, "The second time?" And so on.

I also asked."Did you get into it (marijuana use) immediately or gradually?"

I coded the responses to questions about "getting high" according to whether the subject had indicated they had experienced the marijuana euphoria on his initial, second, third, or subsequent occasion of use. Some subjects never experienced the expected euphoria.

I coded the responses the questions about "getting into" marijuana use according to whether the subject had responded, "immediately," or, if not, the length of time separating his initial marijuana use from the time he became involved with marijuana, if ever. I then dichotomized the responses into the categories: "Involved within six months" and "Involved within six months to three years." I analyzed the results according to current degree of drug use. The results of both sets of analyses are shown in Table 13.

TABLE 13

MARIJUANA EXPERIENCES AND INCREASING INVOLVEMENT WITH MARIJUANA BY DEGREE OF CURRENT DRUG USE

	Heavy Users (n = 31)	**Regular Users** (n = 11)	**Light Users** (n = 20)	**Non-Users** (n = 2)	**Total** (n = 64)
Experienced "High"					
1st Time	55%	18%	20%	0%	38%
2nd Time	16%	55%	35%	0%	28%
3rd or Subsequent Time	29%	9%	15%	0%	20%
Never	0%	18%	20%	100%	14%
Became Involved With Marijuana					
Immediately	42%	18%	10%	0%	27%
Within 6 months	32%	46%	25%	0%	31%
Within 6 months to 3 years	26%	36%	15%	0%	23%
Never	0%	0%	50%	100%	19%

Above subjects who <u>never</u> experienced a "high" by the number of times they have used marijuana.
(n = 9)

Once	*5*
2 to 10 times	*2*
10+ times	*2*

The data indicate some rather interesting patterns. There appeared to be a relationship between experiencing the euphoria initially and subsequent degree of drug use. There also appeared to be a relationship between the point at which the subject became involved in the drug subculture and his subsequent degree of drug use. Heavier users reported perceptions of the marijuana euphoria, or "high," at earlier stages of marijuana use than did light users. Heavier users also reported becoming involved in the drug subculture at a more rapid pace than others.

The data could indicate support for social control theory as well as Differential Association. The subjects appeared to have varying degrees of inner controls (perhaps resulting from peer definitions) which either permitted or inhibited them from experiencing the euphoria of marijuana use and, once experienced, allowing them to become more immediately involved in continued use of marijuana.

These data are also consistent with Howard Becker's interactionist explanation "Becoming a Marijuana User." As Becker explained, the being initiated into marijuana use must first properly consume a mixture of marijuana and air, then perceive the "high," and have the experience defined for him as pleasurable.[5]

The responses of four subjects were of particular interest. They had used marijuana up to 30 or more times without experiencing a "high." I probed them to determine what they had experienced. One had recently purchased his third "lid" of marijuana and was earnestly attempting to experience the feeling which he perceived his peers had experienced. Another had smoked marijuana intermittently, over a period of four years, and could not understand why he had never experienced the "high."

The data indicate the differential rate of involvement in the drug subculture. The explanation of Becker would suggest peer influence within these processes.[6]

In order to examine the process of peer group influence prior to and following initial drug use, each subject was asked, "Have you ever changed groups or the people you hang around with?"

If the subject responded affirmatively, I asked the next series of items,

What group did you leave?
What group did you join?
Were there more drugs, or less drugs, in the new group?
Did you then change your use of drugs?

Did you use more drugs? Or less drugs?
When did each of these changes take place?

I coded the answers according to whether changes in peer groups had occurred "prior to" or "following" initial drug use, and by groups "using less drugs," "using more drugs" or "the same amount of drugs." I coded the change in use according to whether it was in the direction of "more drugs" or "less drugs," or had remained "unchanged."

I analyzed the data by changes prior to, and following, initial drug use and the direction of the change by the individual within the new peer group.

Only one subject reported, entering a new peer group and being initiated into drugs by the new group. He was explicit in his acknowledgment that he had used drugs to be accepted by the new group (the wall "crew"). Four non-users entered new peer groups but the new the degree of drug use in the new group did not differ from their previous peer groups. None of the four began to use drugs after changing groups. One subject reported that his two closest friends during junior high school had been heavy users of drugs but that he had never used drugs with them. In high school, he joined a new group of peers, composed of very light users and non-users. He felt more comfortable in the new group and remained a non-user. Overall, changing peer groups did not appear to have a significant influence on initial use of drugs.

Twenty-two individuals, however, reported changing peer groups after their initiation to drugs. Only two of these subjects did not change their drug patterns in conformity with the new group. One of the two moved to a new group that used drugs with the same frequency as had his previous peer group. Another began to associate with a new group that used drugs less than his previous peer group but did not change his pattern of use. All subjects who moved into new groups that used drugs more frequently than their previous peer groups subsequently increased their own use.

Eight subjects reported changing groups several times. They changed increased or decreased their user of drugs according to the new peer group they had joined each time.

There were a wide variety of reasons given as reasons for changes in peer groups. Many of the reported changes were the result of changes in area of residence. Is some cases the subjects reported changing groups for the purpose of changing their own drug use. In other instances, an indirect influence related to both a new peer group and changing drug patterns appeared to be operating. The following are some composites of portions of several of the responses,

> "Yeah, I moved from Alta Vista down here. That's when I began to hang out at the wall. When I got down here, I quit using reds, 'cuz nobody down here used them."
>
> "I move all over the place. For a while, I hung around with surfers. That's when I smoked the most. I jes' kinda didn't like the scene there. Ya know, like they own the place an' are too good for anybody else, so I began hanging out north of the pier. There was a lot less pot there. I was getting tired of it anyway . . . But, anyway, ya know, the soshes were too stuck on themselves, so sometimes I got down to Lime Avenue in the summer, or hang around with the jocks during football . . . Oh, jocks? They use less than the surfers, but they're too busy playing football and doin' other things. But they go to parties and stuff a lot more than some of the guys. You know."
>
> "Oh, yeah, since I been gittin' into soccer, I hardly ever hang around with them guys anymore . . . Oh, yeah, less drugs . . . Yeah, that's what I mean, I don't smoke or drink as much any more as I used to."
>
> "I guess you could say a new group. When I started workin' at Berger's (restaurant), all the guys there were takin' speed, so I started to, too. I was 16, in 10th grade."
>
> "Well, I guess you could say with me it was the opposite. I mean when I quit doin' drugs, I still hung around with the same group, but then, gradually, I began to hang around with other friends. I still have friends at Lime Avenue and go down there a lot . . . but you couldn't say I hang around them anymore."

Some said they had changed peer groups because changes in their religious life, others because of surfing or sports. Still others indicated that they, more or less purposively, left or entered a group because of changes in their own drug use or the desire to change their patterns of drug use. It was obvious that the young males were quite aware of the patterns of drug use within the various groups and of the influence of each new group upon their own behavior.

The data suggest rather stable drug patterns within groups comprising the youth subculture in Golden Beach, with individuals often changing groups and their own drug patterns for various reasons. At the same time, there were a few cases in which youths entered groups aware of the potential peer influence regarding drugs. They were confident of their own "inner" defense mechanisms to resist this influence. In each of those cases, the youth was initiated into drug use by the new peer group.

Nevertheless, some youths who had never used marijuana responded to my queries about the peer pressures they felt, as follows,

> "I have (felt peer pressure) for pot. Not for beer."
>
> "Yeah, but I promised myself, after what happened to my brother (a heavy user, killed in an auto accident under the influence of marijuana) that I would never use pot, and I never have."
>
> "I used to feel peer pressure when I was littler, but not anymore. All my friends and people that know me know I don't use it."
>
> "I tell them that I used to smoke and my best friend got busted so I quit."

The data, thus far, suggested that peer influence was considerable. The influence was apparent in the process of introduction to various substances. It was also apparent in the movements both out of and deeper into the drug subculture.

Church groups, sports activities and family influence.

Two types of peer groups were particularly effective in influencing young people to conform to conventional behavior and in influencing them to either not use drugs or to decrease their drug use. Participation in these groups appeared to have been influenced by families and factors related to families. The groups were church youth groups and sports groups. As I came to realize their importance I concentrated on them in far greater detail than I had originally anticipated.

During the early stage of the field research, I observed that activity in church youth groups were, for the most part, concentrated among three congregations. The first was the previously described fundamentalist-evangelical group who claimed success in rehabilitating former young drug users. The second was the St. Patrick's Catholic youth program, "Drop-In," in which young people exercised a considerable amount of planning and direction. The third was a Baptist youth program which had been very active in Golden Beach but, four years earlier, had sold its property to St. Patrick's and moved to Alta Vista. Other church youth groups, an older, more established fundamentalist group, a Lutheran group and a Methodist group, had been more active five years earlier. Their influence and attendance had declined considerably. Youths from the more established fundamentalist group began to attend the meetings of the newer fundamentalist group. The same was true of many from the Baptist group. Some Lutheran and Methodist youths attended the Catholic youth group. The three groups met on Wednesday evenings.

I attended meetings and services at both the fundamentalist-evangelical church and the Catholic church. I played the role of an adult leader at St. Patrick's, but was not an official member of the organizing "team." The groups had several differences and similarities,

1) Both groups were directed toward young people and young people held leadership roles within them.

2) The fundamentalist group drew from a wide area of San Diego, was located in Alta Vista, and drew an average attendance exceeding 1,000 each Wednesday. It included those of all ages, but its main appeal was to those in their late teens and 20s. St. Patrick's was located in Golden Beach. Attendance at Drop-In varied between 75 and 110 each week. It was limited to those of high school age. There were separate organizations for junior high and college-age youths within the parish. Attendance at Sunday Masses in the parish exceeded 1,200 each week.

3) The fundamentalist group featured rock bands playing "Christian - Rock" music before, after and during the services. Individual socializing individually took place after the services, frequently in small gatherings at restaurants. The Catholic group's music was provided by its own members who played guitars and bongo drums during services and other activities. The Catholic group interwove religious services and social activities each week. Outside recreational activities were held at various times during the year. Each youth was encouraged to become closely acquainted with each other member.

4) Both groups downplayed "denominationalism" and encouraged those of all faiths to join them. However, the fundamentalist preacher often

criticized other religions. It appeared that youths with fundamentalist and Baptist religious backgrounds gravitated toward this group, and those with backgrounds in more institutionalized religious backgrounds, Catholic and non-Catholic, gravitated toward the Catholic group.

5) The fundamentalist group, in both prayer and sermons, relied heavily on the Bible, and, at times, ridiculed the social and behavioral sciences. The Catholic group prayed from and read the Bible, but often incorporated sociological and psychological "games" to encourage members to "share," "express themselves" and "interact."

6) Each week, the preacher at the fundamentalist group ended his sermon with an emotional appeal for "repentance" and individuals were encouraged to "accept Jesus," have their sins forgiven by raising their hands, come down the center aisle to be "saved" and receive a free copy of the Bible. The preacher's arguments about the "approaching end of the world" led up to these closings. Catholic youths were provided opportunities to make private "confessions" regularly during the year separate from Drop-In. Sermons were brief, less emotional and the general tenor one of optimism and hope. Emotions during the Wednesday night Drop-In sessions were heightened by "sharing" with each other, holding hands during the recitation of the Lord's Prayer and by hugging each person during a "kiss of peace" ritual.

7) Most males who attended the fundamentalist meetings were former drug user or those seeking to reform. Total abstinence from all drugs was required to be a "Christian." Anyone who used drugs was "not a Christian." Although the entire spectrum of drug use behavior was represented, Drop-In typically attracted light and non-users of drugs. Drugs were not condoned, but there was not a specific call for a commitment of total abstinence.

8) The fundamentalist preacher, who had been heavily involved in the use of hallucinogens several years earlier, strongly condemned alcohol and other drugs each week. Alcohol and other drugs were rarely given specific mention during Drop-In's activities.

The fundamentalist group appeared to continuously attract new members who drastically reduced their drug use. However, there was a constant turnover and many youths left the group to resume their former patterns within a few weeks to several months.

The Baptist group appeared to attract some new members, but most of the group's members had been associated with the church from their childhood. This Baptist group also condemned the use of all drugs.

The Catholic group's membership appeared quite stable. A majority of its members had been members of the parish since childhood. Those who were not Catholics and attended more than one meeting appeared to develop regular patterns of weekly attendance as well. Heavy users, Catholic and others, seemed ill-at-ease among the group and, typically, did not attend more than once or twice. They were heard to remark that they had not enjoyed the "head games" or the physical contacts during the exercises and religious services. Many referred to the group's members as "snobs." The group did not make claims that they were successful in reforming drug users. The priest-moderator felt the program was "preventive" and "not equipped" to deal with heavy drug users and "kids with a lot of problems." Phil, once a heavy user, credited this group with his curtailment of drug use. Another subject claimed that the group, and his girlfriend who attended with him, had prevented his deeper involvement in the drug subculture.

During the interviews I attempted to quantify these patterns. I asked, "Are there any other clubs or activities you are or were in, outside of school? Have you belonged to any church youth groups?" I analyzed the results according to whether or not the youth was currently active in a youth group and his degree of drug use. The results indicated a very strong relationship between current activity in a church youth group and degree of drug use, with a very large, positive gamma of .89. However, this interpretation has to be qualified because I used church youth groups as a source to obtain non-users for the sample.

In addition, I examined the responses for trends in drug use compared to involvement in the three church groups. The results indicate that those subjects active in the fundamentalist group had all used marijuana, and all but one had immediately quit using drugs upon joining the group. Those who left the church group returned to their former patterns of drug use. Three of the five subjects who remained active in the group at the time of their interviews continued to abstain from drugs. One continued to use drugs but to a lesser degree than previously. One remained in the group but returned to his former patterns of heavy use. There were similar trends among the Baptist group members who joined that group and later ceased their involvement with that group. Those who remained in the Baptist group, however, continued their previous drug patterns (light or non-use). These three subjects had attended the church since childhood and no major conversion had taken place in their lives. Subjects who had been involved in the Catholic group did not typically change their drug use patterns upon entering or leaving that group.

Thus, involvement in church youth groups affected the subjects' drug use according to the emphasis placed upon drug use within the particular group. Nevertheless, dramatic and instantaneous "conversions" were rather rare in bring about long-term cessation of drug use.

Given these patterns, I decided to examine the data, controlling for parental practice of religion. I had asked each subject if either he had or his parents, currently or in the past, had regularly practiced any religion.

TABLE 14

ACTIVITY IN CHURCH YOUTH GROUPS BY PARENTAL PRACTICE OF RELIGION

	Parents Practice A Religion (n = 50)	**Parents Do Not Practice A Religion** (n = 22)	
Subjects Active in Church Youth Group	*34%*	*9%*	*n* = 20
Subjects Not Active in Church Youth Group	*66%*	*91%*	*n* = 52

Q = .67

	Parents Practice A Religion	**Parents Do Not Practice A Religion**	
Subjects Joined Group and Quit	*18%*	*71%*	*n* = 9
Subjects Joined and Continued to Participate	*82%*	*29%*	*n* = 20

Q = .84

The results, shown in Table 14, indicate a substantial relationship between parental practice of religion and current activity in a church youth group. Q is a substantial .67. However, there was an even stronger relationship between continued long-term participation in such groups and parental practice of religion, with a Q of .84. Thus, the data produced evidence of another connection to family background. Family background both affected participation and continued participation in religious groups. At the same time, participation in the groups was associated with lesser degrees of drug use.

Team sports.

Participation in team sports *was the* second aspect of peer group activity which appeared to be associated with a lesser degree of involvement in the drug subculture. I asked each subject who was currently enrolled in high school, "Do you participate in any team sports?" If the subject had graduated from high school, I phrased the question in the past tense.

The data indicate a very strong and consistent, negative relationship between participation in sports and degree of drug use. Gamma, a negative .76, reflected this. Both light and non-users had more than an 80 percent participation rate in sports. A majority of the regular users (64 percent) participated in one or more sports. However, only 19 percent of the heavy users had ever participated in team sports.

My observational findings indicated that sports activities served as control mechanism, so that youths decreased their drug use when they were participating in sports. Eight-six percent of the non-users and 83 percent of the light users had participated in team sport yet only 19% of the heavy users had ever participated in team sports. Moreover, 12 subjects who were using drugs said they had participated in sports in the past, but withdrew from school sports. Four withdrew from sports prior to their initial drug use. Four withdrew after they began to use drugs. I was unable to determine the exact sequence of four others because they withdrew from sports at approximately the same time as their initial drug use. It is possible, therefore, that the two variables were interacting, so that increased participation in sports served as an incentive to decrease drug use and decreased drug use increased the potential for sports participation.

I made an additional to determine the extent to which prior family socialization may have influenced participation in sports. I controlled the data for three family factors, "Father absence," "Father adequacy," and "Overprotective mother." In addition, I asked the following two questions,

> "Do you and your Dad (or whoever had been named as a father figure) ever talk about sports?"
>
> "Do you and your Dad (or whoever had been named as a father figure) attend sports together?"

I recorded as positive responses all cases, past or current, in which the father figure had discussed sports with the son or attended athletic events with him in the past. Thus, the responses reflected all prior socialization regardless of the age of the subject. I included Mrs. Gilroy as a "father figure" for the two items because she had been described as such by each of her four sons. The results of the analysts are shown in Table #15.

The data indicate that the mere presence of a father was not significantly related to participation in team sports. However, the presence of an adequate father figure was significant. Sixty-eight percent of all subjects who had a father figure both present and adequate participated in team sports. Those subjects who reported that they perceived their mothers as overprotective were more likely to participate in sports than others. On the other hand, those subjects who had stated that their mothers were overprotective and that they lacked an adequate father figure were least likely to participate. The Q is a rather strong, negative .74 in those instances.

Both the discussion of sports and attendance at athletic events were very strongly related to the son's participation in sports. The strength of the Q in the latter instance, in fact, indicates an almost total correspondence of the two variables. This type of relationship could indicate that both variables are measuring the same phenomenon. This may be the case so that if the son participated in sports the father was likely to attend to see his son perform in the events. On the other hand, it may well be that the last two items are measuring interactional effects of parental response to the son's activities and continuing performance by the son in response to the parental attention he has received, and so on.

Overall, the data show a relationship between participation in sports and degree of drug use. Moreover, they indicate a relationship between family variables and participation in sports. In this and other data, the link between familial socialization and peer group associations was quite obvious.

TABLE 15

FAMILY VARIABLES AND PARTICIPATION IN TEAM SPORTS

Family Variable	Number Reporting Positive to Family Variables	Percent Participating in Sports	*Q*
Father Present	*51*	*57%*	*.28*
Father Present & Adequate	*40*	*68%*	*.60*
Overprotective Mother	*29*	*59%*	*.20*
Overprotective Mother & Lack of Adequate Father Figure	*19*	*21%*	*-74*
Father Figure Discussed Sports	*46*	*76%*	*..86*
Father Figure Attended Sports With Son	*34*	*94%*	*.98*

Finally, although I did not count them as "father figures" in the above data, I should reiterate that coaches were the persons most often named by the subjects as substitute father figures. The young males viewed the coach as a role model who provided guidance and structure for them. I found that the coaches typically did not realize the degree of influence they had on the young men.

School and family.

In addition to academic achievement and rates of truancy, there were other facets of school which related both to degree of drug use and family factors. Those subjects who lacked an adequate father figure were more likely to use drugs before school (gamma of .48). The same was true for those that lacked discipline or who had only experienced severe discipline (gamma of .52).

The most significant link appeared to be parental interest and discussion of school with their sons. Those subjects who stated that their parents were interested in their performance in school were less likely to be heavily involved in drugs (a negative gamma of .55). Moreover, 78 percent of sons whose parents discussed school progress with them expected to obtain a college diploma. Only 27 percent of those whose parents did not discuss school with them expected to obtain a college diploma. Fifty-nine percent of the sons whose parents did not discuss school expressed disenchantment with school.

CONCLUSIONS REGARDING THE RELATIONSHIPS BETWEEN PEER AND FAMILY FACTORS

In this section I examined the relationship of peer association and degree of drug use. The role of peers seemed to be a very important factor affecting the subjects' degree of drug involvement. Likewise, specific peer groups associated with religious and sports activities played a part in controlling drug use.

In addition, the data demonstrated that there was a relationship between family situations and association with peers who were less likely to be involved with drugs. There were links between family factors and participation in religious and sports activities. Further, the data indicated that older siblings played a substantial role in the introduction of subjects to various drugs.

Finally, parental interest in their children's education, as measured by discussion of school with their sons, appeared to positively effect the sons' expectations to attend college. The lack of such discussion appeared to increase the likelihood of the son's disenchantment with high school.

The data provide very strong support for Sutherland's Differential Association theory as an explanation for differing degrees of drug use. The "learning" regarding use and non-use of drugs appeared to begin in the home and continued in peer groups. The "differential association" between primary groups in the home and peer groups were apparent.

The application of Differential Association is particularly significant if considered on conjunction with social control theory. This "theoretical convergence" has been shown by Harwin Voss. Voss demonstrated that Reckless' social control model and Differential Association were both describing the same basic concept, socialization. Voss combined measurements of each to illustrate their greater explanatory power when both mechanisms of socialization are taken into *account.*[7]

Likewise, involvements in and commitment to conventional activities, such as church youth groups, sports and school provide support for Hirschi's model of social control.[8] In addition, these activities and their links to home factors can be seen as congruent with the "containment" factors described in Reckless' model of social control. It would appear that both the "external" and "internal" components of containment are found in the results.[9]

Data from the interviews complemented the findings from observational research in one other way. The data confirmed that the "external" controls exercised by public officials were not effective in reducing drug use and other deviant behavior. Twenty-nine of the subjects had been arrested. Twenty of the arrests were drug-related, including alcohol offenses. Twenty of the arrests were of heavy users. None of the subjects reported decreasing their use as a result of the arrest. Eleven of those arrested felt they were "stupid to get caught." Another five felt they had been "persecuted." The offenders received varying degrees of punishment, detention, fines and reprimands. Only two of those arrested for drug offenses adopted any form of a negative label (such as "stoner," "druggie" and so on) as a result of the arrest. Obviously, the internal controls resulting from caring parental discipline and peer influence as well as the external controls provided by involvement in church, sports and school activities were far more effective than police, probation officers and the courts. These results support a far greater emphasis by families, schools, communities, school, government and others on the "supply" side as opposed to the "demand" side of drug control.

A FINAL NOTE

The total findings demonstrate the primary importance of family and, particularly, the role of an adequate father figure in the lives of young men. The critical aspects of the role of parents were, first, love (caring) and second, communications of care through words and example, and third, interest in the young person's life. True caring was demonstrated most directly through firm and caring discipline. These factors, the essence of socialization, provided the young person with both internalized controls as well as external structural constraints from the allurements to which he was exposed. Parental care and interest influenced the likelihood that the son would become involved in church groups, sports activities and school. Thus, the son was more likely to become a part of peer groups who shared his parents' values. The quantified data complemented the observations and descriptions I have described in previous chapters. Likewise, in this chapter, the qualitative examples and cases complemented the statistical analysis of the subjects' responses.

There was very limited support for the McCord-Chein model. The relationship between an overprotective mother and degree of drug use was limited to a few cases. In spite of the strength of family factors and the evidence of sexual difficulties among heavy users, the sequence of events did not support that envisioned by the model. Likewise, the data called into question some theories regarding the youth subculture. There was evidence that labeling occurred. However, there were only limited examples of individuals who adopted a negative label. On the other hand, both Differential Association and social control theories were strongly supported by the findings.

In the following chapter, five families and a very special single-parent will be described. Their stories and others will unfold in the final chapters of this book.

End Notes

1. For more details see Jeremiah Lowney, Dissertation. *Drug Use Among Young Males*, Lexington, Ky: University of Kentucky, 1976.

2. I had very little difficulty in determining the presence of a "mother figure" in the lives of the subjects during their formative years. It was not necessary to make these distinctions as was the case with father figures. In only three cases were subjects placed with their father following a divorce. In one of these cases, the divorce was recent and the youth had lived with his mother during the previous, "formative years." In another instance, the father who had custody had not remarried and the subject had considerable interaction with his mother. In the final instance, that of the Roe family, the siblings had one step-mother for the larger part of their lives and considered the step-mother to be a "real Mom."

3. Gerard A. Dewit. *Symbolism of Masculinity and Femininity*. New York: Springer Publishing Company, Inc., 1963; Eleanor E. Maccoby and Carol Nagy Jacklin. *The Psychology of Sex Differences*. Stanford, Ca.: Stanford University Press, 1974; American Medical Association Committee on Human Sexuality. *Human Sexuality*. Chicago: American Medical Association, 1972.

4. Travis Hirschi. *Causes of Delinquency*. Berkeley: University of California Press, 1969, p. 108

5. Howard S. Becker. "Becoming a Marijuana User," *American Journal of Sociology*, LIX (November, 1953), pp. 235-242.

6. Ibid.

7. Harwin L. Voss. "Differential Association and Containment Theory: A Theoretical Convergence," *Social Forces,* IIL (June, 1969), pp. 381-391.

8. Travis Hirschi, *Causes of Delinquency*, Berkeley: University of California Press, 1969.

9. Walter C. Reckless. "Containment Theory," in Barry Krisberg, and James Austin (eds.) *The Children of Ishmael: Critical Perspectives on Juvenile Justice.* Palo Alto, Ca: Mayfield Publishing, 1978, pp. 187-192.

Chapter 9

Five Families and a "Super-Mom"

In previous chapters, I introduced five families. I selected the families to provide a more complete picture of the similarities and differences involved in various parent-child relationships. More than one brother from each of the families was a subject of the research. They allowed me to make comparisons and contrasts between and within the families. Their stories summarize key elements of home, school and peers. In addition, Mrs. Mary Gilroy, a single-parent mother of four sons provides additional insights and wisdom from her experiences as a "Super-Mom."

THE DUNN FAMILY

Martin, 14, a heavy user (initially a non-user).
Norm, 16, a heavy user.
Toby, 17, a heavy user (a non-subject).

Originally, I chose 14-year-old Martin Dunn to compare his life history and perceptions with those of his older brother, Norm, 16, one of the wall rats. The primary purpose of adding Martin as a subject was to obtain some indication as to why Martin did not use drugs although Norm and another older brother, Toby, were heavy users. By late summer 1975, however, Martin also became a heavy user.

Both Norm and Martin recalled the serious conflict which took place prior to their parents' divorce. However, Martin's perceptions of home life were more harsh than those of Norm. They both recalled their father's "temper," and both indicated that their parents' divorce ended most of the conflict and brought a more pleasant home situation. The conflict and the father's temper apparently made stronger impressions on the younger brother, Martin. He described them more vividly and with greater detail and emotion than Norm. However, Norm's perceptions may have been tempered somewhat by later interactions with his father. Norm frequently spent weekends camping and riding motorcycles with his father. Martin resented the greater attention received by Norm. Mr. Dunn also raised marijuana and smoked it with Norm during the weekend trips.

None of the brothers had been active in team sports although they followed some events with interest and took part in neighborhood sports activities. They had not been raised in a religious faith, although Norm and Toby had been baptized Catholic and attended church prior to the divorce.

Norm's academic performance had always been somewhat mediocre. Martin had been an honor student until eighth grade when his grades began to decline. Martin began to smoke marijuana at the beginning of ninth grade. By the close of the first semester, his grades had declined even more dramatically. The youths interacted frequently with neighbors of their same age. These neighbors included the Roe brothers and several other youths whose parents had been divorced. Each Dunn brother had one friend close to his age who was a member of an intact family. However, the majority of their contacts were with youths with home situations similar to their own. Two separate groups, one aged 13 and 14 years, the other of 15 and 16 years, gathered at unsupervised homes in the neighborhood to smoke marijuana after school and on weekends. Mrs. Dunn dated regularly. Thus, the Dunn home was often a center of this activity.

Neither youth felt they experienced any extraordinary psychological discomfort and neither had used drugs other than marijuana and alcohol.

THE ROE FAMILY

Chuck, 16, a heavy user.
Bart, 17, a heavy user.

Chuck Roe, 16, was also a wall rat and one of Norm's closest friends. Both Chuck, and his 17-year-old brother, Bart, were research subjects. The brothers had lived in several homes during the early years of their lives. Their parents had divorced when Chuck was 1-year-old and Bart was three. They had lived with their mother and five different stepfathers over the next five years. The last of these stepfathers was described by Chuck, "That last one, he used to stick his fork in my hand if I put my elbows on the table! He was an asshole! But I guess it is hard to be a Dad, though."

The biological father remarried and eventually obtained custody of his two sons. Their stepmother was perceived as a "real Mom" by both youths. The brothers each downplayed the stepmother's drinking patterns but felt their father "might" be an alcoholic. Chuck often bragged to other wall crew members that his "Mom"fixed a "hot breakfast" every morning.

Both admitted that some conflict existed in their home, but each differed in his perception as to the relative degree of the conflict. Chuck said, "Yeah, There's jest your basic 'Shut the fuck up!' occasionally, but nothin' too big."

On the other hand, Bart responded, "Yes! All the time! But with my real Mom I remember even more. Then, she once threw an oak chair at my Dad and hit him on the head."

There were relative differences in their responses to interview questions regarding discipline. Chuck stated,

> I get a little more slack than most kids. They're more lenient than most folks. They don't care if I smoke pot . . . My old lady screams a lot and my old man backs her up. My Dad found out I smoked pot eight months ago. I guess he had figured out I smoked already and figured out I was going to be a brain surgeon . . . No, I know I'm glad they weren't stricter with me.

The following is a composite of quotes by Bart regarding discipline,

> My Dad tries to (discipline me). It's yelling mostly. They used to be physical. They can't give me restrictions. I won't take them . . . I used to not think about things, 'cuz I wasn't close to 18. Now I do. I guess because that's the age I can get arrested or get kicked out of the house . . . I think it's good that my Dad lets me run around but it would have been better that he didn't smoke pot, then he could get down on me more. Like the other day, he came into my room an' I was smokin' an' all he could say was, 'What if I was a cop, and came walkin' in here? You'd be busted.' But, he really can't do anything about it or make me stop, because he does it himself.

Neither of the Roe brothers had been active in sports during high school. Chuck was somewhat active in some team sports in junior high.

Both youths began to smoke marijuana during ninth grade. Both had been "A" students through most of elementary and junior high school. Chuck's grades declined to "C's" in the 10th grade. Bart's grades declined during 11th grade. Neither brother planned to attend college.

Neither of the youths had any religious training. Both expressed some psychological discomforts about "worry" and "depression," but neither viewed these as abnormal. Both had used a variety of drugs, including hallucinogens and cocaine. They both smoked marijuana daily and engaged in rather extensive drug "dealing."

THE BAYER FAMILY

Morris, 17, a heavy user (a non-subject).
Gil, 19, a light user.
And six sisters, including 16-year-old, Alise, and 13- year old, Colleen.

Gil Bayer, 19, was a "light" user. He had not used marijuana or alcohol for more than three months before his interview.

Gil's 17-year-old brother, Morris, was not "officially" a subject of the research as far as the formal interviews were concerned. As I have indicated in Chapter 6, I made a decision not to include him because of my previous interactions with him and the other two members of the "trio." I exercised this caution so that their inclusion would not contaminate the results. Nevertheless, I continued to have many interactions with Morris. Morris was a heavy user of drugs. He had experienced many difficulties with law enforcement and school officials, involving drugs and other illegal behaviors.

The Bayer family included six other children, all girls, ranging in ages from 12 to 23. Three of the girls were older than Gil and Morris, and three were younger. Dr. Bayer was a professor of Biology. His wife, Rita, had five years of higher education. She was a registered nurse, but had remained a housewife since the birth of her first child. I was able to observe many interactions in their home.

Dr. Bayer consumed large amounts of alcohol during most evenings. Morris had been disturbed by his father's drinking for several years. He expressed concern that his father was an alcoholic and that the drinking patterns would affect his father's ulcer. On many occasions, Morris openly expressed the desire that his father "do more things with him." Each time that Morris had difficulties with legal or school officials, Dr. Bayer resumed responsibility for his son's discipline. Mrs. Bayer often became emotional and criticized Dr. Bayer's lack of consistency in enforcing the discipline as well as her husband's aloofness from his children's daily lives.

Gil had only one criticism of his father, "He's not real affectionate. I think he could be more thoughtful and more affectionate."

Gil had been known as "Mr. Perfect" in high school had been selected as "most likely to succeed" as early as ninth grade when he served as student body president of the junior high. During high school, he had been an "A" student, an officer in the Catholic youth group, a "star" football player, a wrestler and a member of the soccer team, He worked following high school to save money to travel before attending a university from which he had received an athletic scholarship for the following academic year. Morris, on the other hand, often referred to himself as "a doper," and "a dumb shit."

As I have previously indicated, during the year when Gil was not attending Golden Beach High School, Morris reversed several earlier patterns. His grades had previously been mediocre. It was doubtful that he would graduate and he had never participated in team sports at the school. Morris continuously had judged himself by his ability to not perform as well as Gil. In the fall of 1975, however, Morris went out for football. As a senior, he was entitled to be on the team regardless of his ability. Morris was usually in each game for only two or three plays. He spoke, however, after each game about what "we" had done and considered himself very much a member of the team. His former friends criticized him for becoming a "jock," and they noticed that he had changed peer groups. Morris' drug use declined somewhat but did not completely end. His interest in the school, including academics, picked up considerably. Mr. Wilcox, the vice principal, was among those who noticed the change and expressed hope that Morris would graduate from Golden Beach High School.

Morris' communication with his father appeared to increase during this period. His parents attended the games each week. On one evening, Mrs. Bayer was unable to attend. The game was not a "home" game and it was necessary for Dr. Bayer to drive to the game alone. Dr. Bayer sat next to me. Morris was in the game at the kickoff. He noticeably turned sideways and surveyed the stands before the opening whistle. He nodded his head as his eyes located his father. He smiled broadly, and faced forward to begin to "play ball."

When the football season had ended, Morris' drug patterns continued to fluctuate, but he did not return to his previous peer group. After school his afternoons were free, and he and some of his classmates occasionally "taught" their younger neighbors, including Norm Dunn and Chuck Roe, how to play football, at a nearby park.

The long term stories of Gil, Morris, Colleen, Alise Bayer, as well as Dr. Bayer would eventually become a most significant aspect of my research.

THE JONES FAMILY

Terry Jones, 16, a non-user.
Todd Jones, 19, a light user, a former heavy user.
Bill Jones, 20, a heavy user.
Pete Jones, 21, a regular user, a former heavy user.

The four Jones sons lived at home with their parents. The parents were devout Baptists and their sons had been raised accordingly. Neither parent drank nor smoked. Mrs. Jones sang in the church choir.

The sons all members of the wall crew. Pete and Bill were both employed, part-time, and attending a junior college, also part-time. Todd attended a Midwest Bible college. Terry was in high school. Pete, Bill and Todd, each separated in age by a single year, had been particularly close during their earlier lives. They "discovered" marijuana together when Todd was in ninth grade, Bill in the 10th, and Pete in the 11th. They began to surf at approximately the same period of time. They each became heavy users and initiated Terry when he discovered them smoking marijuana in the garage. They admitted that they urged Terry to smoke pot so that he would not be able to inform their parents. They reasoned that if Terry took part in their activities, he would be as "guilty" as they. Terry experimented with the marijuana only on a few occasions during that period of time. He was then in the seventh grade.

The three older brothers had various disciplinary problems at school prior to their use of marijuana. After they began to smoke marijuana, their academic grades declined. They attributed the decline, variously, to "pot," "surfing," and "hangin' around with different people." Terry had some behavior problems in junior high school, but his grades remained above satisfactory into senior high.

None of the brothers had been very active in sports. Before they began to use marijuana, Pete and Bill had both quit the high school wrestling team. All of the youths said that their father had discussed and attended sporting events with them, but they reported this in terms of "a little" and "not a whole lot."

The three older youths, who had become heavy users, differed from Terry in some other aspects of their lives. Likewise, their perceptions of their home life differed from his. Each of the three older brothers viewed Terry as "spoiled," or "getting special privileges." The most dramatic differences centered about the period preceding their initial use of marijuana and the following year. This period was described, in separate terms, by each of them as a period of "rebellion" against what they viewed as their parents' "strictness." The three stopped attending church services and took other measures to assert their "independence" and "freedom." Each disclosed the storm of the controversy surrounding "haircuts," the apparent symbol of parental restriction and sibling "freedom," at that time. Each of the three also referred to the fact that Terry had always been allowed to let his hair grow and they had to "battle" for the privilege three years earlier.

Following this period, Pete and Todd began to attend the fundamentalist church services which I described in preceding chapters. When they were attending the services regularly, their drug use decreased. However, the pattern was somewhat erratic, particularly for Todd who had become the heaviest user in the family. At times, Todd averaged 30 marijuana cigarettes per day. Todd later quit using any drugs and increasingly became devoted to church activities. Eventually, he attended a Bible college to prepare himself for missionary duty. In all conversations, Todd expressed himself in terms of the Bible and "The Lord," regardless of the topic. Pete eventually settled into a pattern of somewhat moderate though regular drug use.

Terry continued to worship at the Baptist church on Sunday and the Wednesday meetings of the youth group.

Bill often expressed his belief in God and religion. Toward the end of this phase of the research, he attended the fundamentalist services a few times, but did not stop using drugs. He had some doubts about the degree of his parents' concern for him. Bill felt he had received differential treatment in comparison with his brothers. Bill frequently mentioned that his brothers were given extensive vacations for high school graduations' presents and he had not. He also noted that he had never received the birthday presents he had been promised.

In addition to these perceptions of Bill, the most striking differences in the four brothers' interviews centered around the roles of their parents.

Other members of the wall crew, including two who had lived in the Jones' household for some periods of time, spoke of Mrs. Jones' domineering personality and the passivity of Mr. Jones. In general, the youths resented Mrs. Jones and were fond of Mr. Jones, who often received their sympathy. I had opportunity to view some family interactions after bailing Bill from jail, and on four other occasions which were less emotional. Mrs. Jones appeared to be high-strung and domineering, but some of the young people's assessments appeared to be somewhat exaggerated.

Mr. Jones had a previous, brief marriage. Both he and Mrs. Jones had retired from service in the U.S. Navy. Mrs. Jones had a higher rank in the service than Mr. Jones. Mrs. Jones was currently employed in a management position. Mr. Jones was a clerk at an insurance office. They lived in a rather expensive home with a view of the bay.

Terry, the youngest who had not been involved in the drug subculture, viewed his father as the head of the home and the major disciplinarian. He viewed his mother as participating in the discipline. He felt his father was a completely adequate father figure. He stated that his mother was "not overprotective," although she treated him "like a baby, a lot," and tried to make plans for his future. He said his parents had some conflict but these were "not big." Thus, in Terry's eyes, his home life was quite normal. He stated he worried "sometimes," but did not express any other psychological discomfort.

Todd, formerly the heaviest user of the four, had similar views regarding discipline in the home, the adequacy of his father, and his father's role in the family. He felt, however, that his relationship with his father had improved considerably in recent years and that he admired his father more than he had previously. He did not view his mother as overprotective, but admitted that she tried to plan his future, often interfered with his father's disciplinary measures, and attempted to make excuses for his behavior. He perceived that conflict took place in the home "once in a while." Todd stated that he had experienced many psychological problems when he was "doing drugs," but that they ended when he stopped using drugs.

Pete, a former heavy user and later a regular user, perceived the conflict as "pretty regular." He mentioned that his mother was "getting more' crabby," particularly around his friends. Pete perceived both his parents as taking part in discipline "but my mom more." He stated that his father was the "boss in the home," but lets his mother "put up like she is." Pete described an incident, later verified in Bill's interview, in which his father had finally "put his foot down" and "locked my mom in the bathroom" so he could "talk to my sons." Pete described his mother as "very protective" and "very emotional." He stated he had never doubted that either of his parents had cared about him. He expressed several forms of psychological discomfort, including depression, loneliness and anxiety. He stated these feelings occurred infrequently and did not overly concern him

Bill, the heavy user, stated that his parents "fight all the time." He viewed discipline as shared in by both parents and that his father was an adequate father figure. He described, as mentioned earlier, certain doubts regarding parental concern. He felt his relationship had improved with his father because, as he said, "He doesn't mind my hair, anymore, an' he's not totally against my sport anymore, surfing."

Bill said that he formerly had doubted that his father was head of the household, but he then "looked at it" and felt that his father was now more of a "man" and had undergone some changes. He then described the incident in which his mother had been locked in the bathroom by his father. Bill's strongest comments dealt with his mother. He felt that she, "treats me like a baby, all the time," and that he has to "stop her short" when she attempts to make excuses for his behavior. He described his mother as frequently emotional and upset, and that she increasingly had moods during which she "screams and yells" at her sons. Among the four, Bill reported the most extreme and frequent psychological discomforts.

The Jones brothers illustrate differing perceptions, within the same family, in regard to home factors. The perceptions were grounded in differing historical or other changes affecting their objective reality. They also demonstrate that such perceptions may correspond to differing psychological discomforts as well as differing and changing drug patterns. They indicate how many variables interact, and, consequently, the difficulties in establishing "cause" and priority with regard to variables, such as, academic performance, sports activity, psychological discomfort and drug use.

THE GILROY FAMILY

Mark, 16, a light user (formerly a heavy user).
Reed, 17, a non-user.
John, 18, a light user.
Ron, 20, a heavy user.

I selected the Gilroy family in order to ascertain how Mrs. Mary Gilroy, a Mexican-American and a divorced single-parent, had raised her four sons. The drug patterns of the sons were as skewed to the "non-use" end of the spectrum as the Jones sons had been to the "heavy use" end of the same spectrum. Ron, the eldest, had been a heavy user but his use decreased considerably during the 1975 and 1976. He was of the same "generation," as the older Jones' brothers. Unlike Mrs. Jones, Ron's mother had been more lenient on matters such as surfing and hair-length. Mary Gilroy admitted that she had overreacted to Ron's use of drugs, but what she had learned from that experience helped her to deal with the situation when she sensed that her youngest son, Mark, was using drugs. After Ron was arrested for possession of marijuana, Ron and his mother visited a family counselor together, Ron did not see these sessions as beneficial, but Mrs. Gilroy felt they had helped her understand matters and gave her confidence to handle later difficulties. In ninth grade, Mary Gilroy insisted that Mark receive counseling. Mark resisted the treatment and the prescribed tranquilizers, but admitted the counseling had been of some benefit in helping him to "understand himself better." He attributed the reversal of drug patterns to his involvement in the Catholic youth group and to the influence of his mother and older brother, Reed.

Mrs. Gilroy and her husband were divorced shortly after Mark was born. Ron was the only one of the children who remembered the conflict that had preceded the divorce.

Ron differed from his brothers in other ways. He expressed a greater alienation toward teachers in school. He did not plan to go to college. He had some difficulty in relating to females. He had not participated in high school sports. Ron had been active in the Catholic youth group that had preceded Drop In. He was currently employed at St. Patrick's parish, but did not attend Sunday Mass.

The four sons and Mrs. Gilroy expressed similar opinions regarding the absent Mr. Gilroy. The father and husband had a "drinking problem" that had contributed to the divorce, was irresponsible, and had abandoned a second wife and children. He paid alimony sporadically and rarely visited his sons. Still, he was not despised by the family, who had been forced onto the welfare rolls. Mrs. Gilroy underwent a training program for welfare recipients and became permanently employed. Ron's attitude toward his father was similar to that of his brothers, "He's a nice guy, but confused. He's searching for what's happening. He has a lot of potential, but he's not using it to the fullest . . . I want to get to know him better. I used to resent him. Now I guess I'm indifferent."

None of the brothers expressed doubts regarding the concern their mother had for them. All described her as a "strict" disciplinarian who used a "switch" when they were "little," and later placed them on "restrictions." None of them felt their mother was overprotective. Only Ron indicated that she was, at time, overly emotional.

The three youngest brothers planned to attend college. Mark felt he lacked some degree of attention when Reed and John continuously were praised with "Wows" for their "Straight-A" report cards and he only got, ''Gee, that's nice's," for his ''B's.''

The three were involved in many team sports, in and out of school. Mrs. Gilroy was known as "the loudest mouth at the games" in cheering her sons at almost every event in which they participated. She was active in parent-teacher organizations, chaperoned dances and had been a co-director of the previous church youth group.

At various times, each of the three youngest sons were board members in Drop-In, the current Catholic youth group. Reed was the director during 1975 and 1976.

John and Reed had steady girlfriends during this period of the study. Mark made several attempts to follow in their footsteps. Ron was currently living with a young woman.

The closeness of the entire "family" was evident on my frequent visits to the home. Mrs. Gilroy insisted that everyone be together during holidays. She frequently hurried home from work to fix dinner before attending a football game, a band recital or a parent's meeting. She was 5 feet tall, but never appeared to have a discipline problem. She would frequently switch moods and tone of voice instantaneously to reprimand one son as she was consoling another. She did not drink alcohol but offered wine to guests in her home. Her laughter was frequent, open and unconstrained. Each of the four sons stated that there were very few things that they had missed by not having a father present. Ron and John indicated that their mother had been open in her discussions regarding sex, but that "certain things" would have been better handled by a male. Each of the brothers named Mrs. Gilroy as a "substitute father figure," and agreed that the reason they had not missed having a father present was because their mother had played both roles so well. They each stressed this particularly as regards to her role in discipline and sports. In regard to the latter, Reed stated, "I even remember Mom tryin' to teach us how to bat a ball when Ron and I went out for Little League."

I asked Reed if his mother know how to bat a ball. He laughed and replied, "No. But she tried to, anyway!"

Mrs. Gilroy was interviewed after I had completed my interviews and observations of her sons. Although the limitations of space do not permit me to provide the total transcript of her remark, the entire two-hour interview might be helpful to many parents. I have selected quotes from the interview which seem most appropriate to the factors under consideration. These remarks provide an appreciation of parent-child relationships in a single-parent home.

I have supplied the emphasis in italics and written the question or topic above each of Mrs. Gilroy's responses.

Excerpts From Mrs. Mary Gilroy's Interview

The Divorce:

> He (Mr. Gilroy) just kept drinking more and more. He was a wonderful fella, but was one of those who couldn't cope with the day-to-day realities. There was more and more arguing . . . Until I finally thought, 'This just isn't any good. This is doing more harm to these kids, than, you know, if the marriage lasted,' so I finally wrote my folks and asked them for the fare and brought the kids home. The only one old enough, to require an explanation was Ron, and he remembers us fighting, so I told him that we didn't want to fight any more . . . I really didn't go into much detail with any of the kids. I guess they just grew up with it . . . Later on, when they'd ask, *I tell them, you know, that their father truly loves them*, but he just couldn't take the responsibility of a family, and, then, they saw it when he married another girl, with four children, and they had two children and he left her when she was expecting.

After the Divorce:

> It was miserable! Oh, I *felt very, very guilty* for a long time. I felt *they were missing out on a great deal by not having a father.* You know, being boys, and being active. I felt they were missing things that they could have done with a father. But, after a while, I began to think I couldn't spend the rest of my life feeling guilty about it.
>
> I've told the kids that I've seen too many cases where people have come from handicapped backgrounds . . . but, no matter what, there's no excuse for mediocrity in your life because of a handicap. If you're gonna make something of yourself, you're gonna make something of yourself regardless of your background and circumstances. If you don't do something with yourself, you can always find excuses, you know, like, 'My Dad beats me,' or "I don't have any shoes.'

Playing "Both" Roles:

To a degree. Probably more than playing both roles, what I *have tried to do is be Super Mom, in lieu of trying to be Momma and Dad . . .* I try to be extra readily accessible to my kids. If they have problems, I try to get them out in the open and get them to discuss them. I have tried to let them know I'm available, regardless of when. *If they call me at work and they have a problem, I'm going to stop and listen.* And, they know they come first, because there have been times, when they were littler that I had to stop.

Two of the sons had also told me the following story in their interviews:

Like, one time, I think it was Reed, called me at work and told me Ron was chasing John around the house with a pair of scissors. So, I said, 'Okay,' I hung up the phone. I told them, 'I got to go home.' I went out, got in the car, drove home. I was so furious! I was so mad! I said, 'Okay, everybody, line up at the bathtub, pull your pants down!' and I hauled out and beat the snot out of all four of them. An', Mark and Reed said, 'We didn't do anything!' I said, 'I don't care, just in case!' So they knew that if any crisis occurred or arose that I would be there. Like when John broke his arm at school, I was at work, but as soon as they called me, I got in the car, got him, took him to the hospital. Even though t couldn't be there physically, they knew I could be there if they need me.

I have tried to keep communication open between us, so that if they wanted to come to talk to me about sex, or whatever, we could discuss it. I found it really wasn't uncomfortable with them about sex. I could tell them about night dreams, or whatever. I really didn't feel uncomfortable about it.

We were on welfare. My caseworker said that it would be good for me to get out and get off welfare. So they sent me to vocational guidance classes . . . As soon as I got out of school, I went to work at the drug store, and I have been there ever since.

Religion:

I always made them go to catechism classes, and *we went to church together.* You know, I taught them their prayers and, when they were smaller, we would say night prayers together . . . When the kids were older, and didn't feel like going to CCD (religion classes), *I didn't really push it.* I asked them to go and try out some of the classes and see if there was anything they might like.

I really never pushed it. I think I always made it plain my faith was important to me that it served me in good stead, through good times and bad . . . We haven't discussed a lot about religion. It's just something that's always been there, expected of them, and, like I say, they could see it was important to me . . . At times, I have stressed to them that, because of your religion, this is important or that is important . . . There was a time when I thought they shouldn't go steady, for instance, too early. They church says, and I agree with the fact that, if you start going with someone too early, you know, it leads to other things and that you also should have the experience of meeting other people. It was more things like that, which I stressed.

Holidays:

I'm a big holiday person! Holidays are family days. I'm really, really upset if our family can't be together for any holiday, Christmas, or Memorial Day, or Birthdays. To this day, I still fill their stockings for Christmas. The Fourth of July without fireworks is nothing for me. (Laughter) We go up to Alta Vista and watch the fireworks and we usually have a picnic. I really, really get upset if our family can't be together for the holidays.

Sports:

I have always told the kids, if they were interested, fine, if they weren't interested, fine. If you don't want to play, if you don't want to participate, fine; but, one thing I did insist on, and something I have feelings against is that once you have signed up, you aren't going to say, 'I don't like the coach,' or 'I don't wanna play,' and quit. One thing I always hated was a quitter. That can be in anything.

Sure I enjoy watching them play sports. You know. It's a source of pride to me. I'm not going to deny that, especially if they do well. But, if they didn't want to, good. Nobody was going to push them. *I felt that sports were good for them.* I felt it was important for them to be part of a team, and learn something. If they did something deliberately bad, it reflected, not just on them but on the team. Like, you were out in left field, and playing around, and not paying attention and a fly ball came to you; if they tried and they missed it, well, okay, there wasn't any more you could do. If you go to bat, and you strike out, well, you tried. You tried, but you can't do any more than that. A lot of people strike out.

And, also, they had some male companionship playing sports, and a male figure they kind of look up to. I'm sorry I didn't get the kids in the

'Big Brother' program. That was my fault. I was always so busy. But it is good for them to be able to relate to a man.

I just think that *sports give them that male figure, that male image.* I thought that was one good thing they got out of sports.

Drugs:

I first was aware that Ron used pot when he was about 16. He was on acid or something. *Oh, God, was I scared!* He was weaving. I didn't know what was going to happen to him. I called the priest who was in charge of the youth group then. He came over. We talked to Ron for a while. He said someone gave him something and he didn't know what it was. And, I believed him! I didn't know, and they tell you what you want to hear, and 'Oh, no, I'll never do that, Mom.' I was really upset.

After that, I became aware that he was smoking pot, and, when he finally admitted to me, I guess I just didn't want to believe that he would do anything like that. I may have seen signs of it earlier, but *being the first one and not wanting to believe, I may have overlooked things.* I went to the classes at school where they had a drug display, and talked to you, and you looked at it. *It's amazing to see how normal they can appear when they're stoned. Or seemingly normal*, because he started smoking when he was in the seventh grade, so he was using a long time before I was aware of it. Finally, I thought, 'Baloney! You're smoking it!' So, finally, he admitted to me that he did. I really don't know if he's taken anything harder than that. I'd like to believe he hasn't, but I don't know. I know that he has smoked pot with hash oil. I don't know if that makes any difference. It makes it smellier! (Laughter) I know that at parties, even then, in ninth grade, there was beer and liquor at parties. Ron doesn't handle it well. In many ways, he reminds me of his father . . . I pray he can find himself! Before he loses himself! If he does smoke pot, there is nothing I can do about it.

I feel so sorry for people who need a couple of drinks to have a good time. I think, 'Oh, God, I have a great time without it! I wish there was a way to communicate this to my kids, *but I got to fight that peer-group pressure!*

One time, he (Ron) was so upset because I found his grass and flushed it down the toilet. He said, 'Don't you know how much money it costs?' I said, 'You shouldn't be wasting your money on stuff like that. Do you know how hard I have struggled to support you guys for years on 90 dollars a week? You go out and throw away money!' I said, 'I don't feel the least bit sorry for you!'

John is the kind that wouldn't (use drugs). I knew he has drank beers. He is one of these guys that, once he has made up his mind abut something, it is like a wall. So I don't worry about him. I'm as certain as anybody can be about their kids. He'll take a beer, or wine.

I don't think Reed ever has (smoked marijuana). I really, really don't. Oh, he might have tasted a beer, but I know he doesn't smoke.

And, Mark! (Laughter) I knew he was smoking pot. I was smarter by that time. I had learned. I think Mark was giving him (the counselor) a snow job. He was probably giving him the biggest con job! He helped Mark realize certain things, things about himself, his feelings. It definitely helped, but not in the way he thought it would help . . . From that time on, he joined the youth group, I have seen the most change . . . He is still argumentative. He still keeps me in line on a lot of things. The other night, he wanted to go to the ball game. He wanted his supper early and he wanted it now. Well, I told him, 'Listen, mister, you just wait. I just got home.' He called me 'a bitch.' Oh, God! I was so mad! Well, I slapped him across the mouth! Then, I gave him the cold shoulder. I was furious! Well, he came home from the basketball game and he apologized to me. Then, when I came home the next night, he had cleaned up the bathroom and done some dishes. So, we very often disagree, but he will take me to task, once in a while, when I need it. But, I don't appreciate being called, 'a bitch.' (Laughter) But, I don't worry about him anymore, like I used to. I do trust him again.

I think marijuana was very, very prevalent a few years ago, but, I think it has slowed down a little bit . . . I think there are more kids drinking, wine, beer, . . . I think there has been a slowdown in most drugs other than alcohol.

If I had caught it (Ron's use of marijuana) sooner, I think I could have done something about it. We did go, one time, to a drug counselor, but it really didn't do much good because he said everything I had been saying, right along, but it was good for me. I was never quite sure if I was doing the right thing, whether I was handling things right. But, he said things I had been saying all along. So, I knew that if I followed my own instincts, I was on the right track. So, it gave me more confidence, so that I could speak more authoritatively with the other kids. If I had known sooner, I would have definitely done something while I had more control over Ron.

Advice for Others:

As much as possible, *be honest with your kids*. Let them know that you are in need. Let them know that you hurt, and it doesn't hurt to cry, once in a while, and let them know you are really hurting inside . . .

Let them see that they're loved. Love a lot!
Don't be afraid to discipline your children. Please! Don't be afraid to discipline your children! I feel very, very sorry for some children, because they are children that people can't stand to be around. They're obnoxious! They're nasty! They're rotten kids! And, it's not their fault! It's their parents' fault! Because they are either too lazy, or, in the name of not wanting to stifle a child's creativity, or whatever reason, they have not been disciplined. They are really not doing their kids any favors at all.

What do you do when the kid is larger than you?

Well, hopefully, by the time your kids bigger than you, they have respect for you as a person, so that he knows, or she knows, that you love them, and the best possible thing that you can do for them is what you are doing for them. They will respect that fact.

How tall are you?
"About five feet."
How tall is Ron?
"Oh, about five-nine"
And, John?
"Five-eleven."
And Reed?
"Five-eleven."
And, Mark?
"Just under six-foot . . . "

I have always tried to show my kids, not just by words, but by my actions, that, *if I am disciplining them, I love them, because I want what's best for them,* and I don't want them to grow up as undisciplined, unusual human beings. I tried to teach them that discipline is an important part of our lives. Like, with Mark, when he said that (bitch) the other night, he said he said it because he was mad. I said to him, 'Well, honey, do you think just because you are mad, you can just open your mouth and let anything come out. You have got to learn to discipline yourself, so that, even though you may be thinking that in your mind, it doesn't just run out of your mouth.
I think discipline is love. It's hard for me to explain, but I know that's the way I've done it.

Given the emphasis Mrs. Gilroy placed upon discipline and love, it is well to recall that none of her sons doubted her care for them, and all felt she had played both the "mother" and the "father" roles well. They expressed that they had missed nothing, especially discipline, by not having a father present. To close this section, it would be fitting to quote the responses of Mrs. Gilroy's four sons to my questions,

> When your Mom disciplined you, did you feel it was because she cared about you?
> Have you ever doubted this? When?

The four Gilroy sons responded, as follows,

Ron, 20,
Oh, I knew she cared. That's why she did it . . . Oh, I may have doubted it at the time, when it hurt, but not later on, when the hurt quit

John, 18,
Yes, I knew.
No, only when she was beating on me for something I did bad, at the time, but I knew she was tryin' to train me, for my own good.

Reed, 17,
Yes . . . Yeah, when I couldn't see it was to my advantage and I thought someone was doing it to influence my life. Not my mom so much, but other discipline, like in school. I guess I never doubted my mom at all, even though I didn't think I always deserved it. (Laughter) (Reed then related the story of his mom returning from work and giving all four a spanking because of the misdeed of Ron and John misdeeds)

Mark, 16,
Sure, I knew. I might have protested, at times, but that was when I was being rebellious. The way I see it is that *it would be a lot easier just to let your kids go, but, if you care about them, you are going to discipline them.*

Yeah. At the time when she was hitting me. Now I realize it, though, as I grew older.

CLOSING REMARKS

The five families provide some interesting contrasts. In the Dunn and Roe families, there was very little discipline. This was particularly apparent in regard to the sons' drug use. One parent in each of the two families used marijuana. The parents gave their sons no particular encouragement to participate in sports. Neither family had strong religious ties. In both families there had been parental conflict preceding the initial divorces.

The Bayer family was marked by somewhat inconsistent discipline by the father, heavy parental drinking and sibling rivalry. Morris accepted the negative labels placed on him. Morris' patterns fluctuate accordingly.

The parents in the Jones and Gilroy families had strong religious convictions. However, for a period of time, three of the Jones sons rejected their parents' faith. Two had eventually joined to a religious group which differed slightly from their parents' religious beliefs. Ron Gilroy had once rebelled against his mother's religious beliefs and drug attitudes, but was gradually becoming less adamant in his resistance.

Pete and Bill Jones were the two brothers most affected by parental conflict. Both became heavy users. Ron Gilroy was the only son in his family who remembered the conflict that preceded his parents' divorce. Ron became heavily involved in drugs and remained a heavy user.

Pete and Bill Jones believed their mother was overly emotional and overly protective. They became the two heaviest drug users in the family. Ron Gilroy perceived his mother as overly emotional. He was the only heavy user in his family.

Mrs. Jones was not aware of or did not admit to the extent of marijuana use in Golden Beach or by her own sons. After Bill's arrest, she believed his story that he was simply holding a single marijuana cigarette for a friend when he was apprehended. Mrs. Gilroy admits she was initially naive, but acted on her "instincts," once she had greater confidence in them.

The two Jones sons who had the most ambivalence regarding the role of their father as "boss" in the home, at least until a particular incident had occurred, were also the two heaviest users of drugs. There was no doubt that Mrs. Gilroy was head of her household, but this was deemed appropriate, because she was considered to be the "father figure" by her sons.

Mr. Jones lived at home with his wife and children. All four of his sons expressed regret that he had not given them more sex education or taken more interest in sports. There was no adult male present in the Gilroy household, but the youths and Mrs. Gilroy reported that sex education was provided for and sports activity was encouraged.

The Jones sons expressed some doubts about the degree of care their parents had for them. Bill Jones, in particular, stated that there were times when he felt that his parents did not care about him. His doubts centered, to a large extent, around material items. The Jones family was financially secure. The Gilroy family had far less in the way of material goods, but none of the youths doubted their mother's concern for them. (The four sons bought Mrs. Gilroy a new dishwasher for Christmas 1975.)

The comparisons of these families give a more complete picture of some of the interacting factors and processes which are involved in drug use and non-use. They give insight into differing effects of divorce and father absence. Likewise, they shed more light on the importance of caring discipline and the roles of sports and religion in the lives of children.

In recent years, several books and research findings have been published which report findings similar to my 1976 research. One is the very thorough and acclaimed work by David Popenoe, *Life Without Father.* Popenoe cites considerable evidence as to why "fatherhood and marriage are indispensable for the good of children and society."[1] William Pollack's *Real Boys* describes research about boys growing up in America, their needs, the special role of the father and the particular way that fathers show love to sons through father-son activity.[2] In *Raising Cain,* clinical psychologists, Kindlon and Thompson, describe their research findings regarding the unmet emotional needs of boys in our society. [3] A report by the National Center on Addiction and Substance Abuse at Columbia University in February 2001 found substantially lower rates of teen use of marijuana among those young people whose parents were "engaged" with them. The "hands on" approach included restrictions, curfews, daily involvement with children and clear messages about marijuana use.[4] Judith Wallerstein and her colleagues reported their findings on the long-term effects of divorce on children in "The Unexpected Legacy of Divorce." It is particularly appropriate to this research, because the Wallerstein study began in 1971. The period covered in their research overlaps the time of my research. [5]

In subsequent chapters I describe the longitudinal findings regarding the sons in these five families and others. The five families became particularly significant in the long term research findings. Eventually, I would meet Les' challenge and discover where he and others were 20 (and more) years later. First, however, I will describe what occurred in the years immediately following 1975-76, and the findings regarding the young women whom I would include in my study.

End Notes

1. David Popenoe. *Life Without Father*, NY: The Free Press, 1996.
2. William Pollack, *Real Boys*, NY: Henry Holt and Company, 1998.
3. Dan Kindlon and Michael Thompson. *Raising Cain,* NY: Ballentine Books, 2000.
4. The National Center for Addiction and Substance Abuse at Columbia University. *The 2000 CASA National Survey of American Attitudes on Substance Abuse VI*, NY: Columbia University, February 21, 2001.
5. Judith S. Wallerstein, Julia M. Lewis and Sandra Blakeslee. *The Unexpected Legacy of Divorce,* NY: Hyperion, 2000.

Chapter 10

Dichotomies 1976 - 1980

INTRODUCTION

In February 1976, I returned to the University of Kentucky to complete my dissertation. I heard from many of the young people in Golden Beach by mail and phone. Over the years, some came to visit. Gil Bayer drove across country on a motorcycle in late spring, 1976. He spent two days in Lexington. Two years later, his brother Morris would pay me a visit in Richmond, Virginia following an extremely dramatic set of events. In the meantime, I completed my dissertation and defense, and accepted a position as assistant professor of sociology at the University of Richmond, in July 1976. A year later, I received a summer research grant from the university to follow-up my earlier research in Golden Beach and to add females to the study. I continued my contacts and renewed my role as a nonparticipatant observer.The four years, from 1976 to 1980, were ones of contrasts. Many of the young people graduated, went on to college, married and traveled the road to success. Others became more deeply involved in drugs, dropping out of school and followed paths that lead to violence and even death. The lives of the young women revealed the dichotomies of background and future direction perhaps more distinctly than did those of the male subjects.

EARLY REPORTS, 1976-1977

During the months immediately following my return to Kentucky, I received cards and letters from many of those who had been in my study. These initial messages were typically upbeat. At the same time, the letters tended to come from opposite ends of the spectrum. I heard frequently from the non-users and light users who were anxious to discuss their educational progress, sports and church activities and girlfriends. Likewise, I received many from the heavy users, particularly members of the wall crew, who kept me abreast regarding drugs, increasing violence and their buddies.

For several years, non-user, Brendan, 15, was the most frequent correspondent. Eventually, he would become a truly successful "star". He wrote on June, 10 1976,

Dear Jerry,

I am now writing from my bed. Isn't that interesting? I have many thoughts in my mind so I thought I would write to a good friend. Sorry I have not written to you in a longtime but many things have happened. While trying to get my grades up I accomplished shot put, JV track, and been elected junior class vice-president. Some of my goals are finally materializing. It was hard work that it was worth it. Your ideas have helped me a lot. Work has been fine....Graduation is this coming week and I am going to have to miss it because of work. My trouble with girls is hard to explain. (But that is as usual). I'm praying that I do good on my finals next week, They're going to be hard . . . Now for the bad news. I hope you and your paper are now a success. I am still pushing for you. I hope you come this summer. It sure would be great. Oh yeah I got my permit last week. I finally feel legal driving. Richard, Phil, and everyone are fine. Also, Ned is going to U.S.C., to be an actor. He will be good. That's all I can think of right now, so see you this summer.

Love, Your good friend always,
Brendan

P.S. Everyone misses you, hurry.

I heard from many of the wall crew. The first letter was written by Bill Jones. However, others put their remarks in as well, including Carl. The letter was decorated with art work and diagrams. Highlights of the six-page letter follow:

March 22, 1976

Hey Looney,

It's about time, huh? Things that really been happenin' round here.

We've been having good weather for the past five days, as opposed two weeks of rain. Everybody is getting tan, and having a good time. There has been a lot of excitement around here, I'll start with the red freaks. It was a Sunday afternoon, sunny, no wind, <u>everybody</u> was down here. This one red freak was sitting on the wall, drinking beer and throwing the cans on the ground. So I went around picking up the cans and throwing them in the trash. Than I told him to put his trash in the can, cause his dirtying the place up! He grunted at me and kept drinking. (He's a thicko-type with long hair, the same clothes everyday, mustache like Kyle's and bad disposition.) He drank a few more beers and then threw the cans at the trash can, and missed. This time Mick told him to pick up the trash and the red freaks said he didn't f–king feel like it, so Mick fired on him about 6 times. One more red freak jumped in on Mick, so Luke grabbed him and cocked his fist back. He cooled it. The flight broke up and Mick went to get more beers. Than the red freak started hassling Paul and me. He called Paul a punk and kicked the door in his car. Paul and I were hassling them a lot while Leo was puggin' him. He wuz acting as hard as a rock, so Paul and gave him the same. All of a sudden, Mick comes running up with the cops behind him, grabs the red freak and shoves face into the car and yells out, "You're under citizen's arrest for littering!" The cops grabbed the red freak and took him away. (At least 10 cops!!)

CUT-IN!! By Carl.
Dear Loon,

Man, you really are a great friend and I appreciate you helping me out. It seems that everything is starting to work out for me .I have a job waiting for me in Switzerland so Paul, Mick and I are going in June. I'm really excited about it. I'm working at a gas station in Diamond Heights and I really like it. Hope that everything is working out the way you planned. We're all rooting for you. Well, Jer, I will let Bill get back to telling his story.

Good luck, luck, PROFESSOR, Love and kisses,
Carl

(Continued by Bill Jones)

Getting back to the red freaks, another day we were sitting around the shed. We heard something at the wall, we look down and saw Ken's chick getting punched by a red freak could she wouldn't kiss him. Ken was in the water so we had a lifeguard call him in and we told him what happened then he exploded!. The red freak was still sitting on the wall! (Dumb shit!) Ken wasted him (I mean wasted!) Then he went and talked to his girl friend who was crying, and he really got pissed when he heard the whole story. Meanwhile, the red freak crawled to his car and locked the door. Ken yanked on the door and opened it. (Muscles baby!) Grabbed the red freak by the ears and proceeded to mash his head on the side of the door. We told him not to kill him and he finally let him drop! Spaced huh!!

Then the "pissed de resistance" (French). Yesterday, Mar. 21, '76 we saw a blue pick-up truck drive up the wall behind this Mexican's Camaro and stopped. Both drivers flashed on each other, you know like maybe one guy burned the other for drugs or something. The pickup threw his stick in reverse and backed up all the way to Bay Boulevard at about 50 mph. Meanwhile, The Mex ran for his car, opens up the trunk, took out a .22 caliber rifle, ran down the street and shot at the truck! Insane!! Everybody hit the ground. The Mex ran back to his car and went after the truck that was burning down Bay Boulevard, south. Really spaced!! And the guys in the truck came back later carrying pistols looking for the Mexican. Wow what a trip! Well, enough of the light weight stuff.... continued...

They say a lot of good pot going around....Quacan (Mexican). Leo's got pounds, so does Bart, Joe and me (if I wanted to..could) Pat's got a job washing telephone booths (casual). By the way, Shane got a job at the motel a few minutes ago. Hee, hee!! The ratz are cool, nobody's blowin' it. Hey, I almost forgot! Last week, Melissa entered the Golden Beach contests. She didn't do too bad. She won!!! What a flash!. She wuz looking good! Bathing suit, evening gown, poise, style, overall bitchiness, you know! I am rally freaking out! Leo's beeb wuz in it too. She lost. She wuz pissed!! She spent $250 on an evening gown, and who knows how much on the other junk. Melissa spent $30 on hers! It wuz defective, so she fixed it and customized it. It wuz right-on. Help me!!

You missed Up-town Saturday Night. That was outrageous!! We were looking so kool!! I wuz in black velvet and white silk, hats, caps, tars, ha ha !! It wuz un-real! (Hey ran out of paper. I'll get back to ya!)

Bill Jones,

(Also signed by Paul and Art)

On March 23rd I received a note from Norm Dunn on the back of what appeared to be a school art paper:.

Jerry,

What's going on over there? Not much happening here. No waves. A lot of <u>good</u> stash going around. I haven't got a job yet but I'm still looking. Sorry it took me so long to write but I just couldn't find any time. Chuck Roe will probably write you soon.

When are you coming back? I need a job!! We have a lot of rain for awhile but we've also had some good sun. I saw your deal in the paper.

Not bad! Not much news has happened. Same old parties. Me and Chuck haven't been going to many any more.

We've been doing a lot of bowling, every Sunday, and Wednesday. Everybody is doing good, Skip, Jones's, Bart Roe, Rusty and everyone else. No one's been busted either.

Keep it cool, Jer,

Your friend,

Norm

When I completed my dissertation, I sent a copy to the Gilroy family to review so that they could check for accuracy as well as anonymity. I sent an additional copy to the Golden Beach branch of the San Diego Public Library. I asked the Jones family to review that copy before I delivered a copy to Golden Beach High School. The responses were favorable.

A card signed by the members of the Jones family read:

Hi Jerry!

Hey, everybody has been camping in the library for the last week, reading your book on us. Everybody is trying to guess who they are and who everyone else is. Happy Holiday! I send our tape back with something else on it. Later Bro,

Bill Jones,

(Signed) Terry, Todd, Pete, Bill, Mrs. Jones

(Rather than using his own name, Bill Jones had signed the card with his pseudonym, "Bill Jones," which I had used in the dissertation. Many of the wall crew members did not recognize themselves. Moreover, despite their many attempts, they have never guessed the identity of "Jim".)

Mrs. Gilroy told me by phone that their family liked the dissertation and all were comfortable with it. I received a letter in late August from Reed Gilroy en route to Brown University,

Dear Jerry,

We received your dissertation about a month and a half ago. Now that everybody in the family has finished reading it, the consensus of opinion seems to be one of awe, admiration, and praise. Really, Jerry, we all loved it. It was thorough, in-depth, and, at the same time, very readable and interesting. Overall, an excellent job. I'm proud to be able to say you are my friend.

If my writing appears to be a little bit sloppy, it is because I am composing this letter and a 20 ft. U-Haul junket bound for Chicago. Right now, we're (Grandpa, Aunt Phyllis and myself) passing through New Mexico on Route 10 and plan to arrive in Chicago on Sunday...I plan to stay in Chicago for a couple of weeks at the most before I have to report for school on Sept. 13th (I am going by bus to Rhode Island.) So, I'm sorry, but due to tight funds, I won't be able to visit you before I start school this year. However, as of yet, I have no plans for Thanksgiving and would love to "get-together". (My break for Thanksgiving is from November 24 to 28.) Also, at you can come see me whenever you get the "itch" And maybe, if its economical, I'll go back to San Diego with you at Christmas.

My Christmas recess begins at 6 p.m., December 17th and goes through Jan. 4th.

While it's almost my turn to drive so I'll close for now. I'll be hoping to hear from you soon my address at Brown will be.

Until then I'll send you a course guard from somewhere along the route.

Take care. I'll be thinking of you,

Reed

Reed and I met in New York that Thanksgiving to watch the Macy's Thanksgiving Day parade.

I received two letters from 19-year-old Carl, of the wall crew. The first was from Switzerland. Paul and Mick did not travel with him. He described his visit of several months and how much peace he had found there. In early December, I received a six-page handwritten letter. Carl told of his tour of Paris, England, Spain, Italy and Greece. Then he described his dramatic adventure after leaving Athens:

.... The group decided to the head north to Germany, to drink beer, but I had heard a lot about India and was really intrigued by it. So I decided that's where I wanted to go. I only had $200. Well, I had a train pass that took me as far as the Turkish border. Then, from there on I was paying. The first stop I made was Istanbul. I stayed there for 2 days. Right off the train, I was confronted with every kind of "Mugger, whore or pusher" you could imagine. I was just a small preview of what was lying ahead in Istanbul. I bought a bus to get to Deli, but one which allowed me to get on off in Iran and Afghanistan for however much time I wanted. Well, I stayed one day in Iran and left. It was a pit, overpopulated with cars and people and "oil".The Persian culture trying to live with Western-style. I didn't fit! So I directly moved onto Afghanistan. There I went through the lowest and toughest valley I've ever experienced in my life! The place had a reputation for its "Black Afghani hash" and it definitely lived up to its name. I had arrived only five minutes and found myself in a small room with a stick of hash about 6" long by 4" wide in my hands. In America for only a gram of the shit it would cost you $15.00, but in Afghanistan the "whole thing" was only 35 bucks! 45-50 grams! Then the man who was selling the stuff brought out a bag of opium. It was just unreal! I just never imagined myself holding so much yet. Well from then on, I was stoned, I was also getting really low on money. I hadn't anticipated all the expenses, so I was only mainly eating nuts, fruits and bread which had brought on the street corners. Well, I continued on down to Kabul then stopped, planning to stay a while. I was feeding real shitty! I had no energy and was getting really dizzy and short winded. Due to the lack of sleep and good food, and maybe a little bit had to do with beings stoned all of the time. Then, all at once, everything came down on me. I got SUPER SICK with dysentery and on top of that, high temperature. Then I ran out of money therefore I had no place to sleep and nothing to eat. At that time I really felt alone, helpless, but luckily I met some "Children of God" people who took me to their place in their place to sleep and pumped me full of water, apples and rice. I was out-of-it for eight days. The first two days my temperature was really hot and during that time I had terrible hallucinations. Evil demon-like images running at me, laughing screening. It was terrifying! Well it all slowly passed. Those people were great. They "literally" saved me. When I got back on my feet I went to the embassy to see if I could get any help. The only thing they would do was send me directly to the USA, but my home, at least for this year, is in Switzerland so I declined. The next day I made arrangements with a bus company allowing me to turn my ticket around to head back to Istanbul. So I got on the bus without any money, food or any idea if I would even ever really make it. When I got to the border of Iran my Visa had just expired. So they said I could not into the country. So I was stuck between Afghanistan and Iran without anything, money etc. Can you imagine how I felt? I've never felt more alone and helpless. I just grabbed my passport from the officer and ran straight to the "Head Bitch" there. I completely fell apart and literally begged him to let me through. Well, after I told him my story, they all talked, threw up their hands and shook their heads but let me through. As the trip progressed on, I met two guys from Austria who were going back to Austria on the same bus as I. They really befriended me and helped me. They bought me for my first meal in three days. Then when I got to Istanbul, I was planning to hitch hike home. When they found out, they insisted on paying my way and took me with them to Austria. We had been traveling by bus for four days and nights with only shortstops for the toilet and lunch and dinner. So we hadn't the opportunity to get much sleep, and it was the same the first night on the train.... Than the next day we all dropped "speed." (Don't ask me why?) So the next night we were completely wired. We arrived in Austria at 6 in the morning and I was completely exhausted but right off we smoked some more dope with some of their friends and partied all day and on into the night. I was just kind of reacting. The next day I was in such a state of depression and total exhaustion, that I really thought I had flipped myself out completely. Then, at that time, I stopped and looked at myself and all I had accomplished with my life. I had left my family friends and a girl who I was in love with....Then, I directed my thoughts towards the future and the direction that I was heading now. Man, Jerry, everything was just spinning so fast that I didn't even what end was up or even why I was living. Well I stayed on with those guys for about five days. I got a lot of sleep, ate some good food and I stopped smoking and I started feeding a lot better. So I hitch-hiked back home. Man was it good to get home! There was a time that I really never thought I make it. Well, all that I've gone through was in the past and from then on I decided to start moving forward. I made so many STUPID mistakes, I'll ever let myself get into a pit like that again.

I just thank GOD for watching over me and protecting me.

So now I'm on the farm working again and will be moving up to the Alps and spend the rest of the winter working on a ski resort. I plan to come back to Chicago in May or June. You said in your letter that you might be heading to San Diego about that time. Maybe I could come to Richmond and we could make the trip together. Is just a thought from the top of my head.....

Well, Jerry, I'll never think of written as long letter before, but I really wanted to let you know a little bit about what's been happening as I believe you really care and you are interested in me. I'm really glad to be able to know you, Jerry. You're a very special person and friend. If you get the time to write any more just address it here... Okay, I guess I'll see you in Spring or Summer then.

Take care always,

Carl

When Carl and I visited each other in July 2000, his letter became a topic of conversation that involved his own 18-year-old son's desire to travel. In the meantime, Carl returned to the U.S., married and became a successful businessman.

Overall, I began to hear that many of the younger wall rats and others were experimenting with more potent drugs.

I planned a train trip from Richmond to visit my family home in Butte, Montana, and then to San Diego during Christmas and semester break.

CHRISTMAS BREAK, 1976-1977

I arrived by train in San Diego, December 28, 1976. I remained until January 1, 1977. I was a guest in the Bayer family home.

I soon learned that clear-cut patterns were developing that, once more, separated the light and non-users from the heavy and regular users of drugs.

I report the findings as taken from my journal in the present tense.

The Light and Non-Users.

Brendan has a new girl friend. He is working. He had a successful football season. He is planning to attend the Rose Bowl with Ned who is studying acting at the University of Southern California. Ned began to use alcohol during college.

Phil is dating Bridget. He injured his leg playing football at the University of the Pacific.

Alex played football at Golden Beach High school. He is dating a new girl friend.

Roger is attending the U.S. Naval Academy. He decided not to play football. He says that Annapolis is not like he thought it would be.

Barry is working as a gardener.

Rick was accepted at Oregon State. He is waiting to see if he is accepted at Arizona State. If not, he may wait a year before beginning college.

Jeff is a senior at Golden Beach High. He began to drink at parties, counter to his vow, following the death of his brother, never to use alcohol or drugs. This upsets Brendan.

Steve is still dating Bridget's sister, Marie. He attends college in the East, but is home to visit her for Christmas.

Jack is staying with the Gilroy family. He went to Louisiana to train for deep sea diving. Due to curvature of the spin he is unable to do so. He hopes to be a supervisor instead.

Heavy and Regular Users

Albert, who had played football in high school and hosted the party described in Chapter 6, is working, but he parties frequently.

Sol was enrolled in high school, but dropped out again.

Ron left home and lives with one of his buddies' parents. He is unemployed but attends a lot of parties.

Carl is drunk, drunk and drunk. He is incoherent most of the time. He hangs out at the wall.

Rusty went to Hawaii.

Tom has been unemployed for two months. His patterns remain the same.

Art now lives with a girl in San Francisco.

Lonnie is in New Mexico for Christmas to be with his father.

Butch attends a community college. He no longer plays football. He parties a lot.

Andy, a frequent user of hallucinogens, is "spaced out".

Eric quit high school. He is unable to return to Golden Beach High. He says he will enroll next summer. He is working. His father "fell off the wagon" again. Eric still uses pot and drinks alcohol at times. He did not recognize himself in the dissertation.

And, Among the Wall Crew.

Matt hardly recognizes me. Other guys say he is "spaced out".

Skip is also "spaced out." Using hallucinogens, Quaaludes and cocaine.

Jim left for another part of the country.

Matt is living with two women. He skies a lot. He is still employed.

Julian and his wife, Lois, are drunk. They play volleyball at the beach. Both are unemployed.

Les continues to be a practicing "Christian." He is in Arizona to help take care of his grandfather.

Luke has a new girl friend. She is a "Christian."He is, "somewhat of a Christian," but very drunk on New Year's Eve.

Greg graduated from high school, but is unemployed. Pat says, "Another success story at the wall."

Pat lives with Sherrie. He is working, but continues to drink heavily.

There is a lot of drinking!

Some Special Cases and the Five Families.

The younger rats became involved with an older, wealthy man. I will call him Bill Dimaggio. It appeared that he may have taken advantage of their need for an older father figure. In 1976, I had heard of Bill Dimaggio. One younger rat mentioned him but another responded, "Don't talk about him!"

Bill Dimaggio's became involved with all of the sons in the Roe and Dunn families. He began to introduce them to cocaine and cocaine dealing. In addition, he introduced them to and supplied them with Quaaludes.

Quaalude was a brand name for methaqualone introduced in the U.S. in 1965 as a sleeping pill. It was approved and marketed as a substance that did not produce physical dependence. By the early seventies, it was clear that methaqualone was very addictive and extremely dangerous. It became popular in the drug subculture, known also as "ludes" or "soper". It was known as a "love drug" with aphrodisiac qualities. Many deaths, including the mixture of methaqualone and alcohol and suicides, were traced to the drug. In October 1973, methaqualone was listed as a Schedule II drug and, by 1985, was no longer produced as a prescription drug.[1]

Norman Dunn moved from his mother's home to live with his father. He tells me he "gets high with his Dad every day." He does not skip school frequently because he was not near a beach and "there is nothing to do if I skip." Norm is selling minor amounts of cocaine through the Dimaggio connection. He has saved over $250.

Norm's younger brother, Martin, is glad to that Norman is not at home because "he beats me up." Martin tells me their mother found Toby's marijuana plants and was upset.

I see Toby Dunn at the beach. He appears listless and has no drive. He is with others, but acts like he wants to talk to me. I did not see Toby again until the next summer. He, too, is involved with cocaine.

Bart Roe had been arrested for theft of motorcycle parts. He spent thirty days in jail. He had also been charged with the theft of a small car.

Bart's younger brother, Chuck, Norm Dunn's close friend, is increasingly involved in dealing cocaine as a "runner" for Bill Dimaggio. He now uses Quaaludes. He frequently skips school and is receiving "F's" in school. When he skips school, he surfs, then goes to Leo's house. Leo is also dealing cocaine and using Quaaludes. Leo had been arrested for outstanding warrants and spent a few days in jail. I learn that Leo buys Quaaludes tables for $1.75 each. He has given them to 17-year-old Betty.

A younger, 14-year-old, wall rat, Kyle, is more closely involved with Bill Dimaggio than are the other rats. He does not have a father and frequently mentioned he does not like to be at home. His mother is frequently absent. During my visit, Kyle tells me he has been using cocaine for two years. He began to use Quaaludes the previous fall. Bill Dimaggio supplies the drugs. At times, Kyle sleeps overnight at the Dimaggio residence. Kyle frequently skips school with Chuck Roe and they go together to Leo's house to use drugs after surfing. Kyle tells me that he uses Quaaludes to have sex with Debbie, another 14-year-old and the daughter of two alcoholic parents. Kyle assures me saying, "I always use rubbers."

I fail to contain my emotions when I learn what has been occurring. I express strong anger at Leo and Chuck Roe. The older wall crew members want me to "give them hell." Interestingly enough, Leo and Chuck, both say afterward that they had wanted me to "give them hell."

Paul is now 17. He wakes me one morning to ask to talk to me. He lives with another friend's parents. His mother is still in Arizona and, without a father, he says he needs direction. He has been involved with the Chuck Roe, Norm Dunn, Kyle, Leo and Bill Dimaggio. He continues to study in high school, but does not like his situation. He says he would like to leave Golden Beach. He would like to go to college. He says he doubts he is loved. He resents the fact that his step-Dad and mother give him no support and he has to pay his own way through his father's social security payments. I discuss "external" and "internal" control concepts with him. He is very bright and values education. He reiterates his belief that he needs to leave the area to succeed.

I begin to view Bill Dimaggio as an older man who satisfies a need to those young people who were without an adequate father figure in their lives. He becomes the first of what I term, not just an "inadequate father figure," but a "damaging father figure". The story of the Dimaggio connection will continue through the summer of 1977 and beyond.

Morris Bayer and his brother, Gil, are moving in opposite directions. Morris has been in jail twice for public drunkenness. He has moved from home and lives in Sand Beach. Gil is attending San Diego State University. He receives "A's" and "B's". He dates, but always returns by 10:30 p.m. to study. He tells me he is very pleased with his lifestyle. Gil's and Morris' younger sister, Alise, "hangs out" with Betty at the wall. Anna says she thinks her life style is "great."

Trent, one of the "Trio" along with Morris Bayer and Rich, phones me at the Bayer's. He was jailed and served time in a county honor camp for four months and 16 days for "Breaking and Entering". He tells me his mother "turned him in."

Rich had also been arrested for stealing. He hired a lawyer and stole more to pay the lawyer $1,500. After paying the lawyer, he was arrested again for stealing. Rich's father complains but Rich's room is filled with stereo equipment and other "hot" items. He was able to avoid jail time.

The Jones sons appear to be moving back to their religious roots. Todd is working as a roofer. He is going to a Christian convention for New Year's. Pete is on a "furlough" at a Bible camp in Oregon. Terry is now a successful salesman at a mens' clothing store. Bill Jones now works for "art shows." He began college, but did not finish the semester. His friend, Barry, a non-user, may put up the money for Bill to buy the art show business. Bill tells me that he no longer feels guilty about sex. He does not use drugs as frequently as in the past. He tells me he "liked"my dissertation.

I spend some time at the Gilroy home. Ron has moved out and is working at St. Patrick's. John is employed at an auto dealership. Reed is home from Brown University for Christmas. Mrs. Gilroy is concerned about Reed's infatuation with a high school classmate, Tara. Mark is doing "ok". He does not have a girlfriend, but knows many girls from "Drop-In" at St. Patrick's. He argues with Fr. Gonzalez, who has taken Fr. O'Malley's place. Mark is graduating from high school, but is undecided about college. Mark is concerned that he will not be able to attend because, unlike Reed, he does not have extremely high grades and SAT scores. Without a scholarship, he believes he cannot afford college.

Vick

I learn at the wall that Vick, one of the Old Wall gang, had what they term a "nervous breakdown." Vick had appeared "spaced out" at times during the previous year. During high school, he had used LSD. There is some talk that Vick is suffering from "LSD-Psychosis." He entered a mental hospital several months ago. He has been in and out of the hospital and halfway houses. Vick has had a difficult home life. His mother suffered from mental illness. Vick expressed great emotion in describing the scene to me. Vick was a "loner." Typically he did not discuss his family situation with his peers at the wall. I am moved when I hear of Vick's hospitalization. He wrote a college paper about me the previous summer, entitled, "The Person I Admire the Most."

The First Death.

In other disturbing news, shortly before the holidays, I learned of the death of Ed, a 17- year-old. Ed and his best friend, Al, were rock climbing.

Both had skipped school and were drinking. Another friend, Rick, tells me that they were probably "smoking a few j's" as well. The two teens apparently made a difficult climb. Ed slipped and fell. He died two hours later on the way to the hospital. Ed had been one of the most sensitive young men in my study. Ed's father had been a minister until he divorced Ed's mother. Ed was 2 years old. His father remarried twice. Both ended in divorce. Ed described the great pain he experienced in not having a full-time father. He especially missed the discipline of a father. However, he appreciated weekly visits with his Dad. Ed had used marijuana "once a day" and drank alcohol on weekends. His only sexual experience had been in the 9th grade. He found that it had "turned him off" toward the girl. Ed seemed to be searching. He felt depressed at times but felt comfort in the outdoors, camping, and especially in rock climbing. He felt very close to Al, his best friend.

Ed's death profoundly affected Al. I phone Al and have a long conversation. In the years that followed, I believe that Al never completed the grieving process involved in the loss of his very close friend. Al continued to drink heavily and smoke marijuana frequently.

A tree was planted in Ed's memory at a Golden Beach park, a short distance from the Bayer home. I frequently stop at the tree to pray for Ed and others.

THE SUMMER OF 1977

During the next six months, I continued to receive news from Golden Beach. Brendan, Ken, Rick, Bill Jones, Reed Gilroy and the Bayers were among those who maintained frequent contact. The news was of graduation and college plans by light and non-users, and increased use of cocaine and other substances by the regular and heavy users.

I continue to use the present tense as I describe my observations during the summer months of 1977.

Once again, with another grant of confidentiality in hand from the U.S. Department of Justice, I head for San Diego. Reed Gilroy broke his leg in a motorcycle accident at Brown University in that spring. He asked to ride with me to Golden Beach that summer. On the way we discuss politics, history, sociology and religion. His grades at Brown are excellent. He now drinks "a little"but not as much as other Brown students. Reed expresses his desire to become more independent. He demonstrates his independence by refusing to allow me to help him with expenses even though he has very little money.

We arrive at the Gilroy home in Golden Beach on June 5, 1977. Mrs. Gilroy gives Reed a big hug. Mark Gilroy is home. He has grown considerably. He now drives a big car with a new, very loud engine. He has a new girlfriend and remains active in "Drop-In".

I stay with the Bayer's for two days until I can move into an apartment. Gil Bayer is working as a carpenter for the summer. Morris has been evicted from his apartment in Sand Beach because of the keg parties he and his roommates had hosted. He fell off a skateboard and cut his hand. Unable to work, he is moving back home. The next night he comes home drunk and falls asleep on a bench in the backyard.

Colleen Bayer tells me that Alex and some of his buddies need to talk to me.

Alise Bayer is now 17 and will graduate this summer. She asks me to drive her to the store. She uses the occasion to discuss her confusion regarding her future and her negative feelings about her father's behavior under the influence of alcohol. We drive by the wall. I note that the area is filled with red freaks, "hippies" and a number of police officers. In the midst of the "hippie" group, drinking beer, is Pat, "the mayor of the beach." Pat hastens toward the car. He is ecstatic to see me. "Lowney," he yells, "It is a great to have you back! Things have not been going too good around here." I will soon learn what Pat means.

A Renewed Acceptance of My Role.

I immediately sense a greater acceptance of my role and presence in Golden Beach. I have now completed my PhD and am "Dr. Lowney." Some of the young people begin to address me as "Dr J." They and their parents have been impressed with my dissertation. I am asked by the Golden Beach Women's Group to address their next meeting to discuss my research findings. I am invited to numerous homes for dinner with the young people and their parents.

Most importantly I discover that some fears other had about my role with young people have been relieved. During the previous years, I frequently was disturbed by the fact that few parents questioned my involvement and the time I spent with their children. It was true that I had many community contacts over many years at St. Patrick's, as a volunteer with the San Diego County Probation Department, as a member of the

Optimist Club and among business associates. It is also true that our society had not yet awakened as to the extent and nature of child abuse. Nonetheless, only once was I informed that a parent had questioned my role. That parent had called St. Patrick's to ask a priest about me. He assured the mother of my character and the nature of my research. The priest told about the phone call. I had expected more questioning.

Now I learned that a few others had concerns. On my third day at the beach, I see Lee. He is on the baseball team. He has a new girl friend. He works at a surf shop and on boats. He asks me into his home to meet his mother. His mother is very happy to meet me. She thanks me, "for all you have done for my son." She told me that she was worried when she first heard about me. She checked with people from St. Patrick's and learned more about me. She stated that she learned how much I had helped Lee and others by "talking to them" and "encouraging them in school and sports."

The next week I talk to Alex. He is very happy to hear from me. He wants me to drop by to see him and his parents. He tells me very proudly that he has been dating the "same girl" for over a year. He is on both the track and baseball teams. I set a time to stop by his house and meet his mother. She tells me how glad she is to meet me and also thanks me for what I "have done for the kids." She informs me that, in 1975, when I was "hanging out" at the beach, she had her older son go to watch and "check-up" on me. Unknown to me, the older son visited the area and inquired of some his classmates who were subjects of my research. He assured his parents that I was "legit" as well.

Finally, in July, I am invited by Theresa, Betty and Marie to speak to two summer classes at Golden Beach High School. Upon my arrival, word spreads across the campus that "Lowney's here!" I discuss drugs and the beach area. I receive cheers and rather wild reception in the second class. The teacher tells me afterwards that he was surprised by my appearance and what I had to say. He says he pictured me "as a young, student, freak-weirdo." He had looked for me on the beach. He asked the vice-principal about me and received favorable comments about me and assurances that I was "legit." He thanks me and tells me he respects me for what I had done and the message I bring to the students.

These assurances mean a lot to me because I realize the vulnerability of those who missed a father figure in their lives. In addition to Bill Dimaggio, I would become painfully aware of other "damaging father figures." Two of these were damaging both young males and young females and I am unaware of it. I would learn of some incidents only after several more years of research.

Changes and "Anomie."

Soon after my arrival, I begin to see and hear many things that indicate major changes are taking place in the Golden Beach youth drug subculture. They are particularly obvious along the beach and, above all, at the wall.

The price of housing in Golden Beach continues to skyrocket. Houses, which had sold for $60,000 three years earlier, are now priced above $110,000. New condominiums spring up. Older apartments become costly. Small established businesses disappear. They are replaced by new franchises and up-scale businesses.

A citizen's movement circulated a petition to the City of San Diego to place a rent-control measure on the ballot. The movement failed and rents continued to increase sharply, particularly in the beach areas.

The boardwalk appears very dirty with trash strewn about. Beer cans and broken bottles are on the beach and on the boardwalk. I find it difficult to dodge the skateboards and bicycles navigated by drunk and stoned teens. Mopeds, illegal on the board walk, occasionally weave through the skateboards, bicycles and pedestrians.

School is still in session, but most of the rats, along with others, skip classes. In part, they are taking advantage of the substitute teachers in the midst of a teacher's strike. In addition, there is a new vice-principal at Golden Beach High School who does not command the respect of his predecessor.

Many parents are less supportive of the school and the school district because bussing of inner-city students to Golden Beach has been initiated. There are many racial jokes and slurs that would have been unheard of when I came to Golden Beach in 1968.

Community seems to be breaking down in Golden Beach. In my sociological mind, I keep repeating the term "anomie." Emile Durkheim first coined the term "anomie" to describe a societal condition typically occurring in times of rapid change. When anomie exists, the former norms do not fit the new situation. As a result, society is unable to provide moral guidelines to individuals. Durkheim studied the rate of suicides as an indicator of anomie. He maintained that divorce was one of the major factors bringing about anomie.[2]

Golden Beach has been undergoing rapid change. Divorce rates skyrocketed in recent years. Wealth and development accelerate. The schools are changing. Even the "Drop-In" and St. Patrick's are experiencing disruptions. Moreover, there are other signs, including changes in the types of drugs used, and the norms that have governed the use drugs used and the norms governing interaction with one's peers in the drug subculture.

I add new terms to my glossary of terms: "cola," "coke" and "c" for cocaine; "crack" for crystalized cocaine; "z" for ounce; "g" for gram; "stepped on" for dilution of drugs, particularly cocaine; "lombo" for Columbian marijuana; "Sensimilla" for the new, highly potent "seedless pot"; as well as "ludes" and "soper" for Quaaludes or Methaqualone. "Pound" replaces the measurement for buying and selling large amounts of drugs instead of "kilos" or "bricks."

The prices of drugs are as inflated as much as the price of housing. The exception is "commercial pot". It remains at $10 a "lid" or $150 a pound. I obtain the following "price list" from several sources:

Regular Columbian	$400 lb.	$35 lid
Columbian Gold	$550 lb.	$45 lid
Oaxacan	$300 lb.	$25 lid
Sensimilla	$550	$50 lid
Homegrown	$25 - $30 lid (if tops) 25 to 50 cents a joint	
Thai Sticks	$160 for 16 to 19 sticks; a single stick = $15-$20	
Cocaine	$1900 for the first lb., $85 - $100 a gram, $1400 for the second lb. The price varies depending on how many times the cocaine has been "stepped on."(Frequently only 20% cocaine.)	
Quaaludes	$2.50 a hit	
LSD (blotter acid)	$2.00 a hit	
Mushrooms (hallucinogenic)	$10-15 a can	
Peyote	$5.00 (if "fresh from the reservation")	

It is obvious there is considerable profit for any entrepreneur who can afford larger quantities and risk breaking that quantity down for smaller individual sales. And, as profits increase, rip-offs and fights become common. Violence and property crime are increasing. The police are responding in kind.

In spite of all the attention being focused on marijuana, cocaine and other illegal drugs, the mostly widely used drug, alcohol, is obviously the number one problem. More and more, members of the drug subculture use alcohol along with other drugs. This is a far cry from the ethic of 1970 that alcohol was unhealthy and its use unwise when compared to the drug of choice of that generation, marijuana.

However, the dichotomy between those involved in the drug subculture and those not involved becomes more obvious. The continued list of those who were succeeding in school, involved in church, courting and marrying might sound somewhat "boring" compared to the "excitement" of the wall crew, the party goers and the "wild" times in the drug subculture. A few simple facts summarize the differences. I count seven light and non-users who are to graduate from Golden Beach High School this June. Only three heavy users graduate, and two of those do not attend their graduation ceremonies. In the previous year, seventeen of the male subjects experienced difficulties in adjusting to college. Eleven of these have dropped out of college. All eleven are heavy users. Six others either remain in the college they are attending or switch to a different school. Only two of those who remain in college are heavy users. All four light users who experience adjustment problems continue their college careers.

The dichotomy may be reflected in other ways as well. Country music is now popular across the country as well as among the over-20 crowd in Golden Beach. The younger members of the drug subculture prefer the new "acid" rock. The hair styles of men, including young men, are shorter (including my own).

Most of the members of the Old Wall Gang decrease their use of marijuana and other illegal drugs. However, there is an increasing amount of evidence that some are abusing alcohol. Their "wild" hair styles of 1970 are replaced by shorter conventional cuts.

The Wall Crew & Others - Drugs, Money, Rip-offs, Parties and Arrests.

My second full day in Golden Beach I go to the wall. It is overcast and not particularly desirable for surfing. A lot of rats are skipping school. I see

Norm Dunn with June. Norm has a lot of money. Paul flashes a $50 bill. Neither Paul nor Nelson plans to attend their graduation. Bart Roe was in jail again - 8 days for stealing a motorcycle. He admits he is dealing cocaine. He dropped out of school. He had a job roofing, but was "laid off."

Bart, Paul and I go to Eric's apartment. Bart stops to buy beer at a liquor store. Eric arrives and begins to smoke Columbian pot. His roommate, Tim, weighs $20 worth of "Thai Sticks" on a scale to pay back what he borrowed from Eric. Tom says he is "addicted" to Thai Sticks. He says, "I have to have three a day. I smoke one first thing every morning." Eric tells me Tim is a "big dealer."

I am invited to Eric's parents' home for dinner. Jeff's Mom joins us. She is very "hip" and admits she smokes marijuana with Jeff.

I go to the beach at 11 p.m. I notice that no one from the wall crew is around. It is very crowded with "red freaks." I soon find that although the wall crew retains their "turf" during the daylight hours, the "territory" is lost to them after dark. The police "crackdowns" of the previous summer eliminated their presence and the "outsiders" have taken over. In spite of city ordinances to the contrary, the police now allow people to sleep on the beach in their sleeping bags.

The next morning I return to the wall. Luke is drinking beer with Sally. He was fired from his job on a fishing boat. His mother urges him to go to Alcoholics Anonymous. He brings me up to date on the Old Wall Gang. Shane and his wife came down from Washington state last month. They have a new baby. Frosty has become a father as well. Kenny is enrolled in a chef's school and working Cunard Lines. Keith no longer deals cocaine. He lives with a girl in a San Diego suburb. Moe is still in Hawaii. One of Luke's friends was busted last week for crack.

Luke is disgusted with the trash on the boardwalk and those who now frequent the area. He says in two weeks they are having a "Golden Beach Drive Clean-up Party" (as he hits his fist hard into the palm of his hand!). I see bumper stickers with the same messages including statements about "red freaks."

Rusty comes by. He tells me that Mario has had a "nervous breakdown." Mario has been in mental wards and now lives with his mother. Rusty says, "He smokes pot all day and collects welfare checks." (I recall Mario's interview last year and his reported use of LSD and other hallucinogens. I wonder if Mario, like Vick, is a victim of "LSD-psychosis." Very much a "loner," Mario had a very low self-image. He had described many "bad feelings." He had used various drugs, including heroin, to cope.)

Rusty tells me that Ralph is now "into coke." Rusty says, "I can't see that, snorting $100 and sit around with your chick. It's too much!"

I call Kyle. His mother tells me he has dropped out of the alternative school. She says Kyle, 14, "won't listen" so she allowed him to go to San Francisco for a week. The guys at the wall are very angry at Kyle. They call him "a little rip-off."

Carl is sitting on the wall as I come by. He returned from Europe after he borrowed $20 in Chicago to cover his fare back to San Diego. His parents are upset that he is "play dating" with Tara. He says he is not yet ready for marriage. Pete Jones comes by and they "go have a beer."

At 7 p.m., I return to the beach for another marvelous sunset. Ron Gilroy is on the boardwalk drinking beer. He moved out of his Mom's home. He broke up with his girl friend and "called off the marriage." He talks about enjoying his freedom and independence.

I smell lots of pot. Soon a fight breaks out. A knife is pulled. Three guys jump on one other and end up kicking him. No police are in sight. A half an hour later, I see three police officers spending twenty minutes to give a ticket to a teen for not having a light on his bicycle. They are very rude. I can see the youth holding in his anger, but later I hear lots of words about "pigs," "fascist tactics," and so on. In the days and weeks following, more incidents occur and I hear more tales.

Dennis is married and has a son. He "had to get married." He works at a local restaurant, which is known as a location to purchase and use cocaine.

Kevin's father died. This deeply affects Kevin and his sister, Norma. Kevin has increased his use of drugs and alcohol. Norma is "in" and "out" of her practice of being a "Christian." She preaches to others constantly, including Kevin and her "off-again" and "on-again" boyfriend, Les. Les says she is a "hypocrite." Les begins to use drugs and alcohol again.

I see bumper stickers reading, "Keep Golden Beach Drive Red Freak Free." Graffiti on the wall reads, "Surfers Rule the Beach. Beaners Rule the Taco Stand."

Chuck Roe admits to me he is dealing coke. He does various "tests" on its purity. He made $2,000 last month and saved $200. He asks me to stay at the wall until 12:30 p.m. so that I can drive him to school. He lets me know he wants me "to make him stay in school." Chuck brags about his "rep" stating, "Anyone orders anything and in three days I could deliver it!" He tells me, "I snorted H twice, but didn't like it."

A few days later, I receive a call from Paul. Chuck Roe and Paul just finished doing "lines" of coke. When I question Chuck about his association with Bill Dimaggio, he responds angrily, "It's all your fault!"

Nelson seeks me out at Billy's restaurant late one afternoon. He is graduating from high school, but does not feel it is an accomplishment because "anyone can graduate from Golden Beach High." He is concerned about his future. I ask why he has been going downhill with grades, drugs, lack of work and not participating in soccer. He blames me! I ask how he can blame me. He replies, "When you were around, I was doing ok. It's all your fault!" A few minutes later, he asks, "Should I go tomorrow morning and apply for that job?" I urge him to do so.

Nelson describes more about the connection with Bill Dimaggio. He tells me he drove Bill to the airport to buy a ticket for 15-year-old Kyle to return from San Francisco. Kyle had lied to his Mom and told her he had been in a car accident. Nelson says Bill Dimaggio is a "big man." A few years ago, his brother was "busted and they paid the judge $20,000 to get him off.." He claimed he had been "set-up." Nelson tells me that Norm Dunn is the "go-between" and Chuck Roe and Kyle are at a "higher-level." They invest money to deal coke and other drugs. Nelson confesses that he had been a go-between in the past few months. He says, about work, "It's so hard though. You bust your butt to ever get $20.00 and I see Norm make that much in a few seconds."

Nelson informs me that Toby Dunn was "ripped-off" by Chuck and Bart Roe. It led to a big fight.

The next day, I meet Paul. He states that Norman is "a rip-off" regarding coke. He says he's got some good stuff and that he has tested it for purity. He says Norm is just looking for someone who wants some and then goes back to see if he can buy it from Chuck or someone. Paul says he feels Bill Dimaggio is "just using Norm and Kyle and Chuck." That evening, I hear Luke Smith confront Norm , "Your cola is only 41!" (That is 41 percent on a test.)

Paul says to me, " See, I told you Danny was a 'rip-off!'. I gave him $100 for a 'g'."

Luke Smith is rolling Thai sticks at the wall. Luke Smith feels he is "safe from a bust." His says his Dad is a "cop." His uncle is also a "cop" and inherited $250,000. His uncle lives in an expensive condominium.

Toby Dunn is on the boardwalk the next day. He tells me he is dealing dope because he "has a connection." He started three months ago with only $35.00. He had $600.00 worth of pot locked in his closet a month ago and "someone broke into it." He states that Bart Roe started "buying with a lot of money afterwards."

On Friday, June 17th, the *San Diego Union's* headlines read "Dr. Mandell on Drug Charges with the San Diego Chargers." Elsewhere in the news that day are reports of massive arrest for cocaine in Sand Beach. The residents of Sand Beach protest "police harassment." Finally, a small headline states that "San Diego is Fourth in the U.S. in Heroin Addicts."An employee of Lilly and Company sits next to me and tells me that his company donates methadone to Calexico, Mexico, but they do not ship "reds" to Mexico City because some people were imitating their capsule and selling imitation barbiturates on the illegal market, including in San Diego.

Monday, June 20, I begin to sign-up a number of female subjects. As I walk the boardwalk at midday, I smell marijuana nine times.

I learn that Eric "beats up" Bridget, Marie's sister. He gave her a black eye yesterday. Eric has, in the past, beat up a former girlfriend. Eric, the son of two alcoholic parents, frequently takes up collections to "throw a kegger."

Marie asks me if I use drugs. I respond that I do not use pot, would never think of using substances like cocaine and I use alcohol very infrequently. She responds, "Good, I feel much better about you, and am more confident then about your research."

Linda and Helen, both 16, see me at Lime Avenue. Linda tells me how happy she is to see me and how happy they are to be in my study. She tells me where the parties are. I frequently see her at parties. She and Marie tend to hover near me when males approach them flirtatiously. I view this behavior from them and other females as part of my role as a father figure and a "protector." (Again, only in the years to come, I would realize the true significance of these behaviors.)

Lonnie, now 16, works at a popular restaurant. He tells me that he no longer goes to the boardwalk. Regarding the red freaks, he states, "If I knew karate, I'd bust their noses. Someone should take some dynamite and blow them up!" He says he doesn't smoke as much pot as he used because, "It's too expensive." Instead, he drinks more beer.

The next morning, Chuck Roe slept in and missed school. He wants me to start calling him in the morning to "urge" him on. I tell him to set his alarm and practice getting himself up in the morning. He tells me that his brother, Bart, got ripped-off for $800 in a deal. Chuck says, "Maybe I'll get out of it (coke dealing)."

On Saturday, I chat with one of my newest subjects, 16-year-old Jeanie. Jeanie is the younger sister of Nelson. She is with Jeri, Kent and Red. Jeanie has used a number of drugs. She states that she has "no communication" with her Mom, and that her Dad "does not care." She says, "I want to go to Oregon or back East, but my mother says I would get into too much trouble. Then, I don't come home for two days and she doesn't do anything!"

Kent, 16, talks of his mother kicking him out of the house, so he stays "with chicks."

Red, 17, discusses the difference between regular pot and "more expensive pot." He does coke and Quaaludes. He drinks beer with Quaaludes. Red says he "gets stoned with his mother." He says, "She gets me drunk when she wants to find out something." A thirteen-year-old rides upon a bike and tells me, "Don't talk to him (Red). He is an alcoholic."

I leave after an hour to meet Luke who said he wanted to attend an A.A. meeting. Luke does not show.

That night and the next I attend parties and observe a number of police actions.

At 8 p.m. I see Jeanie again. She is with Linda and Kent. Randy Wong comes by. He sells a half of a lid of Columbian to two sailors for $45.00 (twice the going price). We all go to parties. The first is off of Wellspring Street near the Alano building.(I realize that an A.A. meeting is going on inside that building.) The price for the party is one dollar. There is a band, but very few locals. I see Albert, Al, Paul, Luke Smith and Mary Beth Smith. There is a large crowd outside.

Al and I go check out the other parties. The next party is at a house on Wellspring with very young kids. No one is there. We hear that the party has been moved to the city park. We go to the park and nothing is taking place. Two police vans and two cruisers were there earlier and told everyone to leave. The young people are upset because the band had obtained a permit to play there.

Linda says there is another party on Lime Avenue. There are only thirty-one people present, including Morris Bayer. Jeanie and Linda both become very drunk. They also smoke joints. When they are high they become very flirtatious, especially Linda. When the guys tend to approach them and "move in" on them, they come to me and stand behind and to the side of me, as though I am their "protector." Jeanie says her Mom wants to go to an "analyst." Linda has told her parents she is staying at Jeanie's (but Jeanie is not home).

Kent believes that Jeanie and Linda "do too much drugs and booze." He tells me his father was an alcoholic. He went to Alateen and Alanon when he was younger. Ken ran away from home when he was 14, was arrested and placed in Los Angeles Juvenile Hall. Kent stayed in school until the 12th grade, but did not graduate. He talks to me as though seeking a father figure for advice. Linda and Jeanie both tell him I am "like a father."

The party's host takes up a collection for beer. Shortly thereafter, his father shows up and tells everyone the party is over. Most are angry because they have paid for a keg. Kent eggs them on. The host pleads for everyone to leave. Kent makes tough remarks to him as we leave. A group of "bikers" show up outside. The same two police officers who were at the previous party show up. They say they want "no one else let inside." I leave the kids at Golden Beach Drive and go to Billy's to write my notes.

At 11 p.m. the next evening, I arrive at the wall. The police are there in force. They clear the area of anyone that appears to be a "red freak." Well-dressed people are not disturbed. The police begin to move north. As they approach Main Street, the teens in vans and cars hide their liquor. Many leave, but a large crowd remains. The crowd is very hostile to the police. Some yell out, "Pigs!" An officer sees one young teen drinking. He says, "I'll give you five to get rid of that beer!" The kid drops his beer on the sand at the count of "four." Three police begin to beat him and haul him into a cruiser. Two other policemen force two other teens into another car. I notice that when one of the officers saw me observing their actions, they all seemed to calm down. They left with the two youngsters in the backseats of the cars.

Nelson, Linda's brother, finds me at Billy's that evening. He has been hired at an expensive restaurant as a cook and waiter. He is "stoked" and feels very proud of himself.

Chuck Roe is ripped-off again. A well-dressed man in a Cadillac arranged to buy some coke. He showed Chuck the money. They drove off in the Cadillac and pulled up in front of what he said was his home. He asked Chuck for the coke. Chuck gave it to him. The man took the coke but kept his money, telling Chuck, "I will be back in a minute." He never returned. No one was in the house. Chuck waited in the Cadillac which turned out to be "hot."

On July 4 at 1:30 a.m., over thirty police arrive at a beach party. They wear "riot gear," (masked helmets, batons, and so on) and move into the party. A bottle broke against the wall. Albert claims an officer broke the bottle. The police move in and scatter the crowd. Three officers begin to beat on a Datsun with a young woman inside. She is frightened and refuses to open the door for several minutes. They search her and the car and place her under arrest.

Shortly thereafter, the police were called to another party in Sand Beach. Two girls were fighting each other. A guy went inside and brought out a gun. Everyone scattered before the police arrived.

The next day I attend a party with approximately four hundred participants. The police arrive and approach the band members to tell them to stop playing. The party slows down and breaks up by 5 p.m. I see several subjects including Jeanie (she is on LSD), Linda , Karen (with a new boyfriend), Betty (sober but flirts a lot), Nancy (drinking margarita), Beth and many of the wall crew.

The evening of the Fourth of July is a zoo! Lots of firecrackers. One is thrown about three inches from me. There are drunks on roller skates and bikes. I see lots of drug deals. I small lots of pot. Police patrol on foot and write a number of tickets.

The Fourth of July is known to be the "wildest" part of the summer on the beach. I continue to observe the wall and beach scene, the party scene, and the drug deals and rip-offs throughout the summer. It is not necessary to report all of the details of the remaining weeks. The patterns remained the same.

The Trio and Others.

The "trio" continues to have problems with the law. Morris Bayer is arrested twice, once for drunkenness and another time for theft. I see Morris frequently. He is usually very drunk. Trent and Rich are both on probation with the California Youth Authority (subject to incarceration in a prison for juveniles). Rich was stealing liquor from a liquor store. He did another break-in to pay for his attorney fees. Trent receives five months in jail for stealing cassette tapes. Both were "redded-out" and crashed into a car. They can both be prosecuted for "drunk driving" and have their probations violated. Neither is working in spite of the terms of their probation to be employed.

A few days later, Rich is taken home by police for being drunk on the boardwalk and acting "wild."

Trent told a large group how "cool" I am. He reflects on himself, "I need to get high to talk to girls."

Rich seeks me out at the beach frequently. On one occasion, Budweiser beer is running a promotional on the beach. Rich is one of the few who receive a "Mr. Bud" t-shirt. He gives it to me if I promise to wear it in one of my lectures at the university. (In the years to come, the now-tattered t-shirt will be, more me, a constant memorial to Rich when I discuss the rest of his story with my students.)

Those, males and females, not involved in the drug scene continue to go to summer school, plan for college, date, hold summer jobs and remain involved in a variety of activities. They seek me out frequently for my advice regarding school, relationships and their future. Often our conversations center around politics (Ford's pardon of Nixon, Carter's energy policies, the need for increased college loans and so on.) I visit them and their parents after church. I attend several dinners in their homes. Once, I drove Brendan by the wall, and he walked a short distance with me. He was shocked at what was taking place. Brendan vowed he would never use drugs.

There is less participation by young people at St. Patrick's Drop-In and increasing dissatisfaction with Fr. Gonzalez. He does not appear to relate as well to teens as did Fr. O'Malley.

Matt's biological father dies. Matt spent most of his non-working hours at the hospital with his Dad. They had just begun to re-establish a relationship for the first time since his mother divorced his father when Matt was 2 years old. Matt begins to "re-connect" with me. He tells others what I did for him as a kind of "foster father."

Matt and other Old Wall Gang members move from Golden Beach. A few are married. They use alcohol and other drugs less than their peers who remain at the wall.

The Females.

Twenty-two females originally signed up to be subjects of this phase of the research. However, one (a "red freak girl") disappeared from the area midway through the summer. Another, decided at the time of the final interview that she did not wish to be interviewed. She told me, "I don't want to tell my troubles to anyone." Both subjects were heavy users. As a result, only twenty remained as subjects during the final interviews. Their responses are reflected in the quantified data.

In order to insure openness and honesty during the final interviews, I chose to use "safe spaces" for the interviews. Typically, I interviewed them in my car during the daylight in an open space where we could be seen but not heard. Other interviews were conducted on a hillside in a park, two were in the front yards of the subjects. Their responses tended to be much more sensitive, but not as lengthy as the males.

In a manner similar to my observational findings, the quantified data demonstrated the dichotomy between those females were either heavy or regular users and those who were light or non-users. I examined the responses of 10 heavy and regular users and 10 light and non-users.

TABLE 16

FAMILY AND RELATED FACTORS AMONG FEMALES BY DEGREE OF DRUG USE

	Heavy and Regular Users (n = 10)	Light and Non-Users (n = 10)
Parents Divorced	6	1
Father Absence	6	1
Father Absent or Inadequate	9	1
Lacked Discipline	4	0
Doubted Parental Care	6	3
Sexually Active	8	1

Their responses followed the pattern that I found among the male subjects, but with even great consistency within the two categories. This produced obvious dichotomies. Consider the data in Table 16 obtained from female subjects with respect to the key factors family factors. The data are consistent with the findings from the male subjects presented in Chapter 8. The family factors, divorce, father absence, inadequate father, lack of discipline and doubts regarding parental care, each separated the heavy and regular users from the light and non-users. Moreover, only one of the light and non-users had engaged in sexual intercourse. All but two of the heavy users were sexually active and one said she "just played around." The median grade level of initial use of drugs by heavy and regular users was 8th grade. The median grade level of initial use of the light users was 11th grade. As with the males, the data are consistent in supporting social control theories as well as Differential Association.

When I examined their peer associations, only one of the heavy and regular users participated in religious or church-related activities. All of the light and non-users were active in their religion. The same was true regarding sports and school-related activities. All of the light and non-users were active either in school sports or student body activities. Only one of the heavy and regular users was active in school sport. Again, there is consistent support for Differential Association as well as social control theories.

Surprisingly, the "overprotective mother" was more significant to the female subjects than was the case with the males. Five of the heavy users and one of the light users reported that their mothers were overprotective. In two of those instances, the perception of the daughters was that their mothers were more protective of them than their brother. My observations of both brother and sister combinations confirmed this. On the other hand, females were more likely than males to express their importance of mothers in their lives.

Some sample responses are illustrative.

Regarding mothers:

"I like her. She is really nice but we do not get along. She wants me to "be responsible" and "wear the right clothes."

"She is too sensitive. She feels I am irresponsible. It has gotten worse lately, the last two years...She does not understand me."

"My Mom disciplines me....All she does is scream."

"My Mom yells at me all the time."

"She makes excuses for me all the time. She blames herself."

Regarding fathers:

"I hate my Dad!"

"My step-dad is too weak. He makes himself vulnerable."

"I don't really have a relationship with my Dad. He hides his emotions and never opens up."

"He's the greatest Dad in the world!"

"My Dad is nice!"

"I didn't miss not having a father, but I think it was something my younger brothers needed."

"Sometimes, I think he tried to make up for me not having a brother. Like with sports and stuff, he pushed me."

Regarding parental care:

"My Dad liked my older sister more than me."

"Sometimes, my Mom cares too much!"

"No, I know they love me."

"Both my parents care about me, even if my Dad doesn't know how to show it sometimes."

"My Mom pays more attention to my little brothers than she does to me."

Regarding the use of drugs:

"There were never any barriers. I began using in the 7th grade...It was always just curiosity...I use pot to fall asleep."

" I drink because I like to get high and get all rowdy. Coke is a good high."

"It's fun...Sometimes I use it (pot) to have sex."

"Pot? For the hell of it. I like it...I never use it for sex."

"I like the high of pot and beer...Coke makes me feel good. It makes my skin breathe."

"I like it! (pot) I like it! (alcohol)"

Regarding lesbianism:

"Once, I heard that our P.E. teacher was a lesbian. It really scared me."

"Yes, it kind of scares me."

"If a found out my best friend was a lesbian, it would scare me off. I would drop her."

"No way, I don't want to be near them!"

"As long as she didn't bother me, I would continue our relationship."

To the question, "What do you think of yourself?"

"I am lazy."

"I'm irresponsible."

"I need to work on it. I'm lazy."

"I'm just average."

"I'm better than most. I am easy to get along with, easy to talk to. I listen."

"I'm crazy and fun!"

One interesting difference between the females as compared to the males was the lack of admitting to the use of drugs for or prior to sex. This was in spite of the fact that at parties and on the boardwalk, the males often "enticed" females with drugs in order to lure them into sexual behavior. The males expressed this ethic more frequently with the increased use of cocaine and Quaaludes. Likewise, the females became much more flirtatious when under the influence of drugs. The relationship between lack of a father and female sexuality and sexual promiscuity have been noted by both David Popenoe[3] and Judith Wallerstein[4] Both indicate that girls seek in sex the love they have not experienced from a father. In addition, Wallerstein notes that girls use drugs to numb their feelings and to inflate "shaky self-esteem."[5]

It must be kept in mind that in 1977 there was not a concept of "date rape." In addition, other "rape drugs" had not yet been "discovered." Not only have the norms changed since 1977, but the norms have been incorporated into law. I often felt disgust when I saw young girls, particularly runaways, being enticed by males, including older males.

Overall, the responses of the twenty females were consistent with those of the seventy-two males that had been interviewed in the previous year and a half to two years. The exception was the degree to which the mother played a more significant role than the father in the lives of the young women. In addition, although the heavy and regular users tended to be sexually active, they were far less likely to view drugs as a means to have sex or to heighten the sexual experience. This was counter to the actions of the males and the perceptions of the males that drugs were effective enticements for females to consent to sexual activity.

In my interactions, the females appear to view me as a "father figure," but not as a disciplinarian as did the males. Rather, they interacted with me as a "protector," a person who "cared" and an educated older male who could advise them about school, jobs and drugs. On the other hand, they withheld from me "girl talk" about guys. If I entered their space when they were discussing the guys, they stopped. I would remind them to continue to act naturally as they had promised. They would give a response such as, "Oh, yeah, but not about the guys we won't!" In short, not matter whatever other indicators I had of my acceptance and rapport, I could never become "one of the girls."

My Final Hours in Golden Beach, 1977.

Saturday, July 30, I go to the beach. Many of the wall crew are present. I learn that Julian was arrested at 1 a.m. for "public drunkenness". Lois could not bail him out. They released him at 7 a.m. He had a Thai stick on him. The police confiscated it but took no action. The much despised Officer Johnson was present for the arrest. Lois said, "They hate each other. Johnson just picked him out of the crowd!" Lois tells me, "Julian is an alcoholic. He has lots of blackouts." I discuss Alanon and Alcoholics Anonymous with her. Lois tells me that Dr. Black , a female physician, prescribes Quaaludes freely. Julian is on Medi-Cal and sells them to others. I go to my car to get a schedule or A.A. meetings for Lois.

Later, I see Julian. He tells me, "I can't be an alcoholic! I only drink beer!" He goes on to say he quit for four days and got "the shakes." I describe the disease, its progression, the types of people in A.A. and the welcoming atmosphere at A.A. meetings.

Bill Jones and others are smoking hashish, but Bill leaves when heroin is mentioned.

Carl is handing out invitations to his wedding. He asks me if I expect everyone to be at the wall when I return.

I help Adam schedule San Diego State University general education courses. His friend, Todd, joins us and also asks my advice about classes.

I go to a party at Sherman's house with Sol. We are early. There are five kegs inside. The cost is $1.00 per person and girls have to pay. (Usually there is no charge for females.) Sherman is a football player and not usually a heavy user. He says he just wanted to raise a few bucks and have friends there for a party. The early crowd includes Michelle and Christi, both 15, Linda, Tara and Diane. Five of the wall crew are present, as well as six other heavy users and two football players, both regular users. The music is turned down low so as not to disturb the neighbors. The mood is somewhat mellow at this late afternoon hour. Linda and Christi ask me to drive them to Hamburger Heaven, even though Christi tells me she hates to leave because of a "foxy" guy that is there. They are very appreciative. At Hamburger Heaven, we discuss home life and guys. Christi says she is still living at home even though she does not get along with her mother. She says, "Alex puts on a show for the guys, but he is really wild!" Christi thinks Lonnie is "a fox." Linda says Andy Scott is, "Wow! And a good kid!"

Martin Dunn sees us. His mother is gone for the weekend again and did not leave any food for him at home. I buy him a meal. They are all very appreciative.

At 9 p.m., I go to the beach. There are lots of people there, all types, but most of the "locals" are now at Sherman's party. There is a lot of dealing going on at the wall. One guy rides by on a bike loudly proclaiming, "Thai Sticks!" Someone asks the price. He says, "$15.00." A 16-year-old at Lime Avenue is dealing. I hear him talking about "$6.50" and "$20." Dean's younger brother is also dealing. Another stranger walks by subtly asking, "Anything to smoke?"

All this occurs while two policemen walk past the area at least six times. When they are coming in one direction or another, the word is passed along.

Paul and Norm Dunn are with their girlfriends drinking a six pack and smoking joints at the wall. The police walk past them twice. Norm drove in from his Dad's tonight so that he could visit with me tomorrow at Billy's restaurant. Tom comes by to smoke a joint.

Luke tells me that he had bet Lois that Julian could not stop drinking. Luke maintains he is not an alcoholic because, "I quit for a while, or at least cut down." He tells me a friend of his joined A.A., but "he had to..His stomach was bleeding." I tell Luke that he is kidding himself. The other members of the wall crew are heading to Tom's house to watch pornographic movies.

At the party, Shane Harding, a 12th grader and a neighbor of the Bayer's asked to visit with me. We made an appointment to meet at Billy's restaurant at midnight. He tells me his mother found pot in the bathroom. He told her that he had quit. His parents urge him to college. He does not want to go but he does not want to tell them. His oldest brother is now going through a second divorce. He does not want to end up that way. Another brother is doing well at Annapolis. We discuss the use of alcohol and pot. He is not supposed to drink because he had hepatitis. He wants to know more about "relationships." We continue to visit, but he is anxious to get home because his mother is waiting for him. He tells me he was glad we have had our "little talks." (Shane was not a subject of the research, and I see very little of him in the next few years. In 1989, I receive an invitation to his wedding in Hawaii.)

Sunday, July 31, I go to 10 a.m. Mass at St. Patrick's. Laura, Bridget and Phil are there. We all meet in the coffee room after Mass. Mrs. Gilroy is concerned about her son, Ron. He is depressed and feels unwanted. He no longer attends Mass. She asks where she can get help. I suggest Catholic Family Services, Pathfinder or the Youth Service Bureau.

Reed Gilroy arrives with Nora. His Mom offers to buy their breakfast, but, independent as ever, he refuses. He is ready to leave but I urge him to stay. He had offered to go to Ron's house last night and stay with him. He gives me a big bear hug as we leave.

Mark Gilroy ushers at the next Mass and we say goodbye on the church steps.

I make my last "good-byes" at the beach. I feel sad. The girls say they "hate to see me go." The younger ones are especially upset. Linda gives me two hugs, one for her and one for her brother, Nelson. Linda stayed at Helen's last night. They got home at 1:30 a.m. I say, "Be careful." Betty says, "You are too fatherly, Lowney!".

I say "Goodbye" to Beth, Martha and Terry Jones.

I call the Bayer's. Morris tells me he "beat up" Rich, his former trio buddy, because Rich stole his surfboard. Morris says, "The guy didn't even fight back - so he has to be guilty!" ...When I try to impress how others feel when he steals, he responds, "But those are not my good friends!" He avoids the reality of it all! I will hear more from Morris about Rich before a year goes by.

Floyd is down from Manhattan Beach for the day with his girlfriend. He is now a carpenter and has become a "Christian." He gives me his address. He is thinking of becoming a police officer.

Paul makes certain I have his address and phone number.

Matt, too, wants to make certain I have his address. Matt comes to the beach with his live-in girlfriend, Jan. He talks about how his mother is such a "perfectionist" and so "controlling" that she never would accept me and my relationship with Matt. He still appreciates my role as a "father" to him after he was arrested and did not have a home. Jan is amazed at the way I could make Matt come home and especially make him help with dishes. She says he helps with chores but "hates the dishes." Matt is more mature. He repeats that he appreciates all I did for him.

Luke is at the wall drinking. He and others are shooting balloons into the air over the beach with a large rubber band. They call it the "E.M.B. (Eat My Butt) Machine".

Pat says he had his "bust" on alcohol and is under control. He says, "I got to stay away from chicks, especially them younger ones. Underage is a "stupid law."

I bid them all farewell and head back to Richmond.

Some Final Notes.

During the nine weeks I spent in Golden Beach in the summer of 1977, I was able to visit with all of the Old Wall Gang and all but nine of the other subjects of my 1975-76 research. Of the nine, five were heavy users and, of these, one, Ed, was dead. Two were undergoing mental health treatment. One had moved outside of the area and did not return that summer. The other four were light or non-users who were away at college and either were taking summer classes and/or working at their colleges over the summer.

The dichotomies between heavy users and others became more and more apparent. Those regular users who had played football, but were similar to the heavy users in family background, began to join the ranks of the heavy users. Those who had been heavy users, but had family patterns similar to light and non-users, began to move from the drug subculture. And Bill Jones was heading in that direction.

A similar dichotomy existed among the former "Wall Gang." The Old Wall Gang members who remained at the wall began to choose alcohol as their drug of choice. Those who were decreased their time at the beach, or who had moved out of the area and were gainfully employed, used drugs less often. They began to show signs of maturity. However, those who had moved out of the area and into meaningful employment were likely to have had family backgrounds which provided them with economic and social opportunities. This was not true of those who remained at the wall.

The most striking dichotomy of all was among the females. The differences between the heavy and regular users and the light and non-users were striking and consistent. Overall, the females, including those from families in which a son was also a subject, were more "protected" and had more consistent discipline than the males. The females were affected by divorce and the absence of an adequate father, but they did not express the same degree of concern as the males about missing discipline and other aspects of the father figure. They tended to be much more influenced by their mothers who were able to maintain stronger discipline and control over their daughters than their sons. Nevertheless, the females appeared to miss the "protection" of a father. Perhaps, this difference and the lack of healthy interaction with a male role model accounted for their sexual activity.

Given the number of arrests and the degree of police activity, external legal controls were ineffective in reducing or deterring drug use and other crimes. As in previous years, what appeared to be effective were negative consequences either experienced directly or affecting their immediate peers.

In subsequent years, the stakes would grow higher and the consequences would be even more severe. In the meantime, it appears that a condition of anomie continued to affect many of the residents in Golden Beach.

1978-1980
SOME CHANGES AND SOME MORE OF THE SAME

I continued to hear from Golden Beach. The Bayers, the Jones family, Mrs. Gilroy, Brendan, Ken, Rick, and Norman Dunn and others stayed in contact by phone and mail.

Brendan seemed to be the most open of all. He was named the "Most Valuable Player" in football. He discussed his work. He improved his grades but was not accepted by the Air Force Academy. Instead, he joined Gil Bayer at Humboldt State in northern California. They became roommates and I was kept doubly abreast of occurrences in California. Brendan discussed his relationships with girls. His openness seemed so apparent that I was shocked to learn in the next decade that he did not tell me the most important matter that were then affecting him.

Rick informed me of his progress in running and, as always, was anxious to receive my advice either by mail or on the phone. Rick was concerned that he had trouble establishing a healthy relationship with the "right" female.

Ken sent me a long letter. He was sorry he missed me over the summer. He has enrolled in the Cinema Department at U.S.C. He had pledged in a fraternity. He was very pleased with his college career. He took a class in religion and became involved in a Bible study group.

Reed Gilroy came to Richmond to spend Thanksgiving in 1977.

Pat, the “Mayor of the Beach”, wrote at Christmas,

Hi Jerry!!!

Greetings from sunny San Diego! How’s tricks? I just thought I’d drop you a line to wish ya a Merry Christmas and all that garbage. Bah humbug! In case you were wondering, everyone is doing well. Everything is fairly under control. To make you feel miserable, I’ll mention that the weather is absolutely dyno. We are in the midst of a Santa Ana condition at the moment and the temperature today was a chilling 78 degrees!.......This is now the seventh month that I’ve gone without smoking. Not too shabby eh? Now all I gotta do is quit drinkin’ and I can be a real live Mormon. Except I gotta go out and score me about six or seven wives. Maybe those guys weren’t as lame as I thought. I wish I had some spine tingling news to lay on ya but I don’t. You’re probably too busy to bother with the local gossip scene anyway. Everyone is employed, at least in “my age bracket.” I’m still on the same job, been here a year and four months. Firmin’ up, huh? I better be careful or I’ll end up with a house full of kids and fridge full of Geritol instead of beers!! Well, Jerry, Buddy, I’ll have to say so long to ya now because I should get back to work. Good excuse, huh? But seriously I hope you have a great holiday season and everything goes according to plan for you. Drop me a letter if you like.

Your bud,

Pat

Mrs. Jones sent me a Christmas card,

Dear Jerry,

....We do want to thank you again for the interest you’ve shown in the boys and the encouraging words to them to “fly right”. The boys are doing fine in general. Bill and Pete are both roofing, but Bill is in “wrong” company, I think. You know more about that than we do, no doubt, so pray for him; Todd is home from “boot camp” with the New Tribes Institute, hating the crummy, rainy weather he thought he had left behind in Oregon; Terry is working at Food Basket as well as going to Mesa College. He seems to be having a problem with his girlfriend at present (better to find out now for himself since parents don’t know anything..Ha! Ha!) Who could tell him?

Our house is coming along very slowly...
Best of '78 to you,
Mrs. Jones & Co.

Nora wrote about how busy she was at University of the Pacific. Phil lived across the hall from her. She told me Phil is maturing. She hoped to see me the next summer and wished me "a Very Merry Christmas and a beautiful New Year."

Norm Dunn called somewhat frequently. On one occasion, he was in tears telling me how he did not have a father and how his mother "never cared about us." (He had denied these feelings in 1976.)

I heard more news about cocaine, expensive marijuana and increased crime and violence in Golden Beach. In July of 1979, Mrs. Bayer sent me copies of the *Golden Beach Sentinel.* The July 5, 1979, headline read, "Beach Crime Soars - Resident, Merchants Expect It." A nighttime photo taken from the lifeguard tower at Main St. graced the front page. A separate front beach story was headlined, "Teen-age Drinking: Sobering Problem".[6] A July 8 headline in the *San Diego Evening Tribune* told of "A Summer of Fun and Fear - Tide of Discontent Rolls in Golden Beach." Details described "....busts of minor drug dealers at the foot of Golden Beach Drive have routed many of those dealing from the area (the wall area!)." One person told the reporter, "It's just a clash of cultures...Someone comes here from a conservative area like Indiana and it blows their minds." Another stated, "People are just a lot looser here and those who come here to visit just have to realize that."[7]

The next day, the lead story in the *Golden Beach Sentinel* was headlined "Man Shot to Death in Brawl at Beach." The story described a fight in a Golden Beach condominium that ended with the shooting death of a 19-year-old.[8]

On August 19, 1979, the *San Diego Evening Tribune* carried a story headlined, "Police Arrest 57 in Sweep of 2 Beaches." The story described police sweeps in Golden Beach and Sand Beach including the boardwalk and the wall area. Most of the arrests were for alcohol violations. Two of the arrests were for possession of marijuana.[9]

A September flyer distributed by the Sand Beach Town Council area invited people to attend a meeting featuring police officers and a city councilman. The flyer described the 1400 arrests in Sand Beach since the police "sweep" began in mid-August.

I heard from members of the wall crew that the police have been "harassing" lots of people so that the "locals" were avoiding the beach at night. I ask myself if the police actions continued to be counterproductive and if they were producing negative, latent effects?

I was very curious as to what was actually happening.

In late August, I learned that Toby Dunn has been stabbed several times. He was rushed to the hospital and survives. It appeared that both cocaine and his relationship with a girlfriend were involved.

Next, I received a letter from Morris Bayer who was in Europe with his sister, Anna. Morris was involved in a fight with a teen in Spain. He won the fight and was able to escape from his opponent's buddies. Morris was not yet aware of what was occurring Golden Beach.

Morris' former buddy, Rich, was dead! Grant used a shotgun to kill Rich. Grant was the young man who once gave the trio, Morris, Rich and Trent, a bottle of barbiturates that we flushed down my toilet when they were in 8th grade. Trent was present during the shooting. They were all high on cocaine and very drunk.

Morris wrote to me on September 12, 1978,

> Hello, Jerry,
>
> You know that I can't type but I can't write so hot either, so here it goes. I'm in New York staying with Margaret (his older sister). The place is about 1½ miles from Central Park on Manhattan Island. I got a job in a squash club. I'm working at the front desk (it's a snap). Well, I guess you heard about all the shit going on back home. Will you write and tell me about Toby Dunn. I heard the guy that stabbed him thought he was Howard Wilson. Now I know what you mean by picking the guys you hang around with. Too bad it took a thing like that to make me realize it was so true. I thought about it with Trent and Rich because Rich was a little shit and Trent will do anything for excitement. Plus Rich stole my surf board so that really split us up. Thank God I was in Europe because I would have been right in the middle of it. You remember Rich, Trent and I were three punks running around at night ripping off and smoking dope. We were buddies. Then Grant moved down from his house and in with Trent. That S.O.B. bought all of his friends. Rich was his friend (?) for a long time. I think all the time we fucked with Grant's guns must have gone to Grant's head. So now Rich's a stiff, Trent is in the slammer and Grant is up for murder 1. I hope they don't let him out because I don't want to have anything to do with him. You know that I don't like the Pigs but I also value human life more than all the cola in the world. Shit, I've been to jail four times and I hate the butt fuckers that work there, but I never waisted anybody so I guess I can't imagine what

Grant is going to go through. He won't last a week in San Quentin. His foster father is so rich he might be able to buy his ass off the hook. Tell your kids what happened to Rich. I know they won't listen, but it's worth a try. When I was their age I didn't listen. I had to find it out for myself. It would have been a lot easier to do what you suggested. Home won't be the same when I get back. Toby got stabbed five times, that's like dying and coming back to life. Rich is dead, I didn't like his ass anyway. What happens if you hold a grudge on someone and he gets killed? I have to forgive him because I can't get my money from him now. I only forgave him because he died, does God count that as forgiven? Kinda spooky ain't it.

Well the shit hit the fan.

I left your address with my friends in Switzerland so I hope you get this. Do the people in Lexington know your address. I hope so.

See ya, later,

MORRIS

Two weeks later Morris showed up at my doorstep. He was going to hitchhike to San Diego. He stopped in Richmond to spend some time with me. He brought a 13-page letter a young lady, Millie, had written to him. Morris wanted me to have the letter. Millie was with Rich, Trent and Grant until shortly before the shooting. She described the drugs, the beer and wine guzzling and the arguments between Rich and Grant lasting until early morning. Millie left prior to the shooting. Another friend stayed and told Millie the details. Grant went into his room and returned to the living area with a shotgun. Grant sat on the couch. Rich was in a chair. Grant picked up the shotgun, aimed and shot Rich. Blood gushed out in spurts. Trent begged Grant not to shot him. Grant went over to Rich's body and slammed the gun on his head said, "If that didn't kill him, I hope this does!"

The police arrived and arrested Grant and Trent. Grant was released three days later on a $250,000 bond. Trent was held because of a violation of his probation. Trent was sent to a county camp for a year, but expected to get out early on good behavior.

Morris and I had a good visit. I had become involved in youth ministry in Richmond. In addition, I was engaged in a minor research project to compare young people in the Richmond suburbs with those in Golden Beach. I introduced Morris to them at a party. Unknown to me, Morris had "ripped-off" a roof garden next to his sister's Manhattan apartment. Morris was looking out the window one day and noticed the garden was filled with marijuana plants. Morris took a garbage bag, made it to the roof and harvested the pot. Morris had the pot inside a large trench coat when he came to Richmond. I learned later that he was selling pot to the high school students at the party. The next morning I took Morris to the Interstate. He said, "Goodbye," and I began to drive off. He yelled at me. I stopped. Morris had left his duffle bag in my car. He departed saying, "I'm such a dumb shit!"

CHRISTMAS BREAK, 1978

During the next Christmas break, I traveled to Golden Beach for a brief visit. Mrs. Bayer told me that Trent's mother told her the police said Grant's family would probably hire high-powered attorneys to get him off. Grant served less than one year. I continue in the present tense from my journal notes.

I go to the wall. Norm Dunn sees me and gives me a big hug. He says, "My mother does want me in the house." He says she put in a new hot tub and other improvements. He bemoans the fact that his mother is a vice-president of a large savings and loan and earns good money, but does not save money. He tells me he does not like living at his Dad's and he cannot talk to his Mom.

I find that cocaine and expensive marijuana are still widely used. On the other hand, among the wall crew, Rich's death and other acts of violence, such as the stabbing of Toby Dunn, have had an impact on others. They begin to reassess their use of "hard drugs." Many have learned that Quaaludes, LSD and PCP (widely used in Virginia at the time) are harmful. I am told, "There is no market for them." When I tell them of the use of LSD in Virginia, Todd says, "Are they crazy?"

Many of those who had moved away from home have returned, including Morris Bayer, Frank, Eric, Tom and Herb.

Nelson still works at the Japanese restaurant. He is more "mellow." So is Lee who avoids his former friends.

On the other hand, Chuck Roe continues to deal. He says, "The danger is over." He brags about how much money he has made.

Some former light and non-users begin to smoke pot. Mark Gilroy defends the use of pot. In addition, he now drinks alcohol. Brendan tells me he has used marijuana four times. He sees it as helpful to make him relax and sleep. Brendan broke up with his girlfriend. (I was not yet aware of the trauma Brendan had undergone.)

Alcohol use is increasingly acceptable even among those who had been non-users and taken for granted among light users and others, regardless of their age.

Roger tells me it that "1977-78 was a bad year at Annapolis." He is unhappy, but plans to continue his education and naval career.

Kyle is now living with Bill Dimaggio, the damaging father figure.

Most significantly, the shed from which Bill Jones operated his surfboard rentals is gone. The owners of the motel sold the space to a nearby resort hotel. The resort did not want Bill's competition. The wall crew is now without a specific "turf." Nevertheless, they "hang out" in the area in the daytime.

The reputation of Golden Beach grows as a desirable location for tourists. Likewise, the reputation of the boardwalk spreads as a desirable location to buy marijuana, cocaine and other drugs. The night is now owned by the red freaks, the outsiders and those looking for "action". Each morning, glass and other debris tell the stories of the previous night which are not reported in the press.

1979, AND ON TO 1980

I continued to stay in touch with as many of the young people in Golden Beach as possible. With letters, phone calls and messages from them and their parents, I was made generally aware of who is doing what and where.

Once again, Mrs. Bayer sent me a news clippings from the San Diego papers. One banner headline was "Police Poised To Wash Out Terrorism At City Beaches". A sub-story was entitled, "Riptide of Violence Grips Residents." It began, "Life in Golden Beach and Sand Beach is described as a 'battlefield' by two businessmen." One businessman described a drug deal "gone sour" outside a local surf shop. One person was shot, another was knifed and another run over by a car."[10]

That spring, I received several graduation notices. Most were from Golden Beach High School, but some are from colleges and universities.

Paul writes:

> Jerry,
> What the hell's happening, Bit Jer? Plenty of sun and fun around here, as always. Graduated with ease taking six classes all year long. Not bad for a Rat, huh, Jer? Hope you're coming down for the ceremonies, or at least the after parties. If not just send the check by mail (just kidding). Are you coming down for summer, Jer? Write back or call and let me know.
> Later, Big Jerry,
> Paul
> P.S. a hundred spot will do.

I was unable to go to Golden Beach that summer. I accepted a new position at Spring Hill College in Mobile, Alabama. In the meantime, visitors were coming to see me in Richmond.

I heard from Marie on July 21, 1979,

Hi Lowntee!

First of all, thanks for the birthday card (a little late). I loved it. Second, what are you doing from August 5th to August 15th? Will you be home? There is a reason for this question. Arlene and I are driving from here to Boston. We're leaving San Diego on August 5th...We will be going through Richmond, Va. somewhere near the 12th, 13th or 14th of August and would love to visit you..providing you still know where all the parties are!! Really, can you put up with two Golden Beach stoner, surf-rats for an afternoon, or maybe even a night? We can sleep on a floor, cook breakfast, wash a few dishes!
Will you be in town?
Please write back in a hurry and tell me what the scoop is.
Thanks. After I get your letter, I'll write or call with the definite date we'll be in town. I have your phone number, compliments of Mrs. Bayer.
I'll see ya,
Love,
Marie

There was a gathering of high school youths the evening Marie and Arlene arrived. I took them. The Virginia guys were agog with the sight of "California Girls" escorted by "old Dr. Lowney." Marie and Arlene slept on a sofa bed in my living room. At about 2 a.m., I was awakened by pebbles striking the balcony window. The Virginia young men were attempting to lure the California girls outside. Marie laughed. I played the protector and sent the youth on their way. Marie and Arlene headed north shortly after breakfast! Marie did not indicate any other problems in her life. I became aware of them in 1995.

I learned that Pat has been arrested, more than once, for cocaine. The judge sent him to jail. Pat says he survived in jail because he was the "only dude that knew how to read." He described how he would read the morning newspaper to "these big black dudes." Some days, he had to read the news more than once. He maintained that, as a result, he avoided the violence that otherwise besets persons placed in the San Diego County Jail. Pat quit using cocaine, but continued his love affair with alcohol.

I moved to Mobile, but continued to follow events in Golden Beach. I spent most of the following summer in Europe to study the criminal justice systems in other cultures.

In 2001, Pat and I discussed the years 1977 to 1980. Pat, appropriately, calls them "The Bad, Old Years."

I would return to Golden Beach in 1981.

End Notes

1. Oakley Ray and Charles Ksir. *Drugs, Society and Human Behavior,* St. Louis: Times Mirror/Mosby, 1990, pp. 142-143.

2. Emile Durkheim, *Suicide: A Study in Sociology*, Translated by George A. Spaulding and George Simpson. NY: The Free Press, 1951; especially pp. 384-386; Steve Lukes, *Emile Durkheim: His Life and Works.* NY: Harper and Row, 1972; John J. Macionis, *Society: The Basics,* Upper Saddle River, N.J.: Prentice Hall, 2000, p. 429.

3. David Popenoe, *Life Without Father*. NY: The Free Press, 1996. pp. 158-162.

4. Judith S. Wallerstein, Julia M. Lewis, and Sandra Blackeslee, *The Unexpected Legacy of Divorce,* NY: Hyperion, 2000, pp. 186-194.

5. Ibid. p. 187.

6. *Golden Beach Sentinel*, Wednesday, July 5, 1978, p. 1.

7. *San Diego Evening Tribune*, Saturday, July 8, 1978, p. A-3.

8. *Golden Beach Sentinel*, Sunday, July 9, 1978, p. 1.

9. *San Diego Evening Tribune,* Saturday, August 19, 1978, p. A-3.

10. *San Diego Evening Tribune*, Thursday, April 5, 1979.

Chapter 11

The Early 1980s - Lots of Dope & Rays of Hope

INTRODUCTION

It is 1981. Ronald Reagan has replaced Jimmy Carter as President of the United States. Prices have increased across the country. A value system based on materialism and taking care of "Number One" has set in. It is called, "The Me Generation." Haircuts are much shorter. Punk Rock and "New Wave" are favorites of the young. Kenny Rogers, Dolly Parton and Loretta Lynn are favored by many of the older generation. Among the young, "Pistols" do not refer only to guns, and "The Police" are not necessarily law enforcement officers. Both are popular rock groups. Golden Beach is no exception. California's Proposition #13 has frozen the assessed value of a home prior to a resale. Real estate taxes decrease. However, housing prices increase and homes in Golden Beach become prohibitive for most families with children. State and local funding for schools and libraries are curtailed.

The cost of illegal drugs inflates along with the general economy. Cocaine now sells for $100 a gram. A freeze-dried psychedelic mushroom (schroom) costs $8. Sensimilla (or "sensem") is the preferred "brand"of marijuana. The going rate for a lid is $48.

The Old Wall Gang members have haircuts almost as short as their parents. Some of the younger wall crew members sport the "New Wave" look. Pat, who once had a "far-out" brillo-like hairdo, is concerned because his niece has a short, dyed "punk" haircut. A few of the wall crew have moved to northern California, purchased land and raise their "cash crop," Sensimilla. Many others remain in San Diego and have well-paying jobs in the booming construction industry. The "Hippies" have been become or have been replaced by the "Yuppies."

Those in their 20s and early 30s continue to party. However, their parties are either in small groups at home or in the many new "clubs" that have sprung up along Main Street. Cocaine is readily available at the parties or snorted inside cars near the "pick-up" bars. Cocaine is too expensive to use outdoors or on the beach where a $10 could be blown away by a gust of wind. Unlike the early 1970s, it and the other expensive drugs are not shared with others, unless one is seeking sexual favors in return.

There are new terms and phrases associated with the popularity of cocaine. "Blow" means snorting cocaine or, as a noun, a snort of cocaine. "Coke and poke" refers to the use of cocaine to have sex, typically a method used by males to induce females to engage in sex. "Meat Exchanges" refers to those clubs reputed to be locations for persons to "pick-up" members of the opposite sex and, frequently, to "coke and poke." "Does it ever snow here?" is used to ask, "Can I get some cocaine from you or do you know a source?"

In some ways, the younger teens have now come "a full circle," back to the early 1960s. They have parties with loud music, but they actually dance at these parties. The new drugs are available to them, but the drug of preference is alcohol. It is consumed in large quantities. Drinking contests are frequent at the parties and they have devised "funnels" for "shotgunning" beer and hard liquor quickly into their bodies. Some overdose on this, the most popular, and legal drug.

These teens have new words in their vocabulary. "Fishing" refers to waiting outside of or near a liquor store to find someone who will purchase alcohol for those underage. "Air head" refers to a person who does not appear bright or lacks common sense. "Awesome" has replaced "cool," which had replaced "groovy" as a word to describe an enjoyable person, thing or event. "Bad" means "good," or, perhaps, "awesome."

The streets are no longer lined with young hitchhikers seeking a ride to or from the beach. Rides are not shared and it is considered dangerous to either hitchhike or pick up a hitchhiker. Trust and community have decreased. Crime and violence have increased. There are fewer teens on the beach.

Business leaders in the Golden Beach Town Council have made efforts to "clean up" the area, particularly the beach and boardwalk. Cosmetically, Golden Beach is much more attractive. Ordinances have been passed to prohibit glass on the beach or boardwalk. A speed limit of 5 miles per hour has been imposed on those on skateboards, bicycles or roller skates. The popularity of skateboards and roller skates has waned. A line has been painted down the center of the boardwalk with directions for pedestrians and others to walk or ride on the right half of the boardwalk and pass on the left. Traffic has been cut off on some of the streets along the beach. Other have been designated as one-way streets. Thus, teens are no long able to "cruise" the area in cars, trucks and vans. Fewer parking spaces result in increased frustration and, on occasion, rage and violence. Some police officers now walk a "beat" along the boardwalk. They wear short-sleeved shirts and baseball style caps. Neither helmets nor batons are evident. They mingle and visit with citizens, ticketing those drinking for glass containers. They frequently target the "red freaks" whose identity may also be referred to by the terms, "hard rocks" or "hardcore." As a whole, everything appears more orderly to the increased number of tourists who fill the new and remodeled motels. The tourists are much wealthier than a decade ago, and they include an increasing numbers of foreigners.

I arrive to this scene on June 20, 1981. Once again, I have a grant of confidentiality from the U.S. Department of Justice, and, once again, have been granted a faculty summer stipend to continue my research. And, once again, as a nonparticipant observer I hear and see what would be invisible to the typical adult resident or tourist.

My own encounter with the high real estate prices forces me into an extremely small, older, studio apartment for my sojourn. In 1970, it had been the apartment of both Pat and his father. I continue my narration, based on my journal entries, in the present tense.

THE OLD WALL GANG

I go to the wall and, once again, the first person I see is Pat, drinking a beer. Pat tells me about a party the night before with lots of "coke, shrooms and beer." Pat received his paycheck of $125 yesterday and spent $50 for coke (1/4 gram) and $25 for a baseball bat. He tells me, "There is lots of money in the beach, coke, Sensimilla and mushrooms!"

Pat tells me that he visited Vick in a jail in north San Diego County. Vick was in for a drunk charge and did not know how to get out. Vick was eventually sent back to a mental hospital and then to a halfway house. Vick's parents have abandoned him. Pat says Vick was so paranoid that he, "Couldn't take it any more."

Pat wears a T-shirt with a message that I will see many times over the summer. It reads, "We have no drinking problem in Golden Beach. We drink. We get drunk. We fall down . . . No Problem!"

At the wall, I meet some of the other members of the Old Wall Gang. Julian has his arm in a sling from a boating accident. He drinks beer, a lot. He is divorced and talks about reenlisting in the army. Julian began to attend meetings of Alcoholics Anonymous with Kramer. He does not continue to attend the meetings. Julian dates Norma. Kramer has been divorced twice (still far from the record, seven, his father had set). Kramer still goes to attend A.A.

Frosty is now divorced but still works and attends college.

Luke, Keith and Barry appear to have stable marriages. Keith and his wife have a child and continue to live in a San Diego suburb. Keith avoids the wall and Golden Beach and has not returned to his cocaine dealing practices. Barry has been steadily employed and is a father. Luke lost his job as a bartender because his boss "gave him a bad time about coke." A car comes by. Luke leaves to buy coke from the driver and returns five minutes later.

Turk lost his job as a disc jockey at a local radio station when the manager entered the sound room and discovered Turk with several lines of cocaine in front of him. Turk's brother is in Los Angeles, working at a X-rated bookstore.

Kenny is in Hawaii. His father is now the fleet commander there. Mo is also in Hawaii, employed as a welder. Beaver is working in Santa Barbara and finishing college.

Most of those who have left the wall and San Diego are "doing well."

THE FIVE FAMILIES

The next day I see Norm Dunn, Chuck Roe and their friend, Rudy. Norm and Rudy had been living in Mrs. Dunn's house. She is evicting them after a "big fight" between Norm and his mother. (Later, I hear that Norm hit his mother.) Norm blames Chuck. Mrs. Dunn was upset because Chuck still deals coke. A few months ago, Chuck stole a purse from an elderly lady and was sent to a work release camp. I visit with Norm a great deal over the summer.

Toby Dunn, who had been stabbed two years earlier, is living at home. Martin Dunn is the U.S. Army, stationed in Germany.

Bart Roe has been working full-time. He still hangs out at the wall and continues to use cocaine and marijuana.

Morris Bayer has again moved from home into an apartment. He is very drunk most of the summer. His brother, Gil, has graduated from San Diego State. Sally Bayer attends U.C. Santa Cruz. The youngest Bayer, Colleen, is in Pensacola, Florida visiting Roger. I had once pulled Roger from a fight at a party. He now has graduated from the U.S. Naval Academy and is in flight training school in Pensacola. Dr. Bayer continues to drink. Sally, Alise and Colleen Bayer discuss their irritation with him.

I am invited to another great Mexican dinner at Mrs. Mary Gilroy's. She now lives in a suburb of San Diego. Mark, John and John's girlfriend live in her home. John now owns a condominium and is a manager in an insurance office. Mark appears to be going through a stage of rebellion. He resents the conversations about drugs. He works for a temporary work agency, but puts in very few hours. Mark spends a considerable amount of time at his brother, Ron's, home. Ron still drinks heavily and uses other drugs. Reed has graduated from Brown and has completed his first year at the UCLA. Law School. He is in Rhode Island visiting the woman he intends to marry.

Mrs. Gilroy, Mark and John fill me in on several of the young people who had attended "Drop-In" during high school. Phil is married and attends San Diego State. Jose is in medical school at UCSD. Ernie is employed full-time. Jack owns a condominium in San Diego. Luke is employed at a supermarket. Matt is in college and is "doing well." Joanie still plays music at St. Patrick's. Marie continues at San Diego State. Tammy did not go to college. She is married. Nora is preparing to go to the University of the Pacific. Teri works and goes to UCSD. I will visit with most of these subjects over the summer.

THE "YOUNGER" WALL CREW

Most of the younger wall crew have graduated from high school. Some have dropped out. A few are going to college. Bill Dimaggio's continues to be involved with Kyle.

For the most part, the younger rats have become a part of the older wall crew. Their life is centered around surfing and partying. Cocaine and marijuana are used at their parties, which are much smaller than three years earlier. Alcohol is always present.

It appears that the wall crew has permanently surrendered their turf at the wall after sunset. Instead, the red freaks (hard rocks), sailors and others buying and selling drugs. (One evening, two sailors are walking the boardwalk. I hear one say to the other, "If you can't score [drugs] here, you can't score anywhere!") Nevertheless, younger and older wall crew members tend to stick together. Even those who have left San Diego and no longer use drugs stay in contact with their friends at the wall.

The stories of a few members the wall crew provide more depth into their lives during the summer of 1981.

Norm Dunn.

Norm has graduated from high school. He did not go on to college. After my initial contact with them, Norm and Rudy did not leave Mrs. Dunn's property. They simply moved into the garage. Mrs. Dunn threatens to get a bench warrant against them because she claims items have been stolen from her home. Rudy says, "She can't prove anything. She can't prove anything was stolen."

Norm and I are supposed to have lunch together my first Saturday in Golden Beach. Norm, in a pattern that is consistent, does not show. I do not call him. The following Thursday we meet and go to lunch. Norm is upset that I had not called him. He is worried that I am going to "dump him." I tell him I am still his friend, but he has to take responsibility and should apologize. He says he is "sorry."

Norm then tells me about his coke dealing. One day Chuck Roe was arrested, told the police he was Martin Dunn and said to the police, "You can check with my brother, Norm." Chuck then gave the police Norm's address. Norm had $2,000 in coke in his apartment. Norm told his roommate, Dale, to take the coke and the scales to Dale's house. Dale took the coke. He cut the coke in half and, when the coast was clear for Norm, Dale kept half and returned the other to Norm. Norm had been fronted the $2,000 for the coke so he took $1,000 from his savings account and sold the remaining coke for another $1,000. Norm claims he has not dealt coke or bought coke since, but uses it when it is given to him. In addition, Norm's friend, who "looked like a red freak," was busted for coke at the wall. The police told him if he provided them with the names of thirteen other users of cocaine his charges would be dropped. Norm and others were "scared for a long time."

Norm has been working as a tile setter for one year. He has $375 in savings.

The following Tuesday is my 40th birthday. Norm leaves a message at the wall for me to meet him there. Norm buys me dinner. Norm tells me that his mother is upset that he wants to remain at home. His brother, Toby, does the laundry and now camps out in the garage. Norm had camped outside in a tent for two months. His mother remodeled the house so that there is only one bedroom for her and one room for a guest. Her boyfriend uses the guest room as an office. Her boyfriend also sells pot.

I encourage Norm to continue to work and become independent.

Rick.

Rick grew up within a block of Norm and Chuck. Early in high school, they had been close friends. After they all had been arrested for a number of burglaries, Rick drifted from them and became a closer friend of Al. Rick had been jealous of Al's closer friendship with Ed. When Ed died rock climbing, Rick and Al renewed their friendship. Overall, Rick felt a need for close relationships. He had written to me of his need for a healthy and close relationship with a female. In 1975, Rick had been a "light user." However, in subsequent years, he occasionally used cocaine and other drugs. His drug use varies according to his degree of depression, which is usually associated with difficulties in relationships. Rick will be a senior Oregon State in the Fall.

The Friday morning following my arrival in Golden Beach, Rick awakes me. He had just been to his "girlfriend's" house. He went to go to her room, when his girlfriend's roommate said, "I wouldn't do that if I were you." Rick asked, "Who is in there? Elliot?" She responded, "Yes."

Rick is emotionally drained. As he tells me the story, he begins to cry. He is upset with the girl, with his mother and his brother, yet he blames himself for having poor relationships. He has a bad temper. He tells me that his father had a problem with his temper and his first stepfather used to beat his older brother. He tells me that his mother had problems with her family. Her father never kissed his grandmother.

Rick talks a great deal about sex and relationships. He feels the need for a girlfriend but sees that he always "blows relationships."

Rick's anger is largely aimed at his mother. He tells me, "You know, she never went to one sports event me or my brother were in. Then, she says she cares! ...She tries to possess me and won't approve of any girl!" (I recall to myself how ecstatic Rick was when I attended a soccer match to see him and others play five years earlier.)

The next Monday, I find a note on my apartment door from Rick. He wants to talk to me. I head for a pay phone and see Al on the way. Al tells me he supports Rick, but he is afraid of being close to someone who "can turn on you like a Doberman Pincer." Al says Rick can be calm one minute, and his temper rages the next. He tells me, "A woman would blow his head off!"

I phone Rick. He is depressed. He asks to meet me at my apartment and offers to buy me dinner after we talk. He describes more details about how he learned that his girlfriend "cheating on him" with Elliot. Rick also feels guilty about stealing. He had stolen some books and some New Orleans Mardi Gras souvenir coins from his friends at Oregon State. I suggest he try to return them. He tells me that it is now impossible. He asks me what to do. He wants me to take the coins "to help kids." I suggest that he give me the coins and I can sell them in Mobile (where they are more valued than in San Diego) and give the money to Catholic Charities. He is eager to do so.

I suggest that Rick seek counseling and give him the names of local resources. I tell him that I think he might particularly benefit from group sessions. He agrees. Rick also sees a need for religion in his life. Again, I give him some resources.

I would receive many letters and phone calls from Rick over the next 20 years.

Eric, Paul and their friends.

I meet Eric on the boardwalk. He now sports a "punk" haircut. He is dating two different girls.

Eric wants to tell me about his family. He tells me that his parents have both "fallen off the wagon, five or six more times." He has been working with his Dad in his Dad's bakery, but lives in his own apartment. Each time his Dad got drunk, Eric took him to A.A. or back to the rehabilitation unit at the hospital. Eric says he would like to save the family bakery but, "I won't do it for $5 an hour. I will for 40 or 50% of the business." Eric uses coke some, but claims he does not drink much.

The next week, Eric's parents invite me to dinner. Tom's mother is also invited. She mother tells me that Tom bought 40 acres of land in Humboldt County for $32,000. Tom put $8,000 down, $5,000 of which she provided as a loan to him. He plants eighty Sensimilla plants, each worth $2400 per year. She explains that after the plants are dried, he receives $1200 for the buds and $1200 for the leaves. He had been working for only $4.00 an hour in a lumber mill. "Now," she says, "He earns $50 a day planting marijuana!" She says that they use solar electronic equipment to avoid detection. In addition, a neighbor hang glides to obtain an aerial view. The neighbor then tells them where not to plant in order to avoid detection by the D.E.A. Tom's partner in the venture is Art. Art is married and has two children. Art's wife and Tom's girlfriend live in town. Art and Tom live on the acreage in a mobile home. Tom's mother tells me she is totally against the "system," the mayor, San Diego Light and Electric Company and others. She believes someday pot will be legal.

Eric's Mom tells me that Paul had borrowed money from her and refused to pay it back. He had been living there. One night, after he had a party at the house, she "threw him out."

Eric tells me that Mel was in the U.S. Coast Guard, but "got busted" in Santa Barbara for "possession of drugs."

Eric and his girlfriend do not remain to socialize following the dinner.

Paul's behavior begins to change over the summer. Paul had lived on his own receiving only his deceased father's social security benefits throughout high school. He now employed and remains committed to obtaining a college diploma in spite of the financial hurdles that have been brought about by President Reagan's program to decrease financial aid and to cut off social security for those in college after their 18th birthday.

THE FEMALES

The females are less visible. This is particularly true of those who had been classified as "light and non-users" in 1977. Seven of the ten are enrolled in college. Five work in the San Diego area during the summer. Nora is working at St. Patrick's. Marie attends San Diego State, works in an office and lives at home. Two are working outside the San Diego area Christi is employed as a fashion designer in Los Angeles. Lacy is in New York with her father.

Laura attends San Diego State and is married. Barbara is married. She did not go to college.

I see these young women either at church, while shopping or at their place of employment. I do not see them at the beach or at parties.

I see most of the other ten females, "heavy and regular users," at parties and at the beach. Only Linda is in college. Laura calls herself a "beach bum." Linda dates an older businessman. Helen dates a man several years her senior. Betty is married to an older man. Karen was working for a cosmetic firm, but quit on June 25. She dates a "punk" boyfriend who is very jealous if Karen talk to other males. Patti works at a bar-restaurant that is reputed to be a "Meat Exchange " where cocaine is readily available. Cindy is part of the "punk" set. She is employed as a dancer in a "pick-up" bar. Two of these young women have been beaten by boyfriends since my last visit. Another, Martha, divorced her husband after he began to beat her.

Colleen and Alise Bayer are at some parties. Alise says she does not understand why people are "down" on "schrooms" and other hallucinogenic drugs.

In all, the females continue to follow the two extremes of either deviant or conventional patterns of behavior. They differ, not only in drugs and recreational activities, but in work and academic pursuits. Moreover, the differences in their relationships with males are striking and, in some instances, very disturbing.

SOME OTHER TRENDS OF "DOING WELL" AMONG MALES

Several other males are "doing well"in 1981. Some cases are of significance.

Brendan is at the Sorbonne in Paris. He now hopes to become an actor in Paris and London.

Brendan's friend, Ned, is studying at Oxford in England.

Nelson is no longer one of the "wall rats." He is still working at the Japanese restaurant where he became employed following our chat in June 1977.

I see Frank on the boardwalk one evening. He is surprised and glad to see me. He is in his second week in firefighting school. He has "mellowed out." He no longer could be described as a "heavy user" or even a "regular user." He is rarely out at night anymore. He cut his very long black hair. He is very happy with himself.

One afternoon, John rides up to me on a bicycle on the boardwalk. He is with a girlfriend, Lorene, who is on roller skates. He tells me how happy he is to see me because he wants me to know how proud he is of himself. He had been one of the wall "rats." He just completed his second year at the University of San Diego, a Catholic University. He is an accounting major.

He now goes to a Catholic Church every other week. He had been raised a Catholic, but had not been to church in many years. He realizes his parents were right about a lot of things, "but not all." He has a paper route and pays for his education along with federal grants and scholarships. He says, "I don't come to the boardwalk much and never go to parties any more." He recalls the old days (1975-76, when he was a "heavy user"). He remembers when I went to the concert with him and Nelson. He tells me that at first he thought I was a cop. Then, he tells me, "Dan said, 'He's cool. If you ever get into trouble, he'll help you.'" He asks me if I ever get frustrated. He sees, as I do, all the runaways at the beach, his friends who are now involved with cocaine and wonders what will happen to them. We exchange addresses and move on. Later, I write in my journal, "He looks great! Very mature! And a good kid!"

I see Lonnie who is now 20 years old. He is more than six feet tall. (He was shorter than my 5'3" in 1976 and now makes fun of my height!) When Lonnie was 14, he used pot daily and was a regular at the parties and along the wall. He tells me he hardly ever comes to the beach anymore. He rarely drinks or smokes. He said when he used to his Mom would "amp out." He is working and she is "cool" with him. Besides, he says, "My Dad has moved back to the area and I have to behave or he would get me!" Lonnie says he wants to go to Hawaii and "travel some." He is concerned about the overcrowding in Golden Beach. Like others, Lonnie is maturing.

AND, THOSE WHO ARE STRUGGLING

Some others who had not used drugs or who, in 1975, would have been classified as "light users" now deal with problems in their lives by drinking or using cocaine or marijuana. Rick's pattern has already been described. But, there are others.

Kevin had used alcohol and marijuana very sparingly. The death of his father was followed by a dramatic increase in his use of marijuana and alcohol. Now, 20 years old, Kevin is described by his friends at the wall as "an alcoholic." When he drinks, Kevin acts "wild" and others shun him. Although he works in the family business, he frequents the beach in the late afternoons and on weekends, drinking and attempting to "pick up chicks." Although a fairly handsome young man, Kevin's intoxicated behavior usually makes him very unappealing to females during these encounters. At times, he succeeds in having sex, but is unable to form a lasting relationship. He tells me, "I am addicted to girls."

Lee, had also been a light user in 1975. He was one of those who frequented Lime Avenue. In 1979, he was involved in sports and was happy with his life. He was working and introduced me to his mother. Lee's parents begin to have marital problems. He begins to use coke at those times. Two months ago, his parents "split up." Lee says this was very difficult for him and he used coke, "a lot." He has been dating Karen, a heavy user. He admits that he uses coke for sex.

At the sunset ritual on the boardwalk a week later, I see Lee. His parents went to counseling and have "gotten back together." He says he is "stoked." He tells me he is doing better and has a meaningful job with good pay.

In these and other cases, the findings indicate even stronger support for the relationship between family factors and the use of drugs and other deviant behavior.

SOME NEW FACES

Because all of my subjects are now out of high school and into their 20s, I tale the opportunity to meet other young people along the beach. Some have heard of me or are introduced to me by others. Still others, somehow, sensed I was "cool." Some are runaways or those searching for the "California Dream." I find that their stories are similar to those I have been hearing since 1970. Some examples suffice.

Tyrone.

Tyrone, 16, is staying with his mother and stepfather at their summer home on the beach. During the school year, he lives inland. His seems to hurt a lot. His mother is an alcoholic. His father died when Tyrone was 2 years old. Tyrone says, about his mother, "She runs the home." He tells me that when his mother is sober, he likes her. However, when she drinks, which always occurs on weekends, he "wants to leave." He tells me,

> Her personality changes. She argues with me and fights with my step-Dad. I don't feel a part of the family. They all have their thing and I'm separate . . . It is the same with some of my friends. We used to be close, but not now. Sometimes, I feel obligated to be with them, but I want to be alone . . . Sometimes, I have a hard time sleeping.

I describe the characteristics of alcoholics as well as those of children of alcoholics. I tell him about Alanon for those who are in similar situations as his. Tyrone admits he drinks when he can and does so to "get drunk."

On my final day in Golden Beach, I bring Tyrone pamphlets on Alanon, Alateen, a local counseling resource and the schedule of meetings for Alanon and Alateen. He is very appreciative. He says I helped explain a lot of things. He says he will write to me. I tell him I will also pray for him.

Kane.

Eric had introduced me to Kane, 16, shortly after my arrival. Kane seemed very shy. One day, I see him alone in a somewhat remote location on the beach north of the swimming areas. He is smoking a bowl of Sensimilla. He tells me that he had been in "C.Y.A." (The California Youth Authority, a prison system for youthful offenders). Kane had stolen a car. His father is a physician, but his parents had a great deal of conflict in their marriage and divorced three years ago. Kane was sent to live with his "grandma."He says, "That is when I started doing things . . . pot, and stuff." He feels that he was "thrown out" by his parents. He tells me, "I smoke grass when I am lonely."

Kane supports himself by working at an amusement park. He sometimes stays at Eric's, and other times he finds some place to "crash." Over the summer, I see Kane at various times either by himself or "hanging out" near others at the wall, but always shy and reserved.

THE PARTIES AND THE BEACH, SUMMER, 1981

As noted, the house parties are smaller. At night, the beach becomes a much more "wild" scene. The ratio of males to females at the beach after dark is now more than 15 to 1. In the daytime, the beach is very crowded and symbols of wealth abound (name labeled clothing, sports gear and so on.) I write in my journal, "The lower beach is a playground for the rich in the day, and almost a 'skid row' at night. 'Locals,' not looking for 'action,' tend to stay north of the boardwalk."

I go to a party on Sailor Street. There are about thirty people present. There is a live band and lots of dancing. The beer is in bottles rather than in kegs. Some mixed drinks are served. I see a lot of former "Junior Beach Rats." They are happy to see me. There is a ratio of two males for each female. This is very different from in years past. At various times during the evening, a female and one or more males "disappear" into one of the bedrooms. They appear to be very "high" afterward. George says, "They're doin' coke."

I leave to go to another party north of the pier. Eric was supposed to set up the party. I go to the location, but there is no party. Did the police break it up?

A few days later I attend another party with George and Seth. The party is some distance from Golden Beach. It is held in a warehouse. The organizer is Seth's brother. There are twelve kegs of beer and four bands. Three of the bands play for free, the fourth charges $150. The entrance fee is $3.00 (triple that of two years earlier). There are more than nine hundred in attendance. Those in charge stamp everyone's hands and keep a count of those entering. I calculate the profit with Seth. The total gross at the entrance is approximately $2,700. The expenses are about $300 to $400, for a profit of between $2,300 and $2.400. Most of the crowd is younger, five males to each female. I see Cindy, Anna, Eric and Paul. Many of the party goers tell me they are on "schrooms."

On weekend night, the boardwalk is a party in itself. I smell lots of pot. Drug dealing is far more open. Police enforce the ordinance on glass containers, but there is lots of alcohol. At least every fifty feet, there are small gatherings of young people. Despite the sex ratio, guys tell me they are here to "pick up tourist chicks."

The Police.

Just over a week after my arrival, on June 28, a Sunday, I am invited by the Bayer's and other prominent members of the Golden Beach Town Council to a "Police Appreciation Evening" at a luxury hotel. I discover the officers present are not Golden Beach beat officers. Rather, they are "public affairs" and desk officers from the division. The affair is very formal.[1]

Morris Bayer is there. To the consternation of his mother, Morris is the only person in a T-shirt. Morris dances and jokes with everyone. Even though I learn little new information from the police officers present, Morris informs me of the status of nine of the subjects I have not yet contacted.

Morris tells me that, after Trent's arrest at the time of Rich's death, Trent completed his sentence on the parole violation. He is now in prison for holding up a convenience store with a knife.

I begin conversations with some of the police officers in attendance. A member of the "Investigative Unit," a detective in charge of violent crimes, tells me that he sees most of the violent crime as "drug related." He says, "There is less a problem with coke than other drugs. We leave coke enforcement to the State and the D.E.A."

His wife works at the emergency room of a local hospital. She tells me that she does not see "overdoses like in the late '60s" when "reds" were popular. She states, "There are a few from coke, ludes and Valium . . . Physicians take a lot of coke!"

The Division Head, whom I interviewed in 1976, says,

> People have begun to realize it's profitable to have a nice beach area . . . There are no problems on Beach Boulevard since we blocked it off. . . . Coke is no bigger a problem here in the beach than any area . . . It's a drug of the affluent . . . The troublemakers at Beach Boulevard are outsiders.

A few days later, I observe Officer Michael O'Neill "bust" a 15-year-old girl. He places her in the car and tells me, "She'll just go home, but the others here will get the message." I ask him about coke on the beach. He says, "It is too windy. It would blow away so they do it in their apartments. I'm not concerned about it."

He claims the problems are those of "the outsiders," according to arrest records, "Beach people want to keep it clean. Others are busting bottles and pouring out their booze."

Officer O'Neill says he would only arrest someone for marijuana if the person was a juvenile, "It's only a $25 ticket for an adult."

He gives me a specific address in Sand Beach where a person can "find anything . . . heroin or whatever." He does not like to wear shorts like the officers who ride bicycles. He goes back to the car to drive the girl home. He tells me that I am welcome to take a ride-along with him anytime. I do not take him up on his officer. My presence in a police cruiser would, without a doubt, seriously endanger the rapport and credibility I have gained in the subculture.

Police are visible on foot. I see police on bicycles for the first time. Cruisers do not "sweep" the area by driving the length of the boardwalk but pull up to the boardwalk from the side streets. They seem to show their presence without making "sweeps" or mass arrests. The police are much more likely to break up large house parties than they had been previously. More than once, they arrive before I do and I miss the party.

Overall, the policy is more realistic regarding the limitations of law enforcement to control the use of drugs. Moreover, although there are times when some officers "single out" individuals apparently based on "profiling," The techniques employed are less likely to provoke anger, violence and distrust from young citizens.

Departing, Once Again.

My final full day in Golden Beach, I attend the annual, "Over-the-Line" festivities. Other-the-line is a form of softball requiring three members on each team. It originated as beach activity. Once a year, a tournament is held. It has been moved to a barren peninsula for crowd control. The weekend is known more for the "institutionalized deviance" that takes place than for the softball games. In some ways, it reminds me of Mardi Gras in Mobile or New Orleans. Drinking is a given. Drugs are plentiful. There are sexual overtones. The names of the teams are so "x-rated" they are not listed in the local newspapers. I park and take the shuttle bus to the area. Many of the young people had asked me to come to see them play. The crowd is estimated at more than 50,000, about 90 percent males. I am unable to find anyone I know. I make a note that the event seems to reflect the cultural values of the beach area.

The local newspaper reports that the city has cut the funds for the alcohol counseling program in Golden Beach. The program will be closed. I shake my head!

I stop by the Bayer home that evening to give my good-byes. Mrs. Bayer tells me she read in *Reader's Digest* that drug use is disappearing. Dr. Bayer has a drink in his hand and is very angry because Mrs. Bayer made a mistake in preparing dinner. Alise and Colleen are disturbed by his outburst.

I too feel emotional. I still consider the Bayer's almost as a "second family" to me. I have talked to Mrs. Bayer about the need for A.A. or other treatment for both her husband and her son, Morris. She seems to be in denial to name them as "alcoholics," but is frustrated by their drinking and resultant behavior. I do not tell her that I had taken Dr. Bayer to an A.A. meeting a few years earlier. He was pleased intellectually with the meeting. However, he felt he was "not that bad off" (when compared with those who spoke). I pray for all the Bayer's and others.

Some Final Comments.

The increased prosperity in Golden Beach has affected its sense of community. The influx of tourists and others subtlety force families to seek other areas to reside. Cocaine use reflects the wealth in Golden Beach and the importation of new values.

I am able to contact 75 percent of the total (162) subjects. I obtain reliable information about twenty-five of the remaining thirty-nine subjects. In the back of my journal I list each subject according to their original category. About 20 to 30 percent of the former heavy user have decreased their use and are now either light or regular users. One former regular user is now also a light user. On the other hand, a few light users and two of the non-users have increased their use and are now heavy users. In addition, 20 percent of the former regular users are heavy users. It is noteworthy that those subjects who are "doing well" or "better" have both mothers and fathers involved in their lives. This is evident in the cases of Frank, John and Lonnie. On the other hand, those without the support of two parents, such as Rick, Norm Dunn, Kevin and Lee are experiencing problems, including increased use of drugs. In each instance, their difficulties are related to their past and/or present home life.

Home factors continue to provide the greatest insight into the lives of the young people even as they enter adulthood. At the same time peer associations weigh heavily on those who either move and "do well" or remain at the wall and in the Golden Beach "scene."

I am on the road to answering Les' question, "Where will we be in twenty years?" Many things seem evident. However, there are factors operating that I will not realize for years to come. Eventually, I will examine where they were "30 years later."

BETWEEN VISITS, 1981-1983

Shortly after my return to Mobile, I receive a letter from Rick. Rick is on what he calls "an emotional roller coaster." He is having a difficult time letting go of his former girlfriend. He tells how he tried to help her overcome smoking tobacco and pot. He feels her new boyfriend, with whom she now lives has a negative impact on her. He thanks me for talking to him and being his friend. He adds a postscript asking if he could send me the stolen coins so that I can sell them and have the money go to "a place where I know it will be of some benefit." He sends the coins. I sell them in Mobile and donate the money to Catholic Charities to be used for needy children. I call Rick and let him know that it has been done according to his wishes. Rick has not utilized the counseling resources that I had suggested.

In early August, the youngest Bayer daughter, Colleen, drives to Mobile from Pensacola one day to visit me. She is very serious about Roger who is still stationed in Pensacola. She later writes from Golden Beach and thanks me for showing her the highlights of Mobile and the seafood lunch. She tells me the photo she took of me in front of my house is now on the family bookcase in Golden Beach, a place reserved for "beloved friends," so "You should feel honored."

I receive mail from Europe later that year.

The first is a card from Brendan, now in Paris, telling me he is pursuing his dreams of being an actor. His father and mother have divorced and Brendan's mother, born in France, has returned to Paris to be near her family. Brendan is upset. He assumes some responsibility for his mother, father and, to some degree, his younger sister. I realize that Brendan, previously a "model" student, athlete and non-user, has been affected by the change in his family. However, Brendan has not yet shared another trauma that had impacted his life.

Ned sends me a letter from England. He is enjoying his study in England. He says he is having a "very worthwhile experience, not to mention a great time."

My parents had retired from Montana to a southern suburb of San Diego. Over the next several years, I visit them. My time is the area is divided between them and my friends in Golden Beach. I continue to keep in contact with those in Golden Beach especially with the Bayer's, the Jones family and the Gilroy's. In addition, I receive messages from Norm Dunn, Pat and others.

In 1983, Matt, my "foster son," marries Jan. They move to Lake Tahoe and buy a house. Matt works as a stationary engineer in a large hotel-casino. In February, I receive a postcard from Hawaii,

> Hi Looney,
>
> The wife and I are taking it easy (as in not having to dig snow) in Hawaii. We're visiting the folks on Maui before they move to New Orleans. It's very nice and sunny here. We've got to see the whole island in the 8 days we've been here. We've 4 days left on Oahu. Hopefully, we'll see half of that island. Back home, the job's going well along with everything else. We're trying to plan already for an '84 Mardi Gras in Mobile and New Orleans. We'll write later,
> Love, Matt & Jan

Matt's marriage is short-lived. He and Jan were married less than a year before they divorced. Matt and I communicate mainly by phone.

SUMMER, 1983

I return to Golden Beach on June 13, 1983 for a ten-day visit. I stay as a guest of the Bayer's. There are some changes, but most follow the trends I observed in 1981.

The General "Scene."

Community policing is in vogue. Police now are assigned to neighborhood "beats" rather than rotating periodically. They set up a "Neighborhood Watch" system. Mrs. Rita Bayer is active in the program. The police now wear bicycle helmets, short sleeve shirts and short pants when they patrol the boardwalk twenty-four hours a day. They have no guns or batons.

The beach area is much more attractive. Several streets along the beach are now blocked off to traffic. Walking paths and landscaping replace the streets "cruisers." Expensive restaurants line the boardwalk where establishments that featured "family dining" or "inexpensive specials" once stood. A national motel chain has built on the location where seaside cabins once catered to families, teens and young adult tourists.

The tourists tend to be either older, retired or semi-retired couples, or younger, upper-socioeconomic singles. I see very few "red freaks" or "hard rocks." On June 17, I am along the beach from 11:30 a.m. until 6:30 p.m. and from 8 p.m. until after midnight. I smell pot only twice, in the afternoon from a group of surfers in their 30s and 40s, and after sunset from a group in their late 20s and early 30s. There are very few teens. I note how "mellow" the boardwalk is throughout my stay.

The 20-to-40-year-old groups frequent the clubs among Main Street as well. I go to the best known of the "pick-up" clubs. There is a lot of drinking taking place, and a number of persons "doing coke."Males outnumber females only slightly.

I learn that inflation continues to force up the price of cocaine, Sensimilla and Thai sticks. Quaaludes seem to have disappeared from the drug scene. "Schrooms" are available, but "You have to know who to ask." "Speed" has returned, but not in a big way.

House parties and "keggers" usually take place on Friday and Saturday evenings. I attend two. They are less than forty at each. The participants tend to be "New Wave" and more formally dressed than in years past.

The beach is crowded during the daytime, particularly on weekends. I note that as U.S. society has become more materialistic and conscious of market values, so has Golden Beach. Real estate prices continue to climb higher than the national average. There is less of a "vacation mentality" among the local residents. I no longer see signs or graffiti proclaiming, "Tourists Go Home." Rather, residents work hard to obtain money from the tourists. Golden Beach has "matured." It enjoys economic prosperity, is physically more appealing, but is less colorful. Many of the "characters" (mimes, street "theater," "weirdos" and others) who entertained passers-by along the boardwalk and on the beach have vanished. Somehow, Golden Beach is more aesthetically pleasing, but less "laid back," less friendly and, perhaps, not nearly as much "fun."

The Subjects.

Most of the subjects continue along the same course they have been in recent years. Nonetheless, there are some changes.

The siblings in the Bayer family are maturing and leaving home. Colleen Bayer and Roger are planning their wedding. Gil Bayer has obtained his M.B.A. He is married and teaching woodworking at a high school. Gil does construction work on the side and during the summers.

Morris Bayer works on fishing boats. He continues to drink heavily. Sally attends UCSB. She tells me how prevalent mushrooms are in Santa Barbara. Dr. Bayer continues to drink.

The Dunn sons come and go from their mother's home. Norm Dunn works for his father in construction. He spends much of his free time at his mother's home and with Chuck Roe. Martin Dunn is home from the army. He had been a non-user at age 14 in 1975, a light user in 1976, and now appears to be an alcoholic who uses many other drugs. I see him at the beach drinking heavily and, at times, very "spaced out." Toby Dunn is living in Mrs. Dunn's garage with his girlfriend and their infant child.

Chuck Roe has been sentenced to five years probation for burglary. He is in possible danger of violating his probation and being sent to prison. Recently, Chuck stole carpets and faces additional charges. At age 24, he dates a 31-year-old woman with a 14-year-old daughter. His language is filled with references to "smoking" (pot) and "fucking" women. His brother, Bart, lives at home.

The four Jones brothers continue to be active in their church. Reed has obtained his contractor's license. He and his wife, Theresa, have a nine-month-old son. Occasionally, I see Reed drinking beer. Both Todd and Pete are working in the roofing business. The youngest son, Terry, works at a local surf shop. He specializes in beach and surf wear.

Mark Gilroy attends college. During the summer he works near the beach, and usually stays with his oldest brother, Ron and Ron's girlfriend. John Gilroy has remained in his present employment for almost four years. Reed has graduated from UCLA law school and is in New Hampshire waiting to take the bar exam. Mrs. Mary Gilroy has remarried and lives a considerable distance from Golden Beach. Mark and John do not feel her home is as much "their home" as it used to be.

Most of the females have finished college and most of those are married. Three of the "heavy users" are pregnant and unmarried. One, Jeanie, is pregnant for the second time outside of wedlock. She is physically abused by her new boyfriend. Jane tells me she is a "new person" and credits her use of speed to her "improvement.". Lucy is concerned about her brother, Max, who, although employed, drinks heavily and continues to use other drugs.

The wall crew continues to follow a variety of life courses. Pat works "off" and "on." He tells me he "gets bummed" with the world. He drinks heavily. Kevin drinks heavily and continues to act "wild" when drunk Bill Jones says, "He (Kevin) just went wild after his father died." Skip, is 23. He lives with a 16-year-old girl. Vick has been diagnosed as "schizophrenic." He continues to be in and out of mental institutions. At times, he lives in a downtown San Diego hotel. Eric expresses bitterness toward life and blames his mother. He claims that when she drinks when she is home alone. He wants me to talk to her. Eric continues to drink as well. Leo no longer sells drugs. He is in Mexico selling condominiums to "gringos." Keith, the former cocaine dealer, also no longer sells drugs, but specializes in sales of construction supplies. Keith lives with his wife in a rural area of the county. They have a second child.

Jeff is working in construction. Mike has moved to Maine and operates a restaurant near a beach on the coast. Frosty completed his bachelor's degree and is employed. He has not remarried. Les surfs a great deal but avoids drugs. He frequently has dinner at the Jones' home Paul is taking steps to improve himself and pursue his dream of a college education. He is employed repairing surfboards. He attends college in the evenings. Paul is pursuing a major in computer science. He receives excellent grades. Paul tells me of his accomplishments with great pride. Matt owns a home in Lake Tahoe. He has obtained a contractor's license. Our bond continues. Carl no longer associates with most of the wall crew. His main contacts with the wall crew come from interactions with the Jones family at church. His tour of Europe and Asia has been forgotten. He studies engineering at SDSU. He and his wife have a one-year-old son. (I will come to know Carl's wife and his son well by the year 2001.)

Other members of the wall crew do not appear to have changed to any substantial degree. Rick continues to have problems with relationships. Some toy with Alcoholics Anonymous, but do not make a full commitment to the program.

Many others, outside of the wall crew, likewise choose to follow varying paths. Albert, like Frank, is a firefighter. Unlike Frank, Albert's drinking continues to increase rather than decrease. Stu has been married five years and has obtained a contractor's license. He is kept busy during the current construction boom. Andy is married and has two children. He lives in Santa Cruz but tells Joseph that he "wants to talk to me." I give Joseph my phone number and address in Mobile. (I am unable to get to Santa Cruz at this time. In years to come, I will regret that I was unable to visit with Andy.) Lee asks to talk to me. After their attempts at reconciliation failed, his mother and father divorced. He is very "bummed out." Once again, he is using coke. He has been with his present employer for more than three years. Brendan is on the road to his goal. He is gainfully employed as an actor in London.

Most of the former non-users, light users and regular users have graduated from college, are employed and several of them are married.

Some Final Notes.

In a brief ten-day period, I visit or receive reliable information on more than half of the subjects. For the most part, the patterns of behavior have not changed. Family and peer associations remain the most important factors related to drug abuse. It is increasingly clear that alcohol is the substance most frequently abused and the number one "drug problem." Politicians and the media continue to focus on cocaine, heroin and marijuana. Another "War on Drugs" is waged. This one by President Reagan. The street prices of cocaine and marijuana continue to climb. They are available and those who wish to purchase are able to do so. Thus, profits increase for the drug dealers.

1984-1985

I return to Spring Hill College in Mobile. My contacts with those in Golden Beach remain. I return for brief visits during my Christmas breaks in 1984 and 1985.

When I arrive in 1984, I ask Mrs. Bayer where I can find Brendan. She responds, "I don't know where you can find Brendan, but I know where you can see him." I ask what she means. She informs me that television commercials are advertising a major motion picture with Brendan in a leading role. Brendan has "made it."

A few nights later, I attend a party at the apartment of Norm Dunn. All three Dunn brothers, Mrs. Dunn and several of the form "wall rats" are present. There are ample supplies of beer and marijuana. A group, including, Mrs. Dunn pose so that I can take slides to show to my students at Spring Hill College. Mrs. Dunn has sold her house. She told Mrs. Bayer, "It was the only way I could get rid of my kids."

The following summer, Norm Dunn calls me to ask me if he can spend an evening and overnight at my residence. Norm is flying to Florida to pick up a very rare sports car for payment. Norm arrives shortly after he received a $75 speeding ticket in Florida. We enjoy a good gulf coast seafood dinner and catch up on old times. We attempt to enter Jimmy Buffett's club, but Norm is turned away because he is wearing shorts, forbidden in formal Alabama. He is incensed. On the other hand, he enjoys his tour of Mobile and takes several pictures of the brick buildings, which are extremely uncommon in Southern California. When we return to my home, Norm asks me to smoke a joint with him. I did not realize he had it in his possession, but was not surprised. I tell him that I do not want it used in my home. He begs me to allow him to smoke it so that "he can sleep." I refuse and apparently he slept well. The following morning, he hugged me, "Good-bye," and continued his cross-country journey.

Gil Bayer leaves teaching to operate his own general contracting business. He is successful, but develops ulcers. He remains extremely conscientious.

In the meantime, my find that much of what I have learned in my research is valuable. In a course on alcohol and drugs as well as others areas of sociology, there is great interest by my students about my findings in Golden Beach. In addition, my background knowledge is of tremendous value in the youth ministries in which I am involved. Frequently, I am asked to conduct workshops on alcohol and drug abuse. The young people are particularly interested in the "Parent-Teen" workshops I conduct to allow high schools the freedom to communication freely without threats of reprisal. All else continues, but I am about to make a major change in my own life.

For several years, many people asked why I did not become a priest. I tried to avoid any thought of the suggestion. Instead, I consoled myself by the "good works" I was accomplishing through my teaching, my involvement with my students and my efforts in youth ministry. On one quiet Sunday in Mobile, I finally allow myself to consider the possibility. When looked at it objectively, I could not deny that I could continue to teach and utilize my knowledge about young people, their struggles, drugs and alcohol as a priest. I wrote to the bishop of my home diocese, Helena, Montana. I thought I would surprise my Irish pastor, Fr. Tim Deasy, when I told him of my decision, he responds, "Well, what the hell took you so long to decide?"

I am surprised that others besides Fr. Deasy were also not surprised, including those in Golden Beach.

In August 1985, I enter the seminary to study for priesthood at Catholic University of America, in Washington, D.C.

How will this decision affect my future research?

End Note

1. I realize how out of place I feel with these my long-time friends. I become engaged in a discussion with the Republican congressman about the cuts in federal aid of education, Mrs. Bayer is shocked that I would question the congressman. Another female friend kisses a former city councilman that she once called a "crook." I hear complaints about school bussing and words such as "nigger." "spick,"and so on. Many of these very formal people are ones that I have known since my arrival in Golden Beach in 1968. At that time, they had long sideburns, were considered "liberal,", and wore leisure suits. In 1969, I and some of them volunteered to assist a parish in the predominantly Black area of Southeast San Diego. They had been supporters of Robert F. Kennedy. How times have changed! What is more stressful is that I know which of their sons and daughters are abusing drugs or dealing cocaine. I am aware of the denial by more than one mother that her husband and/or son is an alcoholic in need of intervention.

Chapter 12

The Late 1980s & Early 1990s - Keeping Contacts, Priesthood & Applying the Findings

INTRODUCTION

I remain in the seminary at Catholic University of America from August 1985 until May 1988. During this time, in addition to my own theology studies, I teach part-time in the Sociology Department. I regularly teach, "Alcoholism, Drug Abuse and Dependency Behavior." The students share their own experiences with me and invite me to their own parties. (I must say they are as wild as any parties I had witnessed elsewhere.)

First Lady Nancy Reagan promotes her "Just Say No" program. She speaks at the University. "Crack" cocaine use is reported to be an "epidemic" sweeping America. When I drive from downtown Washington to the seminary, I witness inner-city drug sales first-hand. If I am required to come to a stop at some intersections, a number of young black men approach the car to offer me of a variety of drugs. A white person driving a Honda Accord late at night is apparently assumed to be a willing customer. Nonetheless, the perspective of Nancy Reagan, the media and an unsophisticated white person do not necessarily correspond to what is occurring nationwide. The use of cocaine is declining.[1]

In 1986, one of the public relations officers at the university makes an appointment to interview me. Her purpose is to contact an "expert" faculty member at the university. She assumes my perspective would match that being proclaimed by politicians and the media. My word would provide publicity for the university. I tell her the facts about cocaine and other drugs. I point out that in my research, as well as in other data, it is evident that the greatest problem among American youth is alcohol abuse. I state that alcohol is the drug that is increasing among high school and college students. She expresses disbelief. Nothing is published, but early the next year she asks for a second appointment. She tells me that she did not believe what I had said several months earlier. However, she had taken the time to study the issue further and had, indeed, found evidence of what I had said. She interviews me about my research. Articles based on the interview are published in many U.S. newspapers. In the fall of 1987, the university public relations office contacts CNN. I am interviewed on air for 10 minutes on Thanksgiving Day. The commentator concentrates on my methodology and use of cocaine and harder drugs. Little attention is paid to the comments about alcohol use. It is not "good copy" to state that the truly effective preventive measures lie within the family and the community. The "war on drugs" continues. Media coverage of interdiction, confiscation and raids on crack houses seem to be evidence that America's is winning each battle. All but ignored are the needs for meaningful jobs, support for families and recreational opportunities for America's youth.

On the other hand, Mothers Against Drunk Driving (M.A.D.D.), are successful in raising awareness of the problem of teen-age drunk drivers. The U.S. Congress enacts legislation to force states to increase the drinking age to 21 years of age.

In the meantime, I am in contact with Golden Beach. During my summers, I am assigned to parishes where I conduct workshops for parents and teens.

1985-1987

I receive many letters and cards from Golden Beach. At Christmas 1985, Mrs. Jones writes:

> Jerry,
> A quick run-down on some of the wall gang - Pete, Bill and Todd own a roofing company. Terry is a catalog buyer for "International Male." Barry works for his Dad in construction, married, 2 children. Carl is an architect in a firm up the coast. Milo works for a company repairing boats. Dick is a San Diego Police Department Patrolman. Pete is married with one son. Bill is married with two sons. Todd is married with two sons. No daughters! Everyone appears "normal" on other fronts as well.

The Bayer's and I are in frequent contact. Colleen Bayer has married Roger. They live in Virginia not far from me. Colleen is a flight attendant for a major airline. Alise Bayer comes to visit Alise and they visit me at the university to see me and tour the campus where their parents first met.

At the end of my summer assignment in 1986, I drive "the long route" back to Washington, via San Diego. I stop in South Lake Tahoe, California to visit Matt. He is a stationary engineer in a large hotel casino. Matt does not want me to go near the casinos alone. He apparently is afraid that I will be "taken in" or become "addicted" by the gambling.

We spend the most quality time together that we have since 1971. Matt takes me on hikes into the beautiful high Sierra's. We discuss many things. In regard to his sojourn with me in 1970-71, he says "I don't know how anyone could live with me the way I was back then." Matt admits he had used cocaine after his divorce. He is doing well now, but tells me how widespread the drug is in the area among the "20s to 40s" set. When a waitress asks, "Oh, is this your father?" Matt responds with a blush, "Well, kinda." Matt dates many young women. He does not quite understand what they "see" in him. He is fairly content with life and his work. Like me, he has taken up an interest in photography. He enjoys the outdoors. Still, I sense that he has a longing for a permanent relationship with a woman. He admits his childhood and his mother's divorces cause him to shy away from another marriage and "bringing children into this kind of a world." In his "rebellious" teens, Matt argued with me about many issues. Now, it seems, we are very much in agreement on politics, unions, peace, justice and the environment.

In San Diego, I am, once again, a guest of the Bayer's. Morris and Dr. Bayer continue to drink heavily. I discuss an intervention program with Mrs. Rita Bayer. She does not act, but she discusses what rehabilitation facilities are available through their health maintenance organization.

Gil Bayer has two children. His contracting business flourishes. One day I drive to one of his job sites and visit with him and Norm Dunn. Norm is a subcontractor for Gil. Norm invites me to a party that evening.

I go to Norm's party. More than thirty people in their late 20s are present. The music is very mellow. Someone tells me that Norm is in one of the bedrooms. I open the door and view a few people huddled together. One is Norm's latest girlfriend. I realize they are snorting coke. I leave. When Norm comes to the living room, he is very high. He puts one arm around his girlfriend and another around me and keeps saying "Jerry Lowney!" He tells us both how much he loves us.

Pat, Kevin and Martin Dunn are frequently at the wall, drinking.

Mrs. Mary Gilroy tells me that not much has changed with her sons. John and Reed are married. Reed is practicing law. Mark and Ron are both working.

I am told that Chuck Roe has been in prison. He is not at his home.

Brendan is playing a major role in another movie, filmed in London.

On a Sunday afternoon, the older Bayer daughters plan a picnic at the beach. I join them and many of their daughters' friends for the afternoon. Many of the young women were in my earlier research or in the area when I was attending parties and other functions. Several beautiful "California girls" pose with me for pictures to show my classmates at the seminary.

The next October, Mrs. Bayer comes to Washington. Her daughters, Sally and Colleen come to visit me along with Colleen's husband, Roger. We celebrate Mrs. Rita Bayer's birthday along my favorite Irish pub district.

Rick writes somewhat regularly. At Christmas 1986, I receive a card,

> Dear Jerry,
>
> I moved back home. The next time you are out here, I would like to get together to talk. I have not written much because I felt that I would be dwelling on my personal problems too much and who wants to read that garbage? Actually I'm fine. I am healthy and like myself, but I still have not fully gotten over Lucy. You told me God doesn't punish us for our screw-ups (namely the bad treatment of Lucy) but only one girl I've been interested in since then has shown any reciprocal feelings. That was just in the last couple of months and she has already lost all interest. I'm very lucky in the sense that I have so many friends but, at the same time, I feel very lonely and a failure. I still feel I'm being punished. I also still love Lucy. She's long gone, however . . .
> Anyway, I've always respected and appreciated your friendship and support.
> I hope you are well and happy, Jerry. Merry Christmas and Happy New Year,
> Your friend,
> Rick

I respond to Rick and receive a lengthy letter a month later. In it, Rick thanks me for my "thoughtfulness." He describes, in detail, his last relationship with a young woman who was "an alcoholic and takes Valium to combat her depression." He assures me,

> Also, I want you to know that I am OK. I'm not going crazy or about to commit suicide or anything stupid like that. I'm just scared and insecure and don't really know how to go about correcting it. Amazing, isn't it, I am so lucky to have friends, family, food, shelter, job, etc., and here I am screwed up upstairs. Right now I am living at my grandmothers' house (mail still goes to my Mom's) and working in Los Angeles. During the week, I stay at my step-dad's. He works up here too . . .
> I still run. However, since I ran a fairly good marathon in October (2:46:15), I have difficulty in strength and endurance . . .
> Thanks for your friendship, Jerry!
> Your friend,
> Rick

A "BOMBSHELL"

In March 1988, I travel to London. After making reservations for my Spring break, I call Brendan in London. Brendan is delighted I am coming and invites me to use his "flat." During the first two days, he takes me on tours of London. He must leave for Paris the next day to dub his latest movie into French.

In our final few hours together, Brendan tells me something he had never mentioned in any of our conversations or letters. He tells me that, in 1978, he mistakenly arrived on a scene that had scandalized him. He found a prominent member of the clergy engaged in sexual activity with some "surfers." Brendan never told anyone about what had occurred for many years.

I am horrified! Brendan tells me it was not long after the event when his parents divorced. He has not only longer stopped going to church, but also doubts the existence of God. I tell Brendan how shocked I am and try to assure him that one person, with individual weakness, does not negate all the benefits of religion and does not represent God. Nonetheless, Brendan expresses the degree to which he has been scandalized. When Brendan leaves the flat, I write a long letter to him. I again express my sorrow at what happened. I attempt to explain to him the connection many make between "Our Father" in heaven, and our earthly fathers and father figures. I point out the human weakness of all human fathers and ask him not to reject his heavenly Father or allow what occurs to damage his faith. I realize that Brendan wanted to share what had occurred before he left for Paris.

Brendan respects my decision to become a priest and our friendship endures, across the miles. Brendan now uses marijuana frequently.

After I returned to the States, I began to reconstruct some events from my research between 1976 and 1980. I reread my journals. I find some minor entries regarding a few individuals, only one of whom was a subject of my research. The young men, all more than 18 years of age, joked about drinking whiskey with the older clergyman. They used a nickname in reference to him that now makes sense to me. One of the young men had told me that the clergyman had allowed him to "drive his car" out of the garage when the youth was then13 years old, and without a father. Finally, I find an entry of August 1975. In it I described that the same young man asked to meet with me. He wanted to tell me in private, "Something that will blow your mind!" I went to his apartment at the appointed time and no one answered. When I questioned him during our next encounter on the beach, he told me it was "nothing" and not "to worry about it." The young man was not a research subject. I did not have another opportunity to follow-up.

I realize that there was another instance of a "damaging father figure." As of yet, I do not comprehend the extent of the damage on other individuals. Likewise, it is not to be the only instance in which I will find that I had been unaware of a "damaging father figure" during my earlier research.

"YOU ARE A PRIEST FOREVER"

On June 4, 1988, I am ordained a Catholic priest at St. Helena's Cathedral in Helena, Montana. I make my vows to my bishop. My hands are anointed with the holy oil. The bishop and the priests of the diocese lay hands on me. The words, "Jeremiah, you are a priest forever according to the order of Melchizedek" are proclaimed. My mother and father robe me in the vestments for Mass.

In this most joyous moment of my life, many friends join me and my family. Among them are Mrs. Rita Bayer, "a second mother" to me, and Matt, my "foster son." (Very few priests are ordained who can introduce their "sons" to the congregation.) Matt never practiced a religion, but he realizes how important this occasion is for me. He meets my family and friends. He joins us in the related activities. I can tell he is very happy for me and proud of me. Mrs. Bayer rides with Matt to Butte for my "First

Mass." Later, she tells me how proud I should be of Matt. She recalls how she and her husband had frequently advised me to "throw the bum out." Now, she says, "He is such a fine young man!" I am very proud of Matt!

The Bayer's arrange another "Mass of Thanksgiving" and reception for me. In the church that had once been a branch of St. Patrick's, where "Drop-In" met on Wednesday evenings, I celebrate Mass in Golden Beach. I look out on the congregation and see the entire Bayer family, Mrs. Mary Gilroy, Sr. Basil and others who had been involved with "Drop-In." Standing in the rear of the church with a big grin on his face is Bill Jones whom I once bailed from jail, now a Baptist Sunday School teacher.

I see others at the wall and along the beach. When they learn that I am now a priest, a common response is "Well, that figures," or "You know that fits; you will make a good priest.".

Les, who once told me that I was "the only Catholic he liked," asks, "Isn't that not as good as being a Franciscan?" I respond in that it is and assure him I remain both, a priest and a Third Order (lay) Franciscan.

I am surprised again that my new, added vocation, surprises no one.

YOUTH MINISTRY OR "APPLYING WHAT YOU LEARNED FROM GOLDEN BEACH"

My bishop assigns me to the Cathedral parish as had been planned. However, I learn that he has made one adjustment. During the summers, I am to serve as spiritual director at a church youth camp. I find my knowledge of young people, enhanced by my years in Golden Beach, is of great help. When summer ends, and I begin my ministry at the Cathedral, I am assigned to work with the high school youth ministry and confirmation programs. Once again, I apply my background and begin other programs. I have passed the several examinations necessary to be certified in Montana as a Chemical Dependency Counselor. Realizing many teens want safe places with healthy activities, I begin a Sunday afternoon gym program for all teens in the area, males and females. The community responds with volunteer labor, equipment, basketballs, pool tables, a scoreboard and a ready cadre of volunteer referees. As gym space becomes more scarce in the coming years, I struggle to make certain, "Fr. Jerry's Kids" have a place to play basketball each week. I soon discover that many of the teens who come to the gym do not participate in school sports. I come to realize many of them are unable to afford athletic shoes, physicals or the necessary fees. My research in Golden Beach demonstrated the positive effects of extracurricular activities, including athletics. I organize the annual "Holiday Classic Benefit Basketball Games" between Christmas and New Year's Day. Alumni and alumnae of the two local high schools play each other, and members of the media take on the politicians (including the governor, the attorney general, a supreme court justice and others). Once again, the community responds and it becomes a highlight of the holiday season in Helena. We have ample funds to take care of most of those in need. I realize that by providing wholesome activities, positive role models, and community involvement in the public schools, the young people are less likely to engage in drug use and other deviant behavior. What is accomplished is an application of my own research in Golden Beach.

In part because of my role in the programs, I am invited to a prayer breakfast at the White House. However, the greatest honor for me is the response from Golden Beach when the wall crew hears about my activities. Mike, doing well in business, sends me a large check. Pat feels left out and asks me to send him a request. He donates as well. Soon, Bill Jones and others hear what "Jerry is doing." They too support our efforts in Montana.

I feel my own role is overemphasized. I am blessed with insights gained from the generosity of those who participated in my earlier research. The community of Helena, Montana deserves the credit for their response. Hundreds of volunteers serve in various capacities and hundreds open up their checkbooks.

I cite all of this here for two reasons. First, I wish to emphasize what any community can do and that such action can be a true "war on drugs" and "war on delinquency." However, rather than a war on anything or anyone, I choose to call such involvement a "communication of love to our children." Second, I am humbled to admit that I avoided priesthood for so many years with the excuse that I was doing "good things" outside of priesthood. Catholics and non-Catholics respond with greater trust to "Fr. Lowney" than to "Mr. Lowney" or "Dr. Lowney."

Perhaps, in reading this, some young men and women will give deeper consideration to what they can accomplish in ministry.

AND, BACK AT THE BEACH

In the summer of 1989, I receive a long-distance phone call at the youth camp. It is from one of eldest of the Bayer daughters, Nell, who is very distraught about her father's drinking and changing behavior. She asks my advice. I describe the process of "intervention" to her. The process involves seeking the assistance of a certified drug counselor to facilitate an intervention session between those who are significant (family, friends and employer and others) in the life of the alcoholic. The counselor gathers data regarding the patterns of alcohol abuse, consequences the alcoholic has suffered, specific effects the person's drinking has had on family members, job performance, and so on. A time is set up to meet with the alcoholic and those involved in the session. Beforehand, a suitcase is packed and arrangements are made for the alcoholic to be transported to an alcohol rehabilitation center at the end of the session. The alcoholic is brought to the session unaware of what is about to take place. The loved ones then confront the alcoholic with what his or her drinking has caused in their lives and his. They are supported and guided by the facilitator."Love" and "confrontation" are emphasized. They express their hurt, their anger and their concern.

I tell Nell that her parents are enrolled in an HMO which provides this type of assistance. I give her the guidelines. Nell gathers her siblings and their spouses. They approach Mrs. Bayer and enlist the assistance of the HMO. The intervention is very successful. Dr. Bayer enters treatment. He continues to attend 12-step group aftercare for some time. He is sober.

On my next visit to San Diego, Dr. Bayer shares some of the letters his sons and daughters wrote to him expressing their feelings. I am very moved.

In 1990, Morris moves to Florida to "get away from Golden Beach." Initially, he lives with his sister, Jenny, and her husband. In March 1991, Morris makes a big step. He goes to an Alcoholics Anonymous meeting and enters their program. Morris is sober.

Rick calls me several times from Portland. He continues to have difficulty with relationships. He meets an older woman and lives with her and her teen-age daughter. He requests a source for counseling. One of my classmates in the seminary is now a priest in Portland and has considerable background in counseling. I put Rick in contact with him. It appears that Rick benefits from this arrangement.

On another trip to San Diego, I visit Matt once again. Matt lost his job at the hotel-casino when it was bought by a conglomerate. The union contract became void and management purged union activists from its payroll. Matt works as an independent contractor and is pleased with his situation. He has become more involved in photography and specialized in "sports photography." Some of his photos have been featured in skiing magazines. On the evening that I arrive, Matt and two other photographers sponsor a showing of their work as part of a charity drive for a park for young people. There is a door prize in which the winner is allowed to choose any of the photos. The photo will then be enlarged, matted and framed. My name is drawn. I pick one of Matt's slides. Due to the difficulty in shipping framing, I will have to wait to my next trip to Lake Tahoe to claim my prize. Once again, Matt and I hike trails and have time together. He continues to do well.

During my four years at the Cathedral and the youth camp, I teach as adjunct professor at Carroll College. In 1992, I am assigned to the college full time. This allows me more time to visit San Diego. The failing health of both of my parents necessitates that I spend more time with them and less time in Golden Beach. Nevertheless, I maintain contact with many of those who have truly become my friends in Golden Beach. I keep journals of our contacts.

Some of my friends in Golden Beach, including members of the wall crew, begin to discover the peace of A.A.

Others go to prison or jail. Others are homeless. They and others are more deeply involved in the drug subculture.

Still others are happily married and raising children. Many become more involved in church groups. Many are successful in business and other professions.

In the latter half of the 1990s and into the 21st century, I will set out to investigate more about "who" is "doing what" and provide a more complete answer to Les's question.

End Note

1. National Institute on Drug Abuse (NIDA). "Overview of the 1990 National Household Survey on Drug Abuse." Rockville, Md.: National Institute on Drug Abuse, 1990. A discussion of the cocaine and crack "epidemic" is found in Erich Goode, *Drugs in American Society,* NY: McGraw-Hill, 1993, pp. 245-255.

Chapter 13

Where Are They Now? 1996-2001

INTRODUCTION

Between 1996 and April 2001, I made a dozen visits to Golden Beach. Each July, I spent approximately three weeks in research activity. As a priest, I was able to supplement limited faculty development funds by staying at St. Patrick's rectory and serving the parish. Each December and January, I returned to Southern California to make an annual retreat with the Franciscans at Mission San Luis Rey. I stayed with the Bayer family before and after my retreat, and, once again, helped at St. Patrick's. In April 2001, I returned to Golden Beach to be certain I was current about the status of as many subjects as possible and as to "what is happening." In addition, I located many subjects by phone, mail and the Internet. I visited others who were residing outside of the San Diego area. I filled more than 450 pages of notes in my journals.

During this time period, I was able to contact 80 percent of all of the subjects in person. I obtained reliable information on all but a handful of the other subjects. I verified any information that was not first-hand through two or more sources. In addition, I interviewed the children of three of the subjects, and several other teens.

In this chapter, I summarize the changes that have occurred in Golden Beach and summarize the overall status of various groups. In addition, I provide updates of key subjects who are of particular note and those who have received special attention in earlier chapters. When appropriate I summarize material over the entire period. In some instances, the specific time sequence of events presents a more clear picture. Most information is edited from my journals. Thus, I continue to describe the events in the present tense.

GOLDEN BEACH AND THE BEACH SCENE INTO THE 21ST CENTURY

Golden Beach continued to grow in population and in wealth. In July 2000, the *San Diego Union* reports that only 22 percent of San Diego residents are able to afford a median priced home of $269,650. The rate was down from 34 percent previous year and 20 percent below the national average.[1] The median price of a new house in Golden Beach is $320,000. In April 2001, it is reported that the median price of homes in San Diego had risen by $30,000 in the previous year, and $5,000 in the previous month.[2] The demography of Golden Beach has changed from a community that was oriented toward families to a haven for single and wealthier retired individuals. The population of Golden Beach has increased to 41,268. Less than 11 percent of the population is less than 18 years of age. The median age is 36 years. Two thirds of the residents are either single, divorced or separated. Of the 21,550 residential units in Golden Beach, 70% are rental units.[3]

The beach and boardwalk are much more esthetically attractive. Only one block of Ocean Boulevard is open to automobile traffic. The streets, where once young drivers cruised in their cars, trucks and vans, are now paved and graced by walking lanes, bike paths, lawns, benches and shrubbery. Larger, more convenient and attractive restrooms and change rooms are available to beach goers.

New ordinances ban or restrict the hours for skateboarding or walking dogs. Alcohol is banned on the boardwalk or alongside the wall during the early 1990s. On April 17, 2001, the city passed a 18-month "experimental" ordinance to ban all alcohol at the beaches in Sand Beach and most of Golden Beach.[4] Police patrolling on bicycles along the boardwalk and in all-terrain vehicles on the sand strictly but courteously enforce the ordinances.

The crowds along the beach reflect these changes. On my early morning and evening walks, I see many surfers. However, surfing is no longer the sole domain of males in their teens and 20s. There is wide age range of male and female surfers from those in their early teens to those in their fifties. In the mornings, I see many retired and middle-aged individuals and couples. In the afternoons and evenings, a younger crowd is evident. In the late evening and night hours, many of those who are called "hard rocks" by the "locals" dominate some areas. And, throughout the day and night, another group is present to enjoy the amenities that the beach, the restrooms, showers and change areas afford. They are the homeless. The homeless are evident along the new walkways, on the benches and on the lawns. Some of the elites of Golden Beach are upset at this "invasion." I ask myself, "If I were homeless, what would be a better location?" The homeless stand in stark contrast to the other residents of Golden Beach. They include a few subjects whom I studied in previous years.

Coffee stands and coffee houses sell the more expensive and potent forms of the drug caffeine. An outdoor restaurant serving coffee and breakfast muffins is located at the wall where "the shed," once operated by Bill Jones, had stood. Coffee houses draw some crowds from the clubs along Main Street. However, particularly on weekend nights, many young single adults still flock to the clubs in Golden Beach.

The old skateboards of the late 1970s and early 1980s are "out." New, more versatile expensive models are "in." It appears that the "skaters" occupy a similar social status to that once held by the surfers in 1970. Like surfers, they "hang out" together. Their clothing is distinctive, baggy pants, baseball caps and large athletic shoes. Their "boom boxes" blare their favorite music, Rap. Those outside their subculture assume that they use drugs. They receive informal social sanctions and it is obvious that the police are far more likely to stop, question and ticket or arrest them than others on the boardwalk.

"In-line" skates have replaced the old roller skates. More expensive brand-name bicycles have replaced the older, more simple bikes. Many of those in the younger generation have beepers, pagers and cell phones.

A hostel located on the boardwalk near Lime Avenue is the target of opprobrium by many in the community. The police respond accordingly. The hostel caters to the young from various nations and overlooks an area of the boardwalk frequented by skaters, hard rocks and those once called "red freaks." Nearby is a club with a patio. It is often crowded and its patrons, in their 20s and 30s, create considerable noise. I view no police activity at the club.

The former members of the Old Wall Gang have dropped the term "red freaks" and have now labeled a new group who frequents the territory at the "wall" area as the "Golden Beach Vermin Gang."

In 1996, tatoos and body piercing are in vogue. There are several tatoo parlors along Main Street and elsewhere. Some of these offer body piercing as well. Tatoos appear on all parts of the body and, it seems, there are no body parts which are exempt from piercing and adornment with rings. By 1999, the same businesses advertise tatoo removals. By then, a clean-cut, non-pierced body is deemed attractive. When I walk the boardwalk on Easter Sunday, 2001, I ask myself, "Where have all the tatoos and piercing gone?" Among thousands of people, I count five males with arm-length and/or upper body tatoos, and only two persons with pierced eyebrows. A number of people have smaller, unobtrusive tatoos. Pierced ears and ear rings are in fashion among some males in their early teens.

A variety of music emanates from radios and CD players. Popular types and artists include Rap, from Marty Marks to Eminem and 'NSync; Country-Western, from Alan Jackson and Garth Brooks to Shania Twain and the Dixie Chicks; Pop artists, from Bruce Springsteen and U-2 to Brittany Spears and the Backstreet Boys and the "new" sounds, from Celtic and New Age to the Latin rhythm of Ricky Martin. Members of the Motley Crue have undergone treatment for heroin abuse and remain popular.

The drug scene varies as well. In 1996, methamphetamine, also known as "crystal meth," "crystal" or "crank," is widely used. It appears there is a repeat of the pattern in 1970 when amphetamine, "speed," had similar popularity. Within two years, methamphetamine takes the same turn as amphetamine had in the mid 1970s. Its negative effects become evident. It is frowned on and its use becomes taboo, even in the drug subculture. On the other hand, ecstacy, also known as "xtc," "x," "Adam," "hug" and "beans," arrives in force. In 1996, a new subculture has developed. The members use ecstacy at clubs and "raves." The locations and times of raves are passed from one member of the in-group to another. By the year 2000, raves grow in size and frequency. Tens of thousands flock to remote rave locations to use ecstacy, called "rolling," wave "glow sticks," sniff menthol, suck on pacifiers, and dance through the night to earsplitting music. A number of deaths and overdoses are reported. Those who use ecstacy claim deaths and "bad trips" are the result of other drugs and/or adulterated ecstacy. Some authorities claim otherwise. As with other illegal substances, there is no control by the Food and Drug Administration. Thus, there is a lack of evidence to completely resolve the issues surrounding its safety or the possibilities of side effects. By 2001, the popularity of ecstasy seems to wane slightly. On the other hand, I learn that cocaine and heroin are being used by a small, but increasing number of upper-class teens. OxyContin and other prescribed pain relievers are available on the illegal market.

The price of marijuana continues to rise. The more potent varieties of "weed" are preferred. A single gram costs $40. Five joints sell for $20. I calculate that the price is 1400 percent higher than the 1970 cost of "commercial" marijuana. Although marijuana is readily available, its use is not as nearly as conspicuous as it had been in previous decades. Many days and evenings I walk the length of the beach area without smelling marijuana.

Alcohol remains the preferred drug to get "high." Most of the alcohol is consumed at home or in the clubs. Until the April 2001 ban on alcohol at the beach, there are frequent beach parties. A common practice is to bury the keg (s) in the sand to keep the beverage cool. A frequent weekend scene is "tent party." Delivery trucks deliver kegs to preset locations on the beach. Others purchase six and twelve-packs to drink on the beach. Glass is not permitted. The police reacted quickly if alcohol is observed on the wall or boardwalk. For those under the legal age, alcoholic beverages, as well as marijuana, are available. Many travel across the border to drink freely in the clubs of downtown Tijuana, and obtain other drugs. At times, large parties of up to 70 or 80 are held in one of the area's parks. House parties are common especially when parents are out of town. Beer is the focus at the parties even though marijuana is frequently present and used by some. The house parties in Golden Beach vary. Sometimes, there are as few as 10 present. At other times, there may be upwards of 50 participating. It is reported that parties are much larger in nearby Diamond Heights, a community even wealthier community than Golden Beach, and somewhat smaller in Alta Vista, where family incomes are slightly lower. Many of underage youth pay the homeless to purchase alcohol for them.

The fear of AIDS has changed the social scene. One local, Marty, tells me "You can't have any fun anymore. You can't trust anyone any more."

Those whom I began to study in the 1970s now range in age from their early 40s to more than 50. Many have children who are now the same age as their parents were when I began my research. Their stories will answer Les' observation, "Where we are twenty years from now is what really counts."

1996

I return to Golden Beach on July 3, 1996. I drive by the beach at 7:50 p.m. hoping to watch the sunset. It is impossible to park nearby due to the throngs of people on the eve of the Fourth of July. The next day I note how orderly the boardwalk is compared to the Fourth in 1976 and 1977. One of the first persons I meet is Sam from Arizona. Sam is 18 years old. His girlfriend brought him here from Arizona to help him "stop using crystal meth." He has no intention of giving up beer and pot. He tells me his mother has been married and divorced twice and an active member in A.A. Sam is

Catholic. When I reveal that I am a priest, he asks where I "practice." I describe my teaching position as a sociologist and describe the history of my research in Golden Beach. I am amazed at how open Sam is with me. I had been afraid that I might have "lost the touch" and that my priesthood might interfere with the openness I had previously been accorded. I will discover that others, like Sam, are more open to me when they learn that I am a priest, once they realize that I do not moralize or condemn them. The next day I see Sam sitting, very lonely, on the wall. He tells me that his girlfriend is paying his way back to Arizona. She has a new boyfriend and the new boyfriend wants Sam "to go home." I encourage Sam to seek out a program, such as Narcotics Anonymous and/or Alanon-Adult Children of Alcoholics. This is the last time I will see Sam. However, I continue to meet young people who, like Sam, have had troubled family backgrounds, became involved with drugs and found their way to Golden Beach.

I walk to the wall area and immediately spot Luke who had introduced me to the Old Wall Gang in 1970. Luke tells me that he has just been released from Folsom Prison. He spent three and a half years in the prison for a property crime related to his use of alcohol. He is on parole for one year. Luke had been divorced but is now back with his wife and his 16-year-old son, Ronnie. Luke brags that Ronnie as "a good kid." Ronnie is a "B" student at Golden Beach High School and "does not do anything (drugs)." Luke is in A.A.

Pat is also at the wall. When we talk about A.A., Pat rejects A.A. saying, "Some can handle it (alcohol) and others can't."

Pat and Luke update me about others who had been members of the Old Wall Gang. Ty, who was addicted to heroin, died in prison. The cause of death is uncertain. Ty is the third of my subjects to come to an early death. There is speculation that he may have died of hepatitis or as the result of prison violence. It is rumored that Bart Roe also died in prison. (Later, I learn that the rumor is false.) His brother, Chuck, is in danger of being declared, "a habitual offender," under California's new "get tough" laws. Chad, who had been excluded from the group several years earlier, "hangs out" north of Golden Beach, lives in a hut and "is kinda like a homeless guy." Kyle who, along with Chuck, became involved with cocaine through Bill Dimaggio has been "in and out" of prison.

Even though the beach is more "mellow"than it had been in the past, it is much more crowded. I notice the effectiveness of the new ordinances regarding alcohol, traffic lanes and speed limits on the boardwalk. There are many groups partying on the beach and the bay. Alcohol is not allowed on the beach after sunset. Most of the holiday revelers remain to view a spectacular display of fireworks.

I retire to St. Patrick's rectory for the night and to ponder what I have learned in my first 24 hours back in Golden Beach. Ty is dead and so, apparently, is Bart Roe. Kyle and Chuck Roe are "in and out of prison." Luke has recently been paroled. Chad is homeless. Some are in A.A. Others are in denial regarding their alcohol and other drug problems. Who else may be dead? Who else is in prison or jail? How many are homeless? How many are sober? How many are struggling like young Sam whom I met today? Sam's story sounds familiar only the names have changed in 26 years.

The following day, Pat is at his usual the spot on the boardwalk near the wall. I recall Norm Dunn's prediction of 20 years earlier, "Twenty-five years from now, Pat will be sitting be on the wall, drinking a beer." Pat tells me he drank heavily last night and needs "a hair of the dog." He tells me, "There are no drugs here anymore. We have seen what they have done to too many of our friends."

Bill Jones joins us. He greets me, "Looney, How ya doin'?" Bill, once a heavy user whom I bailed from jail in 1975, is a Sunday school teacher and has been involved in the men's Christian movement, "Promise Keepers." He tells me that he and his wife have divorced. They have three sons. She left him "to marry a black male dancer." Bill is a mediator for housing construction projects. As he says, "I help people avoid lawsuits." He lives at home with his mother and is able to have his children two or three days a week.

Bill informs me of the status of his brothers. Pete is divorced and has two children. They live north of San Diego. Todd is having marital problems. Terry, the youngest and the only one that had not been involved with drugs, is a vice-president of a leading man's fashion magazine. Each of the Jones brothers is active in their church.

The following Sunday, I meet Bill with two of his sons at the beach. Bill introduces me to his son, Linus, saying, "Jerry has been a friend for a long time. We go way back." Linus asks me, "Did you know him back when he was bad!" I assure him that his Dad is good and there is no one that is "bad."

Having accounted for all the members of two of the "five families," the Roe's and the Joneses, I attempt to reach others. I place a call to Mark Gilroy. Almost the first thing Mark says to me is, "I want to thank you again for teaching me to drive (21 years earlier). I will never forget that!"

Mark Gilroy has been married for six years. He was employed at the college bookstore while attending the university. When cutbacks in the state education budget occurred, Mark began to work in construction. He tells me that his brother Reed, the attorney, and his wife are still in Paris, where Reed sometimes socializes with Brendan, the movie star. John Gilroy is married and has one daughter. Mark gives me the phone number of, Ron, his oldest brother. I leave a phone message for Ron. In spite of their earlier activities in "Drop-In" and other involvements in St. Patrick's parish, Ron is the only one of the four Gilroy brothers who remains a Catholic. John plays music at a "Four-Square Gospel Church" in Los Angeles. Mark and Reed are not active in any church.

An hour later, Morris Bayer and his father, Dr. Bayer pay me a visit me. Morris is returning to Florida that evening. He tells me,

> I am *big* on A.A.! ...the only thing that kept me alive until I became sober was surfing. It was my only physical activity . . . Once I was at an A.A. meeting and this dude starting telling me how he stole someone's surfboard, I really got pissed! It made me so mad! It reminded me of Rich. I am sorry he is dead, but I will never forget how he stole my surfboard.

I give Dr. Bayer and Morris a tour of the improvements to St. Patrick's Church. Morris says, "I go to A.A. now instead of Mass."

A few days later, a very sunny afternoon, I take time to rest on the beach. Some young male surfers in their early teens are nearby. Their loud, gross language and behaviors remind me of the "Wall Rats" of 1975. They talk about sex and parties. A young girl approaches them. She interacts with them at their own level. She grabs her tit and points it to one of them. He grabs his crotch and thrusts it toward her. She returns the gesture and he grabs her crotch. I think to myself, "Well, some things have changed, females are now free to behave like the males!"

Kevin, one of the former wall rats, joins me on the beach. Kevin had been raised as a very strict Baptist. He discusses many things,

> You know, even before you were a priest, you were a 'father' to a lot of guys around here . . . Yes, you can't believe how much people here admired you! . . . You have the heart to be a priest . . . I was doing great when I was in Hawaii for five years. I was living as a Christian. The first two years were the greatest. I never felt so good, but, you see, the two things I have to have are beer and sex. I just love sex! So, the last three years were misery. I couldn't keep living as a hypocrite. I needed sex and

> beer! ...I realize how my Dad's death (in 1975) is tied together with my heavy use of alcohol and pot . . . The more time goes by I realize how controlling my mother is. She is remarried and controls my Step-dad . . . She *always* tries to control me and manipulate me! I have to stay away and live in my own apartment. I love it!. . . Also, my Mom tries to control my sister and brother and she has Norma and my brother in the palm of her hands. She tries to control me. I hate it and she keeps trying! . Why do people do this?. . . There are people who go to church and sit and look nice, but they try to control everyone. Others, don't go to church, but they never hurt anybody, but are good to others . . . I am going with this girl. She is 33 years old and has two children. She's now going through a divorce. She has been separated for two years . . . I couldn't marry her because she is not sexually attractive . . . She is a brunette and I like blondes . . . I want blond children . . . Chuck Roe never shows his face around here. We don't allow drugs here. We have seen many of our friends' lives messed up . . . Pot and beer are different. I mean crystal meth, cocaine and LSD!

Early the next week, Kevin introduces me to his girlfriend, Patti. He tells her I have been his "friend for twenty years." She addresses me as "Father Jerry." Kevin asks her if they can go to his apartment for a "massage." She says, "I don't think we should be talking about premarital sex in front of a priest!" Kevin responds, "Jerry's ok with me."

Throughout the summer of 1996, Kevin and his girlfriend are "off again" and "on again." She appears to patronize him. He resents this but does not want to give up the opportunity for sex or forego Patti's cooking. Yet, his friends advise him that she is "unhealthy" for him.

Kevin owns a motor home that he parks near the beach. He refers to it as the "new shed," as a substitute for the "shed" that Bill Jones operated during the mid-1970s. He and others use the "shed" to change clothes or store surfboards or have "private time" with a woman. Kevin moves the van once a week to avoid as many tickets as possibly. Eventually, he moves from his apartment and lives in the "shed."

Over the next five years, Kevin and I will have many conversations and interactions. He comes to the beach each Friday after work and spends most of the weekends on the beach, drinking beer and attempting to "pick up chicks." He continues to struggle with his conflict between what he sees as the Christian ideals and his personal behavior regarding sex and alcohol.

That evening I am invited to the Bayer's for dinner. Jeanie stops by. Her daughter is 15 years old. Jeanie is studying to become a registered nurse.

She was arrested for stealing drugs at a hospital and was sent to a drug treatment center. Her younger brother is active in A.A. Jeanie says to me, "I would never want my daughter to know what I did!"

The atmosphere in the Bayer household has become dramatically more cheerful. Dr. Bayer's sobriety and pleasant demeanor have changed the mood of the entire family. Everything is more positive.

Later, I tour the boardwalk. There are many skateboarders and in-line skaters on the boardwalk, even though the activities are illegal after 10 p.m.

The next day I see some very young boys, about 13 years old, buying crystal meth from some older men (whom the wall crew would have classified as "red freaks"). Later I see some others, perhaps 15 or 16 years old, "shopping" for alcohol and drugs among the many homeless men on the boardwalk. The following morning, the police come to the area and arrest one person, give tickets to others and order some others to clean up the beer cans and trash.

Mike, whom I have not seen in more than 19 years, phones me. He tells me, "Well, I didn't turn out so bad! You were very instrumental in changing my life. I talk about you to people all the time and the influence you had on me . . . Can we get together for dinner? I'd love to see you."

The next afternoon, Mike and his girlfriend, Lisa, come to Mass at St. Patrick's. Afterwards, he drives us in his Porsche to an upscale restaurant, the "Grub and Pub." Lisa says Mike "talked about you many times." Mike now owns a surfboard factory. He has just purchased a brand name label which he wants "to turn more into a clothing line." Mike has 14 employees in his factory. He races Porsche's as a hobby.

Mike discusses his past drug use and some of the former wall crew. Mike used cocaine over a 10-year period, but now avoids drugs. When Les' wife had a nervous breakdown and Les was left to care for their two children, Mike hired Les, an Old Wall Gang buddy, to work in the factory. However, Mike tells me, "He had a terrible work ethic!" Mike fired Les. Later, Les and three other former employees of Mike moved to Washington State where they opened a "wind surfing" board business. Floyd has two children and another "in the cooker." Mike says, "Jeff is a functional drug addict (using crystal meth)." Floyd "is a miracle." Three years earlier, Floyd was involved in an accident at a construction site. (Pat had told me that Floyd "was on cocaine" at the time.) He fell and a pipe entered his skull. He was on life supports for some time. Floyd recovered and is undergoing physical therapy. He married a year later. He has two children. Mike states, "He has no problems no except he forgets some things sometimes."

Mike and I continue our contacts over the next six years. He remains a very successful businessman. He will later marry another woman, not Lisa.

After Mass the next morning, a woman introduces herself to me as Rick's mother. She tells me that she is upset that Rick is still "living with that older woman" in Portland. I ask her for Rick's address and phone number. She phones the information to me that afternoon. Many years earlier Rick had told me his mother would "never approve of any girl I liked." Rick's older brother confirms this perspective that summer.

Gil Bayer and I talk on the phone frequently. He is very busy with his contracting business and his family. Gil and his wife, Shannon, have three children, two daughters and a son. They are active in their Catholic parish. Gil invites me to dinner one evening. During the course of the evening, I will be brought up to date on many of Gil's friends, classmates and acquaintances of the 1970s who were subjects of my research. Through the information Gil and Shannon provide me, I locate many of the individuals. As the conversation begins, however, They drop another "bombshell" on me. Shannon begins the conversation,

> Well I am sure you are aware of the sexual relationships that have been taking place in the Barone family . . . Walter Barone was having sex with all three of his daughters and even some with his two sons while they were children and growing up. It all came to light when Ruth Barone called me to tell me never to let Walter near Elizabeth (Gil's and Shannon's oldest daughter).

Gil and Shannon explain that Ruth had married unsuccessfully. Following her divorce she went to counseling. Apparently, Ruth had undergone "Repressed Memory Syndrome." After the incidents came to light, the other siblings confirmed their own experiences. Walter Barone continues to deny that anything occurred. He and his wife are excluded from many social events.

(Once again, I am horrified. And, once again, I note a "damaging father figure" who I had not recognized in my midst. The Barone's had been pillars of the community. My mind races back 20 years earlier when Ruth Barone would stand near me for protection at parties. I had wondered why she behaved certain ways back then. Later that night, I review my journals from that period of time. As in the case with those involved the "damaging father figure," clergyman, it seems to make much more sense.)

Gil and Shannon Bayer provide me with other, more positive information about others, most of whom had been light or regular users. Frank is now a 18-year veteran of the San Diego Fire Department. He divorced and remarried and his second wife recently gave birth to a child. Albert never married. He inherited the expensive home where he hosted his 1975 party. He is an engineer with the San Diego Fire Department. Howard is a contractor. He never married. He was active in A.A., but relapsed recently. Al is married. He is an architect in Utah. Phil is married and manages a supermarket. Stu has been married for many years. He now owns several restaurants. Robin is a Certified Public Accountant. He and his wife have two children. Steve owns a boat shop. He is married with three children. Nelson works as a bartender at the "Grub and Pub." His parents either "arranged the marriage of" or "introduced" Nelson's sister, Linda, "to" a Japanese medical student. Linda went to Japan and married the student. They live in Japan and have three children. Cliff is a "major alcoholic." He is divorced but has not remarried. He has been convicted twice for D.U.I. He had been employed by Gil, but Gil had to fire him. Brendan stops by to visit Gil and Shannon when he is in San Diego. The couple had watched a recent evening television movie starring Brendan.

Gil and Shannon Bayer's children are very lovable, bright and well behaved. Gil introduces me to them as "Uncle Jer." Beginning that summer I give each of them a Carroll College T-shirt from Montana. Each year thereafter, they expect "Uncle Jer" to arrive with new t-shirts.

The following evening, I visit Doctor and Mrs. Bayer. Dr. Bayer shares some of his experiences in alcoholic treatment with me. I read to him some of the passages from my earlier journals in which I noted the symptoms of his progressive alcoholism. He is intrigued by one remark which he made about me in 1981. I had recorded Dr. Bayer statement, "Everybody else sees these guys at the beach as a bunch of bums. You see them as people to be rehabilitated." We all laugh at the "old times."

On July 19, I talk to Marie who with Arlene had visited me in Richmond in 1978. She tells me she is divorcing Pete. She says he has problems he has to work out. Her close friend, Betty, has four children and is "doing great." Helen is married with three children. Arlene has not married. Arlene's brother, Max, has "begun to clean up his act (regarding drugs and alcohol use)." Judy is also married and "doing well."

That afternoon I phone 16-year-old Ronnie, Luke's son. He confirms the information I had obtained at St. Patrick's about high school parties at a particular spot on the beach. Ronnie says he does not participate. He tells me he has "bleached out" his hair. Luke thinks Ronnie "looks like a hedge hog." (I recall Luke's "hippie" appearance in 1970.) Ronnie skateboards. He works at a car wash. He tells me his Dad said that I "was cool" and it would be fine if we got together sometime.

The next day, a hot sunny Saturday, the wall crew schedules a "surfer's reunion." Bill Jones, Pat, Jeff, Tom, Mike, Luke and I have breakfast together. When Luke tells Tom I am now a priest, Tom gives what seems to now be the standard reply, "Well, that fits."

Jeff told Pat, "I no longer do crystal." Later, Pat and Mike tell me they do not believe him. They do not fully accept Jeff or his brother as members of the wall crew because of this perception. In 2000, they come to believe that Jeff has "put down" the drug. They accept him back into the group.

Many others are surfing and others show up as the day progresses. I note several things. First, is the degree to which the Old Wall Gang and the older members of the wall crew remain a cohesive group. At certain times, the wall is still a gathering place. Second, is the degree that drugs, excluding alcohol, are frowned upon. Cocaine and methamphetamine are particularly taboo. Marijuana is tolerated, but not used by the group itself. Third, is how basically wholesome they are in spite of their family background. Pat was very much on his own when I met him in 1970. Yet, he is doing relatively very well. Bill Jones tries very hard to be "a good father." Mike is successful in business, but willing to share with those who are less fortunate. Mike asks me to pray for Jeff because "he is the only one from our group that is still using drugs."

In my sermon that evening at St. Patrick's, I discuss how we, as Christians, may sometimes be tempted to get rid of the "wheat" along with what appear to be "weeds." I describe the group that I once knew who "People thought they were 'bad' or 'weeds' because they were young males who surfed and had long hair." I mention some of the positive traits I see in them today. Mrs. Rita Bayer notices a long-haired male who is not able to stop laughing. It is Mike. Mrs. Bayer mentions this to me as I she leaves the church. I introduce her to Mike. Mrs. Bayer is slightly embarrassed, but relieved when Mike enjoys another laugh, which we all share.

The next morning, Kevin, my "struggling" Baptist friend, attends the 7:30 a.m. Mass. He leaves before I can say goodbye. I will talk with Kevin many times within the next year.

Before leaving Golden Beach, I follow up on the information that I have been provided by Gil and Shannon Bayer, Pat, Luke, Mike and Marie. I am able to talk with most of the individuals involved. In the remainder of this chapter, I will concentrate on new information and major changes in the person's lives. The overall patterns remain constant. Among males and females alike, those who grew up in stable, caring families, are "doing well." Those who experienced disruptive and/or uncaring lives in childhood, have problems with alcohol and other drugs, difficulties in their relationships and marriages, and are less likely to achieve and retain meaningful employment. There are exceptions and intervening factors, including religion, Alcoholics Anonymous and other treatment programs.

1997

On New Year's Day, 1997, I celebrate Mass at St. Patrick's. Mrs. Bayer and I go to breakfast at a restaurant near the wall. When we exit the building, Pat is in his usual sport at the wall. I introduce them and Pat tells her that he knew several of her children. As we depart, Mrs. Bayer remarks, "Well, what a handsome, fine young man he is!" I remind her that Pat was "one of the bums you and your husband told me not to hang out with back in the '70s."

I return to the beach that afternoon before my flight to Montana. Pat tells me that today is "Luke's first day off parole. This will be the test. He has been 'doin' good', surfing and stuff. I hope he does well. He is on his own now."

The following summer, I drive to Golden Beach by way of Lake Tahoe to visit Matt and with the hope of contacting Paul.

I arrive at Matt's house amidst a June snowstorm. Matt is still working as a contractor in construction jobs. He remains a free spirit and seems content although, at times, somewhat lonely. He is now 45 years old and has had a few health problems. Matt is no longer a part of the "coke" scene in Lake Tahoe, but continues to use marijuana. For some time, Matt had been dating a woman from Sacramento. In 2000, they become engaged.

That afternoon I call Paul and drive to his home after dinner. Paul, one of the wall crew "rats," had lived on his own using his social security payments throughout high school. He completed a bachelor's degree in computer science. Paul worked his way through college by repairing surfboards during the daytime and attending evening classes. He now coordinates the computer system at a ski resort in Lake Tahoe. He is married to Beverly. They are expecting a son very soon. Beverly is a registered nurse. She is a Catholic and they attend Mass together each Sunday. Paul is filled with questions for me about the Catholic Church. We discuss computers and I am amazed at Paul's knowledge and intelligence. He is doing very well. Although I enjoy my visit, I do not remain long because I realize that Beverly's pregnancy is physically discomforting. We remain in touch with one another. Eleven days later, Paul and Beverly become parents to a son, Peter. I ask myself in my journal how Paul had the strength to succeed so well and to come so far. The same may be said of Matt.

I arrive on, July 3, I arrive in Golden Beach. The beach is not crowded that evening. I stay at St. Patrick's.

The morning of the Fourth of July, I have a conversation with, Mark, one of the high school students who serves as a receptionist in the office during weekends and evenings. (I will find that these workers are my most reliable sources for information regarding the current high school scene.) Mark does not attend Golden Beach High School because "it is filled with 'gangsters,' into rap music, baggy pants and drugs." He tells me some grass can be purchased for $10 an ounce, but usually there is "lots of homegrown" available. Although many others claim, "Homegrown is no good," Mark says "It is all right, if they don't use 'Miracle Gro'." Most of the parties that Mark attends are "smaller, fifteen to twenty people," but he has been to one in Diamond Heights with more than three hundred teens present. Mary says, "There is usually beer and pot, but sometimes there is 'jungle juice'(fruit juice spiked with various alcoholic beverages, usually vodka and gin). Mark says, "The police only break up parties if there are other things going on or people resist what they tell them."

He tells me that there are lots of bongs for sale, especially at a local music store. We discuss the dance clubs in Tijuana. (In 1992, a student from Helena, Montana attending a San Diego college took me on a tour of Tijuana and the "dance clubs" on a Friday night.) Mark says that many high school students still go to Tijuana on weekends. Some go to dance and drink. Others go to drink. Still, others go to drink and to buy other drugs.

The beach is very crowded. There are many "tent parties." There are throngs of people, most of whom are in their 20s and 30s. Some are with families. I see only a few teenagers. (Mark told me most of them will be in a beach south of Golden Beach.) It seems there are fewer skateboards and in-line skates than a year ago. There are many surfers in the water.

I learn that the wall crew (who sometimes now referred to themselves as "The Sea Wall Social Club") is having a party at the bay. I go to the location, but only Pat is there.

I return to the wall and meet Max. I have not visited with Max in 17 years. Max has been "sober" for more than three years. He had worked for a local television station, then on fishing boats where he began to both make and deal methamphetamine. He also used cocaine and heroin. He tells me, "One time the cops had me at gunpoint. The DEA and others busted into my house. They took what I had. I never had much. They took what I had, especially the coke, and left . . . Three times I was at gunpoint from others. One was when I was just walking down the boulevard. I thought I was a goner."

Max kept repeats several times, "God was protecting me!" and, "Someone was watching out for me." He informs me that his grandmother, a "saintly" member of St. Patrick's, died five years ago, and that three years ago his family "begged me to go to the hospital." Finally,

> I agreed to go for just five days. When I was ready to leave with six quarters in my hand, for bus fare, I could only think of 'God'. I prayed to my grandma and stayed in the hospital . . . I really messed up my life and the lives of others. I have a bad pancreas and liver . . . I go to A.A. three times a week . . . Once, I almost slipped. I drank half a beer and I stopped at a store to get another and then got a Gatorade instead.

Max works as a baggage handler for a major airline for $6.50 an hour. He states, "Before I had so much money that I never would have worked for $6.50. I'm content now . . . I live at home."

As Max's story unfolds, I reflect on the difference between him and those that had committed fewer serious offenses but served time in prison. Some died there. His pivotal journey involved family and a spiritual renewal. He tells me that he finally, "accepts God." The next Sunday he comes to the Mass I celebrate at St. Patrick's. It is his first time in many years, but he remembers his grandmother's devotion. I see Max frequently over that summer. He remains sober, employed and active in A.A.

Pat and Kevin arrive at the wall. Kevin now lives with Patti. Kevin was in bed with another girl and Patti caught them. Kevin says he is "addicted" to Patti. Referring to the relationship, Pat tells him, "Put down the heroin!"

Pat tells me that Julian continues to be active in A.A. and is now no longer homeless, but gainfully employed. Dean is the vice-president of a technology firm in Indianapolis. Blake is married. He works in San Francisco, but comes to the beach frequently. Barry, still a light user, has been married for 19 years. He owns and manages the hotel he inherited.

That evening I am unable to locate the "Sea Wall Social Club" party during the fireworks display. I see Pat, but he is "zonked" and does not recognize me.

The next morning Pat is suffering from a severe hangover. He left his bike somewhere on the bay last night and it is not there today. He says he will quit drinking for a month. I suggest A.A. He says, "I went once, and I didn't like it. I don't need a crutch!"

Pat tells me about his three arrests for cocaine. He was "let off" the first time. The second time, the testimony of U.S. Marshall's and that of the San Diego Police contradicted each other. The third time, the judge says, "You have to do time!" Pat repeats the story of his survival in jail because he could read the newspaper to other prisoners.

Pat describes his graduation from Golden Beach High School. He was smoking marijuana in the men's room in his graduation gown. He inhaled deeply and held his breath longer than usual. He fainted and hit his head. He was taken to the emergency room to have stitches.

I see Mrs. Mary Gilroy at church. She tells me that Reed and his wife have returned to the U.S. He is practicing law in Massachusetts. She is concerned that her son, Mark, is "turning away from God and the Church." Max greets me after Mass and leaves for an A.A. meeting.

At sunset, Bill Jones visits with me on the beach. His former wife has divorced again. Bills' brothers, Terry, Todd and Pete, are about the same. The next day, Sunday, Bill's two sons, 14-year-old Linus, and 12-year-old Michael, are at the beach with him. They and others surf, play volleyball and enjoy themselves. Bill tells me that Linus stole a bike a few weeks ago. Bill disciplined him and made him pay for the value of the bike. Bill insisted that Linus no longer wear baggy pants and other "rapper" clothing. On another occasion Linus took $5 from Bill without Bill's permission. Kevin's and his girlfriend, Patti, is nearby with Patti's two children. They have a cooler filled with beer. Kevin, Patti and Pat drink a great deal of beer

(That morning, at Billy's restaurant over breakfast, I overhear a teenage son tell his father, "You did worse things that when you were a little kid!" I muse over the statement as I write in my journal about Bill Jones, Luke and their sons.)

Luke, who has completed his parole, is running on the boardwalk preparing for a marathon the next week.

Pat gives me Keith's phone number. I call Keith that evening. Keith quit dealing cocaine 21 years earlier. We plan lunch the next day.

Keith and I have a long conversation. He and his wife have three children. One is Keith's stepdaughter, aged 26. Another daughter is a senior in high school. His 14-year-old son is in 9th grade. Keith proudly shows me their pictures. He describes his life. After he met his wife, they moved to the outskirts of San Diego for several years. Fourteen years ago, when he and his wife were having "problems," Keith joined Alcoholics Anonymous. The pastor in his church helped them. On a weekend church gathering the pastor prayed over Mark and he "had a Pentecostal experience."

He says, "I felt a rushing. I prayed that God would take my anger away from me."

"Six years ago," Keith says "I reevaluated my sobriety. I realized that coke, not alcohol, was my drug of choice."

Keith inherited his parents' home in the wealthy community of Diamond Heights. He also inherited a house in Mexico and some rental properties. For six years, he had a business at a shopping mall in Golden Beach. He is currently "between jobs."

Keith is now an elder in the church in which his parents had been active. Keith, a rebellious youth in the 1970s and a member of the Old Wall Gang, was the one most heavily involved in cocaine trafficking. Keith now admits his parents were "awesome." Keith tells me he never made the trip to South America which he was planning at the time of our 1975 interview.

Keith praises me for what I did for him and the group, "We really felt we could trust you and you never, never ever moralized to us!" He tells me that in 1973 he and Luke, "Beat the crap out of Turk when he welched out on that money he owed you . . . We told him, 'How can you do that to Jerry?' We took him down to Salmon Court and the two of us just beat the crap out of him!"

In the next few years, Keith and I will have various discussions as to which generation is "worse," his own or his son's.

I had attempted to contact Andy several times. I knew he had married, moved to Northern California and had two children. He became more heavily involved in drugs and his wife divorced him. Andy was committed to a state mental hospital in the late 1980s. The hospital prescribed Lithium for Andy. Andy had fathered another child. Recently, he began to attend A.A. meetings. I finally reach Andy at his sister's home. Andy remembers me and that I "interviewed" him. He does not seem to remember other matters. He tells me about some of his former friends. It seems that Andy is somewhat "out of it." I talk to his sister. She remembers me well. She and I talk about the 1970s. She tells me that Andy is "having a bad time." I raise several questions in my journal. I know that Andy had used a lot of LSD and other drugs in the 1970s. Does he suffer from LSD Psychosis? Some of his former friends were involved with the now-deceased member of the clergy who scandalized Brendan. Has this affected Andy? I wonder how it affected others. In the year 2000, I will learn more.

There are two very memorable conversations during my summer stay of 1997.

On July 10, I have dinner with Luke's son, 17-year-old, Ronnie. Ronnie tells me,

> My Dad left us when I was five years old. He was in jail two times. The last time I was not surprised . . . When he got out, he needed a home, so he is just 'rooming' with us. He has no right to discipline me but he yelled at me when I went to an Alta Vista party last year . . . There were 200 kids there. They were all from different groups. There was a fight when they ran out of kegs. A gunshot was fired. The D.J. tried to get his material out and the cops held him at gunpoint. They let him go when they found out he was the D.J.. . . . I first drank last summer, also smoked pot. An older guy, in his 20s, a brother of a friend and his best friend gave it to us and did it with us . . . I D.J. at parties for money. They charge a dollar a person for some parties, $2 for some. There is beer and pot there, nothing else. I want to go to a rave party for music. They set them up in warehouses. There are usually Ecstacy and stuff there, but I only want to be there for the music . . . I have seen the invitations. They charge $5. They make money from people coming. They don't provide beer or anything . . . Different groups have different parties. Jocks have theirs. Soccer players have theirs. There are more toward the West (beach area) than in the East (Inland). The jocks party a lot! Especially the football players!

It seems that Ronnie really is "a great kid" as his father had described him. We stay in contact over the next few years. I will learn much more from him about "raves" and ecstacy.

I finally reach Norm Dunn by phone. He invites me to lunch with him and his girlfriend on a Saturday afternoon. We meet at an expensive seafood restaurant north of San Diego. Norm greets me, once again, with a big bear hug. He introduces me to his girlfriend, Lucy. Lucy's 15-year-old nephew visiting from Utah joins us.

Norm operates his own tile contracting company. In the restaurant, a patron is wearing a T-shirt with Norm Dunn's business logo on the front. Norm asks about Chuck Roe. Norm has lost contact with Chuck who was once his "best friend." They along with Harold, Sol and Skip were "wall rats" in the mid 1970s. Harold has worked for Norm for several years.

Norm tells me that he had hired and fired both Sol and Skip. Sol had acquired six drug driving convictions and lots of problems. On one job, at the home of a policeman, Norm's work crew moved the refrigerator outside the house in order to lay tile on the kitchen floor. Sol removed beer from the refrigerator and was drinking on the job. The wife of the policeman called Norm who then fired Sol. Norm is no longer in contact with Sol or Skip.

We discuss Norm's trip to Mobile. He tells me that he received two more speeding tickets on his return to San Diego. We laugh about his anger about not being admitted to Jimmy Buffett's club because he wore shorts.

Norm gives me his mother's address and phone number. Martin Dunn no longer lives with his mother. I tell Norm that I had talked to his older brother, Toby, who is now married, steadily employed and providing for his wife and child. Toby and his family once lived in his mother's garage. They now rent an apartment not far from the house where the Dunn brothers were raised.

Norm does not want me to talk about his use of marijuana in Mobile. He says he does not use coke and rarely smokes marijuana. Norm is obviously reserved about these issues in front of Lucy. Within two years, I will hear more about Norm's use of cocaine.

Norm invites me to join him at his job site, but I have to return for confessions at St. Patrick's We take pictures of each other in front of the restaurant. Norm hugs me again and promises to come to visit Montana.

Earlier, I had learned that Martin Dunn's alcohol problems have worsened. Martin and his best friend, Anthony, went to the Summer Olympics in Atlanta. Anthony received a free T-shirt. A very drunk Martin demanded that Anthony give the shirt to him. When Anthony refused, Martin broke a glass and stabbed Anthony. The two former "best friends" drove back to San Diego speaking only as necessary and have not spoken to each other since the incident.

I find it of interest that the younger wall rats of 1975 (Nelson, Rick, Pete, Norm, Sol, Skip, Martin, Harold and Anthony) are no longer friends and lack the cohesion that is so evident among the Old Wall Gang and older wall crew members of the early 1970s.

That evening a rally is scheduled in Sand Beach to protest the recent action by the San Diego City Council to impose a 10 p.m. curfew on those under the age of 18. I drive to the area but there are very few in the "rally." Instead of observing what there is of a rally, I walk the boardwalk. I speak with a police officer on a bicycle. He tells me that the department has had to allow exceptions to the requirement of a college degree for officers. Many high school graduates are now considered. During the 1970s, most of those hired as officers possessed a master's degree."No one wants to be a policeman these days," he states, "but to be promoted to lieutenant an M.A. is still required.". We discuss San Diego's progress in promoting community policing. He feels police on bicycles is an essential part of community policing and getting to "know people." He enjoys working with female officers and wishes the department could retain more females.

At various times, I notice that the officers on bicycles and all-terrain vehicles, are noticeably more courteous and professional than in years past. Likewise, they are noticeably more courteous and professional than the officers in cruisers. Several times, I note instances in which the officers leave their cruisers to single out Hispanics and blacks from a crowd. On one occasion, two officers stop a van driven by a young Hispanic male who is playing loud music. They force him out of the van, search the van and detain him for over an hour, before releasing him with a ticket for noise violation. On another occasion, there is a crowd of approximately 70, mostly whites, watching a young man "perform" on roller skates on the boardwalk. The officers drive up just as the performance ends. The officers do not seem to realize why the crowd had gathered. There are many people sitting on the concrete fences outside of the homes on the boardwalk. The officers single out the only black man in the area. I watch for a half hour while they search the man hold him before they ticket him for "trespassing" on private property. On the other hand, when minor violations are discovered on the boardwalk by bicycle patrol persons, or on the beach by those in all-terrain vehicles, the officers simply ask the person to move the alcohol to the sand, rather than on the wall or boardwalk, or remind the violators to place a leash on their dogs. The citizens typically react in kind. They are courteous, frequently thanking the officer as they obey. Community policing is far more effective than the "dragnet" tactics of officers in riot gear during the 1970s and the 1980s.

Upon the advice of the high school students working at St. Patrick's, I visit other beach communities. In the areas south of Golden Beach, there are many more teenagers on the beach than in Golden Beach. The proportion of minorities is considerably higher. In some areas, south of Golden Beach, blacks and Hispanics are in the majority. The northern portion of San Diego County grows rapidly. Many of the youth I studied in Golden Beach during the 1970s reside in that area. The demographics are reflected in the beaches in that area. The proportion of teens is similar to that of Golden Beach in 1970.

I make a point of striking up conversations with as many of the "new" young people in Golden Beach as possible. Typically, their stories are similar to those of their parents' generation at the beach.

On one sunny morning I meet two surfers, Mick, age 24, and Noel, age 16. Mick begins the conversation by telling me that he is divorced. He did not graduate from high school. He had been "kicked out" of several different high schools in the area. He has used pot, coke, speed, "and lots of shit." He sold various drugs. He brags, "I smoked tobacco, taken acid, got my GED and fucked girls! The hardest drugs to give up are tobacco and caffeine. My step-dad lives here in Golden Beach, so that is how I got here."

Noel is in junior high school. He lives with both of his parents. He began surfing two years ago. Noel is clean-cut. He likes to water-ski and to go fishing and with his Dad He asks me if I do my studies, "To help kids, or just to know? Why do you do it?"

I respond by describing the history of my research and then tell him I am now a priest. I tell him how what I have learned helps me in my ministry by accepting people where they are. When Noel learns I am a college professor, he tells me that he has a GPA of 3.75 and wants to attend either UCSB or BYU. He went to a camp called "Any Town Camp" where he learned tolerance and acceptance of diverse people. He met a Hispanic girl there that he likes and continues to correspond with her. He emphasizes to me that he never uses drugs. He asks me for my address so that he can contact me for more information about colleges.

That evening, I meet Nathan, a 16-year- old from North Carolina. Nathan says he and his sister are here to spend a month with their Dad. Their parents were divorced two years ago. Hel tells me that he went to church "until a month ago, then I was bad . . . I drank and smoked pot." He feels he can't go to church anymore. I tell him God is forgiving and going to church will help him. The time is 9:59 p.m. Nathan worries about the 10 p.m. curfew. His Dad and sister are roller skating somewhere on the boardwalk. I promise to stay nearby so that he is accompanied by an adult if the police question him. Shortly after 10, his Dad arrives. I tell his Dad, "He was getting worried about the curfew. He is glad you're back."

Once again, my final day in Golden Beach is a Sunday. Many of my friends are at the 9 a.m. Mass. They include Mrs. Rita Bayer, Gil and Shannon Bayer and their three children (waiting for their Carroll College T-shirts), Kevin and Patti, Pat and Laura, Mike and Butch, one of the regular users and a former Golden Beach football player. In my sermon, I discuss how many of the things I have learned in Golden Beach are now valuable in my youth ministry in Helena, Montana. I mention my gym program and the holiday benefit basketball games. I tell the story of how I promised a local high school football team that, if they won the State AA Championship I would, like them, get a "Mohawk" haircut. The team won and I got my haircut was featured on the local television and in the newspapers. Pat especially enjoyed the "Mohawk" story. The following Christmas he and Mike send me donations for "Fr. Jerry's Kids" in Montana.

I return to Golden Beach shortly after the next Christmas for three days. I visit with Pat, Mike, Luke and the Bayer's. Little has changed. I await my summer visit of 1998.

1998

When I arrive in Golden Beach, the following July, my first destination is the wall. For the first time, no one I know, even Pat, is there.

Morris Bayer is visiting from Florida. Morris has become a mentor and somewhat of an unofficial "Big Brother" to a 11-year-old boy, Louie. Morris has been coaching a Little League team in Florida. Louie has had a "bad, bad home life." Louie's is one of seven children. His father is a "drug addict"and spends all of his earnings on alcohol. Morris brings Louie to Golden Beach to stay with him at the Bayer's home during Morris' and Louie's vacation. Morris tells me he sometimes attends 10 A.A. meetings a week, and he has been sober for seven and a half years.

The next morning I walk the length of the boardwalk. The previous winter, El Nino brought high tides and pounding waves. The wall is collapsing. In some places, the steel support rods show through the broken concrete.

In spite of El Nino, the overall appearance of the beach has improved since the previous summer. There are more palm trees and, increased lighting. The physical appearance seems to attract tourists who appear upper class and well dressed. The morning paper indicates that home prices continue to rise. I note that there are fewer tatoo parlors. In fact, "tatoo removals" are now advertised. (Another fad has come and gone in Golden Beach.) Those on the beach and boardwalk are older than in years past. A few scooters are evident among the parades of bikes, skateboards and pedestrian traffic along the boardwalk.

I phone Luke. He has a new job. He is content and doing well. He has completed his parole time. He talks about the fact that he is "getting old." He tells me that his son, Ronnie, is attending community college. Luke asks me what Masses I will celebrate at St. Patrick's during the weekend. Luke is present for the 7:30 a.m. Mass the next Sunday.

The Sunday *Los Angeles Times* carries a front page story, "Drugs: Use of Meth Rises in the West." The article describes the decreased use of cocaine and increased use of marijuana among "those arrested." San Diego is cited as having a rate 5 percent higher than other cities.

The article states,

> Methamphetamine use prompted special concern among officials. Noting that San Diego has been 'extraordinarily hard hit,' Riley said at a White House briefing that methamphetamine now surpasses cocaine and marijuana among people arrested in the border city.[5]

I note that the data is from arrest records from the previous three years. My observations are that the rate is lower than it had been in 1996 and 1997. Indeed, amphetamines use decreases in San Diego in 1998. (The opposite is true in Montana and other rural areas.) At St. Patrick's rectory, Mark, says he sees lots of crack cocaine at Golden Beach High School and San Diego State University and less methamphetamine.

I see Kevin on the beach. Pat tells me that he does "not want to be around Kevin." Kevin still lives in his motor home, "the shed." Lucy is in Michigan. Kevin tells me, "After our talk last year about my addiction to her, I broke it off." At times, Kevin attends church with Lucy. He tells me he will come to the evening Mass at St. Patrick's.

The 5:30 p.m. Mass is so overly crowded that Kevin is unable to enter. For many years, the Sunday evening Mass at St. Patrick's has attracted "young adults." Those in their 20s and 30s are increasingly drawn to the services and to the various activities for young singles. Thus, on Sunday evenings, the crowd frequently spills outside onto the sidewalks.

There are other parish ministries to meet the needs of Golden Beach's changing demography. On Saturday afternoons, many of those in the same age group line up for confessions. The pastor, Fr. Paul, is kept busy preparing couples for marriage and presiding at their weddings.

On the other hand, St. Patrick's no longer has its own high school ministry program. "Drop-In" has been replaced by weekly "gatherings" sessions which include teens from four surrounding parishes.

Bill Jones asks me to meet him at the wall. He buys coffee from the stand located where his surfboard rental "shed" once stood. Bill tells me that his brother Terry and Terry's wife are receiving marriage counseling. When their son was seriously ill the physician asked what minister should be called. Terry said, "Our pastor." His wife responded, "My Rabbi." This forced them to seek help in working out their religious differences. Bill says his other brothers are doing "ok."

Bill also tells me that during the past year two murders occurred at motel adjoining the wall. The incidents involved two employees involved in a "love triangle" with the same woman. Bill says, "I guess they didn't work things out!"

Rick's older brother, Travis, joins us. He tells me that Rick is still living with same older woman in Portland. It has been 10 years. Travis says that his mother still does not approve. He says his other brother is "in the same situation." Travis describes various incidents involving his mother's dominance in their lives, "She tells me how to fix my house!" Travis says that Rick still has problems with his temper.

Mike learns I am in town and phones me. He is happy to tell me that he has not had a drink since October 13, 1997. I thank him for the money he sent for needy kids in Montana. Mike is planning to get married and asks me to pray for him. The next day, he is leaving to race a car in Tecate, Mexico. Later, I learn that Mike wrecked his Porsche and walked away from the accident. Mike had paid $70,000 for the car.

It on only rare occasions during my stay that I observe illegal drug use or smell marijuana. On one morning, I see some young teens (possibly runaways) sleeping on the beach before noon. Two hours later, I observe them and another youth smoking marijuana in obvious sight of a lifeguard tower and police who ride past on their bicycles. On the other hand, large amounts of alcohol are consumed on the beach and at the nearby clubs.

I tour some of the nearby areas and find a great deal of underage drinking and use of marijuana. There are some signs posted that advertise parties and admission fees from $15 to $25. I realize that the parties are "raves."Luke's son, Ronnie, tells me that he serves as a D.J. at some parties because he has the equipment. He does not use drugs at the parties.

I call Norm Dunn's. Lucy, Norm's girlfriend whom I met at lunch with Norm a year earlier, answers. Lucy is very upset with Norm. He is out of state working on a construction project. Lucy claims that she found Norm cheating on her. She indicates he is involved in other inappropriate activities.

She tells me, "You had better have a talk with him, Jerry!" Within two years, I will understand more completely what Lucy means.

During the summer, I become acquainted with Don, one of the high school students working at St. Patrick's. Don attends Diamond Heights High School. He asks me about my research. I describe my findings and what I found regarding parties and other aspects of the drug scene. Don says, "Well, it sounds like you're doing a good job!" He tells me his perceptions of the parties he has attended,

> They're usually when the parents are out of town . . . The 'max' at any party I have seen is probably 300 or so . . . There is always beer and alcohol, but there is usually weed too, but those guys are usually outside or in a corner some place . . . I think broken homes are what causes it all. I went on a small group retreat and when we were sharing, I was the only one out of the six that had a dad. The others all had stepfathers or something . . . My Dad went to Golden Beach High back when you were doing your research. He must have been around.

I did not recall Don's father. I leave Golden Beach. Unfortunately, one of the first things Fr. Paul tells me the next summer is that Don's father had died of a sudden heart attack.

1999

My visit over Christmas and New Year's, 1998-1999, does not reveal any particularly significant new information. I receive the usual Christmas cards and holiday greetings from several of those in Golden Beach.

In June, I exchange email with Rick,

> Hi Jerry,
>
> My apologies for not writing earlier . . . It is interesting that my mother still gives my address to those who inquire. We haven't talked in five years . . . Oh well. My life here in Oregon is ordinary. I work for a data processing company . . . Michelle and I are still together. We are technically engaged (for five or six years, hahahahaha), but marriage seems remote. My friends tell me to be glad. I don't know, maybe it doesn't matter either way, but I have always wanted to be married. We live together in her house, jointly own the vacant lot next door, and spend a majority of our free time in the year, gardening. Nothing too exciting, but we get along for the most part (except when I throw a tantrum). I still run, but having just turned 40, it is

becoming increasingly more difficult . . . I really miss Golden Beach. Please say hello to Norm Dunn should you see him, Really nice guy . . . Kevin is a terrific guy too . . . Bill Jones gets along well with my brother. Nice guy. It surprised me that it took Alise Bayer so long to get married . . . I hope Morris is doing well in Florida. Unfortunately, I helped get Morris into trouble in high school . . . His mother was not too happy with me, but she has a short memory and always treated me kindly. I know where Al is, in Utah . . . Unfortunately, he is now divorced. He doesn't have a home phone.

Best and know you are in my prayers,
Your friend always,
Rick

Similar to many of those from divorced background Rick has not been able to make a lifelong commitment to marriage.[6] He is only partially content in his relationship with Michelle. He and his mother continue to have difficulties. Rick's temper remains a problem. His best friend, Al, whose parents were divorced, also has divorced.

I arrive in Golden Beach on July 8, 1999. During my stay, the news is dominated by the story of the missing plane and deaths of John F. Kennedy, Jr. and his wife. Most of my observations during the summer of 1999 indicate little variations in the patterns I observed during the previous three years. However, there are some noteworthy changes and findings.

The crowds on the boardwalk on some sunny afternoons are larger than those on the Fourth of July in years past. There are increasing numbers of tourists. Even though the Hispanic population in Golden Beach has risen substantially, very few are at the beach or on the boardwalk. The children on the beach are typically with their parents or a part of organized groups, such as the YMCA or various "camps." The homeless congregate in the areas near the restrooms and showers. There are still some teens who are either runaways or "throwaway kids."

During the week, the wall crew is not at the beach during daytime hours. They are all employed. Pat and Kevin are there regularly at other times. Bill Jones and Luke, and occasionally others, are present on weekends.

On my first Sunday afternoon at the beach, Pat informs me that Vick is dead. Vick, a member of the Old Wall Gang, had spent a majority of his adult life in mental institutions and halfway houses. The cause of death was not stated in the newspaper and no funeral services were mentioned. It is still unclear whether or not Vick's mental problems had been caused or exacerbated by his earlier use of LSD or other drugs. Vick is the fourth young man in my study who has died.

Luke's son, Ronnie, becomes more involved in his avocation of being a disc jockey. Luke and Ronnie spend a weekend camping in the mountains. I sense that Ronnie and Luke are building a stronger father-son relationship since Luke's release form prison.

Morris Bayer and his "little brother," Louie, are again visiting from Florida. Morris feels "hassled" by his parents. He is amazed by my memory regarding his need for his father's support at football games in 1975, and the instances of sibling rivalry between him and Gil in 1969. One evening, Morris and Louie are surfing. A burglar is shot and killed short distance away. Morris and Louie see the body.

The 20-year reunion of the Golden Beach High School class of 1979 is being held. The Saturday evening dinner-dance at a famous downtown San Diego Hotel is closed to nonmembers. A picnic is scheduled on the bay on Sunday afternoon, but few attend. I go to the bay, but am unable to find the location. Sally Bayer is a member of the class. She tells me, "Almost no one came to the picnic so there was nothing to find." She provides me with an update of the previous night's festivities,

> A lot of people are in A.A. and they can't drink, so it is a bummer. Alex was there. He is *really* good-looking! He divorced 10 years ago. He lives near L.A. He gets his two daughters on weekends and so on. He is doing well . . . But Stu was the best looking. Lee had wind-blown hair and was dressed in casual clothes. He snuck into the reunion at the hotel . . . and then got kicked out! Calvin has a lot of money. He lives in Diamond Heights and is on coke. His nose is in caved in. He deals.

Mrs. Mary Gilroy and her husband take me to lunch. Reed and his wife have become Quakers. She believes that Ron "really needs A.A."

Norm Dunn schedules a dinner appointment with me, but does not show. Norm frequently broke appointments when he was in high school, so I do not concern myself greatly, but I resolve to confront him the next time we talk. When we do speak to each other, several months later, I realize Norm was being forced to deal with some major issues in his life.

Don, whose father, died a few months earlier, is working at St. Patrick's. We chat frequently. He says he enjoys it because, "This job is so boring!" One morning Don is very tired. He tells me there was a Golden

Beach High School party the night before. He had to drive his buddies home. He says,

> There were about thirty-five people at the party. A small group of eight to 10 people smoked pot in the backyard. They were not part of the usual group. They were in and out . . . I tired not to drink too much . . . We went out and got a lot of food. It ended about 1:30 in the morning. I got home about 2 a.m.

Don has been accepted at a state university. We exchange email addresses and stay in touch during the next year.

By the time I depart from Golden Beach that summer, I am under the impression that I have completed as much research as is necessary. I write that it appears there is “nothing more to learn.” I was wrong!

I return to Golden Beach on Christmas Eve. After Mass the following Sunday, I drive by the wall. I heard people pounding on my car and yelling, “Jerry Lowney!” It is Luke and Keith. Luke calls me “a midget in a penguin costume” (referring to my clerical white collar and black shirt).

Keith tells me that his son is “So great! He doesn’t do anything! (Drugs)” He asks me about a college for his son who is interested in films. I suggest U.S.C.

Luke says his son, Ronnie, is doing well. Luke and his wife have moved into a condominium and Ronnie lives in their former residence. He says Ronnie is still accepting jobs as a disc jockey, but is thinking of dropping out of community college because “he has too many things going.” I tell Luke and Ronnie that, at times, I would like to work more closely with young people again. They argue that I should not. Keith states, “These kids today are so bad. They aren’t like we were. We did things for ourselves but did not hurt other people.”

I think of the fights and mention, “The red freaks?”

Keith says, “We were not into anything for profit!”

I do not respond verbally, but raise my eyebrows as I think of his coke deals in the tens of thousands of dollars. Keith seems to sense what I am thinking and responds, “But I never made a profit,” and, laughing, “I blew it all!”

Luke warns me, “You have to be careful about the con. These kids today are really bad!”Both Luke and Keith blame today’s parents. Keith says that he and his wife are together and so were his parents. Luke says, “I have been faithful and with my wife, except for a little stint (referring to his time in prison)."

I refuse to argue but am laughing on the inside. I think of how ironic it is. Luke and Keith were among the "wild ones" in their youth. I remember how those in their parents' generation told me not to "waste" my time and be careful around "those bums" (the Old Wall Gang).

Luke says Julian is now in Seattle and has a job. He is no longer homeless or sleeping in "flop houses."

Luke tells me Kevin continues to drink heavily. Luke took Kevin to a casino outside of San Diego recently. They were "kicked out because Kevin was drunk. He "tried to pick-up on some women." I ask Luke if an intervention might help Kevin. Luke replies that he does not think Kevin is "at his bottom yet." He says, "Kevin's family love (enable) him, and Kevin still is functional."

I tell Pat, Luke and Keith about my intentions to write a book. They all want a copy and Luke wants to know how he can obtain a copy of my dissertation. They remark that they will be "celebrities."

I stay with the Bayer's during my visit. Colleen and Roger have three sons. They are extremely intelligent and well mannered. Alise and her husband have a stepson who is with his mother for the holidays. Gil and his three children visit often. They are very intelligent and well mannered.

Jeanie comes to visit. She married a Mormon, but he does not practice his religion. Jeanie is an emergency room nurse. Jeanie is very strict with her 17-year-old daughter. She proudly describes her daughter as "beautiful" and "refined" I tell her that I intend to entitle my book, "What Were Your Parents Doing Back Then?" Jeanie repeats three times, "I never want my daughter to do what I did!" We laugh and recall stories about the "old days."

I close the millennium thinking about how strict the now "older" generation is with their children. As a result, the behavior of the younger generation is much more conforming than the youthful behavior of their parents.

2000 - INTO THE NEW MILLENNIUM

Gil Bayer and his family host a very large "Y2K" party. Gil, who had been one of the "non-partying" light users in high school, sets up a bar in the back yard. Two bands play. The first is a group of teens. They are extremely loud. There are many complaints. I have hearing problems. (I now wear hearing aids. My audiologist tells me that the hearing damage likely occurred, in part, from the loud music during my earlier research at parties and concerts.) I and other "older" adults tend to remain inside toward the front of the house. Nevertheless, the guests enter from that direction. I am able to meet many individuals whom I have not been able to contact in many years. Cliff and Woody are among those I am able to visit. They are both married with children and doing well.

Dr. Bayer leaves early. Because of the loud music and the fact that I am scheduled for an early morning Mass at St. Patrick's, I leave shortly thereafter. (Apparently neighbors began complaining and, by 9 p.m., Gil asked the first band to stop playing. I am told the second group was "much more mellow and played far better.") I say to myself, "I think I am getting too old to be doing these things!"

On New Year's Day, I call a number of persons. Pat, who had been a mainstay at the wall over the past thirty years, is busy at his new home in Alta Vista. He has been working on the exterior of the house and is "now heading for the inside." He discusses 401K's and retirement. Pat, the last of Old Wall Gang "hippies," begins to conform to the image of a conservative, suburban businessman-homeowner. Pat believes Kevin is "out of it" and "needs to get out of Golden Beach."

Mike was married a few weeks earlier in Vermont. Mike is returning to Golden Beach to run the business for year and then sell the business and join her permanently in Vermont.

Luke's son, Ronnie, asks advice about college. I urge him to remain in school. He says he does not get many jobs as a disk jockey because "everyone wants big names." He had a Japanese girlfriend who was three years older than he. Ronnie says, "She was perfect, but she likes to go to clubs and I am only 19, so she was too old for me." Ronnie's grandfather died recently. He tells me, "I have been thinking a lot about God lately." He says he has had no religion, but talks to his "grandma." I promise to call him again and have lunch. I phone several times, but do not reach him before I leave Golden Beach.

During the next several months, I contact many subjects of my 1975-1977 research by telephone and the Internet. Brendan and I chat the day after the academy awards ceremony. Brendan produced, directed and acted in a film that had been featured on a major news network prior to the awards. I am planning a trip to Ireland and France. Brendan asks me to contact him when I arrive in Paris. Unfortunately, just prior to my arrival, Brendan had to make a business trip to the U.S. Paul and Rick exchange email with me. Norm Dunn and I discuss his situation during telephone conversations. He is appealing a felony conviction for "domestic abuse."

On July 7, 2000, the day I turn 61, I drive into Golden Beach. As I have described in the prologue, my mind takes me back to the first time I entered Golden Beach and I ponder all the changes that have taken place since then. The next morning, I walk along the boardwalk. I find few changes from the previous year except that new ordinances forbid skateboards from Main Street northward. Tobacco use seems to be more prevalent among the 12- to 18-year-olds on the boardwalk. There are a number of infants in strollers or being carried by their parents. In the morning hours, a majority of those on the boardwalk and paths are joggers and tourists. Most area waters are restricted to surfers during the morning. In my two-mile round-trip walk I see no blacks and only a few Hispanics. I estimate the crowd. About 80 percent are in their 20s and 30s, between 2 and 5 percent are teens, 10 percent are families, mainly tourists, and about 10 percent appear to be more than 50 years old.

I meet Pat and have a lengthy conversation. He provides me with updates of 17 of those who had been subjects of my dissertation. In most cases, there has been little change. Nevertheless, the information regarding some persons is of significance. Bill Jones has moved to the northern part of the county to be closer to his three sons. Pat gives me Bill's phone number. Barry went to Las Vegas and won the "big jackpot" at Fitzgerald's. Luke frequents the nearby reservation casinos. Luke is still doing well with "no other relapse." Eric operates an athletic store near the beach. Brett lives in Indiana. Brett's son graduated from Purdue and now lives in Golden Beach. Kramer lives in Las Vegas. Kevin "still has an alcohol problem, and gets blitzed all weekend and is still after young girls." Pat believes Kevin has problems other than alcohol. Pat tells me that Carl lives in the north of San Diego and Pat gives me his phone number.

I stop by the Bayer's. Dr. Bayer has begun to drink again, but vows that he will be able to control his drinking by limiting himself to two drinks each afternoon. Morris is not at the house, but is visiting Golden Beach. Once again, he brought young Louie with him from Florida. Morris plans to remain for a period of time and work for his older brother, Gil. The second eldest Bayer daughter, Jane, is also visiting from Florida. Jane remarks how good A.A. has been for Morris. Mrs. Bayer and Jane state that Morris "is still homophobic." Mrs. Bayer wonders if Morris had ever been sexually abused.

The next morning, I meet Morris on the beach. Morris provides some new and valuable information. Bart Roe is alive. For five years, every one of the wall crew "knew" he had died in prison. Morris says that Woody saw Bart and Chuck Roe at a funeral. Morris knows how I can contact Woody. Trent, the other surviving member of the "trio," has been sober for six years. Morris is not certain whether or not Trent reached sobriety through A.A.

Morris and I discuss religion. During our discussion, Morris informs me that he was aware of the sexual behavior of the clergyman and some young men many years earlier. I ask him how he knew. Morris says, "Brendan told Gil a long time ago. I thought everyone knew."

Morris then says, "One time I saw him (the clergyman) with white spots on his nose. I didn't think anything of it but, later, when I used coke I knew where the spots had come from."

I ask Morris if anything had ever happened to him because he seems to be homophobic. Morris responds,

> When I was 19 years old, hitchhiking on Gulf Boulevard, this dude in a van picks me up. He wanted me to go in the back while he gave me a blow job. I said, 'No way,' and told him to let me off, telling him I lived a block from where we were, but it wasn't near our house. Years later, I saw on T.V. a story about a serial killer that drove a van. I am homophobic!

In the next several days, I learn that cocaine played a major factor in the interactions between the clergyman and the few young adult men. I talk with two individuals who were in their late teens and early 20s 1975. I speak with one parent and one other older adult. As I had known at the time, the clergyman had begun to consume his favorite whiskey in the company of some young men. I look back in my journals and find an entry from 1975 in which a young man told me, "We turned him onto grass!" Later, the older man became involved with cocaine. I am uncertain as to whether one of the younger men, all adults, introduced him to cocaine or he had introduced them to cocaine. Nevertheless, his use of cocaine became extremely heavy. One reliable older adult tells me, "Cocaine actually killed him." This process, which apparently began during the period of my dissertation research of 1975 and 1976, culminated within two years upon the death of the addicted clergyman. I realize how devastating the entire episode might have been to the small number of the young men directly involved. It is uncertain how the scandal affected the faith of many others. Morris' statement, "Everyone knew," does not appear to be true. A few knew, but people were reluctant to discuss the matter. I do not know the complete story of the cocaine connection. However, one person who was close to the scene tells me, "It was a lot bigger than anything around here. It was the scariest part of my whole life." I realize any additional probing may cause unknown psychological harm to some human beings. I do not pursue the matter further except to phone Brendan in Paris during March 2001. I ask Brendan, who had been so open with me in our conversations and his letters, why he did not tell me what he had observed. Brendan replies, "Jerry, we just didn't talk about those things back in those days!"

And so, the extent of harm by one "damaging father figure" becomes apparent. Some aspects of my research which have been unclear for 25 years are now obvious.

On a brighter note, after playing phone tag, I reach Carl. My last contact with Carl had been a year after his stay in Switzerland. Carl had written his lengthy letter to me regarding his trip eastward to the hashish markets of Afghanistan. I reach Carl who lives at the northernmost part of the county. Carl is a mortgage banker. He is also directing the building of a subdivision comprising 26 homes, each selling for more than $500,000. Carl and his wife, Jolene, have been married for twenty-two years. They have three children, 18-year-old, Tony, 17-year-old, Sue, and 5-year-old, John.

Carl seems delighted to hear from me. He says, "Apart from any book (referring to my dissertation), you had an impact on my life in that time of instability. You were a very important force in my life!"

This statement, along with those made earlier by others, including Mike, Kevin and Keith, are somewhat bewildering to me. I had reported in my dissertation that I was treated by some of the subjects of my research as somewhat of a "father figure." Nevertheless, I do not understand why some are so strong in their statements regarding my influence. According to the standards of many sociologists one is supposed to be totally "objective" when doing research and one is to avoid influencing one's subjects to any degree. One member of my dissertation committee had been adamant in this regard. Carl and I plan to have lunch the next day. Among other things, I want to have him clarify what he meant by his statement.

I meet Carl at his job site the next day. We go to a local restaurant and find a private room to have a quiet visit. Carl brings me up to date on his life. He completed a degree in engineering from my alma mater, San Diego State University. At the time he and Jolene had two children. Later, they began to have difficulties in their marriage. Carl became bitter. He was in France and went to his hotel room to read the Bible. Carl says,

> I read a passage from Ephesians dealing with bitterness and forgiveness . . . I realized how much God loved me. I cried for over an hour. I stuck it out. Jolene and I worked it out. Now, we help with the pre-marriage program at our church. We discuss with the couple various methods of how to solve conflicts and communicate with each other

Carl discusses his father, "My Dad was very distant. He would never have thought of getting down on the floor with us and playing. I try not to be strict with the kids and give them space, but, from their earliest age, was down on the floor with them."

Carl and his family are very active in their church. The church is an independent "chapel." However, the theology is close to that of the Baptist faith in which Carl was raised. The congregation supports a group of tribal people in the mountains of Nepal. Carl has been very active in this aspect of the church's ministry. The previous year Carl took his son, Tony, with him on a trip to the mission in Nepal. This year, Carl is busy with the construction project. Tony and another young man are to make the trip to the mission in Nepal. Tony wants to extend his tour and go, on his own, to Thailand and Vietnam. Carl is opposed. I mention to Carl his own trip to Afghanistan and the letter he sent to me. I point out that Tony, as did his Carl, needs to establish his own independence. Carl asks me for a copy of the letter. Once again, Carl tells what an importance influence I was in his life. I ask him to tell me more about why and what he means. He responds,

> First, you were always present to us. You were always there. Wherever we were, you were there. Second, you were not judgmental. You never moralized or advised us what to do. You accepted us as we were. Third, it was your presence. I saw God in your presence because you were spiritual. Fourth, You had values and cared, but you did not moralize or make us feel like we were being analyzed.

After our lengthy lunch, Carl and I agree to stay in touch. He wants me to meet his son Tony. He would like to attend Mass at St. Patrick's and hear one of my sermons.

I am humbled by Carl's statement about my influence on him. I am baffled as how to respond. On my drive back to San Diego I ponder what it means. I am well aware of my own human frailties and sinfulness. I have made many mistakes in my life. I continue to deal with the daily temptations as much as any human. Moreover, I am remorseful for many things that I have done that have or could have brought harm to others. My immediate feeling is that I am being put on a pedestal. Such can lead to pride. "Pride cometh before the fall!" and, the higher one is, the greater can be the fall. I will continue to ponder what Carl says. As a sociologist, it is incumbent upon me to report any effects that I, as a researcher, had on the results of the research. I conclude that if I was non-moralizing, nonjudgmental and present when other adults would not have been present, I was merely doing what a sociologist engaged in "non-participant observation" ought to be doing. It is true that I cared about those in my study. The most difficult part of my role during my research has been to realize what had been taking place among young people, such as Carl. It hurt me to see what they were doing to themselves. I was touched by their struggles given their less than adequate home lives and the everyday world in which they lived. That experience changed my life. I decide that I can learn from Carl's "idealized" view of me. I resolve to be aware of the necessity not to be judgmental and, as a priest, to simply be present to people.[7]

A few days later, Carl's son, Tony, phones me. We arrange a meeting at the wall. We greet each other and Tony says his Dad told him I was "casual" and "cool" to talk to. I ask him more about what his Dad said about "the old days." Carl had been fairly open with him. I give Tony a brief tour of the area, including where the "shed" had stood, Pat's role as "Da Mayor of the Beach," and so on. We go to an open-air restaurant for a soft drink.

Tony tells me that he used to go to parties and had smoked pot when he was 16 years old. Then "Jesus came into my life as my personal Savior."

Tony graduated in May with a GPA of 3.4. On graduation night, he and his sister were in an automobile accident. Tony suffered a concussion and still has some short term memory loss. We discuss his proposed trip to Nepal and Thailand. I urge him to negotiate with his Dad about the cost and the length of the trip. Tony says he will choose the right moment because, "My Dad tends to lose his temper when he is busy."

Tony describes the youth in his community for me. He tells me that he is in a group of 10 of his peers, and he, and "maybe one other," are the only ones that have a two-parent home. The high school parties are large, usually more than 200, when parents are not home. At other times, the mother of the family is present while the party is taking place. I tell him the pattern is very similar to what I observed during the 1970s in Golden Beach.

Tony tells me that there were "three or four" shootings last year in his high school. The police closed the school and did a "sweep" of the entire premises. He provides a picture of the drug scene at the high school, "In the boy's room you always smell pot. In the rest of the school, kids use anything that can't be smelled, acid, ecstasy, menthol cough drops, meth. I used to go to Tijuana clubs where there is underage drinking. I never go to Tijuana now."

Tony wants to attend a Bible college. He is very involved within his church and with a group of other teens who gather, on their own, for bible study on weekday evenings. I am very impressed by Tony. He is extremely sensitive and very devout in his faith.

The following Sunday, Carl, Jolene and Jolene's parents attend Mass at St.Patrick's. We have a pleasant visit afterwards and promise to remain in contact.

On my return to Montana, I photocopy the letter Carl had sent to me regarding his trip to Afghanistan. A few days later, Carl writes to me and thanks me, saying, "Somehow, in my memory I had made it all much more romantic and spiritual." Carl compromises with Tony and allows him to decide if he wants to extend his trip beyond Nepal. Nevertheless, Tony sends me an email telling me that he chooses not to extend the trip due to lack of funds.

The day following my lunch with Carl, I have dinner with Don, who had worked at St. Patrick's the previous two years. Don is now 19. He went to Tijuana with some friends to go to the dance clubs. He tells me that at times the clubs are wild but that it was "not bad" the previous weekend. Don and I had visited frequently on the Internet during the previous academic year. He adjusted well to university life. Don tells me that he had partied "a lot" during his junior year in high school, but less his senior year. Don's father died during his senior year and Don became closer to his sister. Don tells me that, after my visit the previous summer, he went to his first "rave" near Los Angeles. He estimated that the crowd numbered about 14,000, "Half of them were on ecstasy. They call it 'rolling.' You could tell who they were because they were using pacifiers, using that Vick's menthol and waving lights."

Don says the promoters are using "fancy brochures and advertising the names of the DJ's." Don does not fit in with the rave crowd because "I'm not into oversized baggy pants, pierced ears and stuff." He says there are "lots" of parties at the university, and "tons" of beer." Don tells me, "One party had posters advertised '50 kegs, 25 hours'. The cops only break them up if they are too loud or something,"

Don recently broke off his relationship with his longtime girlfriend. He tells me, "I'm getting over it."

I had tried to talk by phone with Woody several times. I finally reach him at work. Woody is a plumber and owns his own company. He has two sons, one is in the U.S. Army and one is in high school. Woody says, "I never tell them what I did in the old days."

One of Woody's relatives married Chuck and Bart Roe's sister. Woody gives me the phone numbers of Chuck Roe, and his brother, Bart, whom many believed had died more than four years earlier.

I contact Norm Dunn. Norm apologizes to me for breaking his appointment the previous year. Norm sold his condominium for $170,000 and bought a new house for $250,000. Norm has ended his relationship with Lucy. Lucy went into alcohol rehabilitation. Then, Norm describes, in detail, the incident we had only discussed briefly by phone a few months earlier,

> Something happened to me, Jer . . . I had this girlfriend, Katie. We had an argument. She stole something from me . . . Well it was drugs, coke. I don't do it often, Jer. But, I was showering. I finished and I asked her where it went. She said she sold it for a party by herself . . . She starting 'freaking out.' Martin (Norm's brother) was there. She wacked me two times. I said, 'When I come back, I don't want you here.' As I was leaving, she grabbed my shirt and hair. I pushed her off me, somewhat hard. I left to go to a baby shower. I spent the night at my friend's house. I just got my things and left my house. I called her a day later. She was not there. I came home. Her stuff was gone. There were three or four messages on the machine that the police were looking for me. There was a warrant out for me for 'Domestic Violence.' I called a lawyer. He told me, 'Yes, there is warrant out for you.' I left for Borrego Springs for two days. Then, I went to my lawyer and to court. I was arrested. I had a two and a half day trial and lost. She made up false accusations and admitted it, but there are these 'recanting law.' She had bruises on her neck. That was cuz she was taking blood-thinning meds so it looked like bruises. I had three charges: first, domestic violence; second, house imprisonment, but it was dropped; and, third, pulling the phone from the wall, and it was eventually dropped. I was found guilty of a felony. I am appealing. She told the police I came at her with a razor. That is a felony, like 'with a deadly weapon.' I don't have a problem with copping to what I did - trying to hurt her. She hurt me worse than I did her because she whacked on my head a couple of times, but she said, 'razor,' and that is a deadly weapon, a felony. And, the courts don't allow a recant. I got forty-five days in jail, twenty days of community service. I did that today. And, I have to go to anger management classes one time a week for one year. I have to pay $25 for each class.

I ask Norm why he had not called me or informed me. I asked him if he had told his Mom. He had not. Norm responds,

> I guess I was embarrassed, Jer. Oh, I know what you are thinking. Maybe coke did lead me into this. Maybe that is the bottom line. But, I am appealing the felony. She signed a letter to my lawyer that this was made up but only after I was found guilty, before the sentencing. She told them before the trial, admitting filing a false police report. The final sentence was about six months later. I paid $12,000 in fines, and have paid the lawyer $50,000. I do the anger management and have done my community service now. Martin couldn't be called as a witness because he has warrants out against him.

I ask Norm, again, why he had not told me. I tell him that I still cared about him.

Norm responds, "That means a lot to me, Jer, to know you care about me. I am also very thankful for all you have done for me and always being there. I guess I was really embarrassed because I knew that."

I tell Norm that I am concerned about him. I ask him if he sees the connection between his behavior and the violent conflicts between his Dad and Mom before their divorce. Norm tells me that he has. I urge Norm to continue to work on his anger management and his use of cocaine. I tell him that, otherwise, he will eventually have more problems even if this sentence is reduced from a felony. Norm agrees. Norm says that he has been going to church some times. He asks me more about the Catholic Church. Norm had been baptized a Catholic, but the family never practiced their faith after his parents' divorce.

Norm and I continue to visit by phone during the next year. He continues to work on anger management.

Over the years, I heard a great deal about Howard, but I had not talked with him personally in more than twenty years. We are able to visit. He works on construction jobs. He tells me that he is seeing a therapist. He had used coke and once joined, "Coke Enders."

> It was like a group thing, Then I was in "Life Springs." We were in a hotel in northern California for seven days. They controlled our food, diet, exercise, and gradually I got into A.A. I have been in and out of A.A. until about a year and a half ago. I have been sober for six years. Now, I am back in therapy . . . I have a problem with A.A. They are too dogmatic. My passion is self-growth, psychology and chat about what I can do and

accomplish . . . When you interviewed me it was just the beginning of my alcoholism. I did not have a concept until "Life Springs." I was twenty-seven. On my 21st birthday, something traumatic happened. I found out about my father. The father, who I thought was my father, was not. My mom had an affair. I have a lot of women's issues and fears of rejection. I seek approval. It was probably because of her finding out. It's like with a dog. You give him a piece of food and, each time you do, you bop him on the nose . . . About a year and a half ago, it was November of '98, I was involved with this girl and fell in love. We broke up. I relapsed into Valium, alcohol and ended up with a therapist. I did not use cocaine then, but drank and used some pot. The biggest thing was "Life Springs." It opened the door to a lot of things. I am good at therapy. I open up. I stay in touch with Gil and Shannon Bayer. I started to read your book, '*Deviant Reality.*' I had a Puritan view on sex. I am fascinated by psychology. I spent two years in 'Toastmasters.' I don't like organized religion. My sister is 'born again.' I am reading Norman Vincent Peele. Who I am is somewhat of a 'nat' - 'rude and crude.' I need to build myself up. I am more like a woman than a man. But the father-thing is what is difficult to accept. I go insane about a woman then go off the wagon. If you don't think I would sell my soul, I would do it. I would. I was never abused physically, you see, but had emotional, intangible abuse. I never looked up my real father.

I ask him, "Why not?" He responds,

I have a fear. I need to be in a place where I am strong enough. My Mom and Step-Dad have been married 27years. I am a 'hath not,' and a conspiracy. I hate their guts for their lies and conspiracy . . . My real father is a 'sperm donor.' Right now, I am good if I stay sober. My Mom still loves me even if she created me out of a lack of action. That's the truth. Still, there is no lack of love. I am on my own now.

Howard gives me directions to the construction site where he is working. He tells me that they are almost finished with the job, but he should be there tomorrow. The next day, I follow the directions but do not find any construction. I leave a message for him on his pager.

I think about how cocaine changed the lives of so many individuals, and how many have to deal with alcohol.

Bill Jones leaves a message for me to call. Bill moved to the northern part of the county, two blocks from his ex-wife to be near his sons. His former wife has divorced again. Bill's oldest son, Linus, continued to skip school and now has to attend summer school to graduate. Linus refuses to go to church even though he had promised Bill he would attend if Bill moved near him. Bills is also having problems with Shane, age 15, his second son.

Bill Jones and I plan to meet at the wall at sunset. I arrive, and a few minutes later, Bill's youngest son, 10-year-old, Greg, is the first to recognize me. I ask Greg if he is having a good time.

He responds, "No"

I ask, "Why not?"

Greg says, "Because I want to be in the water."

Bill asks, "Why don't you go in the water then?"

Greg replies, "No, I want you to be with me!"

Bill discusses surfing with Greg, but Greg wants to jet ski. Bill tells him, "You're too young."

I ask Bill if we could rent a speedboat or jet ski. Bill says, "I don't have the money."

Finally, I recommend that he take Greg into the water. I can meet Bill another time.

Greg is hugging and clinging to Bill as they go into the water. I feel very good about their father-son bonding. I know that Bill tries to be a good father. He moved to be closer to his sons. However, his wife does not support his attempts to discipline the older sons. I encourage Bill to "hang in there." I assure him eventually his persistence and consistency will be appreciated. I tell him about the times Matt tested me. (More and more, I feel like I am now a "grandfather figure" not a "father figure." It certainly feels much better!)

I meet Alise Bayer at the post office. She gives me her phone number and I promise to call that evening. Alise updates me on many of the women and some of the men we both knew in the 1970s. Many of Alise's girlfriends gather periodically for luncheon "reunions." What remains striking about the females is the consistency of their patterns. The females who were "light and non-users" are almost all in stable marriages, and relatively free of problems. Those who were "heavy" or "regular" users tend to be unmarried or divorced and/or having problems with alcohol.

Arlene lives with a boyfriend. She suffers from chronic illness. It is difficult for her to care for herself and the house. Marie's divorce has been finalized. She has custody of her daughter. Helen is married, but "is unhappy in her marriage." She is the mother of three children. She "drinks a lot" and "when the girls get together she is wasted by the time the event begins." Betty has four children. She is president of the PTA. She drinks wine. She has an eating disorder. Nancy is married with two children. She drinks heavily and also suffers from an eating disorder. Carlene is a waitress at a local restaurant. She is unmarried. Jane did never married. She drinks and acts "kinda crazy." Erin has been divorced and is remarried. She "drinks a lot." She does not attend the reunions. Judy is an exception. She is married with three children. Judy had been an agnostic. She is now a Christian and her husband is Jewish. They raise the children "half and half." Alise Bayer herself is married and steadily employed.

I pay a visit to the grandmother of the Gilroy sons. Ron Gilroy is there to work on his grandmother's house. His 14-year-old son, Michael, helps his Dad with the work.

Ronnie, Luke's son, is now 20. He works at a small business where his mother is also employed. The first thing Ronnie says to me is, "Well, I have a new chapter for your book!" He elaborates,

> I wanted to meet more people so, when I go to raves, I use ecstasy. I only tried it a couple of times. At least, one good thing came out of it. 'E' made me think about God more and more. When I touched water, it felt weird, like happiest time of my life, a "100," an "A." I will continue to use when there are a lot of friends and at big events. When I use, I like to sit on the ground and watch and listen, but I am a mover. I move around and meet people. It costs $20 for four hours. I don't use a pacifier and other stuff. I realize how dangerous it is.

Ronnie asks, "Is it addictive?" I explain the difference between physical addiction and psychological and social dependency to Ronnie. He continues,

> Now the parties are not secret parties like before. I wish they were. They are not like on T.V., but are more like rural scenes. Everyone used in L.A. In San Diego, they are more like concerts. I use "Red Bowl," a form of Ginseng. It is supposed to give you energy. I like the small events. Those parties are at a bar or some place that needs business, like a 'dive bar.' It is like a 'rave.' but we call it a 'party.' There is not that much energy. It is in a lounge and is a lower tempo. Everybody is sober. They are not drunk or use 'E.' It is for 18 and up. They go until four the morning. After 2 a.m, the 21 and over show up. Raves are *big* events, from like 2,000 to 20,000. There is lots of energy! At the ones that are 20,000, there are more drugs. The older people, like from the 60s and the 90s show up. They use acid

> more. I am not starting that I just use 'E' and, sometimes, mushrooms. I do not see crystal or meth. I am out of work for three or four months. I am running out of money. Mom paid the last two months rent. She tells me to get a job, but she doesn't push. I am getting bored. In 15 hours, I can earn $300, just scanning photos from catalogues and putting them on the Internet . . . My girlfriend moved to Fresno . . . I am going up there this weekend. There is a big rave! There will probably be about 80,000 people there from all of California. We compare it to the Hippies, and call it the 'Woodstock of the Millennium.' It lasts two days, there will be drugs and 80,000 people, but at night he music is different. Vibes are happier. People are nice to you. Like, when people see you, they like you. Old Hippies show up. Money-wise they rip us off. They charge us $35, and say 'No getting in, if no i.d.' Laws and regulations are changing. They have the curfew laws and closing laws, so we have to keep going farther and farther out . . . I have to go now, my roommate needs the phone. I will talk to you later.

I have several thoughts. First, I find that the rhetoric express by Ronnie reminds me of the rhetoric of the late 1960s and early 1970s, when everything was "love" and "mellow." Within a few years, the mood changed and "rip-offs" and violence entered the scene. Those who used drugs that were considered "mellow" and safe began to experience the side effects, addictions, psychoses and so on. Second, I compare the sons whom I have contacted and their fathers. Carl's son, Tony, had used drugs but now is into bible study. Carl is, once again, active in his church. Tony would like to go to Thailand just as Carl, for different reasons, had traveled to Afghanistan. Linus and Shane Jones, use marijuana as their father, Bill, once did, but Bill tries to deter them. They rebel by not going to church as Bill once did. Bill, now a Sunday school teacher, tries to encourage them to attend. Luke's son, Ronnie, had not partied much in high school, but is now into raves and ecstasy. Luke began using many drugs at a much earlier age than Ronnie. Luke served time in prison. Ronnie does not appear to be headed in that direction. Luke was always very open with me and extremely talkative and sociable, so is Ronnie. I have not met Keith's son, but Keith tells me, "He doesn't do anything!"

At. St. Patrick's, 15-year-old, Ed, visits briefly with me as I work at the computer. Ed attends a Catholic high school. He tells me the school conducts random drug tests, "Every once in a while, you will be in history class and they just enter the class and tell everyone they are going to be tested."

Ed is preparing to go on a church youth retreat in Arizona. He only goes to "small parties," averaging 20 or so people. The parties are, "Only "occasionally, when someone's parents are not at home. There is some beer there, but pot is only used by a few." Ed agrees that the high school parties in northern San Diego are similar to the 1970s parties I have described. Ed appears to be a very sincere and responsible young man.

I receive an email from Pat. The email tells me that there is going to be a "reunion" at the wall the next morning. The time is between the two Masses I am scheduled to celebrate at St. Patrick's. Luke phones me later to make certain that I received the message. Luke tells me, "Wear your collar. Be in your penguin outfit! You won't believe who is coming!"

Following the early Mass, I drive to the reunion of the "Golden Beach Seawall Social Club." Pat presents me with one of the group's souvenir t-shirts. The T-shirt features an obscene drawing encircled by the words "Golden Beach Seawall Social Club, 2000." Pat and Luke want to surprise some members of the former Old Wall Gang by showing the transformation of Jerry Lowney. Jerry Lowney once had shoulder length hair, a full beard and wore cutoffs and sandals. Father Lowney has short hair, wears a Roman collar, and, in Luke's words, "a penguin outfit."

Among those at the reunion are several Old Wall Gang members whom I have not seen in many years. They include Turk and his older brother, Larry, Kramer, Max's older brother, Nate, and the Clinton brothers, Tom and Larry. Turk was just released from jail. He had been in jail for 51 days. He is being charged with hiding a refugee (a "Hell's Angel kind of person"), possession of methamphetamine, being under the influence of methamphetamine, possession of marijuana and being under the influence of marijuana. His brother, Steve, has also been using "crystal meth." Steve is not accepted by the Old Wall Crew members. Tom and Larry are also suspected of using methamphetamine. Pat, Luke and the others are courteous to them, but not totally accepting of them in the long term. Kramer has returned to Golden Beach and is "doing well." The group is very supportive of individuals if they "slip, "as long as they make an attempt to better themselves.

Pat says that Leo, who used to deal marijuana and cocaine, is now selling condominiums in Florida. Leo has progressed from sale of drugs, to sales of timeshares in Mexico, to managing exclusive health clubs in Florida, to selling condominiums in Puerto Rico. Leo and his first wife divorced. According to Pat, his former wife was awarded a great deal of the money they had earned in Florida. Leo is now remarried.

Once again, Keith argues that, "The kids today are a lot worse than we used to be!" Keith's wife and I take pictures of the group. Months later Luke sends me two of the enlarged photos.

I will learn the following January that Turk was convicted of several of the charges against him. Turk has been placed under house arrest and wears an anklet monitor. During the following months, Turk and I chat frequently on the Internet.

Prior to my departure from Southern California, I drive to East Los Angeles to visit with Fr. Greg Boyle. Fr. Greg, also known as "G-Dog," is a priest who has worked with gangs in East. Los Angeles. He has been featured on many television programs including "60 Minutes" and "Nightline." Fr. Greg and I had become acquainted by phone and he is scheduled to speak at Carroll College in September. Fr. Greg has a storefront operation that includes job counselors and opportunities for summer jobs. In the brief time I spend with Fr. Greg, it is obvious that he has a tremendous rapport with the youths in East Los Angeles. I notice the manner in which the "gang members" interact with him. His phone conversations remind me of my own. He is accepting, yet firm, when he believes a youth is in need of drug or alcohol treatment. As I drive back to San Diego, I ponder the thought of eventually working again with youth in a direct manner like Fr. Greg. Perhaps, I will, when I retire from my teaching position at Carroll College.

I leave Golden Beach in late July.

CHRISTMAS BREAK, 2000-2001

I return during Christmas break, 2000-2001. During my brief visit, I have dinners with Mrs. Gilroy, the Bayer families, Carl and his family and I visit Jeanie, Ronnie, Norm Dunn, Bill Jones and Pat.

Morris Bayer has moved back to Golden Beach permanently. He is employed by his brother Gil. Morris is active in A.A. in Golden Beach. He and other members decorate Morris' truck before they visit nursing homes in the area. They sing Christmas carols to those in the nursing homes. Morris contacts the sheriff's department to organize an A.A. group at the jail. A few inmates attend the first meeting. Morris had been in jail several times for his actions under the influence of alcohol. Now, he brings Alcoholics Anonymous to others who are in jail.

Jeanie is a neighbor of the Bayer's. Jeanie's father was in a serious car accident. He is an invalid and Jeanie serves as his private home nurse. His condition weakens during the holidays. He is not expected to live. Jeanie once felt her father was "too distant." She struggled with drug addiction. Now she provides loving care for her dying father.

Bill Jones discusses his sons, Shane and Linus, at length. Shane has been involved with a friend with a "bad home life." They both are heavily into pot. On one occasion, they were in a hotel surrounded by some police. The mother of Shane's friend had given a confusing message to the police. The boys were not arrested. The next evening the two boys were caught stealing at a Golden Beach drug store. Shane was charged with "petty theft." Shane phoned Bill to bail him out of jail. Bill, whom I had bailed out of jail in 1975, did not put up bail for Shane until 36 hours after his arrest. Bill also took the car away from Shane. However, Bill's former wife returned the car to Shane so "he could go to work." Linus is doing better, but Bill is concerned about the girl Linus is dating. Bill continues to demonstrate care and discipline to his sons. I ask if Linus smokes pot. Bill responds, "He's a surfer. Of course, he smokes pot!"

Ronnie, Luke's son, is attending college again. He is working during the holidays. He is proud of his music. He is writing music and he did some recordings in a studio to hand out to get recognized. He tells me there are no raves scheduled during the coming week for me to attend. However, there was "a massive one on Halloween, more than 30,000 in the sports arena, and on New Year's there were a 100,000 at the coliseum. They had 80 overdoses, but no deaths."

Ronnie tells me he remains sober and rarely uses ecstasy. He says, "I need 24 hours to recuperate from ecstasy. I work the next day, so I can't use it."

Ronnie is upset that "younger kids" are coming to the raves, "They are as young as 10th grade. It is legal for them to go to raves. Going is not very wise. It is not like weed or pot. Those kids need to be taught!"

Ronnie is happy to tell me that he has a new girlfriend, "It has been seven months, so hopefully . . . "

Tony and I have lunch one afternoon. Tony is doing well. Tony's Dad, Paul, invites me to dinner at their home in North County. Paul, his wife Jolene, their 17-year-old daughter, Sue, and their 5-year-old son, John, are present. Tony calls midway during the meal. Tony says he forgot I was coming. He is with his bible study group. Jolene asks about my book. She asks why I did not "work to change the kids." I explain the role of a sociologist to her. Her daughter, Sue, is very open about the atmosphere at her high school,

> There are 'jocks.' They party. They use pot and beer . . . Then there are the 'skater-surfers.' They are pot-heads. Every April 20, each year, they have a 'surf and party' day. They skip school and party. Most of them are from broken homes. Then there are the 'honors' kids.' They are into school and stuff. I am not a partier. I really don't belong to any group.

Sue has not heard of the use of ecstasy at her high school. She asks her Dad and Mom, "Didn't you have any friends who were Christians?"

Paul responds, "Well, we went to church on sundays and sometimes on Wednesday nights."

Sue says, "But They did not live like Christians!"

Paul and Jolene were aware that Tony had used pot when he was "hanging out" with certain peers, but felt, "There was nothing we could do about it."

Jolene says, "I was probably one of those 'surfer chicks' around when you were doing your research, but I didn't hang around Golden Beach at the wall."

After a pleasant evening, Paul gives me a big hug as I leave.

I do not see Kevin. Pat tells me that Kevin moved his motor home to an R.V. park. Pat, Luke and Bill say that Kevin is "out of control" with his drinking.

Mrs. Mary Gilroy invites me to dinner at her suburban home. Reed is doing well in his law practice in Massachusetts. Ron is getting married in March. John is coming down from Los Angeles for the wedding. Mark is flying from "Back East" for the wedding.

On New Year's Eve, Morris Bayer attends an A.A. meeting and then comes to Mass at St. Patrick's. After Mass, Morris tells me that Andy was outside the A.A. meeting hall. Morris says, "He is kinda out of it. Do you think I should go talk to him?" I tell Morris to go ahead and I will meet him at the church when I finish closing up. Morris returns telling me that Andy asked if they had food inside of A.A. Morris says Andy remembers me and said, "Oh yeah. Cool guy!"

We have a New Year's Eve dinner at a restaurant. As we sit down to eat, Morris remarks, "Everyone is either in A.A., or homeless!"

The situation among Morris' former drinking and pot smoking buddies is not quite that black and white, but Morris has pointed to the two ends of the spectrum.

THE YEAR 2001

During the following months, I communicate with several individuals by phone and Internet.

Luke and Pat are on my "buddy list." We chat frequently. Both keep me posted on the Old Wall Gang, and what is occurring in Golden Beach.

Pat gives me information about Brett who lives in Indianapolis. After an Internet search, I find Brett's phone number. He is surprised to hear from me. Brett has been married for 28 years. They have two children. Brett sells commercial real estate. His son graduated from Purdue. His son is employed in San Diego and lives in Golden Beach. Brett's daughter is a junior at Purdue. Brett says that, in 1978, he and his wife said to each other, "We and our marriage will never make it in Golden Beach." Brett says, "We picked up and moved to Washington State for several years and then moved to Indianapolis."

I discuss my research with Brett. He says, "This generation is a lot more stable than we were."

Brett gives me his email address and how to locate his web site. Brett's web site has pictures of the couple's wedding (complete with Brett's long, curly hair). There are pictures of the family in Indianapolis and scenes from Golden Beach.

Norm Dunn tells me on the phone that his appeal of his felony conviction is still pending.

On March 6, Brendan and I talk by phone. Brendan asks me if I can come to Europe this year. I tell him, "Probably not." Brendan's films are "making a profit." He directs and acts in his films. The films are shown mainly in Europe. He tells me, "I am a big pot smoker now. I smoke it every day. It relaxes me. It is a good crutch."

Brendan's movies deal with sex, heterosexual and homosexual. He tells me that "People need the freedom to love, to have sex."

During our long international call, Brendan discusses a great deal about sex and drugs. When I ask him why he did not tell me earlier that he had discovered the clergyman having sex with the "surfers," Brendan responds, "Jerry, we just didn't talk about those things back in those days."

On March 16, I phone Morris and Gil Bayer. Morris tells me that he just celebrated his 10th anniversary of sobriety in A.A. Morris says Cliff has been in Golden Beach. Cliff is divorced and the father of two children. According to Morris, the divorce was a result of Cliff's alcoholism.

Paul exchanges email with me. Paul now lives in Northern California, just a short distance from Matt. Paul continues to use his computer science degree in his employment. He now works as a computer technician for his county's district courts. Paul and his wife are expecting their second child. Paul is planning to enter the Catholic Church.

Paul tells me about the influences on him that helped him get where he is in life. I tell him that he accomplished a lot given his odds, being on his own without a family, struggling to obtain an education, and so on. I ask about "father figures" in his life. I mention that I thought, at times, Pat seemed to be a father figure to him. I reminded him of a letter he wrote to me, addressing me as "Uncle Jer."

Paul responds in an email,

> ....I seemed to live in a fantasy world of sex, drugs and surfing. Once in a while there were people I would turn to for a dose of reality. Then, back to sex, drugs and surfing!. . . .Somehow I always doubted myself and thought you just might be serious about your work/book and actually did not represent a threat to me or my friends. I'm glad I reserved judgment . . . One of the biggest negative influences was the Roe brothers. Is there confirmation that they are still alive? I've heard rumors, but . . . Pat and two other older guys were very positive influences for me. At the time, they all seemed like smart and intellectual guys who liked to party, but they also had good morals. 'Don't burn your friends. Don't talk bad about someone unless you were prepared to back it up and always pay for what you get (Don't be a sponge *all* the time).' The other main influence was also not wanting to end up like the Golden Beach 'Toads' who lived from friend to friend, lying, fighting, cheating, stealing and b.s.ing their way through life. A lot of people talk really bad about them behind their backs and I did not want to be known as that type of person. I wanted people to say, 'Hey there's Paul, he's a good guy!'

Paul and I plan to meet when I travel to California the following month.

In early April, I reach both of the Roe brothers by phone. They are indeed alive!

Chuck Roe, the former "wall rat" and friend of Norm Dunn, is delighted to hear from me. Chuck tells me he has been sober since "August 30, 1995." Chuck tells me,

> I got into trouble for 'Forging a State Seal.' I was forging California State Driver's Licenses. I did time. They gave me three years, but I got off for

> good behavior in 19 months. I was in a minimum security place . . . I learned about trees and insect control . . . I joined A.A. five years ago and have stayed clean. I moved up here (to the mountains in Central California) and started a tree service business . . . Hey, I am coming up to Montana to pick up a rig in a month or so . . . Do you remember that time when I had a baggie (of marijuana) in my sock and the cops pulled up and you got all shook up?. . .Remember the time at the pizza place when Norm Dunn kicked you under the table?

Chuck tells me he has never married. His father died two years earlier. Chuck also informs me that Bill Dimaggio, who had been Chuck's source for cocaine, died in a car accident from a stroke, "He was driving, and he wasn't even supposed to be driving. He had a stroke before and he was still doin' coke. It was the coke probably that killed him."

(A second "damaging father figure" is dead at least in part due to cocaine.)

When Chuck and I finish our conversation filled with recollection of 1970s memories, he says, "Bye, and, oh yeah, thanks for watching out for us guys, when we were young!"

The following evening, I phone Bart, Chuck's brother. Bart has a pleasant conversation with me, but later asks that I not give his phone number to anyone else. Bart is living in the greater Los Angeles area. He tells me that he is not working because he "messed up" his leg. He had been in a motorcycle accident and pulled some muscles. Bart is living with a woman, but has not married. He has worked as a carpenter and a mechanic. He has "done time." He points out that his older sister is a "cop" in Eastern San Diego County. Bart says, "She kind of offsets things for Chuck and me." Bart is apparently staying "out of trouble" but not avoiding all substances or "doing well" in other aspects of his life.

A FINAL VISIT TO CALIFORNIA

On April 4, 2001, I arrive by plane in Sacramento. My first call is to Matt. Matt directs me to the house that he and his future wife, Martha, are remodeling. Matt shows me with pride all that he has accomplished. Martha has to retire early. Matt and I have a lengthy visit over a leisurely Italian meal. Matt tells me that one of the reasons he left Lake Tahoe was to "get away from pot." He says, "Up there everyone uses it, the cops, judges, city councilman, everyone! It is hard to stay away from up there. Here I am doing fine and staying away from it."

Matt points out that he never had a problem controlling his use of alcohol or cocaine, but "pot was something else." I remind him of the times he would return to my home with red eyes and wonder why I could tell he was high. We laugh!

Matt and Martha are going to marry when the house is completed. He is very happy with his job as the stadium engineer for a new $500,000 baseball stadium.

The next day, I meet Matt at the stadium. He introduces me to his co-workers and I accompany him through some of his chores to prepare for the opening game of the season. We leave for take-out sandwiches and enjoy our lunch in the stadium seats. There is an obvious bond that Matt and I maintain. I am proud of him.

That evening, I talk to Paul who lives about 30 miles from Matt. Paul says he misses "the glitz of Tahoe and Golden Beach," but is happy with his job and his family. His son is now 3 years old. He and his wife are expecting a baby daughter the following month. He asks me more about the process to enter the Catholic Church that he has undertaken.

I stop in Santa Barbara on the drive south to San Diego. I have dinner with Don, who worked at St. Patrick's two years earlier. Don describes the "wild party" scenes at UCSB and the Isla Vista area. One of Don's roommates was present when a student, under the influence, ran a car roughshod through crowds. The roommate intervened and had a lock on the man's throat. The event was featured on national television. Don says he has not been to any more raves and that raves and ecstasy seemed to be decreasing in popularity. He has heard that cocaine and heroin are being used more frequently at his former high school in Diamond Heights, a very wealthy area near Golden Beach. When I arrive in San Diego, I ask some of the high school students and young adults about this information. They agree and tell me that OxyContin is also being used by high school students in Diamond Heights. Once again, I question whether or not a trend is repeating itself. If so, it would be similar to the cycle of the mid to late 1970s when LSD, like ecstacy, decreased and a brief heroin "epidemic" was followed by a large increase in the use of cocaine.

I arrive in San Diego and, after getting settled at St. Patrick's, I visit the Bayer's. Dr. Bayer appears to have increased his "controlled" drinking. Once again, there are noticeable differences in his behavior. His son, Morris, remains deeply committed to A.A. On a subsequent visit, Mrs. Bayer, Morris and I eat dinner together. Dr. Bayer is on a cruise. Morris says that he is "back to the 9th step" of A.A. He says that he was on the 12th, and final step, in Florida. "I had dealt with all the issues that were there, but now that I am back in San Diego, I have to move back to the 9th step to deal with the issues that are here."

Morris explains that is now "making amends" to those in Golden Beach, including his family, whom his drinking harmed in years past. He describes some of the articles he had stolen for which he is seeking to make the amends. Morris is very helpful to others. He reaches out to the homeless. He is paying for Louie, his "little brother," and a friend of Louie's to come to San Diego for a visit the next summer.

Morris leaves after dinner to attend an A.A. meeting. Mrs. Bayer and I chat about her husband's behavior. I try to point out how the behavior is, once again, a consequence of his drinking.

A few nights later, Gil and Shannon Bayer invite me to their home for dinner. Their children discuss the emphasis their parish priest places on quality time in the family. He decries the overuse of television. Gil and Shannon explain how they try to make that time for their children. They sent the three children to the Catholic schools.

Gil updates me on some of his high school and college classmates. He says that when Brendan comes to San Diego he tends to hang out with one of the "stoners." Judy lost two children and her husband to cancer. She has two other children. Howard sometimes accompanies the couple and their children to baseball games and other activities. Howard, without a family of his own, becomes one of their family. Ruth Barone has remarried and appears to have come to terms with the sexual abuse of her father. The family has made efforts to come together with certain rules regarding the interaction of Ruth's father with his grandchildren.

I go to the beach and discover that the area near the wall is under construction. Young people are handing out free samples of "Pepcid Compleat," remedy for intestinal problems. I think of the differences in free samples that have been distributed at the beach over the years. In 1975, various brands of cigarettes were given freely to persons of all ages. In 1977, Budweiser T-shirts were handed out. In 1995, samples of carbonated caffeine beverages were dispensed. And, in 2001, marketers distribute a remedy for stomach upset which could have been induced by smoking, or drinking alcohol or carbonated caffeine beverages. Rather, ironic!

Overall, I notice once again, that the beach is more orderly, with more regulations in effect. In addition to the usual surfers, those at the beach in the morning hours tend to be older couples or middle-aged joggers. In the afternoons and evenings, tourists and those in their mid-20s and 30s dominate. On weekends, there are increasing numbers of teenagers and those in their early 20s, but they are far fewer than those in the same age range during the 1970s.

Another, nearby beach community has made it known that they do not welcome "Starbuck's Coffee" or other franchises. They seek to avoid the pattern that has developed in Golden Beach and elsewhere. I tour the community and find it much as it had been in 1970s. Music stores and "head shops" dot the main street. Very little new building has occurred. It remains a cohesive and unique community free of upscale shops and residences.

The media covers a debate as to whether a city ordinance should be passed to ban all alcohol on the beaches as well as the boardwalks of Golden Beach and Sand Beach 24 hours a day. The remnants of the Old Wall Gang are in favor of the ordinance. Luke tells me that he does not go to the wall area because, "It is full of drunks!" Pat, who Norm Dunn predicted 25 years earlier would "still be at the beach sitting on the wall with a beer in his hand," says he hopes it passes. Mike, who told me in 1975 he had been high every day for eight years, states that he "does not care." Mike does not go to the beach any more. Mike states, "I can't stand drunks. Oh, I know, that is the way I was, and it may be ironic, but I can't stand drunks!" On April 17, prior to my departure, the ordinance passes on an "experimental" basis.

Ironically, the same former members of the Old Wall Gang and wall crew, who only occasionally get together as "The Golden Beach Social Club," now deride a group of young men, in their 20s and 30s, whom they call "The Golden Beach Vermin Gang." Luke, who served time at Folsom prison, says, "They have tatoos and have been in prison. All they do all day is drink and play horseshoes. If you fight them, you had better be prepared because they re a gang. If you fight one, you will be fighting 20." Bill Jones admits the group is not really a "gang," but still says, "They are vermin!" In my observations, I see little distinguishing characteristics of the group who gather there. Indeed, prior to the ordinance, they drink beer as did many of the people on the beach, but their behavior appeared to be at least as conforming as that of the Old Wall Gang in 1970, if not more so.

Bill Jones asks me to visit his oldest son, 18-year-old Shane, who is in drug rehabilitation. Shane had been arrested several months earlier for "petty theft." His companion was charged with possession of cocaine. Apparently, the other youth was actually dealing cocaine for Shane. Both youths had been in an auto accident. They had received a $2,500 settlement. They had decided that they could use the money to "go into business dealing coke." As Shane became more involved, Bill and his former wife applied pressure and told Shane that if he went to school and "did well," he could use the car. If not, he had to leave. Shane left home, but returned after two days. Shane's parents "forced" him into treatment. After two more days, Shane walked away from the rehabilitation center. In a few days, he returned to the center and chose to "check himself in." Bill tries to make arrangements for me to visit Shane, but is unable to do so during my brief stay. Bill's second son, Linus, continues to date the same girlfriend. Bill worries because her home situation is not well. The youngest son, Taylor, is doing well. One Saturday I meet Bill at the wall area. He and a female co-employee are preparing to go roller skating and bike riding with Taylor and the woman's son. Bill continues to work at being a good father.

Mike and his wife live most of the year in Nova Scotia where they have a bed and breakfast. Mike will continue to work for the corporation he founded in San Diego for several months each year for another year. Mike will continue to own a 25 percent interest in the corporation and, if he wishes, he will be able to work for part of the winter months in San Diego.

Pat, is not sitting on the wall, and he drinks much less. A few months earlier, Pat developed what appeared to be a gall bladder problem. He went to the emergency room and was admitted to the hospital for three days of tests. The doctor told him "Drink less and don't eat spicy foods." Pat stopped drinking for a period and tries to limit himself to one or two drinks a day. He is increasingly successful in his business and spends most of his free time remodeling his house. Pat is very proud of his home and his business accomplishments. Indeed, he has come a long way from his high school days when Pat lived with his alcoholic father in a very small apartment and, for the most part, looked after himself. The Old Wall Gang had been his family and the wall itself very much his "home." He had been the mainstay at the wall. He had proudly proclaimed himself "Da Mayor of the Beach." If anything is indicative that the group, though still a cohesive group of friends, is no longer at the wall, it is the lack of Pat's presence

Luke tells me that Larry is doing well and remains free of "crystal meth," but Larry's brother Tom is apparently still using it. A group of the "Golden Beach Social Club" gathered at a club a few nights' earlier for Tom's birthday party. At times, on weekends mornings some of the group still surfs and meet at the wall area. Luke says his son, Ronnie, is doing very well selling cell phones. Ronnie is very busy. I try to reach him my phone several times, but am not able to speak with him. I am unable to locate Kevin or his motor homed. All of his former friends say that he continues to drink and act inappropriately. Mike says, "Kevin is a drunk!" Mike described an incident on Halloween night when Kevin invited them to a bar for "a drink." After Kevin began to drink, his behavior became obnoxious. Mike and his wife left, embarrassed. Somewhere, it appears, that Kevin is still struggling with his "demons." I talk briefly with Nelson. Nelson is a bartender. He is single. He asks what I am doing. I explain. Nelson, who had sought me out during the late hours at Billy's restaurant, does not seem to want to discuss much about himself. He wishes me well. Later, I learn that Nelson had entered a drug rehabilitation program a few years earlier.

Norm Dunn returns my phone calls. Norm is happy to inform me that he had completed all but 13 of the 52 conflict management sessions as a part of his domestic abuse conviction. He has paid his fines and performed 20 days of community service. As a result, the judge informed Norm that he would reduce the conviction from a felony to a misdemeanor upon the completion of the conflict management sessions. Norm says, "It was a nightmare! I paid over $18,000 to my lawyer, plus fines and court costs. I am glad it is all coming to an end." Norm appears to have gained self understanding as to the nature of his problem and attempts to avoid "being around coke."

Norm's brother, Martin, now lives with his Mom. Their oldest brother, Toby, and his wife and child remain in the apartment near the former residence of the Dunn family.

I meet Barry in his penthouse office overlooking the wall and the beach. Barry had been somewhat of an "older brother" to the wall crew during the mid-1970s's. He discusses his "wild days" at college preparatory high school out of state, "It was the Bible Belt. After 11th grade, they told me they did not want me back. I mainly liked to drink . . . I don't take to crowds very well so after I returned to Golden Beach I never got into parties. I liked to sit in a bar and drink."

Barry and his wife are active in their church, the same Baptist congregation to which Bill Jones belongs. Barry and his wife work with couples to prepare for the lifelong commitment of marriage. Barry says, "I see families and religion as important."

Barry is proud of his 22-year-old stepson, who is completing his teaching certificate. Barry describes how he describes his own past life to his stepson,

> If you and I were walking through a big canyon, up high with water underneath and I was walking in front of you, and I stepped on a rickety wooden swinging bridge with a couple of boards that I saw were weak and

> could give, and yelled back at you to be careful, would you listen to me? He says, 'yes.' So I tell him it is the same with temptations you are going to face at your age. I have been there before.

However. Barry states that he does not know "how to handle" his 12-year-old daughter, "I'll let my wife handle her. She's different." Barry's daughter and a group of her friends surf regularly. I mention that there are far more females who surf today than back in the 1970s. Barry agrees and says, "They are treated better in the water. It was not that when I was in the water. We didn't treat them very nice!"

Barry has inherited his wealth and a large tourist hotel. He comes to the office three days a week for about four hours. Barry and Pat golf together frequently.

I meet Carl and his son, Tony, for lunch at a restaurant north of San Diego. The family is planning a trip to Switzerland where Carl spent several months in 1976. After two weeks with the family in Switzerland, Tony is going to stay behind and tour France, Italy and Greece. We mention Carl's early trip through Europe, but Carl blushes when we discuss his trip to Afghanistan and the letter he sent me following his ordeal with hashish and lack of funds. He says jokingly, "Your book should be published three years from now, not next year." Tony seems very interested in reading about his father. Both remain very involved in their church. Tony had driven to Golden Beach with a friend for Good Friday evening services at St. Patrick's, hoping to see me. I had celebrated the noon services and was not available.

The next day, Mrs. Mary Gilroy joins me for lunch at Billy's restaurant. She has retired. A few weeks earlier, all of her sons were present for Ron's second wedding. She continues to believe that "Ron needs A.A." She is proud of her other sons, but believes that they are too lax in their child-rearing methods. The former "Super-Mom" states, "When they came to my Mom's house, Reed's kids were into everything and neither Reed nor his wife would do anything,"

I help at St. Patrick's during Holy Week. At the Easter Vigil, Fr. Paul receives 50 people into the Catholic Church. Many were young singles who came to the community through their attraction to the 5:30 Sunday evening Masses and the activities for young adults that followed the services.

In spite of what Keith, Pat and others have said about the younger generation being "so much worse" than they were in their teens and 20s, I do not find evidence to support those claims. On the other hand, those who had been in their teens and early 20s in the 1970s are, for the most part, "doing well." The vast majority of those who were non-users, light users and regular users in 1975 and 1976 are gainfully employed, happily married and functioning as caring effective parents. Most are active in their church. Those who have been children of divorce, primarily those had been heavy users, are less likely to have ever married, less likely to have a successful marriage and, if married, less likely to become parents. Nevertheless, many of them have matured to a point that their daily lives mirror those who had not used drugs as frequently. Almost all of the members of the Old Wall Gang, the wall crew and others who had been heavily involved in the drug subculture are steadily employed, some quite successfully. Although some of them drink alcohol in moderate amounts, most no longer use other illegal drugs. Some simply "matured out" of drug and alcohol abuse.[8] Many underwent a variety of struggles to reach this stage in their lives. The struggles included jail and/or prison sentences, physical problems, marital difficulties and financial consequences. Many were assisted in their journey by increased opportunities for meaningful employment and/or inherited wealth. For many, a significant step in the journey was to leave the wall, Golden Beach and/or San Diego. A few successfully completed drug treatment programs. Overall, the most successful "treatment" has been and continues to be Alcoholics Anonymous. A return to the individual's religious faith, many times combined with A.A. or another 12-Step program, has been an important factor in the success they have achieved. Those without the benefit of a 12-Step program or religion and with the least amount of family support are more likely to continue to struggle with alcohol and drug abuse as well as the consequences of that abuse.

The final chapter, provides more details about these and other conclusions.

End Notes

1. *San Diego Union*, July 14, 2000, p. 1-A.

2. *San Diego Union,* April 18, 2001, p. 1-A.

3. *McCormick Guide, San Diego County, 1999.* Martininez, Ca.: 1999.

4. *San Diego Union,* April 18, 2001, p. 1-A.

5. *Los Angeles Times*, "Drugs: Use of Meth Rises in the West", Sunday, July 12, 1998, p. A-1 and p. A-20.

6. See, for instance, Judith S. Wallterstein, Julia M. Lewis, and Sandra Blakeslee, *The Unexpected Legacy of Divorce: A 25 Year Landmark Study,* NY: Hyperion Press, 2000, pp. 148-153.

7. Oddly, it is a struggle. Yet, I realize that simply being "present" to others is the heart of ministry. Indeed, I find it ironic that the mere symbol of the roman collar I wear is often interpreted by many others as a sign that I am moralizing and judgmental. This is not the message, however, received by most. For me and most priests, the experiences of healing and forgiveness witnessed during the sacrament of reconciliation are the most moving and fulfilling moments of our ministry. Having said that I must understand and forgive, in death, the member of the clergy whose weakness and addiction harmed others.

8. See C. Winick, "Maturing out of Narcotic Addiction", *Bulletin on Narcotics,* 14, No. 1 (1962), pp. 1-8.

Chapter 14

Summary, Conclusions & Learning From The Past

INTRODUCTION

The nature of this research lends itself to many insights that would not be possible in a less ambitious project. Chapter 8 described the benefits of combining in-depth qualitative research techniques with quantitative methods. These were enhanced by the longitudinal nature of the project over a period exceeding 31years. If one could compare the results of an in-depth longitudinal research project to a single survey or interview, the result might be similar to viewing a full-length motion picture rather than a single frame of the ongoing drama of the film. Much of what appeared to "facts" at one point in time are altered by the changes taking place within a society and/or a particular subculture. The interactions of persons and the interpretations of such interactions are affected by changing values, norms and laws of the larger social group and society. Such has been the case with drug use during the past three decades. For example, in 1970 the possession of any amount of marijuana was a felony in California, and the laws regarding marijuana were strictly enforced. Young persons were singled out by the police who enforced the laws. As the perception of the harm resulting from marijuana use changed, the enforcement of laws became more relaxed and eventually the laws were modified so that possession of small amounts of marijuana is now a misdemeanor. Today, enforcement of laws regarding mere possession of marijuana is all but nonexistent. These and other changes in society ended the perception by young people that police are "pigs." The interactions of police and young people in Golden Beach are, for the most part, cordial and professional.

Throughout this book, I have described many other changes that have occurred in the lives of the individuals, the community of Golden Beach, and the larger society. I hope they provide a more complete understanding than would have been the case in a less thorough research endeavor.

As described in Chapter 1, my own role, which began as a researcher-interventionist, expanded over time and provided even greater depth. As this role evolved and my rapport with the young people increased, I gained not only more information, but also the opportunity to continue my contacts over the years to an extent that would otherwise not have been possible. In Chapter 1, I noted that some of the Old Wall Gang began to see me as a "father figure." I had not realized the depth of this role until the 1995-2001 period. The bonding between Matt and myself were to be expected. On the other hand, Mark Gilroy's appreciation for my efforts to teach him how to drive, the remarks by Mike, Keith and Scott as to how I had influenced their lives, Kevin's remarks that I had been a "father" to the group long before I became a priestly "Father" and Carl's elaboration of the degree to which I was a non-moralizing, but admired presence, in his and others lives, all brought home to me the degree to which my role had impacted their lives. In many ways, their view of me as a "father figure" is one of the most significant of all the findings. Beginning with the Old Wall Gang, the young men, and later the young women, who reacted to me in that role were the very same ones who lacked a father or any adequate father figure. These same individuals were those most likely to be involved in drug use and who experienced a variety of other difficulties. Thus, given the totality of the findings, it ought not be surprising that these young people would respond to an older male who was accepting of them and present to them while attempting to remain objective and non-moralizing. Sociologists are asked to be aware of any "Hawthorne Effect" or results which occur from the research situation or the presence of the researcher. The Hawthorne Effect, which took place over the length of my research, only serves to verify the most important findings regarding the effects of family, divorce, the role of parents, discipline and caring that are so striking in the statistics, presented in Chapter 8. Likewise, they are evident in the descriptions provided throughout this book.

Summaries of the major findings follow.

THE IMPORTANCE OF FAMILIES

The overall importance of families and the role of parents in the lives of children is evident. It is likewise obvious that the early influence of parents has a lifelong impact, for better or worse, on their sons and daughters. The importance of early socialization has been a "given" in sociology since the inception of the discipline. The family is seen as the most important agent of socialization[1]. This importance has been brought home throughout this research.

One of my initial 1970 findings was that the Old Wall Gang was made up of young males who were distinguished by the fact that almost all (more than 90 percent) had parents who had divorced at least once. The Wall Gang became a "family" to them. There are many previous findings that single-parent or broken homes, low family involvement and inappropriate parental discipline are "risk factors" associated with gang involvement.[2] Lewis Yablonsky found that gangs serve the function for "emotionally needy" youth to have the "feeling of having a family[3]." The development of the Wall Gang is consistent with these findings. The cohesiveness of the original group remains today.

A "younger generation," then known as the "wall crew," was drawn to the group from 1974 through 1976. They were likewise from divorced families. In a manner similar to their predecessors, the wall crew functioned as family for them. They looked upon the older members as "father figures." An example was Paul's relationship with Pat. Paul lived on his own during high school, surviving on social security payments. Pat provided Paul with basic rules and guides which were otherwise absent in Paul's life. For Paul, and many others, the group not only provided socialization into drug use and other deviant activities, but also served as a stabilizing force. Nevertheless, even though the group and some substitute father figures alleviated some of what was lacking in their own home lives, nothing replaced the absence of a stable loving family. In essence, the interaction of family factors and peer group factors supports both social control and Differential Association theories.[4]

An intervening set of factors prevented the younger group from remaining as cohesive as the older Wall Gang. The factors were centered around a "damaging father figure" in the person of Bill Dimaggio who involved the younger males in cocaine and cocaine trafficking.

Family factors were influential, not only among the members of the wall crew, but across the entire spectrum of youth in the study, including females as well as males. Lack of an adequate home life was related not only to drug use, but also to stress, sexual behavior, relationships with the opposite sex, marriage and stability of marriage over the entire length of the study. As stated earlier, these results are consistent with the 25-year study by Judith S. Wallerstein and her colleagues. Their study also began in 1970.[5]

FATHERS, FATHER FIGURES AND DAMAGING FATHER FIGURES

The role of an adequate father was a key factor within the family. Given the high divorce rate in Golden Beach, many children were raised without fathers. Father absence was as important for the females as for the males. David Popenoe's book, *Life Without Father*, has been referenced earlier. In this thoroughly documented review and commentary, Popenoe noted the link between father absence and drug abuse, delinquency, teenage sexuality, physical and sexual abuse of children and violence toward women.[6] I found all of these in Golden Beach among those youths whose fathers were either absent, inadequate or damaging father figures. Popenoe states, "Fatherless girls are generally disadvantaged at a later stage than fatherless boys, but the effects are no less striking."[7] Although the number of females in my sample was small, the dichotomy between those with adequate fathers and those without adequate fathers were, indeed, even more striking than among the males. Mrs. Mary Gilroy demonstrated that a single woman can play a dual father-mother role as a "Super Mom." However, as also noted by Popenoe, it is not easy for a single mother to accomplish this.[8]

In most instances, an inadequate father or father figure was found to be preferable to the lack of any father figure. Such was the case in the Jones and Bayer families, among others. On the other hand, presence of a "damaging father figure" was the least desirable of all situations. There were long term effects on those who were physically or sexually abused by fathers or stepfathers and those who were damaged through sexual abuse by a clergyman. In the latter case, there were also effects resulting from knowledge of this scandal for Brendan and others. Bill Dimaggio's role as a "drug dealing father figure" affected the younger "wall rats." In each of these cases, the degree of long-term damage was evident. Likewise, it should be remembered that cocaine was involved in two of the above situations.

On the other hand, adequate substitute fathers exerted a positive and ameliorating effect on those whose biological parents were absent. Some of these were stepfathers. Others were counselors, teachers and clergy. However, coaches were those most frequently cited as playing such a role. Most of these individuals, including Pat of the Old Wall Gang, were unaware of their influence on younger individuals.

MOTHERS

Although their roles are frequently obscured, mothers were as important in the lives of their children as were fathers. In the 1978 interviews, females were more likely than males to acknowledge the significance of their mothers in their lives. However, both males and females typically reported positive relationships with their mothers. As might be expected, there were many who expressed negative feelings about their mothers during their adolescence, a period marked by struggles for independence. Nonetheless, as the individuals matured, many of these attitudes changed. Examples include both Matt and Pat who, in 1970, expressed hostile opinions of their mothers. Both left their mothers' homes in their teens. By the late 1990s, Matt and Pat intervened to set up care for their elderly mothers and both protected their mothers from perceived threats by other family members.

The concept of an "overprotective mother," as measured, did not have a significant relationship to degree of drug use among males. However, it was a significant factor among the females. This lack of a relationship among the males and other facts did not support the McCord-Chein model. Had I utilized a more specific measurement of "controlling" mother, it is possible that a different picture might have emerged. The case of Rick, whose mother continues to oppose his choice of a significant other, and the case of Kevin, who, as an adult, realized the degree to which his mother's controlling effects his current alcohol use, might provide some evidence of this. Likewise, the lack of a caring or protecting mother, rather than an overprotective mother, seemed to be very important. An example is found in the Dunn family. Mrs. Dunn left her three sons at home without food or money to eat when she traveled for weekends with her boyfriends.

The females, who perceived their mothers as "overprotective" in 1978, did not appear to suffer any long-term negative consequences. Indeed, when some of these females became parents of teenagers, they were lovingly protective and concerned about their daughters. Jeanie expressed such concerns for her daughter several times and feared that her daughter "would ever do what I did!"

THE LONG-TERM EFFECTS OF FAMILY FACTORS ON "DOING WELL"

Youths from stable, involved families were more likely than others to participate in church youth groups. These early ties not only insulated them from deviant activities in the 1970s, but provided long-term benefits as well. They afforded the participants with relationships which were beneficial in later academic and business accomplishments. Most significant were the long-lasting effects of religious faith and affiliation. The cases of Gil Bayer, Keith, Carl and the Jones brothers are illustrative of individuals from two-parent homes in which religion was emphasized. Even though in each of these instances, one or more parent was perceived as somewhat inadequate, all of the siblings retained their basic religious faith. Todd, Bill and Pete Jones, Keith and Carl had "strayed" from the practice of their faith during the period in which they were heavily involved in the drug scene. Terry Jones and Gil Bayer were never involved in the drug scene. All recognize the significant role of religion in their lives. Keith, Carl and three of the Jones brothers credited their religious faith as a major factor in the process of their recovery from drug abuse. Terry Jones and Gil Bayer believed their religious faith helped to prevent them from becoming involved in drug use and other inappropriate behavior.

However, it should be noted that not all religious involvement had long-lasting positive effects. Those who had no previous grounding in religion were only temporarily attracted to religious youth groups. The groups who attracted such individuals through emotional appeals and/or "feel good" activities. One such group was the fundamentalist church ministered to by a youthful former drug abuser who had little theological background. Another was the "trendy" Drop-In youth group operating at St. Patrick's during the mid 1970s. For a few young people, who had an earlier religious background, these two movements served as entry back into their original religious tradition. Such was the case with the Jones' brothers and Carl who attended the fundamentalist group. On the one hand, the young people who had been baptized as Catholics and attended Drop-In during their high school years were less likely to remain practicing Catholics in adulthood. On the other hand, those who were older and had attended a more traditional Catholic religious education program tended to remain practicing Catholics.

Examples are found in the contrasts found within the Bayer and the Gilroy families. Gil Bayer, the older Bayer daughters and Ron Gilroy were only slightly older than their younger brothers and sisters. However, their experience in the parish preceded Drop-In. They remain Catholics, unlike their immediately younger male siblings. In 1977, I received a letter from Mrs. Mary Gilroy criticizing Drop-In. She was disturbed by the "feel good" atmosphere, and the lack of discipline as well as the lack of basic religious instruction evident in the program. I had the similar doubts, but I did not express them at the time. Overtime, the evidence appears to support this view.

Finally, in addition to the clergyman who has been described as a "damaging father figure," two other members of the clergy had extramarital affairs. The affairs occurred prior to the beginning of this research. Sons of each of these clergymen were subjects of the research. The fathers' behaviors did not affect the sons' belief in God or underlying religious faith, but both, for a period of time, heavy drug users.

The overall effects of religious faith regardless of denomination and interactions with clergy were very positive and long lasting. Today St. Patrick's attracts large numbers of young men and women. Many of these men and women appear to gravitate to the parish community as a haven from the Golden Beach "club scene." In spite of the changing demographics and decreased number of families in Golden Beach, the high school youth groups for Catholics, Lutherans, Baptists and Presbyterians appear to be meeting the needs of the teens in their congregations.

In addition, parental encouragement and interest were associated with participation in school activities. Participation in high school athletics had long-lasting as well as immediate benefits for those involved. In addition to providing some participants a male role model and a father figure in the role of a coach, there were other immediate benefits. These included being a part of a group that emphasized the values of a healthy lifestyle and working together as a team. Sports bolstered the self-esteem of many and gave them an alternative to drug use and partying. When Morris Bayer played football during his senior year, his self-esteem increased and there was a decrease in his deviant activities. Moreover, Morris stated, "surfing saved my life" and credited the sport as the only thing that kept him physically fit when he used drugs and alcohol. Rick was involved in running until recently. In junior high school, Rick had taken engaged in burglary, theft and other deviant activities with Chuck Roe and Norm Dunn. As Rick became involved in running, he separated himself from the others. He continued to run into his

40s. Many members of the 1975 and 1976 Golden Beach High School football teams have maintained their social contacts and interact in their business activities. These have proved valuable to them. On the negative side, when the athletics careers of some high school students came to an end, they began to increase their use of drugs and became part of the "party scene." Albert, who hosted his 1975 party with his teammates serving as "bouncers," is the most obvious example.

Other activities, such as drama, were beneficial for some. Ned's involvement in drama influenced his decision to enter USC as a drama major. He eventually went to England for advanced theatrical studies.

More importantly, parental interest and encouragement in school were found to have a major influence on the academic performance of their sons and daughters. The results of this academic achievement are obvious in their long-term financial success.

In addition to the role of parents, siblings had a considerable influence on each other. On the positive side, the cohesiveness of functional families, such as the Bayer family, the Jones family and the Gilroy family, assisted Morris Bayer, the Jones brothers and Ron and Reed Gilroy. Their siblings were supportive in their efforts to overcome use of drugs and/or alcohol problems. On the negative side, many younger siblings were introduced to drugs by their older siblings or friends of their older siblings. Likewise, the Roe brothers and the Dunn brothers were mutually supportive of each other's deviant activities.

The long term as well as the short-term analysis of the families and families' influence on peer relationships support Differential Association theory and social control theories. The effects of groups on the individual are evident in an examination of families, religious groups, extracurricular high school peer groups, the Old Wall Gang and the wall crew.

PATTERNS OF CHANGE IN DRUG USE

Over the 31-year period of the study, patterns of drug use changed considerably.

In the years from 1965 to 1970, teens verbalized an ethic that alcohol use was "unhealthy" and "stupid." The youth subculture viewed alcohol as a substance used only by older and "less wise" adults. They were aware that alcohol killed brain cells, damaged livers, caused hangovers and led to alcoholism. The youths proclaimed that they had discovered the new "wonder drug," marijuana, which had none of these properties. Many used

LSD, which was reputed to have a "trip" to "open one's mind," "lead to increased awareness" and "spiritual experiences." Barbiturates, or "reds," were groovy, and amphetamine's were "somewhat cool" to get one "going." By 1971, alcohol was used when marijuana or other substances were not available to "get high." On the other hand, it was "a waste" to use alcohol before smoking pot because "you can't enjoy the high of the pot." LSD was still "in" and "groovy." Some of the negative consequences of the use of barbiturates had begun to become apparent. In the next three years, speed and reds became "uncool," but cocaine was being used by a few members of the drug subculture and a "heroin epidemic" occurred. Beer and "pop wines" were accepted, but were not yet the major focus of the parties.

During the years 1975 and 1976, beer had replaced marijuana as the most popular drug in the youth subculture. "Keggers" replaced "pot parties." Beer, marijuana and other drugs were used at the keg parties. More potent marijuana became available. The large scale "bust" of a multinational marijuana "ring" brought about a drought in "commercial Mexican" pot. This was followed by increased use of exotic marijuana, such as "Thai Sticks," and "Acapulco Gold," at drastically inflated prices. Within weeks, "commercial" marijuana was widely available, but its price had increased Use of reds and speed became taboo. The use of LSD was acceptable only on "special occasions." Tripping on other hallucinogens, such as peyote and mushrooms, was considered "cool" and "far out" because they were "organic." Needles and heroin were, once again, taboo. Quaaludes were "discovered" as aphrodisiacs and were used by a small minority of young people.

During the late 1970s and early 1980s, alcohol remained the number one drug of choice by those over and under the legal age. However, the increased use of cocaine had the most dramatic effect on the drug subculture. Although both drugs were used at home and in clubs, the cost of cocaine and its effects led to an increase in violence, "rip-offs" and property crimes. Rich was shot to death. Toby Dunn was stabbed several times. Cocaine changed relationships between individuals and within groups. The young members of the wall crew lost their cohesiveness and connectedness with others. Ever more costly varieties of marijuana, especially Columbian, Oaxcan and Sensimilla, were smoked by the increasingly affluent residents of Golden Beach.

By the late 1980s and early 1990s, cocaine began to lose its appeal as its consequences were felt among the drug subculture. As fear of Aids spread, the combination of sex and drugs became "uncool." There was an increasing awareness of alcoholism and receptivity to treatment for alcoholism and drug addiction, including Alcoholics Anonymous.

The mid-1990s saw a return of "speed" in a more potent crystalized form, methamphetamine or "crystal meth." As was the case with amphetamine in 1970, the negative effects became apparent. Its popularity waned in Golden Beach, but not until some lives were severely affected. Expensive marijuana was smoked by many of the younger generation. Alcohol use increased. The "disease" of alcoholism was more widely recognized. Many of those who had been involved in the drug subculture in the 1970s became active members of A.A. Those in their late teens and early 20s found their own new "wonder drug," ecstasy. Raves and the subculture involved in them seemed to reflect the ethic of the early "pot smoking" and "acid tripping" subculture of the late 1960s.

As we enter the new century, there are a few signs that ecstasy and raves may become a passing fad in Golden Beach. There are other indications that heroin and cocaine use may be increasing among upper class teenagers in the surrounding area. The jury is still out, but it is clear that the types of drugs, the varieties of particular substances and the subculture surrounding drugs come and go. Tobacco continues to be the most deadly of all substances, but alcohol remains the number one drug of choice. Although alcohol use has decreased slightly in recent years, alcohol affects the lives of more individuals and families than any other drug. Alcohol is the drug associated with the more violence than any other substance in Golden Beach and in America.[9]

CHANGES IN LAWS AND LAW ENFORCEMENT

A number of significant legal changes have been made in the United States, the State of California and the City of San Diego since 1970. At times, the changes in law enforcement resulted from changes in law. At other times, law enforcement changes occurred independent of legislative action.

In 1970, the possession of any amount of marijuana was a felony. Law enforcement was strict. Police raided "pot parties." Dragnets were conducted along the boardwalk when crowds were large or unruly, particularly if complaints were made by business owners.

During the next five years, possession of marijuana was still a felony. However, courts and, to a lesser degree, law enforcement became more lenient regarding marijuana. Little action was taken when police arrived at a party except to ask the host to turn down the volume or to disperse the crowd. Little attention was paid to underage alcohol use at house parties. A major international drug bust of a major "marijuana connection" occurred in 1975. Dragnets continued on the boardwalk. Initially the police concentrated on the non-locals (called "red freaks" by the wall crew). Later they swept the entire boardwalk citing all violators including those in possession of drugs, underage drinkers and those not in compliance with city ordinances regarding bicycle and juvenile curfews. The wall crew began to lose their territory as the "red freaks" moved into the vacuum that had been inadvertently created by the police.

In 1976, the possession of small amounts of marijuana for personal use was treated as a misdemeanor. Police reaction to the use of marijuana became noticeably more lenient.

During the 1980s, police began to curtail the use of dragnets. They drove cruisers along the boardwalk only on rare occasions. Instead, police rode bicycles to patrol the boardwalk. They maintained a low profile and presented themselves in a friendly manner to the public.

By the mid-1990s, the officers on bicycles became a part of a larger effort by the San Diego Police Department's efforts to institute a model of community, or neighborhood, policing. Police and citizen interactions had improved dramatically since 1970. In 1998, Californians voted to allow the medical use of marijuana with a physician's prescription. The federal authorities have challenged the legislation. In the fall election of 2000, the voters approved Proposition #36, mandating treatment rather than imprisonment for first and second drug offenders. The state is preparing to deal with the increased need for drug counselors and treatment centers. In April 2001, the San Diego City Council enacted an ordinance banning all alcohol on the beach and the boardwalks of Golden Beach and Sand Beach.

THE EFFECTIVENESS OF EXTERNAL CONTROL EFFORTS AND INTERNAL CONTROLS

An examination of the evidence regarding external control mechanisms, such as increased police surveillance, strict enforcement of laws, increased criminalization, longer sentences and incarceration points to their relative ineffectiveness. Matt was arrested as a felon twice within a few weeks for possession of marijuana. Matt continued to use marijuana until the year 2000 when he, on his own initiative, moved from Lake Tahoe and changed his lifestyle. Pops was sentenced to a county honor camp for possession of cocaine. He left the San Diego area and his drug use was under control. He returned and, once again, became involved with cocaine. When he left San Diego permanently, he apparently moved out of the drug subculture. Sean was arrested and convicted on federal drug trafficking charges after he attempted to make a large cocaine deal. His imprisonment at a young age seemed to make him more bitter and increasingly alienated from society. He never renounced his earlier drug activity. Bart Roe has been convicted several times. He does not claim to be clean and sober. Turk, Bill Jones and others returned to their use of drugs immediately after leaving jail. Ty had several convictions for possession and sale of heroin as a juvenile and as an adult. Ty died in prison.

For a few, one or more convictions were steps in a journey toward sobriety or decreased use. Had it not been for their legal entanglements, they might not have faced the consequences of their drug use. Pat served jail time following his third arrest for possession of cocaine. Pat decided that he did not want to continue using cocaine. He continued to drink heavily until physical problems forced him to drink less. Luke was sentenced to three and one half years at Folsom prison. He attended A.A. for a period of time. He now drinks moderately and enjoys visits to the gambling casinos. Chuck Roe was convicted of a drug related offense. He was sent to an honor camp where he became sober. Chuck was trained in forestry. He remains sober and operates his own tree service company. Norm Dunn was convicted of a felony for domestic abuse resulting from cocaine. Norm is completing a year-long anger management course. He has used cocaine only twice in the past year. Jeanie was convicted of stealing drugs at a hospital. She was sentenced to a drug rehabilitation program. She remains drug-free and is a successful registered nurse.

Still, many have achieved sobriety through various other means. The program that has been most successful for the largest number has been Alcoholics Anonymous and/or other Twelve-Step programs. The A.A. program is consistent with an application of Differential Association theory. Morris had been arrested a number of times, but this did not affect his use of alcohol or other drugs. Morris entered A.A. after he moved from Golden Beach to Florida. Morris Bayer is extremely active and involved in A.A. activities. Max had been arrested several times. On one occasion, drug enforcement agents swarmed into his apartment, but Max was never incarcerated. Max achieved sobriety through A.A. He attends meetings frequently. Max felt the religious inspiration of his grandmother was responsible for his recovery. Keith avoided detection by law enforcement in spite of his deep involvement in cocaine trafficking. Keith joined A.A. and later had a religious experience which convinced him cocaine, not alcohol, was his drug of choice. He remains drug-free and committed to his religion and family. He no longer attends A.A. Julian had been homeless and living in single-occupancy hotel rooms in downtown San Diego. He joined A.A., achieved sobriety and has moved from the area. Nelson entered a drug treatment program on his own volition. Bill Jones' son, Shane, admitted himself to a drug rehabilitation clinic.

In addition, I have been told there are many other people who attend A.A. meetings whom I "know." I may be aware of the involvement of some of these. Others may be practicing complete anonymity in A.A., which I strongly respect. I have never attempted to inquire further.

Some make statements such as, "I tried A.A., but it didn't work for me." Pat, Art, Kevin and Dr. Bayer have voiced this sentiment. Pat began to cut back on drinking following his medical problems. Art was in A.A. for a period of time. He remains sober and visits a psychotherapist regularly. Kevin is a "drunk," and all but homeless. Dr. Bayer was admitted to an alcoholic treatment center where a program "similar to A.A." was used. Dr. Bayer remained sober for several years and now claims he can maintain his "controlled drinking."

Andy was sober for some time and active in A.A. He ceased attending meetings. He drinks and is homeless. Andy, however, has other psychological problems, possibly as a result of his LSD experiences. Vick received extensive mental health therapy. His difficulties were apparently the result of "LSD Psychosis." Vick died in 1998.

Many of those who were heavily involved in the drug subculture during the 1970s simply "matured out." Moving from Golden Beach or the greater San Diego was a factor in the process of "maturing out" for many. Increased job opportunities due to the booming San Diego economy, particularly the real estate market, provided an incentive for others. For some of those who had not obtained a college education, this increased availability of meaningful employment made a significant difference. Meaningful employment brought about an increased self-esteem and an increased sense of responsibility. Pat provides the clearest example of this. In addition, some, such as Keith, Albert and Barry, were beneficiaries of very substantial inherited wealth.

Marital satisfaction and the resultant family factors provided stability and social support for many.

For several, their religious faith was the most important factor in the process. Barry, Carl, Les, Floyd and the three Jones brothers felt that their religious convictions led them from their drug involvement. All remain drug-free.

What cannot be overlooked is the role of will power and determination. Mike was grateful for my counsel and advice. However, he sought me out and he made his own decision to leave Golden Beach for a lengthy period of time. Later, without a college education, he returned to apply his talents and entrepreneurial skills to build a very successful corporation. He is in the process of moving into a comfortable retirement with his wife. Paul completed high school without adult supervision or encouragement. He worked his way through college. Paul is now a successful computer technician and is happily married.

A few are dead, and some are still struggling with their use of alcohol and other drugs.

In total, the external legal sanctions have had only a minor impact in bringing about change when compared with family background and family support, Alcoholics Anonymous, drug treatment programs, religion, opportunities for meaningful employment and the internalized control often termed "will power" and "determination."

The results of this research offer far greater support for the "demand side" argument of the current debate regarding America's "war on drugs" than for the "supply side" emphasis of past decades. Families and local communities have a great influence on the development of internal controls that result in lower demand for drugs. On the other hand, police, drug enforcement agencies, arrest and incarceration have little influence on the demand for drugs. In addition, some of the most successful efforts by law enforcement, as witnessed in 1976, only serve to increase the cost of drugs and can be counterproductive. Eventually, the supply meets the demand.

WHAT CAN WE DO?

When I discuss the issues of drug and alcohol abuse, I am frequently asked, "Well, what is the answer?" I try to avoid the complex issues of decriminalization of all drugs. However, I do point out the futility of spending billions of dollars on interdiction. Likewise, I question the efficacy of a criminal justice system that singles out the poor, minorities and males. Not only is this system unfair to the poor, minorities and males, but it also remains blind to the needs of the middle and upper income groups, whites and females. The youth of Golden Beach were not poor and very few were minorities. In incarceration has few benefits when effective drug treatment is not available. It is totally counterproductive to place persons in prisons where drugs are as available, if not more available, than on our streets.

So, let us concentrate on what can be done to increase "internal controls."

Thus, we begin with socialization. We begin with the family. In our own families, we can make children our first priority, above and beyond our job or profession, our income and our own personal satisfaction. This process begins before the family is formed. It begins with developing healthy relationships with the opposite sex and being open to adequate preparation for marriage. Many marriage preparation programs emphasize the need, first of all, for life long commitment. Most, but not all, of these programs are administered by churches. To accomplish their goal, they utilize techniques to demonstrate the obstacles that may arise in marriage. They provide couples with opportunities to improve their communication skills. Communication skills provide the basis to discuss the potential obstacles prior to marriage as well as how to solve problems following marriage. After a couple is married, there are programs, such as *Retrouvaille,* and *Marriage Encounter*, which are set up to improve marriages or assist those having difficulties in their relationships. Likewise, there are many opportunities for marriage counseling and parenting courses. The skill to demonstrate love to one's children, including the need to communicate love through firm but caring discipline is essential. These principles may sound very basic, but they cannot be overemphasized.

Parental involvement in children's activities and parental encouragement for the children to participate in religious activities, athletics and other extracurricular activities are very important.

In addition to what I have described, a 2000 National Survey of American Attitudes on Substance Abuse conducted by the National Center on Addiction and Substance Abuse at Columbia University found that teens "who live with 'hands-on' parents–parents who have established a household culture of rules and expectations for their teen's behavior," are "at one quarter the risk of smoking, drinking and using drugs as teens with 'hands-off' parents."[10]

If a marriage ends in divorce, both parents ought to continue to be a part of the child's life. Fortunately, we have seen an increasing trend toward involving the father, as well as the mother, in custody decisions.

The single parent can learn from "Super-Mom," Mrs. Gilroy. To follow her example may be difficult, but it is possible. Likewise, organizations such as "Big Brothers and Big Sisters" are tremendously effective in provided needy role models for children.

As members of our communities, we can volunteer to become Big Brothers or Big Sisters, as well as volunteer to help in other youth activities, such as, Little League, Pop Warner football and the YMCA. Volunteers are frequently welcome in our local schools. Any one of us may be influencing a young person with or without our knowledge. It might be as simple as offering to take a child fishing, hunting or to a ball game.

Those who work with youth must be especially conscientious in performance of their duties to be good role models to young people. Teachers, counselors, coaches, Boy Scouts and Girls Scout leaders, youth ministers, clergy and others must be constantly aware of the role they have to help or hinder the healthy development of young people.

As communities, we can respond through sharing our time, funding and, yes, taxes to support healthy activities for our young people. This can be accomplished by organizing our communities so that all young people are able to participate in a variety of healthy activities. Our assistance may be in the form of monetary donations to various organizations. Or, it may be by means of our vote in local bond issues to provide funding for extracurricular activities, summer youth programs or "midnight basketball." We can support efforts to provide for those who are unable to afford the fees and equipment to participate in athletic and other extracurricular activities. In Chapter 12, I cited the example of the community efforts in Helena, Montana during the 1990s.

As a society, we must emphasize and support prevention and treatment in lieu of, or, at times, in conjunction with prosecution and incarceration. The recent California initiative is a step in this direction. For such action to be successful, however, adequate funding must begin immediately to train drug and alcohol counselors, and to build adequate treatment facilities. The savings obtained by decreasing inmates would more than pay for this.

Finally, we must never panic and always realize the basic goodness within each human being. Most of our children will, eventually, mature and become healthy, functioning adults. I hope the accounts that I have presented provide some understanding of those who have so generously shared their experiences with me.

I close with portions of an email Paul sent to me, dated April 18, 2000,

This, the anniversary of Jimmy Hendrix death in 1970 . . . funny what a difference 30 years can make!

1970: Long Hair.
2000: Longing for hair.

1970: The perfect high.
2000: The perfect high yield mutual funds.

1970: Keg.
2000: EKG.

1970: Moving to California because it's cool.
2000: Moving to California because it's warm.

1970: Seeds and stems.
2000: Roughage.

1970: Popping pills, smoking joints.
2000: Popping joints.

1970: Killer weed.
2000: Weed killer.

1970: The Grateful Dead.
2000: Grateful I'm not dead.

1970: Getting out to a hip, new joint.
2000: Getting a new hip joint.

1970: Rolling Stones.
2000: Kidney stones.

1970: Peace sign.
2000: Mercedes' logo.

1970: Take acid.
2000: Take antacid.

1970: "Whatever"
2000: "Depends"

Remember, parents, you were once young. Remember, young people, your parents once struggled with their own adolescence in a very turbulent period in America. After all, that's what they were doing back then!

And so I have answered Les' challenge given to me more than 30 years earlier.

End Notes

1. See, for instance, Macionis, John J. *Sociology,* 7th ed., Upper Saddle River, N.J., Prentice-Hall, 2000, pp. 125-145.

2. A thorough review of this literature may be found in Thornberry, Terence P., "Membership in Youth Gangs and Involvement in Serious and Violent Offending," In Loeber, R. and Farrington, D.P., (eds.) *Serious and Violent Offenders*, N.Y.: Sage Publications, pp. 147-166, 1998.

3. Yablonsky, Lewis. *Gangsters*, N.Y.: New York University Press, 1997, pp. 20-22.

4. For other similar conclusions see Sheldon, Randall G., Tracy, Sharon K., and Brown, William B., *Youth Gangs in American Society,* 2nd ed., Belmont, Ca.: Wadsworth/Thomson Learning, 2001, pp. 175-178.

5. Wallerstein, Judith S.; Lewis, Julia M.; and Blakeslee, Sandra. *The Unexpected Legacy of Divorce: A 25 -Year Landmark Study,* NY: Hyperion, 2000.

6. Popenoe, David, *Life Without Father,* NY: The Free Press, 1996.

7. Ibid, p. 143.

8. Ibid, pp. 155-156.

9. For an excellent analysis of the link between alcohol and violence and the extent of alcohol use in America see Goode, Erich. *Drugs in American Society,* 4th ed., NY: McGraw-Hill, 1993, pp. 120-178.

10. "The 2000 Casa National Survey of American Attitudes on Substance Abuse VI:" The National Center on Addiction and Substance Abuse at Columbia University Newsletter, February 21, 2001.

APPENDIX A

UNITED STATES DEPARTMENT OF JUSTICE
DRUG ENFORCEMENT ADMINISTRATION
Washington, D.C. 20537

JUL 1O 1975

Mr. Jeremiah Lowney, Jr.
1128 Felspar #1
, California

Dear Mr. Lowney:

Subject: Grant of Confidentiality

On May 28, 1975, you applied for a Grant of Confidentiality under Section 502(c) of the Comprehensive Drug Abuse Prevention and Control Act of 1970 (Title 21, Section 872(c) of the United States Code) and Title 21, Section 1316.21 of the Code of Federal Regulations., for a research project.

The research project is to be conducted by Jeremiah Lowney in California.

The purpose of the research project is to investigate the nature, incidence, prevalence and patterns of youthful drug abuse and various causal conditions conducive to the use of marihuana1 alcohol and other drugs among youths in California.

Under the authority vested in the Attorney General by Title 21, Section 872(c) of the United States Code, and delegated to the Administrator of the Drug Enforcement. Administration by Title. 28, Section 0.100 of the Code of Federal Regulations, I hereby authorize you to withhold the names and other identifying characteristics of persons who are subjects of research conducted pursuant to and in conformity with the research protocol entitled A Study of Youthful Drug Abuse. You may not be compelled in any Federal, State, or local civil, criminal, administrative1 legislative, or other proceeding to identify the subjects of such research. This Grant of Confidentiality shall apply to all other persons engaged in carrying out the research project and shall cover all persons who are subjects of such research while the grant is in effect.

The grant shall remain in effect until the completion of the research project or until April 1, 1976. Within 30 days of the date of completion of the research project, you shall so notify the Administrator. Upon expiration or termination of the grant the Administrator shall issue another letter stating the date on which the period of the grant was concluded; upon receipt of the new letter, you shall return this letter granting confidentiality.

If you have any questions regarding this letter, please contact Mr. Robert J. Rosthal, Deputy Chief Counsel of the Administration.

Sincerely,

Henry S.Dogin
Acting Administrator

APPENDIX B

Letter of Explanation to Potential Subjects

DATE ________________

TO WHOM IT MAY CONCERN

This is to inform you regarding the nature of a research project I am conducting which you may be asked to participate.

This project will take place mainly in the Golden Beach area of San Diego, California, over the next six to nine months. The reason for the research is to help gain an understanding of young people better. This includes: their use of non-use of drugs, alcohol and marijuana; their home lives; their life in school; their friends; and the way they feel about themselves as well as their beliefs and attitudes in general.

I will be studying a number of other young people, like yourself. I will mix with them, talk to them, see how they act and ask them for an interview near the end of the research. What will be asked of you is merely to ask and talk as you would normally otherwise do.

I wish to especially inform you that all information I obtain will remain FULLY CONFIDENTIAL and that NO ONE will be told anything I learn about you unless you so agree. This includes whether you do or do not use drugs of any form or any other information that could embarrass or bring harm to you. This confidentiality includes not only parents, teachers, and school authorities, but also, under Title 21, #316.21 of the Code of Federal Regulations for research projects, I am entitled to withhold names and any other identifying characteristics from any Federal, State, or local civil, criminal, administrative, or legislative authorities.

The research that will be written will use false names of persons and places. All notes and other material used during the course of the project will use false names except for one code sheet kept under lock.

There are no risks expected to be placed on anyone during the project.

You are free to withdraw from the project at any time without this reflecting on you in any way.

If you have any other questions about the research or my reasons for doing it, please feel free to ask these and I will answer them to the best of my ability.

Thank you for your consideration and for what knowledge you may give to science and a better understanding of young people.

Yours truly,

Jeremiah Lowney

APPENDIX C

Signed Understanding and Consent Form by Subjects

TO WHOM IT MAY CONCERN:

Jeremiah Lowney has fully explained to me the nature of his research project. I fully understand this explanation.

(Signed) ________________________________

(Date) __________________________________

(Witness)________________________________
(Optional)

APPENDIX D

Basic Data and Information Sheet on Each Subject

Name: Date:

Code No:

Age:

Sex:

Race:

Address:

Phone:

School Attending:

Year in School:

Employment:

Employer:

Religion: Practicing?:

Estimated Parental Income:

Father's Occupation___________ Mother's Occupation_________

Home: Broken___ Divorced____ Separated____ By Death____
Intact___

Living With: Both Parents___ Mother Only___ Father Only___
Mother & Stepfather____ Alone____ Other____

When, Where and How Initially Contacted:

Surfs____ Is it like Pot?____________
Formal Interview __________________ Date______________

Category: User_____ Non-User____ Rehabilitated User_________
Explain____________________

Uses:	1st Used	Same Friends	Same Age	New Group	Older?	Frequency Now	Past
Marijuana							
Hash							
Alcohol							
Hallucinogens: Kinds:							
Uppers Kinds:							
Downers Kinds:							
Cocaine							
Heroin or Opiate							
Other Kinds:							

Ever used a legal drug illegally? Explain:

Other comments:

APPENDIX E

An Essay by Phil, A Light User

(Note: The following was written by Phil, a light user, during a meeting of St. Patrick's Youth Group, "Drop In." The members were asked to write, in private, their reflections regarding a picture of a young man whose face was shown behind jail bars. Phil's response was selected to be read at the "Coffee House," described in my "Daily Journal Notes" of January, 17, 1976, as quoted in Chapter 7. Phil had been shy before he joined the youth group. The adults at the "Coffee House" commented on Phil's growth after he had read his essay.")

There was this person, lonely, not much pressure on him, but it was hard for him to relate to other people. There being no one close to him, he was struggling just to talk–that's all he needed, someone to talk to. Instead of finding someone, he would just blame himself. If he was given the chance to talk, he would be able to. But the chance has to be given by himself and not the acts of others. Now this person, with no one, had a problem that was very hard to overcome. It was that people irritated him. Everyone was for themselves, but could only act the way the rest of their friends act or wanted them to act.

APPENDIX F
Drawings by Bill Jones

Note: The following drawings were done by Bill Jones, who at the time in 1976 was a heavy user. We were discussing his future in Billy's restaurant. Bill frequently expressed himself through art forms. He drew these on the backs of menu cards. In 2001, Bill is a Sunday school teacher and active in his Baptist congregation.

GLOSSARY OF SUBCULTURE TERMS

ACAPULCO GOLD: A "brand" of marijuana, supposedly grown in or near Acapulco, Mexico.
ACID: LSD, Lysergic acid diethylamide.
ADDICT: Not necessarily physically an addicted person, but may indicate a strong desire. Although it usually refers to drugs, the term may apply to non-drugs, e.g., "addicted to candy bars."
ALCOHOL: Usually refers to "hard" liquor or spirits, as opposed to beer and wine.
AIRHEAD: A person who appears to "be out of it," somewhat irrational.
ALKIE: An alcoholic or heavy user of alcoholic beverages.
ALRIGHT!: An exclamation indicating pleasure. Similar to "Great," or "Far out!"
AMP: Become excited or emotional, usually with strong verbal expression. (Used primarily by surfers.)
ANGEL DUST: PCP, phencyclidine, a hallucinogenic.
AWESOME: Unbelievably great.
BAD: A word used opposite to its meaning in the larger society. "Bad" means "good," or superior of its kind. In recent years, it has been replaced by "Rad."
BAG: An individual's main interest, as in, "Surfing is my bag."
BAGGIE: The container or the marijuana contained in a small plastic bag, usually sold in one ounce quantity in such a bag. May also apply to small amounts of other drugs, especially cocaine and heroin, contained in small bags.
BAGGING Z'S: Sleeping.
BAIL (ALSO, BAIL OUT): Cease an activity or refuse to participate, as in, "I bailed out of that soccer game."
BALL: A verb, meaning to engage in sexual intercourse.
BARBS: Barbiturates.
BEEBS: Females.
BENNIES: "Benzedrine," brand name of amphetamine (Smith, Kline & French Laboratories, Inc.)
BITCHIN': Good. Highly desirable.
BLOW: Snort cocaine.
BLOWING: Process of snorting cocaine.
BLOW ONE'S MIND: To become overwhelmed emotionally or psychologically, as in, "That girl blew my mind!" Also used to describe results of using drugs as disturbing, as in, "That acid blew my mind!"
BLOWN-OUT: A climatic condition of the ocean in which the waves are closed by the wind; undesirable for surfing.
BOARD: Surfboard.
BOMBED: Inebriated, drunk, under heavy influence of any drug.
BONG: A large bamboo pipe or water pipe for smoking marijuana or hashish.

BOOBS: Female breasts.
BOSS: Good, superior.
BOTTLES: A large quantity (usually 100) of prescription-required drugs, usually amphetamines or barbiturates, usually, but not always, contained in glass "bottles."
BREAD: Money.
BREAKING: The breaking of the waves; usually used with direction, as in, "The waves are breaking north," or "The waves are breaking inside."
BREW: Beer.
BRICK: A compact kilo of marijuana.
BRO: Short for "Brother," used affectionately.
BROWN BAG (ALSO, A VERB, "BROWN BAGGING IT"): Alcoholic beverages stored or kept in a brown paper bag while stored, as in one's locker at school, or while consumed in public.
BUCKS: Money, dollars.
BUDS: The tops of the marijuana plant, or "buds" from the marijuana flower.
BUMMED: Depressed, "down," feeling of anxiety.
BUMMER: An unpleasant experience.
BUM TRIP: An unpleasant experience, often as the result of the use of drugs, particularly hallucinogens.
BURNED-OUT: Tired of a particular activity, frequently seen as "old," in, "Those guys are burned out on surfing." Also, used to describe LSD-psychosis or long-term effects of other drugs.
CAFFEINE: Coffee.
CAR GUYS: Youths who are very interested in cars, (as opposed to "surfers," "jocks," "soshes," and so on).
CAT: A person, usually one who is "cool," or "into the scene." Also used with prefixes such as, "surf-cat," "beach-cat," and so on.
CATCHING Z'S: Sleeping.
CHEMICALS: Synthetic drugs, such as amphetamines, barbiturates, LSD.
CHICK: A young female.
CHILL-OUT: Calm down or "Cool it!"
CHUG: Drink, especially beer.
CHUMP: An undependable person.
CHUMP-OUT: Act undependably, or fail to perform as promised, "He chumped-out on meeting me this morning."
COKE: Cocaine.
COKED-OUT: "Addicted" to cocaine.
COKE AND POKE: Use cocaine and have sexual intercourse with a female.
COLA: Cocaine.
COLD: Unacceptable in referring to behavior, as, "That was cold of you to not invite him to join the party."

COLUMBO (ALSO, LOMBO): A "brand" of marijuana, supposedly grown in Columbia, South America.
COMMERCIAL: Standard, or ordinary marijuana, usually imported from Mexico and sold "commercially." Used to distinguish this from "more expensive" varieties.
CONNECTION: A source to obtain marijuana or other drugs.
COOL: Used to describe persons and/or things that are acceptable within the drug subculture. Acceptable, as in, "That's cool, man." Similar to "groovy," or subsequent expressions, "awesome," and "far-out."
COP: As a noun, a policeman. As a verb, to steal or obtain under questionable circumstances. A person often "cops" a small amount of marijuana when obtaining from a connection for a friend, as a go-between.
CRACK: A crystalized form of cocaine, frequently smoked in a pipe.
CRANK: A crystalized form of methamphetamine. Also, "crystal," "meth," "crystal meth." See below.
CRASH: Go to sleep. To complete a drug experience, particularly if one of heavy use of drugs, as, "I crashed last night after doing coke and partying."
CRUISE: To take it easy. To walk, drive or wander with little purpose or direction. As an adjective, to be easy, "That math exam was a cruise."
CRYSTAL: Crystalized form of Methedrine or Methamphetamine.
DEAL: Engage in drug sales.
DIG: To like or enjoy.
DIME: A $10 purchase of any drug, usually cocaine or heroin.
DINE AND DASH: To eat in a restaurant and leave without paying for one's meal.
DITCH: To be truant, particularly in regard to school. To exit from any activity.
DOG: An undesirable female.
DOGGIE REDS: A contemptuous referral to barbiturates.
DOOBIE: A marijuana cigarette. A joint.
DOPE: Any non-alcoholic drug, usually used in reference to marijuana.
DOPER: A person who uses drugs, particularly marijuana, frequently.
DOWN: Feeling depressed.
DOWNERS: Any sedative, particularly barbiturates. An unpleasant or depressing experience (when used singularly).
DRAG: An unpleasant situation, "It's a drag." Also, a puff from a marijuana cigarette.
DROUGHT: A period of time when drugs, particularly marijuana, are not plentiful.
DRY: Not having any drugs. Also, thirsty. Also, not having any money.
DUDE: A male person.
DWID: An undesirable person. A weirdo, or "nobody."
DYNO: Unusually pleasant or superior; often used in reference to a drug or a sexual experience.

E: Ecstacy. See Below.
ECSTACY: MDMA, a designer drug. A synthetic analogue of amphetamines. Also referred to as **E, X, XTC, HUG, ADAM, BEANS.** See "raves" below.
FAGGOT (ALSO, FAG): A derogatory term in reference to a homosexual.
FAR-OUT: Great, good.
FINS: Fins on a surfboard. Rubber fins used to body-surf.
FINGER: Measurement of an amount of marijuana in a "lid" or "baggie," as in, "a five-finger baggie," or "a three-finger lid."
FISHING: Seeking someone to purchase liquor (for those under the legal age). One usually "fishes" near a liquor store.
FLAKE-OFF: Get lost! Get off my back!
FLASHED-ON: To have thought of an idea, or to remember something suddenly, as "I flashed-on the fact that I left my grass under my bed."
FLAT: A climatic condition describing the ocean as devoid of any sizeable waves.
FLIP (ALSO, FLIPPED-OUT): Temporarily or permanently become or act insane or in an "insane" manner. Also, in surfing, to "flip-out" of a wave by a sudden backward motion allowing the wave to "break" in front of the surfer.
FREAK: A person who is overly indulged or concerned in regard to a particular activity, as a "football freak," a "red freak," or a ''school freak.''
FREAK-OUT: Lose control or be overwhelmed, particularly following an unexpected event, "I freaked-out when the cops showed up at the party."
FREE MONEY: Government transfer payments, such as Social Security , G.I. Bill Unemployment Compensation payments and welfare payments.
FUNNEL: A funnel with a large tube attached to pour alcoholic beverages into a person very quickly. Sometimes referred to as a "Bong."
GATOR: (Short for alligator) A person from the Eastern seaboard, particularly Florida.
GESTAPO: The police or any authoritarian figure.
GIG: Method of obtaining money.
GLASSY: A climatic condition of the ocean or a bay characterized by a lack of wind or waves.
GOAB: (Pronounced "go-ab.") Similar to "dwid" or "weirdo"; an undesirable person. A socially unacceptable person.
GROOVY: A late 1960's and early 1970's term for "awesome," "cool," or "far out." Pleasurable, satisfactory, as in, "It was groovy, man!"
G: A gram. See below.
GRAM: Measurement of a drug. For instance, a gram, or "g," of marijuana, or a gram, or "g" of cocaine.
GRASS: Marijuana.
GRUBS: Older clothing. Work clothing.
GRUNT: A derogative reference to a person who plays football.

H: Heroin.
HAIREY: A difficult or troublesome situation, as, "That was hairey when my Mom found my grass in the closet!"
HALF: As an adjective in reference to amount of a drug, such as a "half-ounce" (or "half-z").
HARD GUYS (ALSO, HARD ROCKS): Persons who use "hard" drugs (particularly "chemicals"). Persons who look or act "tough."
HARE-MO: Unbelievably large or frightening.
HEAD: Frequent user of marijuana.
HEAT: A state of increased police activity. "The heat's on."
HEAVY: In regard to drugs, indicates degree of chemical effect of drugs, that is, some drugs are "heavier" than others. Also, very serious, requiring psychological or emotional adjustment, as, "That was a heavy experience after my Dad died."
HELMET: A male youth from Diamond Heights, usually stereotyped as a surfer, derived from a characteristic haircut in shape of a ''helmet.''
HIGH: The euphoric state brought about by the use of a drug, usually marijuana.
HIP: Aware of what is happening, as in "He's hip, man!"
HIT: A single puff from a marijuana cigarette. A single dose of any drug, "a hit of acid," or "a hit of smack."
HIPPY (OR PLURAL, HIPPIES): By those not "in" the subculture, used in reference to a person who meets the stereotype of a drug user, particularly in his physical appearance (longhair, clothing, and so on). By those "in" the subculture, a person who uses "heavier" drugs, who is more than 18 and continuously unemployed, or lacks certain standards of personal hygiene.
HOMEGROWN: Marijuana that is "fresh," that is, has not been dried and packed into "bricks" or kilos; may or may not have been grown locally.
HOOKED: Similar to "addicted," not necessarily used in reference to drugs or to physical addiction, but somewhat strong desire for or toward something or someone, as "I'm hooked on that chick."
HOOTCH: Alcoholic beverages.
HORSE: Heroin.
HOSE: To have sexual intercourse, as "I hosed that chick last night."
HOSE-MONSTER: A promiscuous female.
HOTEL: An exceedingly large wave.
HUFF: To inhale paint, glue, aerosols or other volatile substances.
HUNG-UP: Concerned, worried, perplexed about. "I'm hung-up on what to do after I turn 18."
HUNK: A very handsome, well-built male. Ordinarily used by females.
HYPE: A person who uses a hypodermic needle to inject drugs intravenously.
HYPER: A very emotional, hyperactive person.
IN: Used in reference to that which is currently popular, as in, "Short hair is in."

INSANE: An exclamation meaning "unbelievable!"
INTO: Strongly interested in, as "I'm into surfing," or "He's been into golf lately."
JIVE: Language particular to a single group, especially in reference to language that is used to disguise the meaning from those who are not members of that group. Also, as a verb, to not be fully honest, as in "He's jiving me!"
JOINT: A marijuana cigarette.
JOCK: A person who frequently participates in sports.
JUNK: Heroin.
JUNKIE: A heroin addict.
KEGGER: A beer party; often used with a prefix to denote the number of beer kegs to be provided at the party, as: "a two-kegger," "a three-kegger," or "a 10-kegger."
KILO: Two and two-tenths pounds of marijuana, usually packed into the shape of a brick.
KIT: The hypodermic syringe and materials used to inject drugs intravenously.
LAY: To have sexual intercourse. In reference to a female, a person with whom one has sexual intercourse, as "She's an easy lay."
LEECH: To live off of others. As a noun, a person who continuously borrows from others, especially drugs or money.
LID: A quantity, approximately one ounce, of marijuana, measured by the width of one's finger, "a three-finger lid."
LIGHTWEIGHT: Easy. Also, a person who is not accustomed to the heavy use of drugs or alcohol.
LINE: The ordinary form by which a single dose of cocaine is snorted through the nostrils, that is, a quarter of an inch by two inch "line" of cocaine placed on a mirror for use. Single "hits" of cocaine are often sold in this form.
LOCALS: Those who ordinarily frequent a particular area, as "The Lime Avenue locals." Also, in reference to residents, as opposed to nonresidents.
LOCOWEED: Marijuana.
LSD: Lysergic acid diethylamide, also known as acid.
LUDES: Quaalude tablets, a strong sedative. Also, "sopers."
MAINTAIN: Act as though not under the influence of a drug particularly when under the influence of marijuana or alcohol. Also, act in a calm or collected manner as though in control of a situation.
MAN: The police. Also, used in reference to the person to whom one is speaking, as in, "It's cool, man!"
MANICURED: In reference to marijuana that has been freed of all stems and seeds.
MARKED: Designated by others.
MARRIED: Have a steady girlfriend.
MARY JANE: Marijuana.
MAUI: An expensive "brand" of marijuana, said to have been grown in the Hawaiian Island of Maui.

MEAT EXCHANGE (ALSO, MEAT RACK): Bars, clubs, coffee houses or restaurants known as places to "pick up" or meet another for sexual activity.
MELLOW: Calm. Collected.
MELLOW-OUT: Be calm or "Calm down!"
METH: Methamphetamine. (See below.)
METHAMPHETAMINE: A potent stimulant, frequently seen in crystalized form. Also, referred to as **"meth," "crystal meth," "crystal," or "crank, "or "ice."** Popular in the drug subculture in the 1990s and 2000s. More potent than the Amphetamine or Methedrine widely used in the 1960s and 1970s.
METHEDRINE: A strong stimulant, often injected intravenously.
MICRODOT: A variety of LSD, characterized by "purple" microdots.
MUNCH: Eat.
MUNCHIES: The state of appetite arousal often following the use of marijuana.
NARCO: In reference to the narcotics squad or enforcement of drug laws.
NARK: A narcotic officer or an informant. As a verb, to inform on others, not necessarily in regard to drugs, as in, "If you don't do this, I'll nark to your Mom that you skipped school yesterday."
NEEDLE: A hypodermic needle used to inject drugs intravenously.
NODDIN' OUT: A term used to describe the state immediately following injection of heroin, often characterized by the individual's head moving slowly up and down.
NUMBER: A marijuana cigarette. Also, something that has been done to someone by another, as in, "That shrink (psychiatrist) did a number on my head."
O.D.: Abbreviation for "overdose," referring to an excessive ingestion of any substance.
OLD LADY: One's mother. Also, one's girlfriend.
OLD MAN: One's father.
ON SHAKY GROUND: A polite reference to a person's homosexuality.
OUT: Used as a suffix in reference to having been "used up" or "too tired" to continue a particular activity, as: "I'm surfed-out for today," or "I'm sunned-out from laying on the beach."
OUNCE: Measurement of an amount of drugs. Most frequently used in reference to marijuana. Frequently abbreviated to "z." For example, a "half-z" refers to a half-ounce of marijuana.
OUT-OF-IT: Psychotic. Also, not able to be believed.
OUT-OF-SIGHT: Great. Unbelievably pleasant or "awesome."
OUT-TO-LUNCH: Temporarily insane.
PAD: One's home. A place to sleep.
PCP (ALSO "ANGEL DUST"): An animal tranquilizer, sometimes used on marijuana cigarettes and in other ways to produce a more potent "high," or to take advantage of another person, most frequently for sexual purposes.
PAPERS: Cigarette papers used to roll marijuana cigarettes.

PEYOTE: A "natural" or "organic" hallucinogen, grown in the desert southwest.
PIG: A policeman.
PIPE: A pipe used to smoke marijuana or hashish.
POKE: Have sexual intercourse with, as: "I poked three chicks tonight."
POT: Marijuana.
POTHEAD: A person who uses marijuana frequently.
POUND: Measurement of an amount of a drug, such as cocaine or marijuana.
PSYCHED-UP: Emotionally excited.
PSYCHEDELIC: In reference to hallucinogenic drugs. Also, in reference to the music and art forms that accompanied the late 1960s and early 1970s within the drug and youth subcultures.
PUSS: Womanly, sissy. Also, a derogatory reference to a male, as below.
PUSSY: The female genitals. Derogatory term referring to a weak or effeminate male.
PUTTING-ME-ON: Lying to me. Deceiving me.
QUAALUDE: A strong sedative. Quaalude is no longer manufactured by pharmaceutical companies. Also, **"Ludes" or "Sopers."**
QUARTER: 1) $25 worth of any drug, e.g., "a quarter-bag of coke" (a *$25* bag of cocaine); 2) Abbreviation for a quarter ounce, such as a "quarter" of marijuana.
RACK: A packet of pills, usually five to ten doses of barbiturates or amphetamines.
RAD: Radical or extremely "awesome."
RAINBOWS: Barbiturates (Usually used in reference to "Tuinal," brand name of Eli Lilly and Company).
RATS: Young surfers (approximately 14 to 16 years of age).
RAYS: Sunshine, as in "I am heading to the beach and catch some rays."
RAVE: Typically very large parties or gatherings where persons dance to rock music for several hours, frequently overnight. Many participants in raves use ecstasy, called "rolling," to enhance their experience. Those "rolling" frequently inhale menthol, suck on pacifiers and wave "glow sticks."
REDS: Barbiturates, strong depressants..
REDNECK: A derogatory term used to refer to those who are very "conservative" or do not appreciate the drug subculture. Also, often used in reference to A Midwesterner or those with a very short haircut.
REEFER: Early term for marijuana.
RETIRED: Unemployed. Also, having ceased performing a particular activity. For example, "I retired from surfing."
RITALIN: A stimulant, similar to amphetamine. Frequently prescribed for learning disabilities. Often sold to classmates of those for whom it has been prescribed .
RIP-OFF: As a verb, steal. As a noun, one who is known to engage in stealing. Also, an unfair business transaction.
ROACH: The small butt of a marijuana cigarette.

ROACH CLIP: Any one of many devices used to hold or "clip" the butt of a marijuana cigarette.
ROIDS: Steriods. Frequently used illegally to enhance body and muscle mass. One result of steroid use is "**ROID RAGE,**" an overly aggressive loss of temper.
ROLLING: Using ecstasy, typically at a rave.
SCALES: Scales used to weigh drugs, usually employed by "dealers."
SCHROOMS: Psychedelic mushrooms.
SCORE: Obtain, in reference to drugs or females, as: "I scored some good pot," and "I scored with this chick last night."
SCROUNGE: A person who borrows frequently; similar to "leech."
SENSEM: Term for **SENSEMILLA** or **SINSEMILLA** marijuana, a seedless variety of marijuana.
SHINE-IT-ON: To deceive. Go along with someone while disagreeing, as: "I shined-it-on with that drug counselor."
SKAG: An undesirable female.
SKARF: To consume or eat. Also, to obtain with little or no payment.
SKIN-POP: To inject with a hypodermic needle into the muscle, as opposed to intravenously.
SLUFF-OFF: Be undependable. As a noun, an undependable person.
SLUT: A promiscuous female.
SMACK: Heroin.
SMOKE-OUT: A lengthy session of marijuana smoking. To use marijuana to the point at which additional use becomes undesirable at that time.
SNAKE: To meet or "pick-up" females, usually with the purpose of engaging in sexual intercourse.
SNORT: To ingest (usually cocaine) through the nostrils.
SOPERS: Quaalude, a sedative. Also, "ludes."
SOSH: A "social climber," or person who is active in school and other conventional organizations.
SPACED-OUT: Acting in a psychotic or "peculiar" fashion.
SPEED: Stimulants, usually amphetamines, also called, "Whites."
SPONGE: Similar to "scrounge" and "leech"; a person who borrows frequently. One who does not pay his own way. Also, anything that is undesirable.
STEPPED-ON: Process of diluting drugs, such as heroin and cocaine, with other drugs or inert ingredients to maximize profit. (Most cocaine and opiates have been"stepped-on" several times before they are available on the street.)
STEROIDS: Hormones used in the drug subculture, particularly by those seeking to enhance their athletic ability and/or build muscle tissue. See "Roids" and "Roid Rage," above.
STICK: A surfboard.

STOKED: Happy about, as in, "I am really stoked that my folks let me go to the concert."
STONED: Under the influence of a drug, usually marijuana.
STONER: A person who uses marijuana frequently. Normally used in somewhat of a derogatory fashion.
STONEY: A less derogatory term for a "stoner," or a person who uses marijuana frequently.
SURFER-CHICK: Females who frequent surfing areas of the beach, or who have surfers as their boyfriends.
SURF-PUPPIES: Promiscuous females who "hang out" in areas frequented by male surfers.
SWAB (ALSO, SWABBIE): A sailor.
TALK TO MOM: Use restroom facilities, as: "Excuse me, I have to talk to my Mom."
TALK TO RALPH: To vomit.
TARS: Tobacco cigarettes.
THC: Tetrahydrocannabinol, the active ingredient in marijuana.
THAI-STICKS: A stock of marijuana, supposedly imported from Thailand.
TIME: Length of a sentence spent in jail or prison.
TOKE: Smoke a marijuana cigarette.
TOTE: To inhale or "snort" a drug, usually cocaine.
TRIP: A drug experience. Also, one's interest, as, "What's your trip?"
TOTALLY: As an adverb, usually modifies extremes, as in, "It is totally awesome!" or "I was totally stoned last night, and it was totally rad!"
TURN-OFF: Become disgusted with, as: "That smell of cabbage turned me off."
TURN-ON: Introduce a person to a drug or to an activity. Also, to share a substance with a person, as in, "He was a nice guy; he turned me on to good pot."
VALLEY: Inland areas of San Diego. In the Los Angles area refers to San Fernando Valley. Also, "**VALLEY GIRLS,**" refers to young females from the area who are, at times, stereotyped as "Airheads." (See above.)
WASTED: Under the influence of a drug. Usually refers to an excessive state.
WEED: Marijuana.
WEIRD: Different. Peculiar.
WEIRDO: A person who acts differently or peculiarly.
WESSON OIL PARTY: A sexual orgy, usually accompanied by the saturation of the participants' bodies with oil.
WHEELS: One's automobile or motorcycle. Also, for those less than 16, one's skate board or bicycle.
WHEELING: Driving, usually in a reckless or careless manner.
WHITES: Amphetamines. (See above.)
WIFE: One's girlfriend.

WINDOWPANE: A clear, uncolored, variety of LSD.
WIPED-OUT: In reference to surfing, overcome by a wave. In reference to drugs, having used a drug to excess.
WOLFING: Eating. Also, beating-up someone.
YELLOWS (ALSO, YELLOW JACKETS): Sedatives, usually referring to "Nembutal," brand name of phenobarbital, Abbott Laboratories, Inc., in the form of a yellow capsule.
Z: Abbreviation for "ounce," a measurement of drugs, such as marijuana or cocaine. For example, "I have a quarter 'z'"(or a quarter ounce).
Z'S: Sleep.
Z'ING: Sleeping.
ZONKED: Extremely "wasted," or having used drugs to excess.

BIBLIOGRAPHY

Akers, Ronald L.; Kron, Marvin D.; Lanza-Kaduce, Lonn; and Radosevich, "Social Learning and Deviant Behavior: A Specific Test of a General Theory," *American Sociological Review*, 44 (August 1979), 636-655.

American Medical Association Committee on Human Sexuality. *Human Sexuality*. Chicago: American Medical Association, 1972.

Aseltine, Robert H. Jr.; Gore, Susan; and Gordon, Jennifer. "Life Stress, Anger and Anxiety, and Delinquency: An Empirical Test of General Strain Theory," *Journal of Health and Social Behavior*, Vol. 41, No. 3 (September 2000) 256-275.

Babbie, E.R. *The Practice of Social Research*. 11th ed. Belmont Ca: Wadsworth Publishing Co., 2001.

Bales, Robert F. "Attitudes Toward Drinking in Irish Culture," in *Society, Culture and Drinking Patterns*. Edited by David J. Pittman and Charles R. Snyder. New York: Wiley, 1962.

_______. "Cultural Differences in Rates of Alcoholism," *Quarterly Journal of Studies on Alcohol*, VI (March 1946), 480-499.

Bandura, Albert and Walters, Richard H. "Dependency Conflicts in Aggressive Delinquents," *Journal of Social Issues*, IV (1958), 52-65.

Becker, Howard S. *The Outsiders*. New York: The Free Press, 1955.

________. *The Other Side: Perspectives on Deviance*. New York: The Free Press, 1964.

________. "Becoming a Marihuana User," *American Journal of Sociology*, LIX (November 1953), 235-42.

________. "Problems of Inference and Proof in Participant Observation," *American Sociological Review*, XXIII (1958), 652-660.

________.and Geer, Blanche. "Participant Observation: The Analysis of Qualitative Data," in *Human Organization Research*. Edited by R.N. Adams and J.J. Preiss. Homewood, Illinois: Dorsey Press, 1960.

Beckett, Katherine, "Setting the Public Agenda: 'Street Crime' and Drug use in American Politics," *Social Problems*, Vol. 41, No.3 (August 1994), 425-447.

Benson, Leonard. *Fatherhood, A Sociological Perspective*. New York: Random House, 1968.

Blalock, Hubert M., Jr. *Social Statistics*. 2nd Ed., New York: McGraw-Hill Book Company, 1972.

Burton, Roger and Whiting, John W.M. "Absent Father and Cross-Sex Identity," *Merrill-Palmer Quarterly, Behavior and Development*, VII, 1961.

Bruyn, Severyn. "The Methodology of Participant Observation," *Human Organization*, XXII (Fall, 1963), 224-235.

Cahalan, Don and Room, Robin. *Problem Drinking Among American Men.* Monograph of Rutgers Center of Alcohol Studies, New Brunswick, New Jersey. New Haven: College and University Press, 1974.

Chein, Isidor: Gerard, D.L.: Lee, R.S.; and Rosenfeld, E. *The Road To H: Narcotics, Delinquency and Social Policy.* New York: Basic Books, 1964.

Cicourel, Aaron V. *The Social Organization of Juvenile Justice.* New York: John Wiley and Sons, 1968.

Cloward, Richard A. and Ohlin, Lloyd E. *Delinquency and Opportunity.* Glencoe, Illinois: The Free Press, 1960.

Cohen, Albert K. *Delinquent Boys.* Glencoe, Illinois: Free Press, 1955.

_______. *Deviance and Control.* Englewood Cliffs, New Jersey: Prentice-Hall, Inc., 1966.

Cohen, Theodore. *Men and Masculinities: A Test Reader.* Belmont, Ca: Wadswoth/ Thomson Learning, 2001.

Davis, James A. *Elementary Survey Analysis.* Englewood Cliffs, New Jersey: Prentice-Hall, Inc. 1966.

Davis, Kingsley. "The Sociology of Parent-Youth Conflict," *American Sociological Review,* V (August 1940), 523-535.

Densen-Gerber, Judianne. *We Mainline Decency.* Garden City, New Jersey: Doubleday and Co., 1973.

DeWit, Gerard A. *Symbolism of Masculinity and Femininity.* New York: Springer Publishing Company, Inc., 1963.

Douglas, Jack, ed. *Observations of Deviance.* New York: Random House, 1970.

Durkheim, Emile. *Suicide.* Translated by John A. Spaulding and George Simpson, New York: Free Press, 1951.

Elkin, Frederick. "The Myth of Adolescent Culture," *American Sociological Review,* XX (December, 1955), 680-684.

Elliott, Delbert S. and Voss, Harwin L. *Delinquency and Dropout.* Lexington, Massachusetts: Lexington Books, 1974.

Erikson, Kai T. "Notes on the Sociology of Deviance," *Social Problems,* IX (Spring, 1962), 307-314.

Eysenck, Howard J. *Crime and Personality.* Boston: Houghton Mifflin Company, 1964.

Fort, Joel and Cory, C.T. *American Drugstore: A (Alcohol) to V (Valium).* Boston: Little Brown, 1975.

Friedenberg, Edgar Z. *The Vanishing Adolescent.* Boston: Beacon Press, 1959.

Fremon, Celeste. *Father Greg and the Home Boys.* New York: Hyperion, 1995.

Gaines, Donna. *Teenage Wasteland: Suburbia's Dead End Kids.* New York: Harper Collins, 1995.

Gilder, George F. *Sexual Suicide.* New York: Bantam Books, 1973.

Gitchoff, G. Thomas. *Kids, Cops and Kilos*. San Diego, Ca.: Halter-Westerfield Publishing Company, 1969.

Glassner, Barry and Loughlin, Julia. *Drugs in the Adolescent World: Burnouts to Straights.* New York: St. Martin's Press, 1987.

Glueck, Sheldon and Glueck, Eleanor T. *Unraveling Delinquency.* New York: Commonwealth Fund, 1950.

Goffman, Erving. *Asylums.* New York: Doubleday and Co., 1961.

Gold, R.L. "Roles in Sociological Field Observations," *Social Forces*, XXXVI (March 1958), 217-23.

Goode, Erich. *The Marijuana Smokers.* New York: Basic Books, 1970.

_______. "Multiple Drug Use Among Marijuana Smokers," *Social Problems*, Vol. 17 (Summer 1969), 48-64.

_______. *Drugs in American Society,* 4th ed. New York: McGraw-Hill, 1993.

Goodman, Paul. *Growing Up Absurd.* New York: Random House, 1956.

Gross, Marion. *Working Mothers.* San Francisco: Jossey-Bass, 1974.

Himmelbach, Jerome; Brashears, Benjamin S.; and Rayfield, John R. "Hedonists and Moralists: Contrasting Cultures Among Green Mountain Town Youth," *A Vermont Youth Study*. Goddard College, 1962.

Hirschi, Travis. *Causes of Delinquency*. Berkeley: University of California, 1969.

_______. and Selvin, Hanan C. "False Criteria of Causality in Delinquency Research," *Social Problems*, XIII (Spring, 1966), 254-268.

Horn, Jack. "Suspension From School: Kicked Out Kids," *Psychology Today*, VII (December 1975), 83-84.

Howell, James C. and Gleason, Debra K. "Youth Gang Drug Trafficking," in *The Modern Gang Reader*, 2nd Ed. by Jody Miller, Cheryl L. Maxson and Malcolm W. Klein. Los Angeles: Roxbury, 2001, 245-260.

Hunt, Larry L. and Hunt, Janet G. "Race and the Father-Son Connection: The Conditional Relevance of Father Absence for the Orientations and Identities of Adolescent Boys," *Social Problems*, XXIII (October 1975), 31-52.

Inciardi, James A. *The War on Drugs: Heroin, Cocaine, Crime and Public Policy.* Palo Alto, Ca.: Mayfield Publishing Company, 1987.

Isbell, Harris. "Medical Aspects of Opiate Addiction," in *Narcotic Addiction.* Edited by John A. O'Donnell and John C. Ball. New York: Harper and Row, 1966.

Jensen, Gary F. "Parents, Peers, and Delinquent Action: A Test of the Differential Association Perspective," *American Journal of Sociology*, Vol. 78, No. 3 562-576.

Johnston, Lloyd D.; O'Malley, Patrick; and Bachman, Jerard G. *Drug Use Among American High School Seniors, College Students and Young Adults, 1975-1990.* Vol. and II, Rockville, Md.: National Institute on Drug Abuse, 1991.

Johnson, J.M. *Doing Field Research.* New York: The Free Press, 1975.
Joyner, Kara and Udry, J. Richard. "You Don't Bring Me Anything But Down: Adolescent Romance and Depression," Journal of Health and Social Behavior, Vol. 41, No. 4 (December 2000), 369-391.
Junker, B.H. *Field Work: An Introduction to the Social Sciences.* Chicago: University of Chicago Press, 1960.
Kalb, Claudia, "Playing With Pain Killers", *Newsweek,* April 9, 2001, 45-57.
Kaplan, John. *Marijuana: The New Prohibition.* New York: Simon and Schuster, 1971.
Kenniston, Kenneth. *Youth and Dissent: The Rise of a New Opposition.* New York: Harcourt Brace Jovanovich, 1971.
Kindlon, Dan and Thompson, Michael. *Raising Cain: Protecting the Emotional Life of Boys.* New York: Ballantine Books, 2000.
Kituse, John I. "Societal Reaction to Deviant Behavior: Problems of Theory and Method," *Social Problems,* IX (Winter, 1962), 247-256.
Klein, Malcom W. *Street Gangs and Street Workers.* Englewood Cliffs, NJ: Prentice-Hall, 1971.
_______. "Attempting Gang Control By Suppression: The Misuse of Deterrence Principles," *Studies on Crime and Crime Prevention.* Stockholm, Sweden: Scandinavian University Press, pp. 88-111.
______. *The American Street Gang: Its Nature, Prevalence and Control.* New York: Oxford University Press, 1995.
Kostlowitz, Alex. *There Are No Children Here.* New York: Anchor Books, 1991.
Krohn, Marvin D.; Skinner, William F.; Massey, James L.; and Akers, Ronald L."Social Learning Theory and Adolescent Cigarette Smoking: A Longitudinal Study," *Social Problems,* Vol. 32, No. 5 (June 1985), 455-473.
Kvaraceus, William C. *The Community and the Delinquent.* New York: World Book Co., 1954.
LeMert, Edwin M. *Human Deviance: Social Problems and Social Control.* Englewood Cliffs, New Jersey: Prentice-Hall, Inc., 1967.
Lennard, Henry L., et al. *Mystification and Drug Misuse.* San Francisco: Jossey-Bass, 1971.
Leslie, Gerald R. *The Family in Social Context.* New York: Oxford University Press, 1967.
Lewis, Oscar. *Five Families.* New York: Basic Books, 1959.
Liebow, Elliot. *Tally's Corner.* Boston: Little, Brown, 1967.
Lindesmith, Alfred R. *Addiction and Opiates.* Chicago: Aldine Publishing Co, 1966.
Lofland, John. *Deviance and Identity.* Englewood Cliffs, New Jersey: Prentice Hall, Inc., 1969.
Lowney, Jeremiah, Winslow Robert W. and Winslow, Virginia. *Deviant Reality: Alternative World Views.* Boston: Allyn and Bacon, 1960.

Lowney, Jeremiah, "The Role of a Nonparticipant Observer in Drug Abuse Field Research," *Adolescence,* Vol. XIX No. 74 (Summer 1984), 425-434.

_______. "The Wall Gang: A Study of Interpersonal Process and Deviance Among Twenty-three Middle Class Youths," *Adolescence,* Vol. XIX No.75 (Fall, 1984), 527-538.

_______. "Correspondence Between Attitudes and Drinking and Drug Behavior: Youth Subculture Over Time," *Adolescence,* Vol. XIX No. 76 (Winter 1984), 875-892.

Lukes, Steven. *Emile Durkheim: His Life and Works, A Historical and Critical Study.* New York: Harper and Row, 1972.

Maccoby, Eleanor E., ed. *The Development of Sex Differences*. Stanford, Ca.: Stanford University Press, 1966.

_______. and Jacklin, Carol Nagy. *The Psychology of Sex Differences.* Stanford, California: Stanford University Press, 1974.

MacLeod, Jay. *Ain't No Making' It.* Boulder, Colorado: Westview Press, 1995.

McCord, William and McCord, Joan. *Origins of Alcoholism.* Stanford, Ca: Stanford University, 1960.

McCoy, Clyde B. and Iniciardi, James A. *Sex, Drugs and the Continuing Spread of Aids.* Los Angeles, Ca.: Roxbury, 1995.

McMorris, Barbara J. and Uggen, Christopher. "Alcohol and Employment in the Transition to Adulthood," *Journal of Health and Social Behavior*, Vol. 41, No. 3 (September 2000), 276-294.

Merton, Robert K. "Social Structure and Anomie," *American Sociological Review,* III (October 1938), 672-682.

Miller, Jody. *One of the Guys: Girls, Gangs and Gender.* New York: Oxford University Press, 2001.

Miller, Marissa A. "History and Epidemiology of Amphetamine Abuse in the United States," in *The American Drug Scene: An Anthology,* 3rd ed. Inciardi, James A. and McElrath, Karen, eds. Los Angles, Roxbury Publishing, 2001, 216-230.

Morris, Desmond. *Intimate Behavior*. New York: Bantam Books, 1971.

National Center on Addiction and Substance Abuse at Columbia University. *The 2000 CASA National Survey of American Attitudes on Substance Abuse VI: Teens*. New York: Columbia University, February 21, 2001.

National Commission on Marihuana and Drug Abuse. *Marihuana: A Signal of Misunderstanding.* First Report. 1972.

_______. *Drug Use in America: Problem in Perspective.* Second Report. March 1973.

Nettler, Gwynn. *Explaining Crime*. New York: McGraw-Hill Book Company, 1974.

Nikkah, John. *Our Boys Speak: Adolescent Boys Write About Their Inner Lives.* New York: St. Martin's Griffin, 2000.

Nye, Ivan. "Adolescent-Parent Adjustment: Socio-economic Level As a Variable," *American Sociological Review*, XVI (June, 1951), 341-349

O'Donnell, John A. and Ball, John C., eds. *Narcotic Addiction.* New York: Harper and Row, 1966.

_______. et al., *Young Men and Drugs: A Nationwide Survey,* Research Monograph Series, Rockville, Md.: National Institute on Drug Abuse, 1976.

Parsons, Talcott and Bales, Robert F. *Family, Socialization and Interaction Process*. Glencoe, Illinois: Free Press, 1955.

Pearsall, Marion. "Participant Observation As Role and Method in Behavioral Research," *Nursing Research*, XIV (Winter, 1965), 37-42.

Peele, Stanton, with Archie Brodsky, *Love and Addiction.* New York: Taplinger, 1975.

Pollock, William. *Real Boys: Rescuing Our Sons from the Myth of Boyhood.* New York: Henry Holt and Co., 1999.

Popenoe, David. *Life Without Father.* New York, The Free Press, 1996.

President's Commission on Law Enforcement and Administration of Justice. Task Force Report: *Narcotics and Drug Abuse*. Washington, D.C.: U.S. Government Printing Office, 1967.

Physicians' Desk Reference: To Pharmaceutical Specialties and Biologicals, 26th Ed. Oradell, New Jersey: Medical Economics, Inc., 1972.

Ray, Oakley and Ksir, Charles. *Drugs, Society and Human Behavior*, 5th ed. St. Louis: Times Mirror/Mosby, 1989.

Rains, Prudence. "Imputations of Deviance: A Retrospective Essay On the Labeling Perspective," *Social Problems*, XXIII (October 1975), 1-11.

Reckless, Walter C. *The Crime Problem.* New York: Appleton-Century-Crofts, Inc., 1950.

_______. and Smith, Mapheus. *Juvenile Delinquency.* New York: McGraw-Hill Book Company, 1932.

_______."A New Theory of Delinquency," *Federal Probation*, XXV (December 1961), 42-46.

_______. "Containment Theory," in Barry Krisbert and James Austin (eds.), *The Children of Ishmael: Critical Perspectives on Juvenile Justice.* Palo Alto, Ca.: Mayfield Publishing, 1978, 187-189.

Reiss, Albert J. "Delinquency As the Failure of Personal and Social Controls," *American Sociological Review*, XVI (April 1951), 196-207.

_______. "Social Correlates of Psychological Types of Delinquency," *American Sociological Review*, XVII (December 1952), 710-18.

Research Triangle Institute, "Some Sobering Statistics About Teenage Drinking," *Hypotenuse*. February 1976.

Robertson, Nan. *Getting Better: Inside Alcoholics Anonymous.* New York: William Morrow, 1988.

Rozak, T. *The Making of a Counter-culture*. Garden City, NY: Anchor Books, 1969.

Rubington, Earl and Weinberg, Martin. S. *Deviance: The Interactionist Perspective*, 8th ed. Boston: Allyn and Bacon, 2002.

Shelden, Randall G.; Tracy, Sharon K.; and Brown, William B. *Youth Gangs in American Society,* 2nd ed. Belmont, Ca: Wadsworth/Thomson Learning, 2001.

Sebald, Hans. *Adolescence: A Sociological Analysis*. New York: Appleton-Century-Crofts, 1968.

Shupe, Anson. *In the Name of All That's Holy: A Theory of Clergy Malfeasance*. Westport, Conn.: Praeger.

Skolnick, Jerome H. *Justice Without Trial*. New York: John Wiley and Sons, 1967.

Smith, Ernest A. *American Youth Culture: Group Life in Teenage Society*. Glencoe, Illinois: Free Press, 1962.

Solomon, David, ed. *The Marihuana Papers*. Bergenfield, New Jersey: The New American Library, Inc., 1966.

Straus, Robert. "Alcohol and Alcoholism," in *Contemporary Social Problems*, 3rd ed. Edited by Robert K. Merton and Robert Nisbet. New York: Harcourt Brace Jovanovich, 1971.

_______. *Escape From Custody*. New York: Harper and Row, 1974.

_______. "The Life Record of an Alcoholic," *Quarterly Journal of Studies on Alcohol*, XXXIV (December 1973 , 1212-19.

Sutherland, Edwin H, *Principles of Criminology*, 3rd ed. Philadelphia: J.B. Lippincott, 1939.

Sutherland, Edwin H. and Cressey, Donald R. *Principles of Criminology,* 7th ed. Philadelphia: J. B. Lippincott, 1966.

Tanner, Julian; Davies, Scott; and O'Grady, Bill. "Whatever Happened to Yesterday's Rebels? Longitudinal Effects of Youth Delinquency on Education and Employment," *Social Problems*, Vol. 46, No.2, 250-274, 1991.

Thomson, James G.; Marolla, Joseph A.; and Bromley, David G. "Disclaimers and Accounts in Cases of Catholic Priests Accused of Pedophilia," in *Wolves Within the Fold: Religious Leadership and the Abuses of Power.* Sharpe, Anson, ed. Rutgers: Rutgers University Press, 1998.

Thornberry, Terence. P. "Risk Factors for Gang Membership," in *The Modern Gang Reader*, 2nd Ed. by Jody Miller, Cheryl L. Maxson and Malcolm W. Klein. Los Angeles: Roxbury, 2001, 32-42.

Trasler, G. *The Explanation of Criminality.* London: Routledge and Kegan Paul, 1962.

Trice, Harrison M. and Roman, Paul Michael. "Delabeling, Relabeling and Alcoholics Anonymous," *Social Problems*, Vol. 17, No. 4 (Spring 1970), 538-546.

U.S. Bureau of the Census. *1970 Census of Population and Housing*. Census Tracts. San Diego, California, Standard Metropolitan Statistical Area." Washington, D.C.: U.S. Government Printing Office, May 1972.

U.S. Bureau of the Census. *1970 Census of Population.* Vol. I, Part I, United States Summary, Section I. Washington, D.C.: U.S. Government Printing Office, June 1973.

U.S. Department of Labor, Bureau of Labor Statistics. *Marital and Family Characteristics of the Labor Force.* Washington, D.C.: U.S. Department of Labor, March 1974.

Vander Ven, Thomas M.; Cullen, Francis T.; Carrozza, Mark A.; and Wright, John Paul. "Home Alone: The Impact of Maternal Employment on Delinquency," *Social Problems,* Vol. 48, No. 2 (May 2001), 236-258.

Voss, Harwin L. "Differential Association and Containment Theory: A Theoretical Convergence," *Social Forces*, IIL (June 1969), 381-91.

Wallerstein, Judith S.; Lewis, Julia M.; and Blakeslee, Sandra. *The Unexpected Legacy of Divorce: A 25 Year Landmark Study.* New York: Hyperion, 2000.

Whyte, William F. *Street Corner Society: The Social Structure of an Italian Slum.* Chicago: The University of Chicago Press, 1935.

Wiseman, Jacqueline P. *Stations of the Lost: The Treatment of Skid Row Alcoholics.* Englewood Cliffs, New Jersey: Prentice-Hall, 1970.

Witters, Weldon L. and Witters, Patricia Jones. *Drugs and Sex*. New York: The MacMillan Company, 1975.

Yablonsky, Lewis. *The Violent Gang*. New York: The MacMillan Company, 1962

_______. *The Tunnel Back: Synanon.* New York: The MacMillan Company, 1965.

_______. *Gangsters.* New York: New York University Press, 1997.

Zelditch, Morris, Jr: "Some Methodological Problems of Field Studies," *American Journal of Sociology*, LXVII (March 1962), 566-576.

Zimmering, P.; Toolan, J.; Safrin, R.; and Wortis, S. "Heroin Addiction in Adolescent Boys," *Journal of Nervous and Mental Disease*, CXIV (1951), 19-34.

Zunich, M.A. "A Study of the Relationship Between Child-rearing Attitudes and Maternal Behavior. *Journal of Experimental Education*, 1961, 30, 231-241.

INDEX

ABOUT THE AUTHOR

Jeremiah Lowney is an Associate Professor of Sociology at Carroll College in Helena, Montana and a priest of the Diocese of Helena. He received his B.A. from San Diego State University in 1972, and, the following year, received his M.A. from the same institution. In 1976, Lowney received his Ph.D. from the University of Kentucky. In 1988, he received his M. Div. from the Catholic University of America, Washington, D. C. He has taught at the San Diego State University, the University of Richmond, Spring Hill College, the Catholic University of America and the University of Kentucky. In 1981, he co-authored the second edition of *Deviant Reality: Alternative World Views* with Robert W. Winslow and Virginia Winslow. In 1983, he received the H. J. Fagot award at Spring Hill College for the faculty most involved in student activities. In 1992, Lowney was certified as a Chemical Dependency Counselor by the State of Montana. In 1997, he received the "God and Youth" award by the Catholic Youth Conference for his efforts on behalf of young people in the Diocese of Helena. In 1995, he was honored at the White House for his efforts in leading an effort to enact the first child labor law in the history of Montana and his efforts to raise funds for needy young people to participate in athletics and other extracurricular activities in the Helena public schools. He continues to be active in promoting youth activities and social justice.